THE
CATHOLIC WORKER
MOVEMENT

THE CATHOLIC WORKER MOVEMENT

Intellectual and Spiritual Origins

Mark and Louise Zwick

Paulist Press
New York/Mahwah, New Jersey

ACKNOWLEDGMENTS

Cover photos of Dorothy Day and Peter Maurin courtesy of Marquette University Archives.

Excerpts from *Dostoievsky* by Nicholas Berdyaev, original copyright 1934 by Sheed and Ward. Reprinted by permission of Continuum Books, London.

Excerpts from *From Union Square to Rome* by Dorothy Day, original copyright 1938 by Preservatio of the Faith Press. Reprinted by permission of Ayer Company Publishers.

Excerpts from *House of Hospitality* by Dorothy Day, copyright 1939. Reprinted by permission of Sheed and Ward.

Excerpts from *Loaves and Fishes* by Dorothy Day, copyright 1963 by Harper & Row. Reprinted by permission of HarperCollins Publishers.

Excerpts from *The Long Loneliness* by Dorothy Day, copyright 1952 by HarperSanFrancisco. Reprinted by permission of HarperCollins Publishers.

Excerpts from *On Pilgrimage* by Dorothy Day, copyright 1999. Reprinted by permission of Wm. B. Eerdmans Publishing Company.

Excerpts from *Therese*, original copyright 1960 by Fides Publishers. Reprinted by permission of Templegate Publishers.

Excerpts from *Searching for Christ: The Spirituality of Dorothy Day* by Brigid Merriman, copyright 1994. Reprinted by permission of the University of Notre Dame Press.

Excerpts from *A Harsh and Dreadful Love* by William Miller, original copyright 1973 by Liveright. Reprinted by permission of Marquette University Press.

Excerpts from *Dorothy Day: A Biography* by William Miller, copyright 1982 by Harper & Row. Reprinted by permission of HarperCollins Publishers.

Excerpts from *Peter Maurin: Gay Believer* by Arthur Sheehan, original copyright 1959 by Hanover House. Reprinted by permission of Random House.

Cover design by Sharyn Banks
Book design by Lynn Else

Copyright © 2005 by Mark and Louise Zwick

Library of Congress Cataloging-in-Publication Data

Zwick, Mark.
The Catholic worker movement : intellectual and spiritual origins / Mark and Louise Zwick.
    p.   cm.
Includes bibliographical references and index.
ISBN 0-8091-4315-1 (alk. paper)
1. Catholic Worker Movement—History. 2. Catholic Church—United States—History—20th century. I. Zwick, Louise. II. Title.

BX810.C393Z95 2005
267'.182—dc22

2004026804

Published by Paulist Press
997 Macarthur Boulevard
Mahwah, New Jersey 07430

www.paulistpress.com

Printed and bound in the
United States of America

Contents

CONTENTS

Introduction

It is our hope that through this book readers will become acquainted with the richness of thought, contemplation, and action that has inspired and characterized the Catholic Worker movement. The chapters are organized by themes according to the philosophers, theologians, authors, and saints who influenced Dorothy Day and Peter Maurin in a significant way.

Dorothy and Peter shared the ideas of these great thinkers and models of Christian witness with readers of their newspaper, *The Catholic Worker*, and applied their reflections to the problems and crises of the day. Like so many saints, they rediscovered and expressed in a new way the gospel and the tradition of the church for their age. They engaged in studies of the early church and its saints of every generation in order to discover within Catholic tradition an expression of the heart of the faith that drew and impelled them to not only write about, but to live the gospel in person and in community with the poorest of the poor. The inspiration of contemporary French personalists and participation in the vanguard of the liturgical, scriptural, theological, ecumenical, and lay leadership movements that prepared the way for the Second Vatican Council complemented their study of the tradition. Peter and Dorothy were not only inundated with the richness of the *ressourcement* (retrieval of the sources) and creative reflection that was a part of these movements; they were also very much a part of creating them.

Some of the positions taken by Dorothy during her lifetime that have been considered radical are now well known. Less well known are the philosophical and theological roots that were the basis for these positions. Peter Maurin brought the fruit of years of study and experience to Dorothy and shared his sources with her and with anyone else who would listen. As Dorothy said in an article in the May 1955 *Catholic Worker*, Peter brought to us "great books and great ideas, and great men, so that over the years, we have become a school for the service of God here and now." Like Peter, Dorothy continued her studies throughout her life. In an article entitled "Obedience" in *Ave Maria* magazine (December 17, 1966), Dorothy declared, "I have never felt so sure of myself that I did not feel the necessity of being backed up by great minds, searching the Scriptures and searching the writings of the saints for my authorities."

Our efforts in bringing this book into print sprang from our growing knowledge of the depth of thought and spirituality of the Catholic Worker movement in the face of challenges and even ridicule of Dorothy and Peter's ideas. They were sometimes considered marginal because they asked so much, not by demanding or criticizing, but by the witness of their lives.

When in the mid-1990s Catholic publications began printing articles and letters stating that the Catholic Worker movement was dead, it became clear that many might not be aware of the great thought that had shaped and undergirded the Catholic Worker, ideas which had brought Peter and Dorothy to their role of transforming, if not transfiguring, the world in which they found themselves, instead of being formed by the culture with all its inequalities and injustices and its separation from the Eternal. At that time we began a series in our newspaper, the *Houston Catholic Worker*, about the roots of the movement, the saints and philosophers who influenced it. Those articles have been developed into this book.

We are grateful to Phil Runkel of the Marquette University Archives for his assistance in so many ways, especially in providing copies of old editions of *The Catholic Worker*. The Dorothy Day Library on the Web (http://www.catholicworker/dorothyday/index.cfm) has likewise been invaluable. We want to express here our appreciation to Dana Dillon and to Laura and James Strzelec for their immeasurable help with footnotes and to James Hanink and Phil Runkel for reading the manuscript. All of the Catholic Workers in Houston have contributed much through discussions and reading of the manuscript chapter by chapter in its various stages, and above all through assuming personal responsibility for the work of hospitality that has made it possible for us to complete this book. We especially want to thank Paulist Press for believing in this book.

We ask forgiveness for incompleteness or other imperfections. We have written the chapters with constant interruptions, surrounded by telephones and the endless needs of people in our Houses of Hospitality for immigrants at Casa Juan Diego, the Houston Catholic Worker.

If this book has any authenticity at all, it is because it was compiled in the midst of the turmoil of trying to carry out Matthew 25 and the "shock maxims of the Gospel" described by Peter Maurin.

Mark and Louise Zwick

Blowing the Dynamite
of the Church

The Catholic Worker movement was born out of the meeting of Peter Maurin and Dorothy Day on the feast of the Immaculate Conception, December 8, 1932. Dorothy and Peter founded the movement and *The Catholic Worker* newspaper in 1933 in the midst of the Great Depression in order to implement a radical renewal of Catholicism and the social order. The roots of their movement were so deep, and some so old, that as Peter Maurin said, they looked like new.

The movement has roots in the New Testament, the philosophy of Christian communitarian personalism, the writings and life of the early church, the charisms of the founders of great religious orders, the models of the saints, the theology of the Mystical Body of Christ and the common good, and the thought of those who sought economic alternatives to both monopoly capitalism and socialism.

The philosophy of personalism, as expressed by such writers as Emmanuel Mounier and Nicholas Berdyaev, especially shaped the movement. The French personalists emphasized the tremendous dignity of the human person, together with a profound understanding of each person's vocation in freedom and personal responsibility. Personalists and Catholic Workers challenged the priority of economics and consumerism in daily life, what at the time was called the bourgeois spirit, and insisted instead on the primacy of the spiritual and generosity in living out one's faith. As Peter Maurin put it, the personalist is a "go-giver," rather than a "go-getter."

Dorothy and Peter believed that while the perspective of a Christian is always beyond time, the Lord meant that things should not be so difficult for so many here on this earth. They wanted to present a renewed vision, a Catholic vision, where hearts and minds would be changed as well as the social order. They and others in the Catholic renaissance and renewal movements before the Second Vatican Council insisted on beginning with a conversion of the heart and on a unity of faith, liturgy, contemplation, and action. In the Catholic Worker, insights from the gospel and the rich tradition of the church were not only studied, but also lived in a very practical, even radical, way. This approach frequently contrasted with that of the dominant culture, which has made the movement prophetic.

The perspective that Peter brought to Dorothy, still a fairly new convert to Catholicism, was distinct from that of secular approaches which promised utopias in this life based on human progress without God. He proposed a radical following of the gospel at a time that he described as chaos. Both Peter and Dorothy had seen that the growth of industrialism during the nineteenth and twentieth centuries involved great injustice and violence against workers when labor unions were illegal and laws did not protect workers. They were aware of the pervasive, mechanistic approach of bureaucracy in which people came to be seen as numbers, rather than as persons made in the image and likeness of God, and the resulting danger of totalitarianism. Preparations for war were always in the background. Dorothy, who had previously explored socialist methods in her concern for the poor and been disappointed in efforts for peace and against war during World War I, became convinced of the importance and transformative power of Peter's program and helped him to implement his vision. It was an alternative that could be a model of faith, nonviolence, and creativity.

Dorothy Day (1897–1980)

Dorothy had questioned since her childhood the injustices she observed while walking through the streets of Chicago and that she knew about through her reading. Her father, a newspaper editor, did not allow picture books, detective stories, or what he called "trash" reading in their home, and so Dorothy read good books, many with social criticism: Dostoevsky and other great Russian novelists, and Dickens, but also Jack London and Upton Sinclair. These novels brought to her consciousness the suffering of the poor, of workers who labored long hours in mindless, difficult work for low wages in places where there were no provisions for safety. Her adolescent reading also included the New Testament, John Wesley's *Sermons*, the works of St. Augustine, William James's *The Varieties of Religious Experience* (in which she discovered St. Teresa of Avila and St. John of the Cross), Thomas à Kempis's *The Imitation of Christ*, and Joris-Karl Huysmans's novels that gave rich detail about Catholicism and liturgy. She read the moving story by Robert Louis Stevenson about Father Damien and the lepers. Dorothy wrote later about her struggle with the ideals presented in her reading and the reality she saw about her:

> Whatever I had read as a child about the saints had thrilled me. I could see the nobility of giving one's life for the sick, the maimed, the leper. Priests and Sisters the world over could be working for the littlest ones of Christ, and my heart stirred at their work. Who could hear of Damien—and Stevenson made the whole world hear of him—without feeling impelled to thank God that he had made man so noble?
>
> But there was another question in my mind. Why was so much done in remedying the evil instead of avoiding it in the first place?...
>
> Where were the saints to try to change the social order, not just to minister to the slaves but to do away with slavery?[1]

Dorothy had always been open to the religious spirit, and her search for the Absolute was accompanied by concern for the poor and a just social order. Even in her childhood there was a spiritual awakening. Dorothy was baptized and confirmed in the Episcopal Church at age twelve and grew to love the psalms as she became acquainted with them as part of the formal prayer of the church. She also came to know Catholic families and described some of her youthful encounters with them, including a neighbor, Mrs. Barrett, whom she found on her knees unself-consciously praying the rosary after the housework was done. She recounted her childhood conversations with a Catholic friend, Mary Harrington, who told her about the saints and inspired her to imitate them. Upon hearing about the saints, Dorothy was filled with lofty desires to be one, and a favorite psalm took on new meaning, "Enlarge Thou my heart, O Lord...."[2]

However, her two years as a student at the University of Illinois undermined Dorothy's childhood faith. She wrote later about the comments of a professor who told the students not to criticize religion because some people, especially the weak, need it. The strong do not. "In my youthful arrogance, in my feeling that I was one of the strong, I felt then for the first time that religion was something that I must ruthlessly cut out of my life."[3]

During her college years Dorothy became involved in secular radical movements in which participants criticized the status quo and spoke of the evils of injustice in society. When her family moved to New York City, she decided to leave college and do so also. She made friends there among radicals, participated in protests, and covered events as a journalist, writing for the Socialist paper *The Masses* and later *The Liberator*. However, as John Mitchell points out, her association with the Socialist Party and with Marxism before her conversion to Catholicism was "more principled than doctrinaire." As he put it, "[The Marxists] appeared to her to be the only people in America committed to improving the conditions of the poor and the victims of bourgeois capitalism."[4] Dorothy noted that they appeared to be more concerned and committed than lukewarm Christians were:

> The Marxists, the I.W.W.'s who looked upon religion as the opiate of the people, who thought they had only this life to live and then oblivion—they were the ones who were eager to sacrifice themselves here and now, they were doing without now and for all eternity the good things of the world which they were fighting to obtain for their brothers. It was then, and still is, a paradox that confounds me. God love them! And God pity the lukewarm of whom St. John said harshly (though he was the disciple of love) that God would spew them out of his mouth.[5]

Dorothy explained late in life, in the May 1978 *Catholic Worker*, that she had never, even during this time of searching, been a card-carrying member of the Communist Party: "Upton Sinclair and his book *The Jungle* inflamed me during my high school days, not the Communist Manifesto."

During the time that she wrote for Socialist papers in New York, Dorothy lived in Greenwich Village and associated with a variety of literary figures. She must have then had some of the presence that Julia Porcelli, longtime Catholic Worker, experienced from her first acquaintance with Dorothy. Comparing her to Greta Garbo, she described Dorothy with her "beautiful jaw and her features and her coloring, beautiful bone structure." When Dorothy entered a room, all noticed.[6]

It was in Greenwich Village that Dorothy heard for the first time Francis Thompson's "The Hound of Heaven," recited to her from memory by Eugene O'Neill, and the poem awakened in her the dormant longing for God that would grow again as the months and years passed:

> It was on one of these cold, bitter winter evenings that I first heard *The Hound of Heaven*, that magnificent poem of Francis Thompson. Gene could recite all of it, and he used to sit there, looking dour and black, his head sunk on his chest, sighing, "And now my heart is as a broken fount wherein tear-drippings stagnate." It is one of those poems that awakens the soul, recalls to it the fact that God is its destiny. The idea of this pursuit fascinated me, the inevitableness of it, the recurrence of it, made me feel that inevitably I would have to pause in the mad rush of living to remember my first beginning and last end.[7]

Dorothy wrote a novel about her bohemian life called *The Eleventh Virgin* (published by Liveright in 1924). From the sale of the book she was able to purchase a beach cottage on Staten Island. This book is hard to find today because Dorothy tried to remove all the copies from circulation. When William Miller, a historian who wrote several books about Dorothy and the Catholic Worker movement, spoke to her about writing her biography, she entrusted all of her papers to him and gave him one of the remaining copies of *The Eleventh Virgin*. He describes the scene:

We moved into the living room. I sat down but Dorothy continued to stand. Walking over to the table, she picked up several books and turned to me. She held out one book and asked, "What should I do about this?" I knew the book. It was *The Eleventh Virgin*, her autobiographical novel. "It's all true," she said. It was a book I knew that she hated and would have rejoiced if every copy could have been consumed in flames and then be forever put out of her mind. But now she stood there, holding out to me one of the few copies left.

I said nothing. Dorothy was controlled, but I could tell by the pale, taut look in her face that the business of turning all of this material over to me was a moment of great stress and pain for her. She was, in a way, confronting history.[8]

In their study of *The Eleventh Virgin*, Keith Morton and John Saltmarsh argue that it is this book that gives insight into the origins of Dorothy's political and social thought and how her earlier life "relates to the religious faith and social activism of her Catholic years," her search for meaning and an authentic way of life, for a synthesis of ideas, spirituality, and action, for family and community. Morton and Saltmarsh point out that it was only in *The Eleventh Virgin* that Dorothy wrote in any detail about her experiences as a young woman "coming of age at a time of cultural fragmentation, experiencing the disconnection of modern existence: mind from body, theory from practice, work from labor, intellect from spirit, knowledge from morals, the individual from community." Dorothy's friendships, discussions, and affairs with the radicals and literary figures of the time failed to answer her quest. Her devastating personal experiences and disappointments in politics demonstrated to her "how badly people can treat one another and how poorly the progressive political interests cooperate."[9]

In 1918, during World War I, Dorothy did not want to participate in a war effort, but she wanted to do something to help those in need. She entered nurse's training in King's County Hospital in Brooklyn and later began a liaison with Lionel Moise, who had been a patient there. When she became pregnant, he insisted on an abortion to preserve their relationship, and then abandoned her. Miller noted that later, at age twenty-six, "she began to wonder if she could still have [a child]—if she had not been made sterile by the abortion. She wanted a child desperately, and the matter seems to have become obsessive with her."[10] The abortion had a devastating effect on Dorothy:

> For the rest of her days this part of her life was kept a secret, around which she erected an impenetrable silence. Even in the closing years of her life only several people knew of it. One was a young woman, pregnant, who had gone to the Catholic Worker house and was thinking of having an abortion. Dorothy wrote her a letter, telling of her own experience and begging her not to subject herself to the suffering that she, Dorothy, had undergone.
>
> The consequences of the abortion were near catastrophic. Ill, she took a room with a German family which, as she later said, treated her with extraordinary compassion. Yet she lived with such desolation that twice she initiated attempts at suicide.[11]

During her time in Greenwich Village, as she became more disillusioned with her life there, Dorothy became drawn to the Catholic Church. She noted that it was visibly the church of the poor and the immigrant, not just of the middle or upper classes, in its incarnation of the gospel. She would walk home in the early morning hours, after a night of poetry and drinking, and see the immigrant women who cleaned offices during the night going to Mass at 5:00 a.m. She would sneak into the back pew of St. Joseph's on Sixth Avenue and be in admiration of those who had the faith, so much better off than she in her sordid life. She suspected that she even prayed, "God, be merciful to me, a sinner."[12]

Several years later, when she was in a common-law relationship with Forster Batterham, Dorothy was elated when she found that she was pregnant. Dorothy wrote that it was the joy in being able to have a child that brought her to her conversion: "I will never forget my blissful joy when I was first sure that I was pregnant—I had wanted a baby all the first year we were together....When I was unhappy and repentant in the past I turned to God, but it was my joy at having given birth to a child that made me do something definite."[13]

The event that had the greatest impact in Dorothy Day's life occurred in 1927 when she became Catholic at the age of thirty, not long after giving birth to her daughter. Her years of flirting with the intellectual and devotional aspects of Catholicism culminated in her seeking baptism, first for her child and later for herself. Since Forster, an anarchist, did not believe in religion, marriage, or having children, that relationship dissolved, albeit very painfully.

Dorothy tried to explain to her socialist friends how she could possibly become Catholic. She reflected on the criticism of the church by secular radicals and why she, who had lost none of her perspective of social criticism, was going over to what they considered the other side: "I speak of the misery of leaving one love [Forster Batterham]. But there was another love too, the life I had led in the radical movement. That very winter I was writing a series of articles, interviews with the workers, with the unemployed....I was just as much against capitalism and imperialism as ever, and here I was, going over to the opposition, because of course the Church was lined up with property, with the wealthy, with the state, with capitalism, with all the forces of reaction."[14]

The question of wealthy industrialists and their relationship to the church had been a stumbling block for Dorothy in her interest in the church, even though she knew it to be also the church of the poor because she prayed at Mass with many poor immigrants. She wrote in *From Union Square to Rome* that Sister Aloysia, the very sister who gave her instructions in Catholicism, lived on property donated by one of the most ruthless capitalists, Charles Schwab: "I could not but feel that his was tainted money which the Sisters had accepted. It was, I felt, money that belonged to the workers. He had defrauded the worker of a just wage. His sins cried to heaven for vengeance. He had ground the faces of the poor....Yet strangely enough, in bitterness of soul these thoughts led me inevitably to the problem: how to have Teresa baptized." Her conviction that the church was divine but that its members were filled with human frailties overcame Dorothy's concerns. Whatever the sins of Charlie Schwab and the failure of church people, she made arrangements for her child to be baptized.[15]

Although she was given instruction in the basic doctrines of Catholicism through *The Baltimore Catechism*, so derided by modern catechists, and copies of the *Sacred Heart Messenger*, Dorothy's extensive reading gave her a broad background from which to understand her new faith.

The nun who instructed her expected her to know the answers in that "old-fashioned" catechism in which she found basic concepts that would support her positions on serious issues such as pacifism throughout her life. She also continued reading *The Imitation of Christ*, St. Augustine, and the New Testament. By this time, Dorothy had come to have confidence in the church. As she explained later, "But I do not know how any one can persist in the search for God without the assistance of the Church and the advice of her confessors, with the experience of generations behind them."[16]

Dorothy had made her decision. She was baptized conditionally (because she had been baptized in the Episcopal Church as a child), made her confession, and received communion. The decision to enter the church involved a dramatic conversion from a bohemian, worldly lifestyle and hope for answers to social problems in socialism to a lifetime of total commitment to Christ, to the church, to the poor, and to peace. Ultimately, she had chosen another way: "If I could have felt that communism was the answer to my desire for a cause, a motive, a way to walk in, I would have remained as I was. But I felt that only faith in Christ could give the answer. The Sermon on the Mount answered all the questions as to how to love God and one's brother."[17]

When Dorothy became a Catholic, she did so with her whole heart, soul, and mind. Her life was changed forever. Dorothy was a full-blown Catholic. She accepted the Roman Catholic Church hook, line, and sinker. Some, including her brother, could not understand how she could stand to be a member of a church they considered to be extremely authoritarian. Ironically, it was in the church that Dorothy found freedom, the freedom to be a personalist, to engage the whole world with her faith, to address persons in an impersonal, fragmented world, and especially to meet Christ in the persons who came to her. It was in the church that she found the spiritual weapons of which she later spoke so often. She declared that she had accepted the church's authority:

> Now the creed to which I subscribe is like a battle cry, engraved on my heart—the *Credo* of the Holy Roman Catholic Church. Before, in those former times, I could say: "I shall sleep in the dust: and if thou seek me in the morning, I shall not be." (Job 7:21) Now I can say: "I know that my Redeemer liveth and the last day I shall rise out of the earth. And I shall be clothed again with my skin, and in my flesh I shall see God. Whom I myself shall see and my eyes shall behold, and not another: this my hope is laid up in my bosom." (Job 19:25–27)
>
> I had a conversation with John Spivak, the Communist writer, a few years ago and he said to me, "How *can* you believe? How can you believe in the Immaculate Conception, in the Virgin birth, in the Resurrection?" I could only say that I believe in the Roman Catholic Church and all She teaches. I have accepted Her authority with my whole heart.[18]

Dorothy shared how she continued her studies after her conversion, often with the help of others. Her first confessors gave her Challoner's book of meditations, books of Karl Adam, a St. Andrew's Missal "so that I could learn to follow the seasons of the Church, the saints of the day, and have the doctrinal instruction containing many quotations from the Fathers of the Church," and showed her how to say the Little Office of the Blessed Virgin.[19]

Becoming a Catholic did not mean that Dorothy lost her concern for the poor and her burning desire to create a more just world. As a single mother, on the advice of Father Zachary, she kept her job writing for the Anti-Imperialist League until she was able to find other work with the Fellowship of Reconciliation and continue her work as a journalist, writing articles for Catholic magazines. In 1932 she went to a massive march of unemployed workers in Washington, D.C., not as a participant, but as a reporter for the lay-run Catholic magazine *Commonweal*. The march had been organized by Communists as part of their strategy of winning the workers to their cause, although the masses of rank-and-file workers were, as Dorothy said, of every political color and creed. At the same time a Farmers' Convention was held in Washington, also Communist inspired, "made up of small farmers and tenant farmers from around the country." *America,* the Jesuit weekly, had asked Dorothy to write an article about the convention.[20] The march and the convention brought back to Dorothy sharp memories of her participation in the struggle for rights of workers before she became Catholic. In her recorded reflections at that time, she confessed to a strong feeling of neglecting the workers and the poor, as if in the joy and discovery of her newfound faith she had almost abandoned those whom she had known and defended. Having spent years reading the scriptures and the lives of the saints, she believed that Catholic Christians as well as Communists should be standing with the poor. Although she felt she could not participate in the Communist-organized march, Dorothy said,

> I watched that ragged horde and thought to myself, "These are Christ's poor. He was one of them. He was a man like other men, and He chose His friends amongst the ordinary workers. These men feel they have been betrayed by Christianity. Men are not Christian today. If they were, this sight would not be possible. Far dearer in the sight of God perhaps are these hungry ragged ones, than all those smug, well-fed Christians who sit in their homes, cowering in fear of the Communist menace.
>
> I felt that they were my people, that I was part of them. I had worked for them and with them in the past, and now I was a Catholic and so could not be a Communist. I could not join this united front of protest and I wanted to.[21]

Dorothy understood something that so many who watched that march did not: that Christ loves the poor with what has since been defined by the church as a "preferential option" for them. She knew that the vast majority of the marchers were not Communists, but were simply desperate. As she often wrote later, she perceived then that the way to respond to Communism was not just to say how terrible it was, but to actively challenge an economic system that created so many poor and to offer solidarity and a greater vision to those workers whose only support had seemed to come from the half-truths propagated by Communist organizers. As Communists described the harsh reality of the social order and gave workers their support, Dorothy understood that their ideology ultimately offered the poor only a flawed hope for salvation through materialism. The possibility that some might confuse involvement in causes for justice with Communism, however, did not lessen her cry that Christian faith could not be separated from concern for those who suffered. Dorothy believed that the church of the Lord who overthrew the money changers in the Temple should be concerned about these poor workers: "I could write, I could protest, to arouse the conscience, but where was the Catholic leadership in the gathering of bands of men and women together, for the actual Works of Mercy that the comrades had always made part of their technique in reaching the workers?"[22]

When the demonstration was over and she had finished writing her story, Dorothy went to the National Shrine of the Immaculate Conception at Catholic University, where the building was not yet finished, and prayed in the crypt. She later wrote in her autobiography, "There I offered up a special prayer, a prayer which came with tears and with anguish, that some way would open up for me to use what talents I possessed for my fellow workers, for the poor."[23]

A second historic event in Dorothy's life was Peter Maurin's discovery of her, immediately after she returned from Washington, D.C. As Dorothy later wrote, "And when I returned to New York I found Peter Maurin—Peter, the French peasant, whose spirit and ideas will dominate...the rest of my life."[24] Peter was waiting for her at her apartment and presented his ideas and his program, not least of which was the newspaper she would edit. The meeting of Peter and Dorothy brought together two of the most important Catholics of the twentieth century. Catholicism in the United States would be changed forever. These two thinkers blew the dynamite of the Catholic faith, as Peter described it in an Easy Essay that he entitled "Blowing the Dynamite." His essay begins:

Writing about the Catholic Church,
a radical writer says:
"Rome will have to do more

than to play a waiting game;
she will have to use
some of the dynamite
inherent in her message."
To blow the dynamite
of a message
is the only way
to make the message dynamic.
If the Catholic Church
is not today
the dominant social dynamic force,
it is because Catholic scholars
have taken the dynamite
of the Church,
have wrapped it up
in nice phraseology,
placed it in an hermetic container
and sat on the lid.
It is about time
to blow the lid off
so the Catholic Church
may again become
the dominant social dynamic force.

Holy Cross Father Michael Baxter has pointed out that the dynamic, explosive ingredient to which Peter referred was from the Greek word *dynamis*, the power of the life, death, and resurrection of Christ. *Dynamis* was to be shared by his followers in their spreading of the gospel message. The problem was that Catholic scholars had taken this dynamic message, "cordoned it off, kept it under wraps, and rendered it socially impotent" by treating theology and the social teaching of the church as if they constitute two separate fields of inquiry, separating the natural and the supernatural, theology and the social sphere, in what Baxter calls a misreading of St. Thomas Aquinas:

The social theory to which Maurin referred in his Essay was dynamic because it possessed an explosive ingredient: Jesus Christ. The image of dynamite jolts the listener/reader into imagining Christ and the Church in temporal rather than in purely spiritual terms. This is not to say that Maurin denied that the Church's mission is "spiritual"; no Catholic intellectual of that era would have denied that; but, for Maurin, "spiritual" signified specific practices and a specific form of social life. In contrast to standard Catholic social theory, his social theory was, in a word, ecclesial.[25]

Most people today know much more about Dorothy Day than they do about Peter Maurin. Dorothy has become a famous Catholic convert and pacifist. In 1972 she was given the Laetare Medal by the University of Notre Dame. On the occasion of her death in 1980 Dorothy was described by Catholic historian David O'Brien as "the most significant, interesting, and influential person in the history of American Catholicism." On her eightieth birthday, New York's Cardinal Terence Cook presented Dorothy with a special greeting from Pope Paul VI. Her picture and articles about her appeared in *Time, Newsweek,* and *Life* magazines. *The New York Times* said she was a "nonviolent social radical of luminous personality." In 1999 James Breig reported in *The Evangelist,* newspaper of the Syracuse diocese, that a panel of church historians and theologians had selected her as the most outstanding lay Catholic of the twentieth century. In the year 2000 Cardinal John O'Connor of New York introduced Dorothy's cause for canonization in Rome.

It is impossible to understand Dorothy Day, however, without realizing the importance of Peter Maurin in her life and having some acquaintance with his ideas.

Peter Maurin (1877–1949)

Peter was waiting for Dorothy when she returned to New York to begin his deluge of information about personalism and voluntary poverty, about his analysis of history, about the prophets of Israel and the fathers of the church, about the saints, about how to blow the wonderful dynamite of the church. He told her about his program of action, of roundtable discussions, Houses of Hospitality for the practice of the Works of Mercy, and agronomic universities. Peter wanted a newspaper to bring Catholic social teaching "to the man on the street;" he wanted Dorothy, a newspaperwoman, to start the paper. The newspaper Peter envisioned would not, as he said, simply print the news, but make the news. He wanted to share his dream of making a synthesis of ideas for a pluralist society as St. Thomas had done in the Middle Ages, a synthesis that included economics for the good of all and the idea of making a world where it would be easier for people to be good. His ideas were not meant just for Catholics; Dorothy said, "His friends were Jews, Protestants, agnostics, as well as Catholics, and he found common ground with all in what he termed the Thomistic doctrine of the common good."[26]

Miller pointed out that unlike many critics of the church, it was in the church itself that Peter looked for his new synthesis: "It is perhaps because he was free and so full of his program that Maurin seemed never to have found it necessary to expend any of his energy as a critic of the Church. Personalist radicalism found the idea of the Church no obstacle to its philosophy or methods; to the contrary, it was only through personalist radicalism that the dynamite of the Church could be ignited. Maurin thus united orthodoxy with radicalism, and this principle was understood and has been faithfully followed by Dorothy Day."[27]

Some people have dismissed Peter as a marginal character, as they did Dorothy before her life and work became better known. Stories abound about how Peter was sometimes mistaken for the plumber, the handyman, the janitor when he went somewhere to give a talk. As Dorothy said, "He never had more than the clothes on his back, but he took the Gospel counsel literally—'if anyone asks for thy coat give him thy cloak too.'"[28] Miller recounts that "workers could tell stories in which Maurin's unconventional attire involved him in cases of mistaken identity. Dorothy Day recalled a time when he went to a Westchester town to give a talk to a woman's club....Several hours after he had gone, she received a frantic telephone call: Where was Maurin? 'Since I had put him on the train myself, I told them he must be in the station. "There is only an old tramp sitting on the bench asleep," was the reply. We knew it was Peter.'"[29]

Some have never gotten beyond this image of him. The profundity, however, of Peter's thought and his sanctity are apparent to those who read Dorothy's writings. In his biography of Dorothy, Miller gives her assessment of Peter, that he was a saint-teacher, "an apostle to the world":

> He made one feel the magnificence of our work, our daily lives, the material of God's universe and what we did with it, how we used it....
>
> He built up a new apostolate. He reached the poorest and the most destitute by living always among them, sharing their poverty and sharing what he had with them....
>
> I do know this—that when people come into contact with Peter...they change, they awaken, they begin to see, things become as new, they look at life in the light of the Gospels. They admit the truth he possesses and lives by, and though they themselves fail to go the whole way, their faces are turned at least toward the light.[30]

It is unfortunate that Peter, who lived the poverty he admired in St. Francis, has acquired the image of a Bowery bum, whereas in fact, he was a brilliant intellectual and one of the best-read men of his times. His commitment to Holy Poverty caused him to dress rather shabbily (although it was a shabby suit and tie as opposed to a pair of blue jeans), which obscured his greatness. He gathered the profound concepts that were the fruit of his many studies and expressed them in free verse, in an often-humorous form that Dorothy's brother, John, called "Easy Essays" and that have been so named since then. Dorothy noted that Peter knew well that, in spite of the title given to them, "his essays were anything but easy. Like those in the Gospel, his were hard sayings—hard to work out in everyday life."[31]

Dorothy and Peter embraced a theology of the incarnation that recognizes both the divinity and the humanity of Christ, and lived out the implications of this theology and spirituality. As Dorothy said of Peter in the May 1977 *Catholic Worker*: "While decrying secularism, the separation of the material from the spiritual, his emphasis as a layman, was on our material needs, our need for work, food, clothing and shelter. Though Peter went weekly to confession and daily to Communion and spent an hour a day in the presence of the Blessed Sacrament...[h]e was dealing with this world, in which God has placed us to work for a new heaven and a new earth wherein justice dwelleth."

Many understood and appreciated Peter's sanctity and genius. Mel Piehl quoted Maisie Ward, wife of Frank Sheed and cofounder of the publishing house of Sheed & Ward, remembering Peter: "At first glance you would probably overlook Peter, yet Peter Maurin was perhaps the greatest inspiration of Catholic America in our generation."[32] Arthur Sheehan recorded several commentaries on Peter by well-known people of his time. Cardinal Cardijn, founder of the Jocist movement of young workers, said of him that his thought is the "purest spirit of the Gospels."[33] Father Wilfred Parsons, SJ, editor of *America* magazine, once said that Peter Maurin was the "best-read man he had ever met." John Moody, of Moody's Investors' Service, described one of his meetings with Peter Maurin as follows:

> Anyone who has met Peter knows that he can, on first appearance, make the shivers creep up your spine when he begins to talk. If, when he starts in, you are leaning back in an easy chair, you will find yourself sitting up erect in that chair before he has talked five minutes. He can cram more truth into your cranium at high speed in a single hour than any ordinary person can do in a week....
>
> His theme was social justice. He gave me, among other things, a gist of Pope Pius XI's encyclical *Quadragesimo anno*, which up to that time I had not digested at all. But Peter had digested it, and he made its contents so clear to me that a short time thereafter I was able to give a brief talk on it to a small group of high-brow Wall Streeters, and actually tell them some things they didn't already know.[34]

Dorothy wrote in the May 1977 *Catholic Worker* that, at the time of Peter's death, "[o]bituaries were found not only in *The Industrial Worker*, a Chicago I.W.W. paper which was on the subversive list, but also in *L'Osservatore romano* in Vatican City, which carried its notice on the front page." *Time* magazine described his funeral:

> Dressed in a castoff suit and consigned to a donated grave, the mortal remains of a poor man were buried last week. These

arrangements were appropriate; during most of his life Peter Maurin had slept in no bed of his own and worn no suit that someone had not given away. But to his funeral among the teeming, pushcart-crowded slums of lower Manhattan Cardinal Spellman himself sent his representative. There were priests representing many Catholic orders and there were laymen, rich and poor, from places as far away as Chicago. All night long before the funeral they had come to the rickety storefront where the body lay, to say a prayer or touch their rosaries to the folded hands. For many of them were sure that Peter Maurin was a saint.[35]

Peter, the oldest of twenty-one children, was born on May 9, 1877, in Languedoc, in southern France, where his family lived on the land. His mother had died when he and his brother were small and his father remarried. Peter's stepmother was a mother to him.[36] It was in his home and his village, and especially with the model of his father, that Peter was formed in the Catholic faith, as well as with the De La Salle Brothers, usually known as the Christian Brothers. As a teenager he went to a Christian Brothers' school and later entered the order as a novice and taught several years with them. The work of the Christian Brothers in France was especially to teach poor children. The founder was an educational innovator and Peter learned about educational methods from the brothers. It was from these methods that Peter developed his teaching and writing style, using simple language and clear definitions to express important principles. He also learned from the brothers that the personal example of the teacher living the gospel was key to the teaching method: "The Brothers were firmly grounded in the theological sciences, dogmatic and moral. Education to them was much more than knowledge....The need for sacrifice would be taught through the personalist example of the teacher."[37]

Peter learned much about church tradition and about particular charisms in what must have been an outstanding novitiate of the Christian Brothers. There St. Philip Neri was presented as a model of joyous asceticism. Much later Peter compared his discussions, which he held with everyone who would listen, to the "easy conversations about things that matter" of Philip Neri.

Peter wrote in an Easy Essay about these easy conversations:

Easy conversations
about things that matter
would keep people
from going to the movies,
from talking politics,
from cheap wisecracking.
Easy conversations
about things that matter
would enable Catholics
to understand Catholicism,
to give an account of their faith,
and to make non-Catholics curious
about Catholicism.

The Catholic Worker was and is a lay movement without official status in the church and without formally defined leadership. As Peter later said, "We are an organism, not an organization."[38] Later, as Catholic Worker Houses of Hospitality grew up in other cities, each house was autonomous, although loosely affiliated with the movement in New York City. Sheehan quoted Peter as saying that "each house should stand or fall on its own merits. He wanted no central control, no vows." This was similar to the words of St. Philip Neri, whose Oratory affiliates were not highly organized: "Let each house live by its own vitality or perish of its own decrepitude," St. Philip Neri had said.[39] Peter also believed the individual House of Hospitality should succeed or fail depending upon the spirit animating it.

As he was teaching in different parts of France, including Paris, and often in poor areas, Peter saw firsthand the poverty of workers in contrast to the much greater wealth of the few. This was at the time of the industrial revolution, when so many people were moving from the farms to the cities and were paid little for working fifteen hours a day. He began to reflect on the questions this raised in his mind and to participate in the study groups that were becoming popular, groups that sought to form lay apostles for Christian action in the world. A lay movement in France that employed this study-group technique, called Le Sillon, started and led by Marc Sangnier, was dedicated to the formation of responsible Christians who would unite workers and students in a democracy. Peter became involved with Le Sillon while he was still a Christian Brother and eventually decided to leave the order before he made his final vows and joined that movement, which was to influence Peter later in the way he envisioned the Catholic Worker. His leaving the order was perhaps influenced by the fact that in France at this time the government closed thousands of religious schools for children. It seemed that the Christian Brothers, like other orders whose schools had already been closed, would not long be able to continue teaching.[40]

Peter rented a room in a poor section of Paris. He sold the newspaper of the movement, *L'Eveil démocratique* (The Democratic Awakening) at meetings, on the streets, and in front of churches, as *The Catholic Worker* was later sold in the streets. Sheehan wrote of the elements of Le Sillon that were similar to the Catholic Worker, where a long-term commitment was not required in order to participate in the movement: "There was no enrollment, no dues, no rules, no elections. One entered freely and left freely. No one received a salary, but there were indemnities for personal needs. The ablest rose to leadership not by being elected but by the sheer force of their knowledge and personality."[41]

In similar fashion, participation in the Catholic Worker movement was not necessarily a permanent vocation. For some it was a lifetime vocation. Others came to stay a few days, a few weeks, a few months, or a few years to join in the work. The Catholic Worker became, as Le Sillon had been, a kind of training ground for living the gospel. Years later, Dorothy Day described this characteristic of the Catholic Worker movement: "If they had a true vocation for this work of love, sharing what they had very simply, they would have persevered through hell and high water, as the saying is. Meanwhile it is a school for them, an exercise and they can only learn by doing. They have yet to find their true vocation. Even so, as an act of love, it is of incalculable value."[42]

Miller pointed out that one of the great similarities between Le Sillon and the Catholic Worker movement was its rejection of the bourgeois spirit "and especially to its presence in the Catholic Church."[43]

Peter Maurin left Le Sillon movement when it became political and because, Sheehan implies, their scholarship was not good enough.[44] Having left that movement and becoming more and more uncomfortable with repeated calls to participate in required military reserve service, Peter consulted with his family and then moved to Canada to homestead with a wave of French immigrants. After about two years there he moved to the United States, and like so many immigrants, worked in manual labor in industries such as construction and mining. He was an undocumented immigrant. At around this time he had some kind of profound second conversion. Later, he moved to New York and became a French teacher. After a time, Peter stopped charging for his French lessons and asked students only to offer what they thought the lessons were worth. He began to write his Easy Essays and to formulate his program.[45] At this time Peter not only refused to work for pay, accepting only what students chose to donate, but also wore clothing that was donated. As Sheehan said, "He began to look less careful of his clothes from his Chicago days, when a picture shows him as being quite stylishly dressed." When a student once gently suggested that he should dress better, Peter replied, "I don't want to arouse envy."[46]

Peter began giving talks in churches and at the Rotary Club about his ideas. One priest published his Easy Essays in the parish bulletin. Another priest, Father Joseph B. Scully, became interested in Peter's ideas, gave him a place to stay for five years, and had many talks with him about his vision. When Peter later began the Catholic Worker with Dorothy Day and Cardinal Hayes questioned Father Scully about him, Father Scully replied, "He knows his stuff."[47]

It was George Shuster, editor of *Commonweal* at the time, who suggested to Peter that he contact Dorothy Day. When Peter had first visited *Commonweal*, the staff was very busy putting out the magazine. John Brunini, an assistant, thought he would be helpful and get rid of him. Schuster's high estimation of Peter was clear when he upbraided his assistant, saying, "You might have been entertaining angels."[48] Dorothy said she probably would not have taken Peter seriously if she had not gone to Washington, D.C., to cover the hunger march and then prayed at the National Shrine of the Immaculate Conception for a way to unite her faith with the social concerns that she had so often expressed before her conversion. Nor would she have responded to Peter if she had not been reading the lives of the saints, "canonized and as yet uncanonized, St. John Bosco and Rose Hawthorne for instance—I probably would have listened, but continued to write rather than act."[49] But she did listen and begin to act on Peter's program.

Coming from a newspaper family and having worked on several newspapers herself, Dorothy understood the need to start a paper, but asked, "Where do we get the money?" Peter's response determined the future of the Catholic Worker movement: "In the history of the saints, capital was raised by prayer. God sends you what you need when you need it. You will be able to pay the printer. Just read the lives of the saints." He told her that St. Francis de Sales "scattered leaflets like any radical, St. John of God sold newspapers on the streets."[50] Rose Hawthorne had started a hospice in New York for the poor who had cancer. Her method of raising money simply by telling people what she was going to do appealed to Dorothy. Perhaps she could start in a small way.

The Catholic Worker Movement

The work began in May 1933 with the first issue of 2,500 copies of *The Catholic Worker*, printed by Paulist Press for $57. To begin the newspaper Dorothy had to imaginatively raise money: "I decided to wait until I had the cash in hand before getting out the first issue. I didn't want to run up any debts. I did no installment buying, although I didn't mind being late with the rent or skimping on groceries to speed the accumulation of enough money to pay the first bill. [Paulist] Father McSorley helped a lot by finding work for me to do. Father Harold Purcell gave me ten dollars, and Sister Peter Claver brought me a dollar which someone had just given to her."[51] *The Catholic Worker* newspaper, based on nonviolence and love, was presented as an alternative to the Communist *Daily Worker*, which advocated violent class struggle. Peter had wanted to call the paper *The Catholic Radical*, but Dorothy insisted on *The Catholic Worker* because of her concern for the situation of workers. With unemployment reaching 25 percent of the workforce both in the United States and in the world at large, both Peter and Dorothy knew that there had to be an alternative to the economic system that had left the social order in such disarray. The first editions of the paper made it clear that the basis for the alternative they presented was their faith, a faith whose richness they wished to present to readers in all its fullness, including the social dimension. Dorothy explained further the reason for the word *Catholic* in the name of the paper in her auto-biography: "Many times we have been asked why we spoke of *Catholic* workers, and so named the paper. Of course it was not only because we who were in charge of the work, who edited the paper, were all Catholics, but also because we wished to influence Catholics. They were our own, and we reacted sharply to the accusation that when it came to private morality the Catholics shone but when it came to social and political morality, they were often conscienceless."[52]

When the first issue came out, Peter was quite surprised that *The Catholic Worker* carried articles by other people, including Dorothy. Having envisioned it as simply a paper to promulgate his ideas and program, he took his name off as an editor, saying, "Everybody's paper is nobody's paper." He and Dorothy came to an amicable agreement and continued to work together, but Peter presented only Easy Essays signed by his own name.

In that first issue of the paper, however, Dorothy was present-ing Peter's philosophy, his insistence on blowing the dynamite of the church, helping readers to understand it in terms of her expe-rience and cultural realities. She responded to the criticisms of religion by socialists and radicals as the opium of the people:

> The fundamental aim of most radical sheets is the conversion of
> its readers to radicalism and atheism.

Is it not possible to be radical and not atheist?

Is it not possible to protest, to expose, to complain, to point out abuses and demand reforms without desiring the overthrow of religion?

In an attempt to popularize and make known the encyclicals of the Popes in regard to social justice and the program put forth by the Church for the "reconstruction of the social order," this newssheet, *The Catholic Worker*, is started.

In the 1930s Communism was intellectually fascinating to many in the United States. The great irony of the life of Dorothy Day is that while she was sometimes accused of being a Communist, she and Peter from the beginning developed an alternative for Catholics who might have turned to Communism in desperation in the midst of worldwide depression. Cyril Echele, one of the early Catholic Workers, has asserted that, unbeknownst to most people, the Catholic Worker movement "may inadvertently have done more to stem the tide toward Communism in the United States than any other concerted effort up to the present time."[53]

The new Catholic Workers were determined to get out the news about their paper and the alternative it offered. Friends and volunteers took it not only to Union Square and Communist meetings, but also to Wall Street to pass out copies after talks there. Dorothy wrote in the June–July 1933 *Catholic Worker* about the response to the presence of Catholic Workers in Union Square that first May Day in 1933, where so many, and especially Communists, were shocked to find Catholics there to refute their claims:

The crowds in Union Square stopped to gaze on May 1, not only at the massed parades, blary bands and various red banners, but also at the caption, THE CATHOLIC WORKER, being displayed and distributed everywhere. Communists who make soap-box speeches were frankly shocked at its appearance, refuting as it did their claim that the Church is interested only in squeezing money from the people to send to Rome. Even more surprising to them was the revelation that Catholicism has a definite social program to aid the worker.

People who read about hospitality in the newspaper arrived to receive it, and the Works of Mercy began. Houses of Hospitality and bread and soup lines for the hungry soon followed. First there were only Dorothy, Peter, and Dorothy's brother John to help, but soon others came to join in the work. Later the farms began. Within three or four months, the circulation of *The Catholic Worker* was 25,000; by the end of a year it was 100,000 and by 1936 it was 150,000.[54] The growth in circulation was not accidental. The paper was sold on the street at a penny a copy and bulk subscriptions were developed at Catholic schools and parishes. Dorothy actively sought bulk subscriptions; many parishes received 500 copies, one Catholic high school 3,000. Miller said it was the personalist approach of the movement that attracted many readers: "In the long run, the continued expansion in the circulation of the *Worker* was due to those who, caught by the attractiveness of its personalist idea, supported it with contributions and through work to get subscriptions."[55]

Dorothy commented in the February 1943 *Catholic Worker* on the initiation of the movement, emphasizing her vocation as a journalist, a vocation that could not be separated from the communitarian personalist life of sacrificial love at the Catholic Worker: "We are called, we have a vocation, we have a talent. It is up to us to develop that. Mine, for instance, is journalism writing, and it is only because of the paper, *The Catholic Worker,* that Houses of Hospitality and farming communes, or even the suggestion of them came into being. That's how the communitarian end of the movement started. People read about our way of thinking and our way of life and want to join us. They come to visit and remain."

In the early years of the Catholic Worker movement Dorothy's first spiritual director was Joseph McSorley, CSP. William Portier pointed out in the September–October 2002 *Houston Catholic Worker* that some time during 1932 she had found Paulist Father McSorley, who assisted the founders in the beginning of the movement and provided spiritual direction to Dorothy for the first seven or eight years after it began:

> Thirty years later, on the occasion of McSorley's funeral in 1963, Day remembered "our dear friend Fr. McSorley, with

whose encouragement and advice Peter Maurin and I launched the Catholic Worker back in 1933...." During the paper's first decade, McSorley published two pieces in *The Catholic Worker*....

In a 1974 *Catholic Worker* column, Day recalled how McSorley helped her overcome her uncertainties about public speaking. Again she refers to him as "my first spiritual adviser":

"My missal opened at yesterday's Epistle, which begins, 'The priests and the elders were amazed as they observed the self-assurance of Peter and John and realized the speakers were uneducated men of no standing.' This immediately gave me comfort. 'Go where you are invited,' Father McSorley, my first spiritual adviser, once told me."

In the years after his death, Day gratefully recalled McSorley as "my first spiritual director" and "my first teacher in the faith, to whom I used to go in the large Paulist church near Lincoln Center."

In addition to his role as Day's spiritual director and sometime confessor, it came about that Paulist Father Joseph McSorley also served the Catholic Worker during the 1930s as an "approved adviser." By the second year of the publication of the paper, people were beginning to complain to the chancery office in New York about some of the controversial stands taken by *The Catholic Worker*. Miller recounts that Monsignor Arthur J. Scanlan, Office of Censor of Books, sent a letter to Dorothy suggesting that it would be good to have a priest to advise her on the publication:

It might be a good idea if Miss Day would give him some names of some priests "who are both interested and sympathetic with the work you are doing." He then thought it would be advisable to have "His Eminence appoint one of them to look over the matter before publication and be responsible for it." This course would "avoid criticism and...be of assistance in the future development of the work." Apparently wishing to avoid the appearance of giving an ecclesiastical order, Scanlan followed up his letter with a personal visit. He was concerned about the "great many attacks" on *The Catholic Worker* he had received, Dorothy Day explained in a letter to a friend.

Dorothy readily accepted Scanlan's proposal, suggesting that her spiritual adviser, Fr. McSorley, be chosen as her editorial adviser. Scanlan agreed to this and then relayed information from Cardinal Hayes that McSorley's name was not to appear in print and that he had "received no official appointment to act as censor."[56]

Monsignor Scanlan's commonsense approach proved to be a good one. Dorothy never had serious problems with the archdiocese; in fact, she later became a good friend of the future cardinal of Los Angeles, James Francis McIntyre, then in the New York chancery office.

The work of hospitality and the Works of Mercy were accompanied from the beginning by reading, speakers, and discussions in what Peter considered an essential part of his program, "clarification of thought." To implement this program Peter invited speakers he knew who were Benedictine or Jesuit priests or professors at universities in New York. Father McSorley gave one of these talks at the Catholic Worker. Although the first advertised programs did not attract the crowds that Peter expected, clarification of thought became an integral part of the Catholic Worker movement. Professors often brought their students to the Catholic Worker; the students became workers; they helped with the physical work of putting out the paper, washing dishes, writing thank-you notes, painting, or whatever tasks came to hand.

In the September 1974 *Catholic Worker,* Dorothy reported on how Peter presented his views on economics to professors at various universities, at *The Wall Street Journal,* and at Moody Investment Services. She emphasized how he was "unique in trying to change the social order by 'appeals, not demands'—appeals to man's intellect and heart (mind and soul)":

> He did not hesitate to go to Columbia University to talk to professors, who, in turn, came willingly to speak at our nightly meetings in 1933 and 1934. He also visited often on Wall Street and talked to Thomas Woodlock, an editorial writer on the *Wall Street Journal* (nicknamed Thomas Aquinas Woodlock by some of his confreres), and Thomas Moody, Catholic convert, who headed the Moody Investment Services. Peter talked to them about economics and money lending at interest (originally forbidden by the "Prophets of Israel and the Fathers of the Church").

Peter invited scholars to speak at the House of Hospitality with workers, because he believed both should share work and thought. As he put it:

> The scholars must tell the workers
> what is wrong
> with things as they are.
> The scholars must tell the workers
> how the things would be,
> if they were as they should be.
> The scholars must tell the workers
> how a path can be made
> from the things as they are
> to the things as they should be.
> The scholars must collaborate with the workers
> in the making of a path
> from the things as they are
> to the things as they should be.

One of the most important contributions Peter made to the Catholic Worker and to the world was his insistence on living out one's convictions, not just reading about them, studying them, or collecting facts and information. He did not recommend waiting to develop five-year plans or blueprints for one's life, but simply to begin to live the gospel and to learn by doing, through existential action.

Peter was a real scholar as well as a peasant. He was taken with the idea of 100 Great Books when he heard about the Great Books program that was being publicized in the '30s. "Why not a hundred books explaining the ideas behind the Catholic Worker?" he asked. A list of forty-nine of the books Peter recommended was published in the now out-of-print *Catholic Radicalism*, a collection of Peter's Easy Essays compiled by Dave Mason and published by the Catholic Worker in 1949.[57]

A study of the Catholic Worker movement reveals the rich scholarship and faith sources that accompanied and gave profound meaning to the Works of Mercy as practiced in the Houses of Hospitality. At first, one might wonder where these two people who were committed to voluntary poverty were able to obtain the books to read for their scholarship. Two examples of gifts show that Dorothy and Peter were given much help by people who believed in their project. Dom Virgil Michel, OSB, a friend who was the leader of the liturgical movement in the United States, secured permission from his abbot to send the editors of *The Catholic Worker* free copies of all of the books from his new publishing house, Liturgical Press.[58] Later, of course, many books were sent in to be reviewed by *The Catholic Worker*. Dorothy Day also recounted this story: "One of our readers in Burlington, Vermont, a woman doctor who admired Peter very much, once told him that he could charge books to her account at Brentano's. For a while, Peter had a field day."[59]

Miller gives a clue to the question of how Peter, so far from France, kept up with everything that was happening there in personalist circles and was able to give information on the latest books in *The Catholic Worker* as well as arranging for French books to be translated. Miller quotes from one of Dorothy's columns, in which she recalls Peter telling her of his contacts: "We must get all material from Paulding—he is literary editor at *Commonweal* now—and he will give us more detailed stuff about the leading personalists in France. There is Mounier, editor of *Esprit*, whose *Personalist Manifesto* was translated by Virgil Michel. There is Davidson or Dennison—I cannot remember his name. He is an historian. There is Landberg, a psychologist, and Jacques Madaule, who ran for police chief in Paris...."[60]

The following chapters are meant to mine some of the richness of the reading, study, and writing of Peter Maurin and Dorothy Day and deepen the reflections of future scholars and workers.

Christ in the Poor: The Works of Mercy

One of the central ideas in the Catholic Worker program is the living out of the seven corporal and the seven spiritual Works of Mercy. The daily practice of the Works of Mercy recommended by Peter Maurin is based on Matthew 25:31 and the following verses and on the earliest tradition of the church and the lives of the saints. In the Catholic Worker this practice was first manifested in the '30s, when so many were out of work, by giving a place to stay to the homeless in the Houses of Hospitality and coffee and bread or hearty soups to the hungry. The Catholic Workers drew out the practical implications of all of the fourteen Works of Mercy.

In her writings, Dorothy listed the Works of Mercy for the benefit of readers who may not have known all of them:

> The Spiritual Works of Mercy are: to admonish the sinner, to instruct the ignorant, to counsel the doubtful, to comfort the sorrowful, to bear wrongs patiently, to forgive all injuries, and to pray for the living and the dead.
>
> The Corporal Works of Mercy are to feed the hungry, to give drink to the thirsty, to clothe the naked, to ransom the captive, to harbor the harborless, to visit the sick, and to bury the dead.

Harry Murray explains that it was St. Thomas Aquinas who codified the list that Dorothy gave. Thomas referred to them as "traditional," although Augustine used a different listing. For the Catholic Worker movement, the Works of Mercy "are commands to be taken literally and are as applicable to the technological society of today as they were to the society of two thousand years ago."[1] Workers often told the story from the Matthew 25:31–40:

When the Son of Man comes in his glory, and all the angels with him, then he will sit on the throne of his glory. All the nations will be gathered before him, and he will separate people one from another as a shepherd separates the sheep from the goats, and he will put the sheep at his right and the goats at the left. Then the king will say to those at his right hand, "Come, you that are blessed by my Father, inherit the kingdom prepared for you from the foundation of the world; for I was hungry and you gave me food, I was thirsty and you gave me something to drink, I was a stranger and you welcomed me, I was naked and you gave me clothing, I was sick and you took care of me, I was in prison and you visited me." Then the righteous will answer him, "Lord, when was it that we saw you hungry and gave you food, or thirsty and gave you something to drink? And when was it that we saw you a stranger and welcomed you, or naked and gave you clothing? And when was it that we saw you sick or in prison and visited you?" And the king will answer them, "Truly I tell you, just as you did it to one of the least of these who are members of my family, you did it to me."

Dorothy spent her life putting flesh on the bones of Matthew 25. If there ever was a mission statement of the Catholic Worker movement, this was it. Through the great mystery of the incarnation, persons in every generation are able to respond to Christ himself in the poor. As Dorothy put it, "He made heaven hinge on the way we act toward Him in His disguise of commonplace, frail, ordinary humanity."[2]

Peter told Dorothy (and everyone else) about the early church and how the Christians performed the Works of Mercy at a personal sacrifice, in self-giving love. The reasons for doing the Works of Mercy, as expressed in *The Catholic Worker*, included the witness Peter featured in an Easy Essay, a witness to the world of what Christianity was all about.

In the first centuries
of Christianity
the hungry were fed
at a personal sacrifice,
the naked were clothed

at a personal sacrifice,
the homeless were sheltered
at a personal sacrifice.
And because the poor
were fed, clothed and sheltered
at a personal sacrifice,
the pagans used to say
about the Christians,
"See how they love each other."

Peter saw that the practice of the Works of Mercy involved more than simply receiving the Lord in the poor, binding up wounds, and the symbol of the washing of the feet, although these certainly were meant and were an incredible work and witness. He understood from the lives of the saints that the practice could also be revolutionary, that living the gospel was a unique method of changing the social order: As he put it, "The social order was constructed by the first Christians through the daily practice of the Seven Corporal and Seven Spiritual Works of Mercy."

In October 1933 *The Catholic Worker* published a talk given by Peter Maurin. It was published at that date so that it might be read by the bishops and archbishops meeting at the National Conference of Catholic Charities in New York. The theme was how one of the early church councils insisted that each bishop provide Houses of Hospitality in their parishes:

We read in the Catholic Encyclopedia
that during the early ages of Christianity
the hospice (or the House of Hospitality)
was a shelter for the sick, the poor,
the orphans, the old, the traveler,
and the needy of every kind.
The fourteenth statute
of the so-called Council of Carthage,
held about 435,
enjoins upon the Bishops
to have hospices (or Houses of Hospitality)
in connection with their churches.

The Catholic Workers did not wait for the bishops to start Houses of Hospitality. As personalists, they started them themselves—putting philosophy and practice together. They began with *The Catholic Worker* newspaper and hospitality followed. There was no franchise, no rules except the Sermon on the Mount and Matthew 25. They simply started.

Core to the implementation of the Works of Mercy was the embrace of voluntary poverty. "First of all," Peter used to say, "one must give up one's life to save it. Voluntary poverty is essential."[3] All Workers were to give their works as a gift. No salaries, Dorothy explained. Only their basic needs were to be met. Peter Maurin's fundamental idea: "Reach the people through voluntary poverty (going without the luxuries in order to have the essentials) and through the Works of Mercy (mutual aid and a philosophy of labor)." Dorothy felt the lack of respect and the condemnation of Catholic Workers as radicals but defended their lives and work through the words of the New Testament: "We still are not considered respectable, we still are combated and condemned as 'radicals.' We are fools for Christ's sake....We are weak....We are without honor....We are made as the refuse of this world, the offscouring of all, even until now. And following St. Paul, I am certainly praying that we continue so...."[4]

Catholic Workers knew from experience how destitution ground people down, how difficult it was for those who had not chosen their poverty. On the subject of the poor and destitution, Dorothy as usual quoted respected authors to support her position. In this case it was Daniel-Rops: "In his book, *The Poor and Ourselves,* Daniel-Rops points out clearly the distinction between the destitute and the poor. The destitute are so hopeless, so removed from ordinary life, that it is as though they had a wall around them. It is impossible to reach them, to do anything for them except relieve a few of their immediate needs. As soon as they have begun to work, to think, to read,—no matter whether they are penniless or jobless, they are removed from the ranks of the destitute."[5]

Living in voluntary poverty was not always easy for the Workers, even as they tried to live in faith. Dorothy described one cold winter in old houses without adequate heat in the February 1940 *Catholic Worker,* encouraging Workers and readers with stories of the saints like the individual who was so filled with the love of God that he melted the snow around him and warmed others.

Catholic Workers saw the poor as "ambassadors of God." The Workers believed that when they served or "washed the feet" of a poor person, they were serving the Lord himself, responding to Matthew 25: "When did we see you hungry, when did we see you naked?" As Peter wrote:

> What we give to the poor
> for Christ's sake
> is what we carry with us
> when we die.
> We are afraid
> to pauperize the poor
> because we are afraid to be poor.
> Pagan Greeks used to say
> that the poor
> "are the ambassadors
> of the gods."
> To become poor
> is to become
> an Ambassador of God.

Daniel Di Domizio describes the spirituality of the Catholic Worker movement as theologically "situated in the biblical conviction of the poor being a profound, redeeming revelation of God's presence and grace." The Workers not only gave to those in need, they received even more. Di Domizio reflects on the unity of voluntary poverty and hospitality in the Worker and its witness to church and society:

> For Peter Maurin, voluntary poverty and hospitality were to have a twofold effect: the sanctification of the Catholic Worker and the transformation of the Church's attitude toward the poor. Former Catholic Worker Ed Willock describes, in Maurin's words to a guest, the Catholic Worker approach to "serving the poor": "I can give you bread and meat and coffee. Yes, I can give you these—but you, you can give me the chance

to practice Christian charity. You are an ambassador of God. Thank you." Willock continues, "Contrary to prevailing norms of social service is this notion that the Worker, the volunteer, is the object of reform rather than the poor."[6]

Dorothy struggled for years with questions about charity (sometimes associated with a condescending attitude) and justice. In their study of Dorothy's book, *The Eleventh Virgin*, Keith Morton and John Saltmarsh point out that Dorothy (as the character, June) "has explicitly rejected charity in her quest for justice, and she has been disappointed." In *The Long Loneliness* Dorothy wrote about how she and her radical friends had viewed this question during her time in Greenwich Village: "[O]ur hearts burned with the desire for justice and were revolted at the idea of doled-out charity. The word charity had become something to gag over, something to shudder at." She wrote: "[C]harity was a word to choke over. Who wanted charity?"[7] As a Catholic, however, she concluded that separating justice and charity was a dualism that did not provide answers or solve problems.

It was the attitude of philanthropy, often confused with the charity of Christ, that was so distinct from the philosophy of the Worker. The practice of the Works of Mercy by the movement was so different from philanthropy as to be unrecognizable to those whose way was philanthropic. James Douglass described the difference: "The condescending tone of the term 'charity' can be avoided only if we sink to poverty ourselves and continue to give from our poverty....The Catholic Worker counteracts these pressures [of the consumer, affluent society] by the protest of the poor giving to the poor, shattering the illusion of the billfold apostolate."[8]

Dorothy Day often reminded others that performing the Works of Mercy is not always easy and, in fact, may sometimes bring unpleasant results to the person performing them. She recounted in the June 1956 *Catholic Worker* that in an attempt to close a Catholic Worker House of Hospitality, authorities had accused her of being a slum landlord. In another article entitled "The Scandal of the Works of Mercy," Dorothy shared the sad experience of a reader of the paper whose efforts at hospitality were rewarded by having his wallet stolen. She described these

negative experiences as a pruning, the comparison used in scripture of a plant that must be pruned in order to grow, and to trying by fire: "The Works of Mercy are a wonderful stimulus to our
growth in faith as a well as in love. Our faith is taxed to the utmost
and so grows through this strain put upon it. It is pruned again
and again, and springs up bearing much fruit. For anyone starting
to live literally the words of the Fathers of the Church...there is
always a trial ahead. Our faith, more precious than gold, must be
tried as though by fire."[9]

Even in the face of the challenges always present in the
Houses of Hospitality and on the soup lines, the Workers were
conscious that the Lord himself was their guest in the poor.
Dorothy emphasized, "Too often we are afraid of the poor, of the
worker. We do not realize that we know him, and Christ through
him, in the breaking of the bread."[10]

The Catholic Workers did not hesitate to emphasize the second half of Matthew's story of Judgment Day in their articles, the
part that describes what will happen to those who reject the least
of the brethren. Dorothy wrote in the November 1949 issue of
the paper about sins of omission and the consequences of them
outlined in Matthew 25, when the Lord tells those on his left to
depart into everlasting fire, for when he was hungry they gave him
no food, no drink, a stranger and they did not welcome him: "I
firmly believe that our salvation depends on the poor. 'Inasmuch
as you have not fed the hungry, clothed the naked, sheltered the
homeless, visited the prisoner, protested against injustice, com-
forted the afflicted, etc., you have not done it to Me.' Christ iden-
tifies himself with the poor."

In the May 1947 *Catholic Worker*, Dorothy wrote that an
important part of Peter's program was "to reach the masses
through the spiritual and corporal Works of Mercy." She pointed
out that when we talk of the Works of Mercy, we usually think of
feeding the hungry, clothing the naked, and sheltering the homeless. "Getting Catholic literature around" also includes quite a few
of the tasks involved in the spiritual Works of Mercy, such as
enlightening the ignorant and counseling the doubtful, comforting the afflicted, rebuking the sinner, and even walking on a picket

line. Dorothy quoted St. Paul to support the Catholic Worker's broader understanding of the practicality of the Works of Mercy, even including boycotts as a method to bring about good ends: "We must never forget that Works of Mercy include enlightening the ignorant and rebuking the sinner. St. Paul was advocating a boycott when he said, 'And if any man obey not our word by this epistle, note that man, and do not keep company with him, that he may be ashamed. Yet do not esteem him as an enemy, but admonish him as a brother' (II Thessalonians, 3)."[11]

The spiritual Works of Mercy of picketing and putting out a newspaper often brought the Catholic Workers into conflict with the dominant culture. Their involvement in the world and its problems where others might fear to tread came from the perspective of God as a consuming fire, the fire of love. In her November 1955 Fall Appeal, Dorothy described their love of God also in these terms:

> The love of brother, that care for his freedom is what causes us to go into such controversial subjects as man and the state, war and peace. The implications of the Gospel teaching of the Works of Mercy, lead us into conflict with the powers of this world.
>
> Our love of God is a consuming fire. It is a living God and a living faith that we are trying to express. When we begin to take the lowest place, to wash the feet of others, to love our brothers with that burning love, that passion, which led to the Cross, then we can truly say, "Now I have begun."

Quoting the great writers of the early church, Dorothy showed that the Works of Mercy are for everyone, not just Catholic Workers. Individuals or families can do so much. Dorothy did caution that husbands and wives and children must be considered when one begins to implement Matthew 25. She commented that in her experience it was especially the poor who were hospitable, those who apparently had the least to share, who opened their homes to the stranger in need.

Some observers of the movement criticized Catholic Workers for helping the "undeserving" poor and demanded that Workers discriminate more scrupulously between those who merited help and those who might be lazy parasites and cheats. Dorothy answered in the March 1947 *Catholic Worker* that Christ loved all the poor, and that the social order should be changed so that not so many suffered: "It is indeed hard to see Christ in the undeserving poor. We admit that there will always be the poor, the wastrel, the drunk, the sinner. But Christ came to save them. He loved them. We just insist that there do not need to be so many of them, the degraded, the twisted, the warped, the miserable ones, employed and unemployed."

In the July–August 1943 issue, in the midst of World War II, Dorothy placed all the activities of the Works of Mercy on the deeper level of reparation, of joining the work and suffering to those of Jesus on the cross. In that year she was very conscious of the destruction caused by the war: "All the activities of the Catholic Worker, all of the Works of Mercy performed throughout the country on farms and in houses of hospitality, are reparation and practices in the work of loving."

Although young people flocked to the Catholic Worker and were attracted to performing the Works of Mercy and the work for peace, it was not always easy to find people to do the necessary practical work to keep the Houses of Hospitality going. Much later, in the December 1965 *Catholic Worker*, at a time when so many were attracted to the movement because of its opposition to the Vietnam War and New York was overflowing with Catholic Workers, Dorothy complained of this lack: "Not only are all the beds full, so that we cannot put them up for the Chrystie Street work, but also, it seems in regard to these we already have that their interest in peace keeps them from the clothes room, or from the paper work connected with the thirty or more subscriptions which are coming in each day."

However much work there was to do, Dorothy said that Peter never became discouraged. She herself continued to find inspiration in *The Imitation of Christ*, noting especially the author's regard for the Works of Mercy and the value of manual labor in finding a balance with human mood swings: "Thomas à Kempis says when we are feeling dry as dust, sad and unhappy, to employ ourselves in exterior Works of Mercy. I know by experience how some good brisk housecleaning can revive one's spirits. Manual labor, bringing order out of chaos, also brings serenity to the soul...."[12]

In placing hospitality in the context of the Works of Mercy, Catholic Worker methods differ from those of social agencies that help the homeless. While social workers usually approach the problem of a homeless person by helping them to adapt to their environment, Catholic Workers questioned whether that environment might better be changed than the person. Peter wrote:

> The training of social workers
> enables them to help people
> to adjust themselves
> to the existing environment.
> The training of social workers
> does not enable them
> to help people
> to change the environment.
> In Houses of Hospitality
> social workers can acquire
> that art of human contacts
> and that social-mindedness
> or understanding of social forces
> which will make them critical
> of the existing environment
> and the free creative agents
> of a new environment.

While working many hours each day responding to crises, doing the work of hospitality without pay, the Catholic Workers depended on God's grace in everything and especially for the possibility of positive change in those who came to the houses. In this regard Dorothy quoted one of the priests who gave the retreat at the Catholic Worker: "Father Farina says that the only true influence we have on people is through supernatural love. This sanctity (not an obnoxious piety) so affects others that they can be saved by it. Even though we may seem to increase the delinquency of others (and we have been many a time charged with it), we can do for others, through God's grace, what no law enforcement can do, what no common sense can achieve."[13]

Dorothy wrote about doing *all* of the Works of Mercy, which included visiting Christ in the prisoner and visiting the sick. She visited the mentally ill, who were truly prisoners at the time before modern psychiatric medications were developed. Sometimes jailed for demonstrating (instructing the ignorant) and standing up for her principles, Dorothy presented to readers the novel view that being in jail was a way of visiting the other prisoners. After a time in jail for protesting air-raid drills, she wrote in the July–August 1955 *Catholic Worker* of the poor being imprisoned for petty crimes while the rich who robbed in white-collar crimes escaped jail through the cleverness of their lawyers. The great numbers of the poor in prison was another case of the bias against the poor:

> What a neglected Work of Mercy, visiting the prisoner.
> "When were you in prison, Lord, and we did not visit you?" It is a hard picture Christ presents. He did not forgive this ignorance. "Inasmuch as you did not visit these prisoners ye did not visit Me."
> "But they are guilty, they are the scum of the earth, they are the refuse, they are the offscourings. They drink, they take dope, they are prostitutes. They are vicious themselves and they make others vicious. They even sell drugs to little children. They are where they belong. Prison is too good for them. We can't pamper them."
> "I have come to call them to repentance. I have come to be with publicans and sinners. I have come for the lost sheep. I am more there with these most miserable ones than with the judges sitting on the high seats." This is not sentimentality. This is truth.

Catholic Workers spoke out against racism and welcomed the poor, regardless of race, to their Houses of Hospitality long before this was acceptable in American society. One house was closed and the Workers arrested because blacks and whites were found to be living in the same house. In an article in the April 1942 *Catholic Worker*, Dorothy went to the heart of the matter, responding to the criticism the Catholic Workers received for doing the Works of Mercy: "The opposition to feeding the hungry and clothing the naked is unceasing. There is much talk of the worthy and the unworthy poor, the futility of such panaceas. And yet our Lord himself gave us these jobs to do in his picture of the last Judgment...."

They also knew, however, and Dorothy wrote in *The Catholic Worker*, that the poor, as individuals, are often far from perfect. Dorothy recounted how sometimes she became discouraged with all the practical problems in Houses of Hospitality and how Peter would remind her of the importance of love for the poor:

> Very often in the course of our meetings I had complaints to make, discouragements to pour out. Peter would look at me with calm affection and in a few words speak of the principles involved, reminding me of the Works of Mercy and our role as servants who had to endure humbly and serve faithfully.
>
> He liked to talk of St. Vincent de Paul. When the film *Monsieur Vincent* came out, we all went to see it. The last lines of the saint to the young peasant sister were words we can never forget: "You must love them very much," Monsieur Vincent said of the poor, "to make them forgive the bread you give them."[14]

Catholic Worker houses were and continue to be centers of the ancient practice of the Works of Mercy. The heart of the movement is Matthew 25 and the Sermon on the Mount; it cannot be separated from the mystery of the poor and Christ's presence in them. Dorothy spoke of the "long-continuing crucifixion" of the poor and the hope in sharing somehow in their poverty. As she said in her Easter meditation in the April 1964 *Catholic Worker*: "The mystery of the poor is this: That they are Jesus, and what you do for them you do for Him. It is the only way we have of knowing and believing in our love. The mystery of poverty is that by sharing in it, making ourselves poor in giving to others, we increase our knowledge of and belief in love."

3

Monasticism:
Hospitality, Prayer, Work, and Study

A first glance at the "Aims and Purposes of the Catholic Worker Movement," and suggestions from Dorothy Day and Peter Maurin for spiritual practices might raise questions in the reader's mind. "What kind of community was this? Spiritual reading at meals? Divine Office or rosary at night? Study groups? Attendance at daily Mass? This sounds like a monastery!"

There is some truth to the statement. While Catholic Worker houses and farms were not monasteries, the early communities did find inspiration in monasticism. In the earliest editions of the paper, Dorothy spelled out the program for Houses of Hospitality. Brigid Merriman comments that Dorothy's description of the movement reflected monastic roots:

> The program was spelled out in an idealistic fashion and carried overtones of a strictly monastic interpretation of a life of service. Prospects for a house were in view, and their purpose at that time was stated:
> "The general purpose of the Houses of Hospitality is to form a center of Catholic action in all fields, to work for, teach and preach social justice, to form a powerhouse of genuine spirituality and earnest educational and vocational work, to dignify and transform manual labor, and to work for the glory and love of God and His Church."[1]

As they observed the movement in the early years, people did ask the question about the Catholic Worker and monasteries. Peter Maurin answered in an Easy Essay that the lives of both the

4

monks and the Catholic Workers came from the gospel: "Someone said that *The Catholic Worker* is taking monasticism out of the monasteries. The Counsels of the Gospel are for everybody not only for monks."

Peter specifically related the three prongs of his program— cult, culture, and cultivation—to monasticism and specifically the Irish monks, who were scholars:

When the Irish scholars
decided to lay the foundations
of medieval Europe
they established:
Centers of Thought
in all the cities of Europe
as far as Constantinople
where people
could look for thought
so they could have light.
Houses of Hospitality
where Christian charity
was exemplified.
Agricultural Centers
where they combined
(a) cult—
that is to say, Liturgy
(b) with culture—
that is to say Literature
(c) with cultivation—
that is to say Agriculture.

Several popes, and especially Pius XI, had called for a reconstruction of the social order in which there were so many injustices and in which people did not find meaning in their lives and work. Peter Maurin pointed out that there had been a great precedent for such a reconstruction during what was called the Dark Ages, a time of great violence and dehumanization after the breakup of the Roman Empire. In several of his Easy Essays Peter showed that the Irish monks had brought light, learning, and faith to the people as they established monasteries all over Europe, changing the whole social order in important ways. The monastic model of living the gospel in community, charity, and voluntary poverty without bureaucracy brought such a response that it changed the culture and the way the larger community was organized. Peter told how the Irish monks lived an ideal synthesis of prayer, scholarship, clarification of thought, hospitality, and work, and how, as missionaries, they carried this synthesis to other countries.

Among the books Peter recommended in *The Catholic Worker* on this subject was *Ireland and the Foundations of Europe* by Benedict Fitzpatrick. Fitzpatrick's book brought together an amazing number of sources into a substantive history of the reconstructive activity of Irish missionaries in Europe from the sixth century to the eleventh, flowing from the great ancient Irish civilization which had become Christian: "Abbeys and schools had arisen on the foundations of Roman ruins or the clearings in German forests. Pilgrims came and went in peace. Universities laid their foundations in the metropolitan centers. Barbarian tribes had grown into nations and the lineaments of Europe had taken the form it was to retain in the ages to come."[2]

The monks who left Ireland, where their monasteries were already well established, to become missionaries to the world taken over by "barbarians" had many similarities in their foundations to those of the desert fathers. Stories are told of one or another digging his staff into the ground in the middle of a forest, where bears and other wild animals roamed, to begin his new monastic life there and relate to the people in the area: "Such piety and love dwelt in them all that for them there was only one will and one renunciation. Modesty and moderation, meekness and mildness adorned them all in equal measure. The evils of sloth and dissension were banished. Pride and haughtiness were expiated by severe punishments. Scorn and envy were driven out by faithful diligence. So great was the might of their patience, love and mildness that no one could doubt that the God of mercy dwelt among them."[3]

The Irish monks carried the learning of their great civilization with them as they journeyed to many different points in what is now Europe, often literally carrying their books on their backs as they walked. At a time when other monasteries were rejecting pagan reading, sometimes insisting that only theology be read, the Irish continued reading and recommending Latin and Greek classics, studied astronomy and geography, and taught all kinds of learning in the schools they set up.

The Irish monks especially valued learning and cultural centers in a way that some other monasteries did not. They were scholars and they brought together workers and scholars. As Peter Maurin said, "Through Houses of Hospitality the Irish scholars exemplified Christian charity. Through Farming Communes the Irish scholars made workers out of scholars and scholars out of workers."

Fitzpatrick differentiates the work of the Irish monks and its impact from the work of other monks of the time in great part because of this scholarship. A major figure in the foundations of Irish monasteries in Europe was Columbanus, who had been formed for a number of years at the school of Bangor under Columcille of Iona in Ireland. "The advent of Columbanus on the continent figures as a minor incident in the conventional history of Europe, but there have been battles, confederations, and births of dynasties and kingdoms, not half so big with consequence. Not the founding of Monte Cassino in Italy but the founding of Luxeuil in Gaul marked the passing of the world of antiquity and the beginning of the world of today."[4]

Without the many historical documents with which Fitzpatrick wove his text, and without Peter's insistence on the importance of the Irish monks, it might be hard to imagine the significance of these foundations. The monks influenced kings and popes and played a significant role in the development of philosophy and theology (not without controversy). Fitzpatrick's description of the monastery at Luxeuil gives some glimmer of what this great foundation must have meant, not only to its immediate area, but throughout Europe and for centuries to come: "In the seventh century Luxeuil was the most celebrated school in Christendom, outside of Ireland. Young monks and clerks and scions of the ruling Frank and Burgundian families crowded to it. Lyons, Autun, Langres, and Strasbourg sent their youth to it. The discipline that molded them under the Irish rule became the most powerful single influence in the surrounding kingdoms."[5]

As Peter Maurin pointed out, the Irish monks were not only scholars and people of prayer. They were very practical, often beginning their work alone. Like the followers of Benedict, they worked as well as studied and prayed and cared for the sick and those who needed hospitality. Fitzpatrick tells of how they brought many skills to the people, including better farming methods such as the rotation of crops:

> Their skill in agriculture made them the chosen patrons of farmers and gardeners; and their knowledge of the breeding and care of animals won for them the spiritual devotion of French cowherds. Their knowledge of leachcraft and medicine developed and transmitted through generations of hereditary physicians in Ireland....They showed the people how to build houses of wood and stone, how to clear the forests, and how to care for the poor, the infirm, and the abandoned....The establishments they erected became object-lessons to the people in farming and gardening, in the raising of cattle and sheep and fowl, in architecture, in the carving of wood and stone, and in miniature painting and the production of manuscripts.[6]

The hospitality the Irish monks practiced was influenced by their own culture as well as the gospel: "Medieval hospitality was not built solely on Gospel injunctions. Medieval Irish monasteries were renowned for their hospitality and were frequently cited by Peter Maurin....Irish monks drew upon an ancient, preconversion tradition of hospitality."[7]

As late as the January 1973 *Catholic Worker*, a few years before her death, Dorothy recommended the Irish monasteries as a model for education centers. Describing the negative effects of following the secular model for schools and universities that involved so much fund-raising and government involvement, she described the possibilities:

> How good it would be to see the Church closer and closer to poverty and the poor; little schools set up on every block, in idle

rooms, in empty buildings, with the students themselves helping repair them and getting meanwhile some sense of the joy of manual labor (and the pains of it, too). And idle Church-owned lands given over to the disorderly poor, the unworthy poor, to build up little villages of huts, tepees, log cabins, yes, even outhouses, which might come to resemble (if a Church of sorts were built in the center) an ancient Irish monastery. Ireland used to be called the land of Saints and Scholars.

Peter suggested to Dorothy when they first met that she read the fathers of the church, including the writings of the desert fathers, from which monasticism grew. A reminiscence by Dorothy in 1975 indicates that she had known about the desert fathers even before meeting Peter from reading Anatole France's *Thaïs*. Dorothy said about it: "[E]ven in that satire the beauty of the saints shone through."[8] She wrote in the June 1943 *Catholic Worker* about the desert fathers, especially Helen Waddell's book, saying "I was converted to being a [Benedictine] oblate by reading and re-reading *The Desert Fathers*."

An important aspect of Dorothy's interest in the desert fathers was that of their flight to the wilderness from the cities to escape military service. She recounted in the February 1944 *Catholic Worker* how Peter had told her also about St. Bernard and how "he took a dozen warriors away from the siege of a city and built up a foundation in the wilderness."

In the February 1943 issue, Dorothy emphasized how much she had learned from the desert fathers about "personalism and communitarianism," telling how "thousands of monasteries began then for people to live together as well as to seek solitary places." She noted that these monks also practiced hospitality. In this context, Merriman brings out Dorothy's appreciation for Ephraem the Syrian (c. 306–373), and includes one of Dorothy's quotes from *The Desert Fathers*: "He was a quiet scholar, and without fail a man of hospitality to all who came to him. In the crisis of famine which visited his countryside, Ephraem 'turned man of affairs, building a rough-and-ready hospital of three hundred beds, nursing and feeding those who had any spark of life in them, burying the dead'"[9]

Dorothy reprinted a prayer of St. Ephraem many times over the years in *The Catholic Worker* in whole or in part as if it were her own: "Sorrow on me, beloved...I marvel at myself, O my beloved, how I daily default and daily do repent. I build up of an hour and an hour overthrows what I have built. At evening I say, tomorrow I will repent, but when morning comes, joyous I waste the day. Again at evening I say, I shall keep vigil all night and I shall entreat the Lord to have mercy on my sins. But when night is come, I am full of sleep."[10]

By her references to "joyous I waste the day," Dorothy meant that she had good intentions to accomplish many things, and the day sometimes passed without their being carried out. Of course, in the midst of a busy House of Hospitality, concern for the persons in need often took precedence over any planned project, and Dorothy traveled extensively to visit Catholic Worker houses in other cities and states and for speaking engagements. Her travels often included visits to monasteries.

In the July–August 1943 *Catholic Worker* Dorothy emphasized the nonparticipation of the desert fathers in war, as well as Ephraem's willingness to leave the desert to care for the sick when there as a crisis: "When times got so bad (when there was universal conscription, for instance), they retreated by the tens of thousands to the desert wastes to pray, to work, and God knows what the world would have been without them. St. Ephraem came out when there was need and retired again to pray."

Merriman puts together the influence of the spirituality of the desert fathers, with its emphasis on the mercy of God, with the positive approach of French personalism for the movement: "The sure confidence in God's mercy which found its way into [Dorothy's] spirituality was based upon a positive anthropology which runs through the Psalms, through the Christian personalists Mounier and Maritain, and upon the image of mercy presented by the Desert Fathers."[11]

In September 1943 Dorothy notified *The Catholic Worker* readers that she would be taking a "sabbatical" from the busy Catholic Worker in order to have a time in the "desert" of quiet to pray. She explained her reasons and her plans for the sabbatical, as well as the plans for the Catholic Worker movement during her absence. Some Catholic Workers and others who knew Dorothy criticized Father John Hugo for this decision, only seeing the connection between her absence and his recommendation to give up some of the things we love the most in order to grow in holiness. However, Merriman points out, "the sabbatical was viewed by [Dorothy] as a desert experience. Her readings then and later included frequent re-readings of *The Desert Fathers....*"[12] Another reason for a sabbatical, of course, was the closure of many Catholic Worker houses because of the young men going off to war. After only six months, however, Dorothy returned to the bustle and busyness of the Houses of Hospitality, continuing her work and prayer.

A modern father of the desert, Charles de Foucauld, inspired Peter and Dorothy as well. In the October–November 1977 *Catholic Worker*, Dorothy remembered that in the early days when she had first met Peter Maurin he had told her about him. Dorothy shared with readers how the Little Brothers who followed Charles now lived: "Away back in the thirties, Peter Maurin gave me the life of Charles de Foucauld to read. He said, 'This is the spirituality for our day.'"

In the August 1950 *Catholic Worker*, Dorothy wrote at length about a retreat she had made that was sponsored by the Secular Fraternity of Charles of Jesus (Charles de Foucauld). In that article she gave a little history of Charles de Foucauld and his successor, René Voillaume. She told of Voillaume's visits to the Catholic Worker and their connection with various groups of the Little Brothers or Little Sisters of Jesus, who lived what they called the silence and simplicity of Nazareth among the poor. Dorothy noted the similarities of the de Foucauld retreat with those of the Lacouture/Hugo retreat, often given at the Catholic Worker: "There were many points of similarity in the two retreats, one of them the nocturnal adoration on Thursday nights, and the emphasis on silence and the work of the Holy Spirit in the retreat. There was the same teaching on prayer that Fr. Louis Farina always gave us, that hour in the desert." Dorothy told readers that she was strongly attracted to the spirit of the de Foucauld family "because of its emphasis on poverty as a means (an emphasis in the

CW movement), poverty as an expression of love, poverty because Jesus lived it."

Dorothy recorded in the February 1944 *Catholic Worker* how Peter had emphasized the fathers of the desert, as well as St. Benedict, quoting the history he gave her:

> In time of chaos and persecution, men escape to the desert. One of the Fathers of the Desert, Abbot Allois said, "A man cannot find true repose or satisfaction in this life unless he reckons that there is only God and himself in the world." That's personalism. On the other hand, "With our neighbor," St. Anthony says, "is life and death." He was another Desert Father, and he was a communitarian. He started the foundation of monasteries, he and St. Basil, who wrote the first rule. Then St. Benedict came along and his rule is still being used by tens of thousands of monks all over the world....This Rule...is still animating the lives of men. And it was a rule, written not for priests, but for laymen. Of course now it is used by priests and lay brothers, but why cannot it be used by the family?

St. Benedict developed his *Rule*, as Peter indicated, from the previously existing monastic traditions such as the desert fathers. Benedict (c. 480–543) was born in Nursia, a region northeast of Rome. His *Rule* for monks required them to provide hospitality to travelers, strangers, and any who needed it—a practice that came from the earliest Christian tradition—and insisted that guests who came to them, especially the poor, be treated with loving care:

> In chapter 53 of his *Rule*, Benedict addressed the reception that was to be accorded guests. He reminded his monks that everyone was to be received as Christ, for on the last day each monk would be told: "I was a stranger and you welcomed me" (Mt. 25:35). All persons, without distinction, were to be greeted with every courtesy, including a sharing in the abbot's table, and an offering of accommodation in the guest quarters. The awareness of Christ's presence ran like a refrain throughout the chapter, with special consideration being given to the lowly: "Great care and concern are to be shown in receiving poor people and

pilgrims, because in them more particularly Christ is received; our very awe of the rich guarantees them special respect."[13]

The spirituality of Benedictine monasteries, including hospitality, liturgical prayer, and manual labor, was a great influence on the Catholic Worker. Stanley Vishnewski, longtime Catholic Worker, declared this source essential: "From the Benedictines we got the ideal of Hospitality—Guest Houses—Farming Communes—Liturgical Prayer. Take these away and there is very little left in the Catholic Worker program."[14]

In May 1940 Dorothy Day wrote in *The Catholic Worker* of the relationship between the hospitality of monasticism and the Catholic Worker movement. She was answering critics who complained about Catholic Workers helping the undeserving poor. Rejecting the perspective of her critics that the poor were poor through their own fault and should not be helped, Dorothy pointed instead to the hospitality practiced in the monastic tradition, showing that the attempt to discriminate between deserving and undeserving contradicted the very purpose of Christian hospitality:

Christ once told his disciples, "I was hungry and you gave me to eat," etc. Since that day, all over the world, pilgrims to holy places, weary travelers, the hungry and thirsty, saint and sinner have been succored in the name of Christ. Hospices, centuries ago, were under the supervision of the Bishops. They were set up in lonely and hostile regions. Lepers by the thousands were helped in the many hospices scattered all over France. The monks of St. Bernard are famous for their hospitality....

The early monasteries founded by Benedict of Nursia designated monks as hospitallers and almoners. The former welcomed guests while the latter fed, clothed, and gave shelter to the needy....

There is no record in the history of hospices and hospitality of discrimination....

Christ exercised His good works among those who today would be lumped with "chronics." Hospitable in His heart, He took in the sinning woman and the thief beside Him on the Cross.

In that article Dorothy showed how contrary modern discrimination against the poor was to the monks' hospitality, quoting Louis B. Ward in Back to Benedict: "[In the monasteries] the poor did not have to sit as they do today for endless hours on the benches of some welfare agency to be subjected to a third degree on their personal lives, treated as crooks and investigated to the point of criminal persecution."

Some criticized the Catholic Worker program for only patching up wounds in a society filled with injustice, and maintaining the status quo. In that May 1940 *Catholic Worker*, Dorothy responded by saying that hospitality was deeply rooted in Christian tradition and that the monasteries that practiced it had had a major impact on social conditions and the way people thought about and acted upon them: "We consider the spiritual and corporal Works of Mercy and the following of Christ to be the best revolutionary technique and a means for changing the social order rather than perpetuating it. Did not the thousands of monasteries, with their hospitality, change the entire social pattern of their day? They did not wait for a paternal state to step in nor did they stand by to see destitution precipitate bloody revolt."

Monasticism was especially suited in many ways as a model for the Catholic Worker, although schedules were never strictly followed. Peter had actually tried to make a schedule for work and prayer similar to a monastic one for the farms. Dorothy noted, however, that one problem with implementing the schedule on a practical basis was that it left no time to prepare meals or do the dishes:

5–7	work in the fields
7–9	Mass
9–10	breakfast
10–11	lecture or discussion
11–2	rest or study
2–3	lecture or discussion
3–4	cold lunch
4–5	lesson in handicraft
5–8	work in the field
8–9	dinner
9–5	sleep[15]

A concept the Catholic Worker drew especially from Benedictine monasticism was the spiritual leadership of an abbot. The Benedictines are not a centralized institute, but are organized into confederated congregations of monks. Each monastery is an autonomous community. The word *abbot*, which described Peter's idea of the leader, came from *abba*, meaning father. (In both the Eastern and Western traditions, there were not only abbots, but also abbesses of monasteries of nuns, who were often very powerful women in the communities in which they lived.) Peter hoped that leaders in the Catholic Worker movement would have characteristics of an abbot: "The *abba*, then, was an experienced monk who knew the life from living it himself. He was a holy man, for he had achieved a measure of success in his personal struggle. He was able to be a spiritual father....He was considered to be a bearer of the Spirit...because holiness was no personal achievement, but the gift of the Spirit of God who dwells in us...."[16]

In Catholic Worker agronomic universities Peter Maurin preferred the leadership to have the quality of an abbot figure, a loving spiritual father who guided things. Dorothy quoted him in the February 1944 issue in an article on "Farming Communes": "He said, 'I do not believe in majority rule. I do not believe in having meetings and elections. Then there would be confusion worse confounded, with lobbying, electioneering and people divided into factions.' No, the ideal rule was such as that of the monasteries, with an abbot and subjects."

The role Peter spoke of was not a model of authoritarianism. Peter knew that a lay community would be different from the monastery; he hoped, however, for some leaders who might resemble an abbot in their spirituality. Like the abbot, the leader must work on conversion of heart: "We must build up leaders. And the leaders must first of all change themselves." That leadership had nothing to do with violence or force. In the September 1948 *Catholic Worker*, Dorothy described the reactions of Peter Maurin to difficult situations:

> On one occasion when two men fought in the office over on Charles Street he threatened to leave the work forever if it ever happened again. In a book by Federov on Russian Spirituality,

there is the story of St. Sergius, who left his monastery for two years rather than impose his authority by force. On another occasion at the Easton farm, one man knocked down another over a dispute about an egg (it is horrible to think of people fighting physically over food), and for the rest of the summer Peter ate neither eggs nor milk in order that others might have more. That was his idea of justice.

Of course, many times life in the sometimes chaotic Houses of Hospitality and farms of the Catholic Worker did not in any way resemble a monastery. Stanley Vishnewski tells about various difficult personalities among the guests or coworkers at the houses and farms. On one occasion at the farm, he said, "Dorothy used to sigh with despair over Mr. O'Connell's actions. She told us that the *Rule* of St. Benedict tells the monks to appoint a wise and kind man to act as doorkeeper to greet the visitors and make them welcome. 'And we,' she groaned, 'have Mr. O'Connell. But then we have to take what God sends us.'"[17]

The monks were farmers and, in addition to their witness to the gospel for the world and the model of hospitality, provided an alternative economic model in the local community. Following Benedict, Peter Maurin presented an ideal integration of work and prayer, liturgy and life, a unity of the religious life and the economic life of the people:

> The motto of St. Benedict was
> *Laborare et Orare,* Labor and Pray.
> Labor and prayer ought to be combined;
> labor ought to be a prayer.
> The liturgy of the Church
> is the prayer of the Church.
> The religious life of the people
> and the economic life of the people
> ought to be one.

Peter often spoke of the idea of a philosophy of work, especially manual labor. Work and prayer meant not only intellectual work, but work with one's hands. Reflection on the meaning of work, together with prayer, was very much a part of the

Benedictine tradition. Dorothy quoted at length in the October 1949 *Catholic Worker* from a pamphlet by Father Rembert Sorg, OSB, a priest affiliated with St. Procopius monastery (Eastern rite), *Towards a Benedictine Theology of Manual Labor.*[18] Noting that the pamphlet could be obtained from St. Procopius Abbey, Dorothy described Father Sorg's emphasis on the importance of manual labor in the writings of the early church fathers and monks: "Father Sorg's treatise goes back to St. Anthony of Egypt who rejoiced in never having been troublesome to anyone else on account of labor of his hands. The great rules of St. Pachomius and St. Basil both called for manual labor. St. Jerome said that the monasteries of Egypt would accept no monks who would not do manual work and in St. Basil the strict rule of manual labor is inculcated...."

As can be seen from her article, Dorothy was enthusiastic about Sorg's booklet. Her only reservation was that he was perhaps too strong on St. Paul's dictum that "those who do not work should not eat," knowing as she did so many wounded ones who were not able to work regularly. Although it was Peter who brought the Benedictine idea of work and prayer to the Catholic Worker, Dorothy had been influenced by Benedictine spirituality long before she entered the church. She told about reading Catholic convert Joris Karl Huysmans's trilogy of novels in which a person becomes a Benedictine oblate: "I read *En Route, The Oblate, The Cathedral,* and it was these books which made me feel that I too could be at home in the Catholic Church....They acquainted me with what went on there....I felt the age, the antiquity of the Mass, and here to find in Huysmans detailed instructions in regard to rubrics, all the complicated ritual, was a great joy to me, so that I went more often to the Cathedral."[19]

Peter and Dorothy were very close to the Benedictines at Saint John's Abbey in Collegeville, Minnesota, in the 1930s. It was perhaps also through their influence that Dorothy eventually became a Benedictine oblate herself. She began her affiliation with the English Benedictine congregation at Portsmouth, Rhode Island, where Ade Bethune, Catholic Worker artist, had based her oblature.[20]

Dorothy became more and more interested in Eastern Catholicism and its beautiful liturgy. Her reading of authors from the East, which she shared with readers of *The Catholic Worker*, included not only the great works of novelists like Dostoevsky, but theology, monastic writings, and history. Helene Iswolsky, who encouraged Dorothy's interest in Eastern liturgy and theology, also introduced her to the Benedictine monks at St. Procopius Abbey in Lisle, Illinois. The monks, some of whom were from "Belorrusia," as Dorothy spelled it, soon visited the Worker and gave days of recollection.[21]

It was in April 1955 that Dorothy changed the locus of her lay affiliation to St. Procopius, becoming an oblate of that abbey. In her April 1957 column in *The Catholic Worker*, Dorothy wrote about her profession: "Now I am a professed oblate of the St. Procopius family, and have been for the last two years, which means that I am a part of the Benedictine family all over the world, and a member of the Benedictine community at Lisle....My special love for St. Procopius is because its special function is to pray for the reunion of Rome and the Eastern Church. Their monks can offer Mass in the Eastern or Roman rite and when Fr. Chrysostom came to give us retreats at Maryfarm, we sang the liturgy of St. John Chrysostom."

Over the centuries several reformed groups of Benedictine monks were formed, including the Cistercians, and later the Order of Cistercians of Strict Observance (Trappists). The Catholic Worker had very early connections (beginning in 1936) with the Trappist monastery at Gethsemani in Kentucky. Abbot Frederic Dunne had responded to one of Dorothy's letters of appeal and over a period of several years assured Dorothy of his and the monks' support through prayer and monetary donations. It was this monastery that Thomas Merton entered in 1941 and he continued the relationship with Dorothy and the Catholic Worker. Merton's writings were often published in the paper and many of his books were reviewed and excerpted in *The Catholic Worker*. Dorothy had to be careful to make sure permission was given by Merton's abbot when publishing his articles or poems in the paper. A 1965 letter from Merton to Dorothy gives some idea of the influence of the Catholic Worker on his life: "If there were no Catholic Worker and such forms of witness, I would never have joined the Catholic Church."[22]

In the monastic way, quick, spectacular results in social change were not expected. After much work and prayer, results were left to God. The impact of living the gospel, however, in the midst of pain and suffering, was great even though not always immediately apparent. As Dorothy wrote:

> The new social order as it could be and would be if all men loved God and their brothers because they are all sons of God! A land of peace and tranquility and joy in work and activity. It is heaven that we are contemplating. Do you expect that we are going to be able to accomplish it here? We can accomplish much, of that I am certain. We can do much to change the face of the earth, in that I have hope and faith. But these pains and sufferings are the price we have to pay. Can we change men in a night and a day? Can we give them as much as three months or even a year? A child is forming in the mother's womb for nine long months, and it seems so long. But to make a man in the time of our present disorder with all the world convulsed with hatred and strife and selfishness, that is a lifetime's work and then too often it is not accomplished.[23]

4

Dom Virgil Michel, OSB, the Liturgical Movement, and the Catholic Worker

If there was ever a happy wedding of ideas, it was the coming together of those of Dom Virgil Michel (1890–1938)—monk of the Order of St. Benedict, brilliant philosopher, theologian, liturgist, publisher, and social ethicist—and the Catholic Worker movement. The Benedictine influence on the movement was given flesh in the friendship of Peter Maurin and Dorothy Day with the Benedictine priests at Saint John's Abbey at Collegeville, Minnesota, who were leaders in the renewal of the Catholic liturgy.

In her 1938 obituary of Virgil Michel in *Orate Fratres* (the liturgical journal Michel founded and edited), Dorothy wrote about his friendship with the Catholic Worker and how overwhelmed they were with sadness by his death. She spoke of him as a dear friend and adviser, recalling how he was interested in everything the Workers were trying to do, and said he "made us feel, at all the Catholic Worker groups, that we were working with him."[1]

Those involved in the liturgical movement, with the leadership of Virgil Michel, worked to renew the liturgy of the church and to educate Catholics on the profound meaning of participation in the Mass, the sacraments, and the Divine Office as the center and core not only of their worship, but of their very lives as persons and as members of the Body of Christ. The excitement of the ideas of the liturgical movement and its implications for the human family and for social justice led to study and many discussions at the Catholic Worker.

As Peter so often did in his conversations and Easy Essays, Michel reminded readers how the lives of the early Christians were transformed, and how their witness convinced others of the love and power of the gospel. His approach to the social order was similar to Maurin's in its rejection of bureaucracy, and its basis in the "dynamite of the Church" understood as the Body of Christ. Arguing that general talk about social programs would not truly transform a society, Michel presented the experience of the early church as the example: "Not paper programs, not high-sounding unfulfilled resolutions once renewed the world, but new and living men born out of the depths of Christianity."[2] He, like Peter, insisted that authentic religion must be implemented in the practical sphere: "What the early Christians thus did at the altar of God, in the central act of Christian worship, they also lived out in their daily lives."[3]

Michel emphasized the formation that should take place at the liturgy and should become a key to renewing the social order: "The liturgy is the ordinary school of the development of the true Christian, and the very qualities and outlook it develops in him are also those that make for the best realization of a genuine Christian culture."[4] Michel put together the ideas of two popes in a thesis or syllogism about the link between liturgy and social responsibility: "Pius X tells us that the liturgy is the indispensable source of the true Christian spirit; Pius XI says that the true Christian spirit is indispensable for social regeneration. Hence the conclusion: The liturgy is the indispensable basis of social regeneration." This syllogism became famous to those in the liturgical and social justice movements; without using Michel's name, Dorothy quoted it in her December 1935 *Catholic Worker* column.

Michel pointed out that the need for social regeneration was related to the individualism which had taken over Western thought for centuries, the secular "doctrine" of classic economic liberalism, which held that the good of society is best attained with every individual looking out for his own best interests. His antidote to materialism, individualism, and indifference to injustice was the Body of Christ at worship.[5] Michel insisted on a revival of the Pauline imagery of the church set forth in 1 Corinthians, chapter 12, and its implications, ideas in remission at the time: "As a body is one though it has many parts, and all the parts of the body, though many, are one body, so also Christ. For in one Spirit we were all baptized into one body, whether Jews or Greeks, slaves or free persons, and we were all given to drink of one Spirit."

This understanding of the church as a living organism with Christ as the head and the Holy Spirit as the soul, as the vine and the branches who "must bring forth the spiritual energies of Christ," meant that members had responsibility for one another, that their prayers and actions affected everyone else.[6]

At a time when there was perhaps an overemphasis on external form in the liturgy, Michel insisted that worship be a unity of the external and internal, of liturgy and daily life. He knew, however, that even with greater understanding of and participation in the liturgy, economic disparities and injustices would not be adequately addressed so long as people were in thrall to what he called the bourgeois spirit and its associate, individualism. He argued that a conversion of Christian hearts and minds to live according to the gospel and a change in economic structures must occur simultaneously, and that these changes would best be inspired through the liturgy.[7]

As Michel, as well as Peter and Dorothy, understood it, the worship of the Body of Christ is inextricably linked with the church's teachings on service to the poor, on charity and justice. Dorothy described this concept in her December 1935 column: "In the Liturgy we have the means to teach Catholics, thrown apart by Individualism into snobbery, apathy, prejudice, blind unreason, that they are members of one body and that 'an injury to one is an injury to all.'" Those involved in the liturgical movement believed that people would flock to church if they had the opportunity to hear the word proclaimed in English instead of Latin—and their lives would be profoundly changed. The emphasis on singing at Mass, for example, was an expression of the unity of people, interconnected with the worshipers' social responsibility. In 1933, Dorothy Day wrote in *The Catholic Worker*, "We feel that it is very necessary to connect the liturgical movement with the social justice movement. Each one gives vitality to the other." In a similar vein, Michel wrote in one issue of *Orate Fratres*: "No one person has really entered into the heart of the liturgical spirit if he has not been seized also with a veritable passion for the re-establishment of social justice in all its wide ramifications."[8]

As if he were writing today, Michel blasted the glorification of amassing of wealth and the ever greater accumulation of goods, which had captured the imagination of the American people, a set of values basically hostile to the human spirit: "It is no wonder then that the culture of our day is characterized as being the very opposite pole of any genuine Catholic culture. Its general aim is material prosperity through the amassing of national wealth. Only that is good which furthers this aim, all is bad that hinders it, and ethics has no say in the matter."[9] To illustrate this point, he presented the words of some of the most prominent businessmen in the United States (often called robber barons), who indicated that the individual need not bother about anyone else, that there is no higher law above the individual: "I owe the public nothing," by [J. P.] Morgan. "What do I care about the law? Hain't I got the power?" by Cornelius Vanderbilt. "The public be damned!" by the later Vanderbilt.[10] Michel pointed out that this "false liberalism...ended in virtual economic slavery" for the great majority, the "propertyless proletariat," and that it was this condition that provided a "fertile ground for socialism."[11] John Mitchell summarizes Michel's objections to economics as it was practiced: "The most glaring deficiency was the fact that capitalism was built on an inverted set of priorities which emphasized the priority of capital over labor." What about the dignity of the worker?[12]

The attitude of the men such as these led Pope Pius XI to strongly criticize economic individualism and the idea of "free" competition without reference to the common good in the encyclical, *Quadragesimo anno*. Michel quoted the encyclical: "From this source as from a polluted spring have come all the errors of the 'individualist' school of economics" (*QA* 206). The Holy Father had especially hard words for those who tried to justify unjust labor practices in the name of their religion when he mentioned those who "profess themselves to be Catholics...but do not blush to oppress working men out of greed for gain," and then hide behind the skirts of Holy Mother the Church (*QA* 217).[13]

"What unconscious blasphemy! As if there were anything really Christian about our modern capitalism." This was Michel, responding in the midst of a worldwide depression in *Commonweal* in 1938 to an article in *Catholic World*, which had called Christ "the first preacher of capitalism as the most workable thesis for society."[14] He found it tragic that Christians who structured their lives according to the bourgeois spirit did not understand that it represented a "vision of human life which was diametrically opposed to the Gospel of Jesus Christ." When he observed that the "bourgeois spirit of capitalism in American society had the power to reach into the very sanctuaries of Christian churches and influence the preaching of the Gospel and the celebration of the Eucharist," he was echoing the denunciations of the prophets of Israel who spoke so strongly about God rejecting the worship of those who bring sacrifices but oppress the poor.[15]

Michel could not understand those who considered efficiency and profit almost a religion, in which all efforts were focused on the attainment of an earthly goal and one's own success and aggrandizement, to the detriment of others' businesses and one's own workers. He, like Peter Maurin, insisted that the Christian could not approach economics in terms of the survival of the fittest:

> Thence we have the ideal of free competition extolled to the skies in such glowing rhapsodies down to our own day. Yet it is this free competition in its unlimited and individualistic form that has justified the use of the phrase "cutthroat competition" and has made of the economic life of mankind a veritable jungle in which the jungle law of a bitter struggle for existence, or rather for amassed wealth, and a survival of the fittest, has prevailed. Is there any surprise that Christian ideals could find no place in this life and that social justice has become a completely unknown entity?[16]

Like Michel, Peter Maurin looked to the life of the church in its great traditions, and especially in the liturgy, for guidance in responding to the social order. He contended that the terrible ills of society are related to secularization, to the separation and privatization of faith from political, social, and economic life. A society built upon the mutual support of members of the Body of Christ would look quite different from one built on individualism. One of Peter's Easy Essays distills his understanding of the implications for one's life and economics of participation in the liturgy of the Mass:

> The central act of devotional life
> in the Catholic Church
> is the Holy Sacrifice of the Mass.
> The Sacrifice of the Mass
> is the unbloody repetition
> of the Sacrifice of the Cross.
> On the Cross of Calvary
> Christ gave His life to redeem the world.
> The life of Christ was a life of sacrifice.
> The life of a Christian must be a life of sacrifice.
> We cannot imitate the sacrifice of Christ on Calvary
> by trying to get all we can.
> We can only imitate the sacrifice of Christ on Calvary
> by trying to give all we can.

One might wonder how a brilliant scholar like Virgil Michel could become such a friend of the Catholic Worker movement, which was seen by some as a radical, marginal group. Dorothy's correspondence with Michel's Abbot, Alcuin Deutsch, and with Michel himself indicates that it was his abbot who first brought the Catholic Worker to Father Virgil's attention. Michel founded the Liturgical Press, where books and pamphlets of the blossoming liturgical movement were published, as well as *Orate Fratres* (now called *Worship*). Articles by or about the Catholic Worker movement and liturgy appeared in the pages of *Orate Fratres* and the monks sent a free copy of each book published by Liturgical Press to the Catholic Worker. Dorothy often quoted Virgil Michel and *The Catholic Worker* printed articles by him.

In spite of the Worker's poverty and often ragtag appearance, Michel noted that in the movement one could find an example of the lived experience and daily practice of the supernatural life. He was well aware of the Catholic Worker's ill repute among some groups who called it an "eyesore and a scandal," as he put it in an article in *Orate Fratres:* "Believe-it-or-not, the old slanders are still circulating and believed, even by some priests. Isn't the Catholic Worker group 'a bunch of Communists' boring from within?" Michel was aware that the perceived scandal of the Catholic Worker's mission mirrored the controversial radicalness of Christ's own message: "Catholic Workers and apostles! You have your faults and shortcomings. But who among us on earth is not burdened with them? If people slander and calumniate you, so did they Christ. If you are a stone of scandal to the self-righteous, so was Christ....Blessed are you if you are among those who suffer persecution for justice's sake, since 'theirs is the kingdom of heaven.'"[17]

While there was a great friendship between Virgil Michel and the Catholic Worker, Dorothy did not always exactly follow his recommendations, as William Portier illustrated in an article in the September–October 2002 *Houston Catholic Worker.* In disagreeing with the friend of the movement, for example, on moving "headquarters" from New York to Easton, Pennsylvania, Dorothy referred rather to the authority of her spiritual director and "approved adviser": She assured him that she had "talked these matters over with [Paulist] Father McSorley, our spiritual adviser, and he agrees with this move which is just a part of our growth. I am very careful at this time to do nothing without the advice of Father McSorley our approved adviser so there will be as much united front as he sees fit. He has been in touch with the work from the beginning and I thank God that we have a priest who is always on hand to tell us what sides to take."[18]

A brief sketch of Michel's background may help to explain his support of the movement. As a young graduate student at the Catholic University of America, he chose as the topic of his doctoral dissertation, "The Critical Principles of Orestes Brownson." Brownson, a convert to Catholicism, wrote on the relationship between Catholicism and culture, and his own commitment to economic justice and lay activism had a deep and lasting effect on Michel. Brownson argued, just as Peter Maurin did, that the church was a dynamic, lived reality.[19]

After Michel became a Benedictine monk, his abbot sent him to Europe to be exposed to liturgical leaders and centers of liturgical renewal. In Europe, Michel met Father Lambert Beauduin, secular priest turned monk, who was imbued with the concept of the Mystical Body of Christ and was at the heart of Europe's liturgical movement. There Michel began to recognize that a community transformed by its worship could ultimately be instrumental in the transformation of society.

After his return from Europe, Michel worked day and night to make liturgical renewal a reality. Here was a man who was "all things to all men," as St. Paul had recommended, who had been an English and philosophy professor, a violinist in Saint John's orchestra, a baseball and tennis star, a coach, a translator, and author. So convinced was he of the value of the liturgical movement to transform American Catholicism, he commenced an intense program of study, promoting and educating Catholics in these ideas. Before long, however, he was forced to admit that "the possibilities of doing good are almost overwhelming us." By early 1930 he was suffering from complete exhaustion and finally suffered a nervous breakdown, after which he was sent to the Chippewa Indian Reservation in northern Minnesota to rest and engage in a minimal amount of pastoral ministry. Michel did at the reservation what one would expect of a man of his stature. Refusing to accept the defeat and humiliation with regard to his diagnosis as a so-called mental case, he used the opportunity afforded by his new life with Native Americans to come to know their culture and develop ways of integrating the experience with the idea of the Mystical Body of Christ. Despite his continued suffering from insomnia, headaches, and depression, he learned the language of the Chippewa, hunted and fished with them, ate their food, worked and recreated with them, and sought them out in bars to invite them to Mass. Michel's suffering became redemptive. He became aware of the many injustices that consumed Native Americans each day in their poverty. In Europe, he had learned about worship and the Mystical Body, but it was at the reservation that his understanding deepened. He never forgot the lesson, as is clear from his later writing on justice and the common good.[20] It was in 1933, the same year that the Catholic Worker began, that a recovered Virgil Michel returned to work not only to teach philosophy, but as dean of Saint John's College.

Virgil Michel and other Benedictine monks visited the Catholic Worker to speak about the meaning of the liturgy, especially the Mass and the Divine Office. Stanley Vishnewski, who joined the Worker at age eighteen and died there many years later, dedicated a chapter in his book, *Wings of the Dawn*, to his experience of the influence of these monks. He told about visits from Fathers Benedict Bradley and Virgil Michel in the early 1930s during which they made the community aware of the living doctrine of the Mystical Body of Christ and the social nature of worship.

"The Church," Fr. Bradley told us, "is not simply a society, an organization; she is an organism, a living and life giving organism, with head and members. The dogmatic concept of the Church is the Mystical Body of Christ. This is the cardinal truth revealed to the world by Christ. It was preached to the man on the street by St. Paul. The early Christians all understood it. St. Augustine urged it insistently and St. Thomas Aquinas taught it...." I experienced a sense of religious awe. I felt a sense of unity and oneness with Dorothy, Peter, Mary, Margaret, Big Dan, Little Dan. I closed my eyes and realized a strong sense of Communion with the Negroes, the Chinese, the Russians. All were my brothers and sisters. We were all one in Christ.

"The Liturgy," Father Bradley concluded his talk, "was once the supreme expression of Christian life and the instrument of the world's conversion. And only through it—the celebration and application to men and women of the Redemption—can Christianity be revived."

Father Bradley's talk was like a Pentecost to all of us at the Catholic Worker. For the first time we became aware of the living reality that was our Faith. It was an awe-inspiring doctrine and we were so enthused—so drunk with new wine—that we wanted to go out on the streets and shout to all who would listen about the unity of the members of the Mystical Body of Christ. I wanted to shout to the people on the streets that you are my brothers and sisters in Christ and that together we belong to the royal family of God.

Dorothy encouraged young Catholic Workers to go to daily Mass. Stanley said that during these talks on liturgy, he began to understand what Dorothy meant: "I began to realize how important my actions and prayers were to the health and well being of the Church. For the first time I understood what Dorothy had meant that cold morning, when she told me that by missing [daily] Mass I was hurting the work."[21]

Stanley told how the singing or reading of the Liturgy of the Hours became part of the daily schedule at the Worker through the influence of Virgil Michel:

> It was Father Virgil Michel, OSB, then Dean of St. John's University in Collegeville, Minn., who came to us one afternoon and told us about the relationship of the Mystical Body of Christ to society. Father Virgil told us that the liturgical movement was the primary apostolate....He emphasized strongly the need for liturgical prayers—the recitation of the Divine Office by laymen so as to bring their minds and thoughts into harmony with the Church.
>
> As a result of Father Virgil's visit the custom of reciting Compline was instituted in the Catholic Worker. He sent us a bundle of Compline booklets that had been published by the Liturgical Press....
>
> Every evening at seven Margaret or Big Dan would start banging on a dishpan or a handy pot and its clamorous noise resounding throughout the store would summon us to the kitchen where, facing each other in two rows, we would recite the office of Compline.

Stanley recounted that even among the Catholic Workers themselves there was not always understanding or agreement over praying the Liturgy of the Hours: "We had a few who objected to the saying of what they called these 'new-fangled prayers.' They would rattle their rosaries in protest. One of them said, 'The rosary was good enough for my parents and my ancestors and it is going to be good enough for me.' One person, but I am sure that he was kidding, stated flatly that the Blessed Mother was saying the rosary when the angel greeted her."

Stanley remembered that someone had even reported the Catholic Workers to the chancery for their odd prayers: "Dorothy told us one evening that she had just returned from the Chancery office. Her eyes were smiling and a trace of a smile was playing about her lips. 'Not again,' I said. 'What's wrong now?' 'Nothing really serious at all,' Dorothy said. 'They just wanted to know what we were doing here every night. It seems that someone sent them a letter about the "long theatrical prayers" that we were saying.'"[22]

Dorothy's love of the Office was a continuation of her prayer of the psalms throughout her life. As a child she had attended the Episcopal Church and learned to pray and love the psalms. In *The Long Loneliness* she wrote that the psalms were what she read when she was in jail: "My heart swelled with joy and thankfulness for the Psalms," she explained. "The man who sang these songs knew sorrow and expected joy."[23] Dorothy loved the pattern of repetition of the psalms. In the March *Catholic Worker* of 1966, she compared it to the teaching method of Peter, "who believed in driving his point home by constant repetition, like the dropping of water on the stones which were our hearts."[24] She related the insights that could be gained from Peter repeating his ideas to the psalms prayed again and again: "It is like reading the Psalms each day in the Office of the Church. Over and over again sudden light shines through on what had been passed over before as obscure." In that same 1966 issue of the paper Dorothy, committed pacifist through her Christian faith, addressed the question of how to pray those psalms that are warlike or even cursing in tone, recommending C. S. Lewis's book, *Reflection on the Psalms*, for a better understanding of them.[25]

One would think that there would be a vibrant theological continuation of the thought and practice of Virgil Michel, Peter Maurin, and Dorothy Day on the unity of Christian faith, liturgy, and concern for the social order. Michael Baxter, CSC, describes Virgil Michel as the "leading intellectual light of the liturgical movement that grew up around the Benedictine community at Collegeville in the late twenties and thirties." He observes, however, that while Michel's name has appeared regularly in liturgical journals for the past six decades and liturgists still speak of him "in reverent tones appropriate to a founding father in liturgy classes, conferences and workshops," his legacy as a social ethicist has been obscured: "Among Catholic social ethicists, his name was virtually unheard of until recently, and even so, his impact has been almost nil."[26]

Baxter attributes this lack of understanding or acceptance of Michel's social ethics (as well as Peter Maurin's) to the dualism of the neo-scholastic paradigm related to nature and grace, where "it was generally assumed that 'Catholic social ethics' flows from philosophical principles grounded in reason alone." This dualism, which affected much of Catholic theology in the period before the Second Vatican Council, may be related to the modern-day doctrine of the separation of church and state, where religion is relegated to the privacy of one's home with curtains drawn. It is like the famous popular expression from the Irishman, O'Connell, who said, "My religion from Rome, my politics from home," and never the twain shall meet. The dominant factor, the place where people look for guidance for their lives, has become what Dorothy Day often called "Holy Mother the State" or "Holy Mother the City," and precious little is accepted from "Holy Mother the Church" in everyday decision making. For Baxter, a key to understanding Virgil Michel is to know that for him social ethics is related to a theological understanding of nature and grace which made it impossible to privatize one's faith in such a way. Aquinas and Augustine did not do so:

> Michel insisted that an adequate account of social regeneration must dispel any notion of "pure nature" in favor of a nature dynamically oriented toward the supernatural, a nature that is supernaturalized. As de Lubac and others associated with the *nouvelle theologie* would eventually show, the notion of "pure nature" should not be traced back to Aquinas but to his neo-scholastic successors, Cajetan and Suarez in particular, who actually distorted Aquinas' (Augustinian) vision of humanity as moved by a single, natural desire for God. What we have in Michel's work is a remarkably lucid, albeit undeveloped, version of this later critique of the neo-scholastic two-tier, nature/super-nature paradigm.

Baxter points out that "the critical edge of Michel's work was blunted by the very neo-scholastic categories he was calling into question, categories which classified his liturgically-shaped account of social life as a form of 'liturgics,'" thus assuring that concepts of justice based on liturgical transformation would remain in the church sanctuary and discussion groups and never see the light of day. This located Michel's thought, which exemplified the unity of the tradition of the church from the earliest times, "at the margins of what qualified as 'social ethics' or, as it was called at the time, 'sociology.'"[27]

It is worth quoting here from Baxter's analysis of the ideas of Monsignor John A. Ryan, "the most prominent Catholic social theorist of his era."[28] His work influenced Roosevelt's New Deal and has become the basis of much of Catholic social theory in the United States, later built upon by the work of John Courtney Murray. These theorists, on whose thought the basis of "public theology" rests, took a very different approach from that of Peter Maurin, Dorothy Day, and Virgil Michel. While Monsignor Ryan visited the Worker and was one of the early speakers at the "clarification of thought" programs, the difference in his approach and that of the Worker soon became apparent—not only in his justification of war, but in his approach to social ethics:

> Working out of the dominant neo-scholastic paradigm, Ryan held that the ultimate norm of morality is the divine reason or essence, but that this reason or essence is mediated through human nature and can be ascertained on the basis of reason alone without the aid of the healing and restorative power of the sacraments. He was therefore able to pursue an overall project that attempted to apply general ethical principles, known intuitively through the inclinations of human nature, to social and economic problems. This project had remarkable currency in the pluralistic social setting of the United States. Grounded on a "universal" reason, Ryan's social ethics could appeal to everyone apart from specific ecclesial beliefs and practices, which meant that its principles could be applied directly in formulating public policy. Moreover, Ryan invoked what he called a "principle of expediency" to argue that the Church should even support some economic and social reforms that fall short of its

own ideal moral norms, thus ensuring the immediate relevance and applicability of Catholic social teaching to the policy making problems of the day.[29]

Baxter contends that, in contrast to the approach of Virgil Michel, Ryan's theory, and following Ryan, that of most contemporary social ethicists, requires another dualism: "While virtually all post-conciliar Catholic social ethicists put forth an integrated construal of the nature/grace relation that is diametrically opposed to the pre-conciliar, two-tier construal of nature and grace, they nevertheless work within the same strictures when it comes to social theory, strictures in keeping with the exigencies of a pluralistic society. The end result is thus the same: a social ethic evacuated of specifically Christian content." The contrast with the thought of Virgil Michel (as with that of Peter and Dorothy) is striking: "For Michel, 'justice' is not derived from the Christ-life. It is embodied in the Christ-life."[30]

Those who have followed Ryan and later John Courtney Murray have sometimes tried to dismiss Michel and the Workers as sectarian or even accuse them of trying to reinstate a theocracy. Nothing is further from the truth. They did, however, reject the "principle of expediency" invoked by Ryan in order to make Catholic teaching adaptable to the American society at large. For Michel and the Workers the way to reform the social order began with conversion of heart, and the economic expression of their social concern lay specifically in subsidiarity, in a local economy. In *The Catholic Worker* 1935, Dorothy described the practical implementation of Virgil Michel's ideas on community and practical economics at Saint John's University at Collegeville where he was dean. It in no way resembled a theocracy:

> St. John's College, in Minnesota, is a most impressive place....I was the guest of Fr. Virgil Michel there and yesterday morning he showed me all over the place. It started with just a few monks and now they have a tremendous plant. We visited the kitchens, where the German Franciscan nuns take care of the needs of the community and college, the flour mill, where the grain from their own acres is ground; the butcher shop and the herds of

steers and pigs, and barns where there are eighty cows; and the Liturgical Press, which we make good use of back in New York.

Those who suggest that Dorothy was conservative in her piety while radical on social issues have it wrong. They perhaps do not know of the dialogue Masses, precursors of Vatican II recommendations in church liturgy, which were celebrated at the Catholic Worker wherever permission for them was given by the local bishop. Dorothy referred to the tradition of dialogue Masses at the Worker in the November 1954 *Catholic Worker*, when she noted that Father Pacifique Roy celebrated a sung Mass each day with them because the diocese of the farm at Easton, Pennsylvania, did not yet permit the dialogue Mass. When a priest was available, liturgies were often celebrated at the Worker. Dorothy and Peter did not, however, develop an exclusive chapel of their own, but always also related to the local parish. As she had when she first became interested in the church, Dorothy identified with the masses of people and was concerned that the liturgical movement reach the average person.

At a time when liturgical experimentation was taking place throughout the United States, Dorothy wrote in the March 1966 *Catholic Worker* about the tremendous impact the liturgical movement had always had on the Catholic Worker movement, reflecting on the meaning of worship, especially the Mass, for the Worker:

> The Liturgical movement has meant everything to the Catholic Worker from its very beginning. The Mass was the center of our lives and indeed I was convinced that the Catholic Worker had come about because I was going to daily Mass, daily receiving Holy Communion and happy though I was, kept sighing out, "Lord, what would you have me to do? Lord, here I am." And I kept hearing his call, as Samuel did, but I did not know what he wanted me to do.
>
> And then Peter Maurin came. A group formed around us, including a young girl from Manhattanville and a young man who had tried his vocation with the Franciscans and was still, as a layman, interested in the Divine Office. So there was added to

our lives within the first few months, the recitation of some of
the Hours, sometimes Vespers, always Compline....

We had our communion procession and even the altar facing the people, as far back as 1937....

In this context Dorothy explained why she questioned some
liturgical practices that had recently taken place at the Catholic
Worker in her absence, especially when instead of a chalice, a coffee cup was used at Mass: "I am afraid I am a traditionalist, in that
I do not like to see Mass offered with a large coffee cup as a chalice." Catholic Workers tell the story that after she returned she
quietly took the coffee cup-chalice to the back yard, dug a deep
hole, and buried it. It would never again be used for coffee.

In her commentary in that March 1966 issue, Dorothy
expressed her creed and affirmed the greatness of the liturgy,
which, she believed, deserved more respect than a coffee cup, even
in an informal place like the Catholic Worker:

"I believe in God, Father Almighty, Creator of heaven and
earth. And of all things visible and invisible, and in His Only
Son Jesus Christ, our Lord."

I believe too that when the priest offers Mass at the altar,
and says the solemn words, "This is my body, this is my blood,"
that the bread and the wine truly become the body and blood of
Christ, Son of God, one of the Three Divine persons. I believe
in a personal God. I believe in Jesus Christ, true God and true
man....

To me the Mass, high or low, is glorious and I feel that
though we know we are but dust, at the same time we know too,
and most surely through the Mass that we are little less than the
angels, that indeed it is now not I but Christ in me worshipping,
and in Him I can do all things, though without Him I am nothing. I would not dare write or speak or try to follow the vocation God has given me to work for the poor and for peace, if I
did not have this constant reassurance of the Mass, the confidence the Mass gives.

Dorothy, in her style of seeking "concordances" and understanding with others, explained that the priest had told her afterward that he was only doing as he was told by the Catholic

Workers and that it was difficult for priests (especially in the '60s) to go against what the community asked of them. She sympathized with his predicament, reflecting further:

> It is one thing for a Father Ciszek to offer Mass, to consecrate the wine in a coffee cup in the prison camps of Siberia. It is quite another thing to have this happen in New York. And yet—and yet—perhaps it happened to remind us that the power of God did not rest on all these appurtenances with which we surround it. That all over the world, in the jungles of South America and Vietnam and Africa—all the troubled, indeed anguished spots of the world—there Christ is with the poor, the suffering, even in the cup we share together, in the bread we eat. "They knew Him in the breaking of bread."

As always, Dorothy's reflections turned to the poor and to the presence of Christ in the Eucharist and in the poor. For her, as for Virgil Michel, the two could not be separated.

Nicholas Berdyaev: Particular Prophet of the Movement

William Miller calls Nicholas Berdyaev (1874–1948) a "particular prophet" in the life of the Catholic Worker movement, one who best provides a philosophical statement of Peter Maurin's ideas, especially those relating to Christian freedom. Although Berdyaev did not influence Peter in an "exclusively primary way," Miller points out that Maurin "read him, wrote digests of his ideas, and in his own teaching emphasized many of Berdyaev's principal points."[1]

> Berdyaev, above all others, is the contemporary world's philosopher of freedom and spirit, and it is remarkable to what degree his ideas have been mirrored in the thought and experience of the Catholic Worker movement....Berdyaev died in 1949 [sic], knowing nothing, probably, of the Worker movement. From the Worker side, it seems that Workers were not extensively acquainted with him. True, there was a time when they studied his books, but young Workers of a later period have seemed unaware of the extent to which the Worker idea is contained in the religious and social philosophy of Berdyaev.[2]

The life and thought of the Catholic Worker movement has inspired many by its example of freedom to radically live the gospel. The ideas of Berdyaev gave Peter and Dorothy support in an understanding of human freedom so different from hedonism and the seeking of power. Young people who were not terribly inspired by a Christianity sometimes linked to and shaped by what Berdyaev called the "bourgeois mind" found fresh insights in the program and ideas of Peter Maurin and Dorothy Day. As so many saints had done before them, Peter and Dorothy were able to bring the dynamism of the gospel to break through the everyday patterns of life and reigning philosophies that limited the possibilities of seeing and living the gospel.

In the May 1951 *Catholic Worker*, Dorothy Day wrote: "Peter Maurin, the founder of the Catholic Worker movement, always emphasized...the liberty of Christ; his message was the active life of the Works of Mercy, and the active life of prayer, of Wisdom which is the most active of all things." She brought out again in the May 1958 *Catholic Worker* Peter's theme of the great freedom of Christians to do good through personalist action in the world: "Peter exalted freedom as God's greatest gift to man, and he pointed to the Gospels and Christ's teachings. We were to lead by example, by serving. We were not to seek leadership, indeed, but to strive to be the least—to wash one another's feet in other words. 'I have left you an example,' Jesus said, when He washed the feet of His disciples...." The perspective of Peter and Dorothy on history and ethics and their personalist response reflected their study of Berdyaev, who wrote, "In every moral act, an act of love, compassion, sacrifice, begins the end of this world in which reign hatred, cruelty, and avarice. In every creative act begins the end of this world in which reign necessity, inertia, and limitation and arises a new world, the 'other world.'"[3]

Berdyaev went so far as to say that "all that is unfree is undesirable to God." He explored the ancient question of how human freedom can be possible within the plan of God and concluded that "destiny depends on freedom," and that God's providence is "neither necessity nor compulsion; it is the...union of God's will and human freedom." Berdyaev placed his understanding of freedom, the antithesis of determinism and individualism, in the incarnation and the drama of redemption, the paschal mystery, which for him was what history is all about.[4]

Neither Berdyaev nor the Catholic Workers accepted a dualism that denied the value of human activity in this world, but rather understood their faith as revolutionary within it, or as Peter Maurin put it, "dynamite." Berdyaev emphasized that Christianity does not depend on constant miracles, but very much on the creative, even daring, activity of Christians in the world, working together with God's grace. "The possibility of the miraculous in human life presupposes human spiritual activity." He reminded his readers that one of his own and Dorothy Day's favorite Russian theologians, Vladimir Soloviev, once said, "It is impious to wait upon God to do that which simple justice could bring about."[5] For the Christian, however, in the exercise of freedom in activity in the world, in the building of the reign of God, one must be careful about means and ends—a good end does not justify hatred or violence as the means: "Seeking for the kingdom of God cannot include the service of evil and injustice resulting from human sinfulness....Christianity differs from outward revolutionaries not because its ideas are less radical than theirs but because it demands that means and aims should correspond—it denies hatred and violence as a means for attaining perfect life."[6]

Within the Catholic Worker movement, action requires decisions based on free will and personal responsibility, but with pure means. In the November 1959 *Catholic Worker*, Dorothy wrote that she could not join with certain people, even for a good cause, because they used different means. Berdyaev knew from experience about the problems of using the wrong means to achieve what were perceived as good ends, and he knew about the danger of the state encroaching on the freedom of its citizens. He had been a professor at the University of Moscow. At first a Marxist, he was arrested by the secret police and deported in 1922 after he had begun to criticize the methods of the Russian Revolution.[7] Rejecting Marxism, and embracing his Russian Orthodoxy, he later lived in France and was a part of the Christian communitarian personalist circles there, meeting at the home of philosopher Jacques Maritain. He published many books and articles, including one in the very first issue of *Esprit*, the personalist journal founded and edited by Emmanuel Mounier.[8]

The Catholic Worker movement had a friend in Helene Iswolsky, the Russian emigré who gave talks at the Worker as well as at Fordham University on Russian literature and thought. Iswolsky had met Berdyaev in Paris, joined the personalist circles there, and later indicated that she felt a "lifelong debt" to his ecumenical spirit.[9]

Helene, who had become a Catholic, spent a lifetime working in ecumenism, especially with those in the Orthodox Church, and found a close friend and collaborator in Berdyaev. She spoke of Berdyaev in her presentations, emphasizing that his thought and spirituality were steeped in his Russian background and Russian literature and that in spite of having been arrested with his wife and exiled by the Communists, "...he retained a deep love of his native land and was entirely imbued with his culture. Dostoevsky, Tolstoy, Vladimir Soloviev were the source of his religious inspiration...."[10]

Iswolsky describes Berdyaev's understanding of freedom, so central to his thought, from the perspective of his disillusionment with Marxism. "Berdyaev gradually became aware that the Marxist theory of dialectic materialism led to the denial of freedom; it led to a closed, collective society. Seen in this perspective, dehumanization was near. The creative power of man which belongs to the realm of the spirit had no chance of remaining alive and expanding." Berdyaev renounced materialism in favor of the "transcendent faith that he had found in Christianity." Helene recounts how he returned to the faith of his childhood and his family, but brought to that faith the ideas of social justice and personalism: "Baptized and raised as a Russian Orthodox by his family, he returned to the traditional religion that he had, for a time, abandoned. But now he sought to infuse it with the humanist, social ideas he had acquired. After he was released from his forced residence, he became one of the leaders of a Russian Orthodox revival...."[11]

In response to critics who contend that religion, especially organized religion, makes a person unfree, that the church interferes with freedom, Berdyaev, Maurin, and Day argued that in Christianity there is a deeper freedom, a freedom beyond the dictates of society or the state. Berdyaev pointed out that those who fear a loss of freedom in making the leap of faith might have not reflected on how unfree they are as they live in "blind obedience to the commands" of their environment and social relations. Even if they believe they are rugged individualists, most people feel that it is absolutely necessary to obey fashions and buy the products society insists are currently necessary—though it may mean the destruction of the environment and the impoverishment of many people through the methods of production. Consumerism, slavishness to style, and peer pressure have a way of defining and imprisoning a person and inhibiting all thought of the creative possibilities of one's destiny. Berdyaev called this the opposite of human freedom: "In order to be able to act, [man] must begin by clearly establishing which are the highest value, aim, and meaning of his life, and he cannot gain a true understanding of them from his environment, either social or natural, for it is to them that he has to impart this value, aim, and meaning."[12]

Marc Ellis has pointed out that Berdyaev described the central historical problem of the age as the ascendancy of the bourgeois spirit: "For Berdyaev, the word 'bourgeois' designated not a social, economic, or ethical condition but rather a spiritual state and a direction of the soul in which the emphasis is always on the material aspects of life, the expedient and the useful." Ellis noted that Berdyaev, with Peter Maurin, "lamented that the will to power and affluence had triumphed over the will to holiness and genius."[13]

Berdyaev and Maurin saw the bourgeois mindset as one that inhibited the freedom of human persons to respond creatively to God's grace. For Berdyaev it was the tragic destiny of Christianity to have been made use of to maintain the bourgeois order. His cutting description of the bourgeois spirit in his book, *The Bourgeois Mind*, was immortalized by Peter in an Easy Essay in the July–August 1935 *Catholic Worker* with the same title. Peter stressed, as did Berdyaev, the writers who had discerned and denounced the triumph of bourgeois mediocrity: Carlyle, Nietzsche, Ibsen, Bloy, Dostoevsky, and Leontiev. These thinkers "foresaw the victory of the bourgeois spirit over a truly great culture, on the ruins of which it would establish its own hideous kingdom." Berdyaev, and thus Maurin also in his Essay, featured Léon Bloy's description of this spirit which had taken over: "The bourgeois, even when he is a 'good Catholic,' believes only in this world, in the expedient and the useful; he is incapable of living by faith in another world and refuses to base his life on the mystery of Golgotha....The bourgeois is an idolator, enslaved by the visible. 'Idolatry is the preference of the visible to the invisible.' 'Business' is the bourgeois's god, his absolute....He is bereft of any spiritual fire, of any spiritual creativeness, but has his own 'faith' and superstitions."[14]

It was not only Peter in the Catholic Worker movement, however, who read Berdyaev. Dorothy studied his book on Dostoevsky and his other works as well. Her October 1938 *Catholic Worker* comments showed the interrelatedness of the ideas of Berdyaev with various Catholic movements: "After the meeting I had supper with [labor leader] John Brophy and we talked for an hour and a half of the labor movement and the Church, of Berdyaev's books, *Christianity and Class War*, and *The End of Our Time....*" Like Dorothy and Peter, Catholic labor leaders like Brophy would have agreed with Berdyaev's contention that "the pitiless selfishness of competition, the turning of man into a thing and of his work into a commercial commodity, are intolerable to the Christian conscience."[15]

Berdyaev dedicated *Christianity and Class War* to the memory of Karl Marx, "who was the social master of my youth and whose opponent in ideas I have now become." He pointed out in that book that what is called freedom for the worker is not freedom when the worker is forced to sell his labor under bad conditions in order not to starve to death. These conditions might exist under both Communism and capitalism: "If the workman is ill-used, if he has to put up with bad conditions on pain of losing his job and consequently his livelihood, though his work may be called free because he can leave it at will, nevertheless there is frightful pressure put upon him and his liberty is an illusion."[16]

While he rejected Marxism, Berdyaev contended that the term *class war*, when closely defined, did describe reality and that Christians must not close their eyes to the social conditions the use of the words evoked. Grinding, involuntary poverty makes a person unfree. Berdyaev also perceived that using the wrong means to try to improve oppressive economic situations for the many in the poorer classes might make freedom even less possible: "Real liberty implies in physical life an economic guarantee for all; it supposes a social regime in which no man is required to make a living at the price of over-arduous or degrading work or of the integrity of his conscience. That is why we must not repudiate a class war.

The point is that it must be spiritualized: it must be kept in subordination to the supreme spiritual principle and away from the control of revengeful passions and relentless violence."[17]

Berdyaev saw that economic determinism is the fatal flaw of Marxism. He noted also, however, that the Calvinist doctrine of predestination that became intertwined with capitalism and views of life and wealth and poverty in what he called the "bourgeois mind," was another form of determinism.[18] He pointed out that this determinism included the attitude that the poor are responsible for their own misery, and those who have much deserve their happiness.

Berdyaev argued that even though the Christian religion does not endorse or establish a particular economic system "that will be valid for everybody, everywhere, and for all time," but leaves social creation to man's freedom, it requires its adherents to work for justice in the economic sphere: "Christians are living in this sinful world and must bear its burden, they may not steal away from the battlefield." This is because of the tremendous value of the human person made in the image and likeness of God:

> Christianity has to condemn the exploitation of man by man and of class by class from a religious and moral point of view, and she has to protect the workers and the exploited, for the Christian faith attaches a value beyond price to personality and to the human soul. Therefore it is impossible for her to refrain from condemning also that regime under which this personality and this soul are turned into a means towards the inhuman economic process.
>
> All this involves Capitalism on the one hand and Communism on the other.
>
> Economics exist for man, and not man for economics. There is nothing more inconsistent with Christianity than the optimistic idea that the economically strongest and most successful are of necessity the best, that wealth is a favour granted to man as a reward for his virtues.[19]

Dorothy wrote in a similar vein in the story of her conversion, where she was explaining to nonbelievers how she could possibly have joined the Catholic Church instead of continuing her interest in socialism. Her embrace of Christianity in no way erased her enduring concern for the poor and for a more just society. In fact, she was attracted to the church because she experienced it as the church of the poor, of the immigrant. She, like Berdyaev, insisted that Christians, while rejecting the approach of Marx, recognize realities that exist in the world and work to change them. The realities are so harsh for the workers, she said, that it is often difficult to forgive those who take advantage of them:

> Class lines are drawn even here in America where we have always flattered ourselves that the poor boy can become president, the messenger boy, the head of the corporation....The line has been fixed dividing the rich and the poor, the owner and the proletariat who are the unpropertied, the dispossessed.
>
> And how to convert an employer who has evicted all his workers because they were on strike so that men, women, and children are forced to live in tents, who has called out armed guards as Rockefeller did in Ludlow, who shot into those tents and fired them so that twenty eight women and children were burnt to death? How to forgive such a man? How to convert him? This is the question the worker asks you in the bitterness of his soul. It is only through a Christ-like love that man can forgive.[20]

These thinkers contended that the limitations placed on human freedom and divine grace by the primacy of the economic in everyday life are paralleled in giving to the state the authority to form all of one's basic values and granting it unquestioning obedience. They wondered why some questioned the church so much at the same time as they gave all their loyalty to the state, which might have very different values than their faith professed. After observing the unswerving, unquestioning obedience of many people to the state in an overblown patriotism, Dorothy pointed out, with Simone Weil, that this was a strange modern phenomenon. She could not accept the idea of giving one's first obedience to what she ironically called "Holy Mother the State." The modern state was not her idea of the ideal: "Every new development of the last three centuries has brought men closer to the state of affairs in which absolutely nothing would be recognized in the whole world as possessing a claim to obedience except the authority of the State."[21]

Some people admired the work of Dorothy Day and the Catholic Worker movement, but could not understand her allegiance to the Catholic Church. Ironically, it was in the church that she found freedom, the freedom to be a personalist, to engage the whole world with her faith, to address persons in an impersonal, fragmented world and especially to meet Christ in the persons who came to her. Dorothy commented that often Catholics did not seem to know that they possess such tremendous freedom to do good in living out the gospel. Speaking of people who have not yet come to a conversion or second conversion, "which binds them with a more profound, a more mature love and obedience to the Church," Dorothy noted that many rebel against church authority or resent it, without realizing their freedom. Her commitment came from her love of God: "Even seeing through a glass darkly makes one want to obey, to do all the Beloved wishes, to follow Him to Siberia, to antarctic wastes, to the desert, to prison, to give up one's life for one's brothers since He said, 'inasmuch as ye have done it unto one of the least of these My brethren, ye have done it unto Me.'"[22]

To those who could not understand giving one's allegiance to God and to the church, Berdyaev explained that it is the nature of the church that makes all the difference: "Only an integral conception of the Church which regards it as the Christianized cosmos, as the heavenly and eternal Church, as opposed to a merely temporal and historic body, can free me from a sense of being oppressed by it or can prevent me from exercising my critical faculty in relation to it. To come into the Church is to enter upon the eternal and divine order of the world. This does not mean that we have to make a break with the world or with history, but rather that we participate in their transfiguration."[23]

Answering Nietszche, who criticized Christianity as being a slave mentality only for the weak, Berdyaev affirmed that it is Christianity that gives hope and power to the person, the right kind of power. His insights show the alternative of Christian personalism to all the misuse of power in the world.

Nietzsche did not know or understand true Christianity. He had before him the degenerate Christian society that had lost the heroic spirit. And he rose with passionate indignation against this decadent, bourgeois Christianity....

What Nietzsche has to say of the origin of morality generally and of Christian morality in particular is very interesting, but absolutely the reverse of truth. The weakness and insignificance of the Christians prevented him from seeing the strength and greatness of Christianity....Christianity is the greatest power of resistance to the power of the world....Christian virtue is not compliance to norm and duty but strength and power....Christianity teaches us how to be strong in the face of life and of death. Only a decadent Christianity leads man to think of himself as a trembling, weak and timorous creature, having neither strength nor capacity to do anything. Sinful man is powerless without Christ, but he is strong in Christ, for Christ has overcome the world.[24]

Berdyaev's thought on freedom relates to the way the Lacouture/Hugo retreat[25] brought people to embrace a radical Christianity, even though the dominant culture was pushing them in another direction. The *metanoia* (changing of heart and mind) preached in the retreat meant that Christianity, with God's grace, should transform one's whole viewpoint to the freedom of the gospels, where one is able to live in a different way than the habits, patterns, and pressures common to everyday life. Like Berdyaev, the retreat called those who made it to "maximalist" Christianity, but did not call the Christian to judge others with the demands one might place on oneself. Conversion must begin with oneself. As Berdyaev said, "Christianity teaches us above all to be ruthless with regard to the evil within us, but in the process of extermination we must be indulgent towards our neighbours. We can be maximalists only in relation to ourselves and not to others. We must first realize the power and beauty of goodness in ourselves and not impose on others what we have been unable to compel ourselves to realize. The lie in the soul which is common to political and social revolutions consists in the desire to eliminate external evils while allowing them to flourish within."[26] Dorothy also often wrote in this way. She used the scriptural expression and the language of the retreat of "putting on Christ" to describe what Berdyaev meant when he spoke of the path to uniting human freedom with divine freedom.

Miller asks the practical question, "And what in the personalist-Worker view did 'putting on Christ' mean?" He gives the answer in terms of freedom, a freedom not weighed down by bureaucracy and old institutional forms, but with the creativity of the incarnation of the gospel in the social order: "It certainly did not mean a further refinement and extension of the analytic temper of the modern mind, so dear to the hearts of those whose first thought was to 'study' the problem....Putting on Christ was an act of freedom which would be a leave-taking in spirit, mind, and even body of the institutional forms, manners, and values of a world of process—of, more particularly, the bourgeois world...."[27]

Like Emmanuel Mounier, Berdyaev contended that each person has a special destiny in this world related to the eternal, to the kingdom of God, which begins here and now. With Berdyaev, the Catholic Workers went beyond the secular philosophies of the past several centuries to an understanding of time and history with Christ at its center. Their focus was the mystery of freedom and God's grace, free will and personal responsibility, the destiny of the person in the world. They also took into account the tragedy of freedom and the cross and the problems of evil and suffering.

Berdyaev, like Peter Maurin, believed that those who put all their hope in human progress within time were mistaken. His reflections on the questions of time, eternity, and destiny refer to a concept which is key to both his thought and the philosophy of the Catholic Worker movement: "The theory of progress is not concerned with the solution of human destiny and history in timeless eternity, beyond the limits of history itself. It is concerned solely with a solution within the time torrent of history, a solution at a particular moment of the future that proves to be the assassin and devourer of the past. The idea of progress bases its expectation on death itself. Its promise is not of resurrection in eternal life, but of the incessant extermination of past by future, of preceding by succeeding generations."[28]

Berdyaev challenged the positivist doctrine of progress of Comte, Hegel, Spencer, and Marx on the grounds that it rejected the value of the lives and cultures of those who had gone before, seeing them simply as "means and instrument" to the goal of an "ultimate humanity in that power and happiness which are denied to the present generation." He was outraged by the dismissal of all the previous generations by those who glorified progress, making it a religion of its own, ultimately, a religion of death:

> The religion of progress regards all the generations and epochs that have been as devoid of intrinsic value, purpose or significance, as the mere means and instruments to the ultimate goal.
>
> It is this fundamental moral contradiction that invalidates the doctrine of progress, turning it into a religion of death instead of resurrection and eternal life....No future perfection can expiate the sufferings of past generations. Such a sacrifice of all human destinies to the messianic consummation of the favoured race can only revolt man's moral and religious conscience.[29]

The Christian view of those who had lived in generations before, best expressed in the idea of the communion of saints, was quite different. Those who took seriously the lives of the saints and the creative ways in which they performed God's work in the world could not disparage them as sad specimens of humanity by comparison to those involved in current and future progress, because they didn't have certain technical advantages.

Berdyaev's understanding of time and his defense of the people who had lived and contributed before the present moment are similar to the ideas that emerge in Dorothy's writings, especially as she prayed for the dead and reflected on the communion of saints. In the March 1939 *Catholic Worker* she wrote that there is no time with God: "I remembered suddenly a young boy I knew who had committed suicide. I had asked a priest afterward as to praying for a suicide, and he said, 'There is no time with God, and perhaps He foresees the prayers you will say and so gave him time to turn to Him at that last moment with love and longing and repentance.'" In the November 1953 issue, Dorothy wrote again on this theme, reflecting on perhaps the same conversation with "this dear and kindly priest, who is dead himself now, God rest his soul...." She repeated church teaching: "It is not a matter of faith to believe that any one is damned to hell, though it is a matter of faith to believe that there is a hell," and reaffirmed her faith in the resurrection of the body:

> When I first read Léon Bloy's *The Woman Who was Poor*, I could not understand what I considered the joy of Clotilde, sitting in the cemetery, praying for her dead. It was morbid, of course, in the true sense of the word. But now that little Charlie Smith has died and has been buried in St. Joseph's cemetery at Rossville, Staten Island, which is a mile from Peter Maurin farm, I can understand that last chapter of the Bloy book. We went there often this summer, and will go there often this month of November, to tend his little grave and those of the two little babies who are buried just next to him in the next plot; and the children all came with us, and ran picking flowers among the grave stones....The sun warmed us, and the breeze spoke to us of God's Goodness and Beauty and there was no sadness there but peace. When there are many who have gone before, and among those so many who are near and dear, then the ties of this earth, the hold this life has on us, is loosened and we look with joy to the world to come. It is not "natural" to do this, it is true, and it is a matter of faith that these bones shall rise again, and that in our flesh we shall see God our Savior.

Berdyaev was not alone in his critique of the "religion" of progress. Christopher Dawson, another of Peter Maurin's favorite authors, wrote extensively about Christianity and culture and addressed in similar fashion the question of "progress." Dawson, like Berdyaev and Maurin, argued that eighteenth- and nineteenth-century philosophers had made a religion—a doctrine—out of the idea of progress, implying that it was an eternal truth that could replace religion. As Dawson said, this theory had become so much a part of modern thought that to criticize it was considered "almost an act of impiety."[30]

In 1929, when Dawson's book was written, disillusionment with the great hopes of progress had set in. Peter and Dorothy noted, however, and one might observe still today, that the average person and particularly the businessmen and the professors of business administration and economics continue to present as doctrine what appears to be the same mindset.

While Dawson recognized some material advances, he questioned whether "the modern advance of material civilization is progressive in the true sense of the word; whether men are happier or wiser or better than they were in simpler states of society, and whether Birmingham or Chicago is to be preferred to mediaeval Florence." He spoke of conditions for the many that were not ideal, of "social parasitism and physical degeneration in the enormous and shapeless agglomerations of badly-housed humanity, which everywhere accompanied the progress of industrialism." Like Peter Maurin, he decried the "destruction of the finer forms of local life, and the disappearance of popular art and craftsmanship before a standardized mechanical civilization as well as the havoc that has been wrought among the primitive peoples by European trade and conquest"—this at a time when the leaders extolling their countries' great progress were profiting from the forced labor of colonialism. He did not neglect to mention the destruction of the environment, by a "system that recklessly exhausts the resources of nature for immediate gain...and dissipates the stored-up mineral energy of ages in an orgy of stench and smoke."[31]

This was the "progress" with which Berdyaev refused to throw in his lot. One could not speak of the perfection of human nature without relationship to the eternal: "The exclusive cult of the future at the expense of the past, which is the feature of the various theories of progress, makes life subservient to a disruptive and deadly principle destructive of all co-ordination and of the integral reality of time. Subservience to the deadly power of time hinders the apprehension of the significance of human destiny as a celestial destiny."[32]

Not only did Berdyaev reject the idea of the world and humanity becoming better with each advance of progress, he rejected the idea of objectification, the Enlightenment dogma that human progress is best measured and served by a view of truth that is expressed in research and studies (and later, opinion polls).

Peter Maurin and Berdyaev understood that in the claims to objectivity in what was called a value-free or neutral (objective) approach to social science, the person was treated as a number, deprived of the dignity of one made in the image and likeness of God. In this "objectified," as opposed to personal, approach, efficiency as a value replaced the philosophical understanding of the importance of pure means and substantive ends. Miller highlights the similarity in the thought of Maurin and Berdyaev in this regard, explaining what both thinkers meant when they contended that "objectification" did not and could not capture the greatness of the human person and civilization and that this phenomenon limited human freedom:

> This passion for the "objective" transfers the criterion of reality from a subject reference, the person, to an object reference, the datum. The "objective," which has become the great driving force behind modern scholarship, expresses its social usefulness in the production of patterns in "hard data" that provide norms to which society, and the person, can be adjusted so that passing time can flow more serenely on its way. Thus the person, who once found a meaning for existence from a value climate that was ordered to the eternal, now finds his freedom and creativity thwarted by the necessity of conforming to the new behavior norms based always, of course, on the latest "new study."[33]

Berdyaev's critique of the ideology of efficiency experts and the development in the social sciences of the objectification of the individual person into a number, an object, or commodity for research studies and polls was echoed in Peter Maurin's Easy Essays.

Miller presents Peter's analysis of the Enlightenment views which left out the whole perspective of the eternal, of Christ as the center of history: "And so Maurin was a radical because he denied the Enlightenment proposition that reality lay in a discernment of order in the object and because he denied the nineteenth century idea that history was evolving toward its own heaven."[34] Peter said with Berdyaev, "History has failed....There is no such thing as historical progress. The present is in no wise an improvement on the past. A period of high cultural development is succeeded by another wherein culture deteriorates qualitatively."[35] Peter understood only too well the historical failures of the human part of the church: "An intellectual revolution was necessary. The truths of eternity had to be made understandable to the minds of ordinary people. Further, whatever part of the Church had been beguiled by time, the mark of its long embrace with the spirit of bourgeoisity, had to be excised."[36] Personalism called for an authentic Christian humanism, which was only possible when philosophy, education, politics, and economics were not fragmented, nor severed from their roots in the spiritual, and therefore from ethics and practical virtues.

In Berdyaev's view, neither the human mind, the human psyche, nor society could keep up with the accelerating factor of fragmentation that came from the singular pursuit of the "objective." Peter knew that fragmentation limited human freedom and personal responsibility. Miller recounts Peter's encounter with a priest "who was a great scholar and a man of power in the world of learning." Peter told Jesuit Father Lord how he had grasped the arm of the priest, shaken his finger under his nose, and demanded, "What are you doing for the Catholic social revolution?" Peter asked Father Lord, "Do you know what he answered me?" He said, "That is not my field." This was inconceivable to Peter, whose view of scholarship did not allow for dualisms, separations, isolation, or fragmentation.[37]

For Peter the mystery of freedom implied immediate personal responsibility for one's neighbors—he did not allow Christians to abandon this responsibility to the government, to the Catholic or any other hierarchy, or to social agencies. The Christian should be a model of love: "See those Christians, how they love one another." As Dorothy said in the May 1955 *Catholic Worker*,

> Above all it was in the name of man's freedom that Peter opposed all "government ownership of the indigent," as one Bishop put it. Men who were truly brothers would share what they had and that was the beginning of simple community....Men were free and they were always rejecting their freedom, which brought with it so many responsibilities. He wanted no organization, so the Catholic Worker groups have always been free associations of people who are working together to

get out a paper, to run Houses of Hospitality for themselves and for others who come in "off the road."

Miller describes what Peter was able to bring to Dorothy, who had sought answers in socialism, left it, and as a new Catholic was still searching. This was his understanding (from Berdyaev and Maritain) of Christian freedom and Christian anthropology. This understanding became very much a part of the Catholic Worker, and helps to explain its freedom and creativity:

> What Peter Maurin did for Dorothy was to reorient her vision from the object to the subject, from collectivism to Christian personalism. He also provided her with something she had not had—an understanding of the meaning of the Church and her position in it. Peter saw the Church as the logical and necessary instrument of re-creation. It was logical and necessary because the whole of human history had been cluttered with the wreckage of lives and of cultures that had been victimized by the ambitions and vision of those who would have their own beatitude in time. No such heavenly city of history had ever been achieved, but were it approximated, it would impose an absolute tyranny upon every person that lived within its bounds. True freedom, true creativity, true humanism could be achieved only when a people were set upon the path to God. The Church provided that path; it was the voice of God made audible in time, giving humankind "an instruction and a way of life."[38]

Berdyaev and Peter's refusal to objectify people in categories, their insistence that each one is a person and is to be treated as such, has had many practical implications in Catholic Worker Houses of Hospitality. Catholic Worker personalism, following Berdyaev and Mounier, means treating the person who comes to a House of Hospitality as a guest. No Worker in a House of Hospitality would call the person who comes for help a client or a case, which implies an objectification of that person and a position of power and supposed expertise over them. Catholic Worker houses avoid bureaucratic forms of organization at all costs in the Houses of Hospitality.

The nonviolent "anarchism" of the movement, which has not always been understood, is the assumption of personal responsibility and love in a world of objects and impersonal structures. The insistence of the Catholic Worker movement on Christian freedom, however, created situations that might have been avoided in a structured organization. "For her part, Dorothy Day in her life with the movement has accepted the divisions and catastrophes that are the part of freedom....From the first, there were those who would have it follow a more moderate course, who would trade the precariousness that went with freedom for an organization of their lives."[39]

Peter and Dorothy, as Berdyaev, knew that an attempt to counteract the bourgeois mind with a freedom or anarchism without spiritual roots would not solve the problem. This may explain the tragedy of the 1960s' rejection of the bourgeois lifestyle by young people who had no roots. That revolution, which began with such great hopes, was doomed to failure because it did not have a profound tradition and spirituality with which to replace what was rejected. It is little wonder that those who had first protested bourgeoisity eventually became yuppies. Many of those who did not destroy their minds with drugs later found solace in becoming bourgeois.

The revolution of the '60s and the disillusionment related to the Vietnam War affected the Worker, especially the farm at Tivoli, where youth gathered who were completely unaware of the roots of the Catholic Worker movement. Some of those young people mistook the freedom of the gospel for license. Dorothy increasingly found things to dismay her. Miller quoted from a letter from Dorothy to her old friend, Sister Peter Claver, at that time:

> On Sunday, of the seventy people at the farm "only a scant half dozen get to Mass at the parish and our own Vespers and Compline daily." When a priest did come to the house for Sunday Mass, "they all go and receive too. (Catholic and non-Catholic—children unprepared and adults unshriven). I'm considered an ancient old fogey, and the more praise given me by the press—by those who do not know me—the more the young edge away from me....I am just not 'with it' any more, and you can imagine the kind of desolation I feel...."

"They 'feel' they are right so they are right." Meanwhile, "they despise the old, who have made such a mess of the world, and with the old—the ancient Church itself. They want to 'rebuild the Church in the shell of the old,' as one of them said."

As for sex, Dorothy wrote, "I must say the new morality is depressing...how much sorrow is being laid up for these young ones." [40]

Berdyaev's freedom is not the freedom for sensual exploration of youth. It is not the freedom of the invisible hand of the market to be as avaricious as the market will allow, it is not the freedom to consume and consume, not the freedom to ignore the victims of one's selfish actions. It is the freedom to love God with one's whole heart, mind, and soul and one's neighbor as oneself, but it is not a freedom without risks or tragedy: "Doubtless this long passage through the experience of good and evil could be made much shorter and easier by limiting, or entirely suppressing human liberty. But what is the value of men coming to God otherwise than by the road of freedom and after having experienced the harmfulness of evil? It is to this view of freedom that the Catholic Worker has subscribed—which it has practiced and which has surely brought it hurt and tragedy."[41]

Those who contend that, without God and simply on a human plane, progress can solve everything, have left out the problem of the power of evil, of powers and dominations. For Berdyaev, an awareness of evil is crucial in exercising one's freedom:

> To deny evil is to lose the freedom of the spirit and to escape the burden of freedom. Our present age has witnessed a terrible increase of evil coupled with the denial of its existence. But man is powerless to resist evil if he fails to recognize it as such. Human personality deceives itself when, having made a distinction between good and evil, it thinks itself competent to delimit evil. When we abolish such limits and when man finds himself in a state of confusion and indifference, his personality begins to disintegrate, for the power of conscience is inseparably connected with the denunciation of evil.[42]

Both Berdyaev and Maurin believed that "reordering institutions in the flow of time, either by 'peaceful' or 'revolutionary' means, could change little in the long run." For these prophetic thinkers, hope and resurrection lay in the spiritual: "The rebirth of the world would occur when the myth of slavery and death gave way to the light of the divine, where life and freedom found their true focus in eternity."[43]

Berdyaev identified the "rising beast of Revelations" with the "spirit of bourgeoisity which signaled the end of history, the final sign before Christ's Second Coming." He wrote that "the spirit of bourgeoisity, by finding its outlet in the creation of systems, turned one of the sources of the joy of life into darkness, for the creative act was a source of joy." Miller summarizes Berdyaev's ideas about the Second Coming, so different from the apocalyptic doomsday stereotype: "'It may be possible,' he writes, 'to await passively the judgment of a revengeful deity, but no such attitude is compatible with the Second Coming....This event will be a transition from historical Christianity, which foreshadows the end of the spell-bound world of ours.' It would be an event characterized, not by 'fear, inertia and frustration, but one of daring and creative endeavor.'"[44]

The eschatology of the Catholic Workers was similar to and influenced by that of Berdyaev. The faith of Dorothy and Peter was based in the incarnation of the Son of God, who had entered history, worked as a carpenter, healed the sick, sanctified human existence, and died and rose again. It was also firmly based in the hope of the resurrection and of the Second Coming of Christ. The Catholic Worker understanding of the freedom of the gospel is a source of great hope. If it is ultimately an eschatological hope, it is also an alternative way of life in love and freedom in the richness of Christian tradition in the here and now. As the Catholic Workers declared in the Aims and Purposes of the Movement, "We are working for a new heaven and a new earth wherein justice dwelleth."

Berdyaev, like Peter and Dorothy, understood the depth of meaning of Christian freedom in relation to the cross and resurrection: "Christ opened up for us a freedom of the spirit and sealed it with His blood for all eternity. Faith in Calvary is faith in freedom."[45] Suffering was very much a part of life at the Catholic

Worker, especially in the suffering of those who were served, but also in the lives of Workers, as in the Christian life. Dorothy frequently wrote: "in the Cross is joy of spirit." As Berdyaev also said:

> Unenlightened suffering, the most terrible of all, is that which man does not accept, against which he rebels and feels vindictive. But when he accepts suffering as having a higher meaning, it regenerates him. This is the meaning of the Cross. "Take up thy cross and follow me." That means, "accept suffering, understand its meaning, and bear it graciously. And if you are given your cross, do not compare it with, and measure it against, other people's crosses." To try to avoid suffering and run away from it is self-deception and one of the greatest illusions of life....This is the deepest mystery of Christianity and of Christian ethics. Suffering is closely connected with freedom. To seek a life in which there will be no more suffering is to seek a life in which there will be no more freedom. Hence all hedonistic morality is opposed to freedom.[46]

The influence of Berdyaev was apparent in Miller's collection of Dorothy's notes from the retreat, where she dramatically affirmed Berdyaev's view that Christ is the center of history and that it is through his cross that darkness is transformed into the light of resurrection, that time is redeemed: "The Cross is the instrument of Christ's suffering and death. It stands at the center of time, a stark and forbidding sign of the evil that time can spawn. It is the point of deposit for all the suffering and all of the death that was or will be. But God, by Himself suffering and dying on the Cross, transformed its dark and torturous meaning into light. The Cross is the portal into beauty, into eternity. There is no figure of human conception so exalted as the Cross, for from out of its desolation life receives its highest due."[47]

The Catholic Workers tried together to live out Peter Maurin's (and Berdyaev's) teaching on freedom and personal responsibility flowing from Christian faith. Peter explained the possible problems as well as the solution to this dilemma of the freedom of loving God and doing what you will:

St. Augustine said,
"Love God
and do what you please."
We do what we please
but we don't love God.
We don't love God
because we don't try
to know God.
And man was created
in the image of God
and every creature
speaks to us
about God
and the Son of God
came to earth
to tell us
about God.

This phrase of Augustine explained Peter Maurin's life. It also described Dorothy, famous for her care for the poor, for her newspaper, for her protests, for going to jail for her principles, so active and engaged in the world's affairs, yet always teaching the necessity for the revolution of the heart for the freedom of the gospel—trying to implement on a day-to-day basis what Berdyaev had said: "Christianity teaches us to work from within to the outward and not *vice versa;* the perfect life, whether individual or social, cannot be attained through any programme imposed externally: spiritual rebirth is essential and it proceeds from freedom and grace. Compulsion will never make good Christians or a Christian social order; there must be an effective and real change in the hearts of persons and of peoples, and the realization of this perfect life is a task of infinite difficulty and endless duration."[48]

Emmanuel Mounier, Personalism, and the Catholic Worker Movement

The September 1936 *Catholic Worker* declared the communitarian personalist position of the young movement:

> We are working for the Communitarian revolution to oppose both the rugged individualism of the capitalist era, and the collectivism of the Communist revolution. We are working for the Personalist revolution because we believe in the dignity of man, the temple of the Holy Ghost, so beloved by God that He sent His son to take upon Himself our sins and die an ignominious and disgraceful death for us. We are Personalists because we believe that man, a person, a creature of body and soul is greater than the State, of which as an individual he is a part. We are Personalists because we oppose the vesting of all authority in the hands of the state instead of in the hands of Christ the King. We are Personalists because we believe in free will, and not in the economic determinism of the Communist philosophy.

Peter Maurin's background in French personalism, which emphasized so much the dignity and destiny, the special vocation of each person, not only gave him a philosophical base for engagement in the world, but also informed his own personal attitude and style. Dorothy Day wrote in *The Long Loneliness* about the vision that Peter brought to the movement:

> Peter made you feel a sense of his mission as soon as you met him. He did not begin by tearing down, or by painting so intense a picture of misery and injustice that you burned to change the world. Instead, he aroused in you a sense of your

own capacities for work, for accomplishment. He made you feel that you and all men had great and generous hearts with which to love God. If you once recognized this fact in yourself you would expect and find it in others.[1]

Peter's presence and approach seemed to be the embodiment of this dictum of Emmanuel Mounier (1905–1950): "One does not free a man by detaching him from the bonds that paralyze him; one frees a man by attaching him to his destiny."[2] By destiny, Mounier did not mean determinism, fatalism, or predestination, but vocation in freedom.

It was Peter who introduced the ideas of Mounier to Dorothy and to the Catholic Worker movement. One of his Easy Essays featured Mounier's book, *La revolution personnaliste et communautaire* (The Personalist and Communitarian Revolution). Peter Maurin knew, of course, that the roots of communitarian personalism were much older in the church than the twentieth century. As Dorothy Day put it in her 1955 *Catholic Worker* article, "He [Peter] loved St. Benedict because he said that what the workers needed most was a philosophy of work. He loved St. Francis because he said St. Francis, through his voluntary poverty, was free as a bird. St. Francis was the personalist, St. Benedict the communitarian." However, the Catholic Worker is incomprehensible without an understanding of the influence of the thought and movements going on in France, and especially the ideas of Mounier and Berdyaev, in applying this ancient vision to modern times.

Mounier articulated a philosophy of Christian personalism, of human persons whose responsibility it is to take an active role in history even while their ultimate goal is beyond the temporal and beyond human history. Mounier expressed it as "a philosophy of engagement...inseparable from a philosophy of the Absolute or of the transcendence of the human model."[3]

Mounier's personalism is based in the value of each and every human person made in the image and likeness of God, and in the mystery of free will. Mounier brought to his country, where the proclamation of "the rights of man" had had such influence and historically had led to the deaths of so many people, the perspective that any movement or effort toward human rights must be based in the affirmation of the value of the person: "If our efforts were confined merely to a defense of man's public liberties or to any rights not further grounded, then our position would be weak indeed; for there would then be danger of defending only individual privileges." It was the person who mattered:

> We are not asserting that the human person is an absolute, although for a Christian believer the Absolute is indeed a person, and in strict terminology the spiritual does not exist except as personal. But we do assert that the human person as defined by us is an absolute in comparison with any other material or social reality and with any other human person. It can never be considered merely as part of a whole, whether of family, class, state, nation or even humanity. No other person, and still more, no collective whole, no organism, can legitimately utilize the person as a means to an end. God himself, in the doctrines of Christianity, respects the liberty of the person, even while vivifying it from within.[4]

For Mounier, the person is never an object, but a subject with presence, to be loved, inspired, encouraged, even provoked into responding to destiny and vocation:

> Whenever I treat another person as though he were not present, or as a repository of information for my use (G. Marcel), an instrument at my disposal; or when I set him down in a list without right of appeal—in such a case I am behaving towards him as though he were an object, which means in effect, despairing of him. But if I treat him as a subject, as a presence—which is to recognize that I am unable to define or classify him, that he is inexhaustible, filled with hopes upon which alone he can act—this is to give him credit. To despair of anyone is to make him desperate: whereas the credit that generosity extends regenerates his own confidence....[5]

Mounier described what he calls the "dialectic of personal intercourse," which "builds up and sustains the being of all who participate in it," as a gift that can be given by respecting others as persons and interacting with them. Centered in love, it is distinct from all individualism:

Love is the one surest certainty that man knows; the one irrefutable, existential *cogito:* I love, therefore I am; therefore being is, and life has value (is worth the pain of living). Love does not reassure me simply as a state of being in which I find myself, for it gives me to someone else. Sartre has spoken of the eye of another as something that transfixes one, that curdles the blood; and of the presence of someone else as a trespass upon one, a deprivation or a bondage. What we speak of here is no less disturbing; it shakes me out of my self-assurance, my habits, my egocentric torpor: communication, even when hostile, is the thing that most surely reveals me to myself.

Thus the positive interpersonal relation is a reciprocal provocation, a mutual fertilization.[6]

In her study of Mounier (reviewed in *The Catholic Worker,* September 1974), Ellen Cantin, CSJ, describes his personalism in terms of engagement and love and respect for the other person. "Personalism does not attempt to be entirely objective. It cannot be understood or appropriated through cogitation alone. The first requisite of Personalism is commitment and commitment is never neutral. It is a commitment that initiates and directs each one's thinking, and it is in a commitment that thought terminates. Hence, the starting point of Personalism is, 'I love, therefore being is,' and not 'I think, therefore I am.'"[7]

Descartes, the philosopher whose assertions turned some ideas in philosophy upside down by his definition of how one defines reality, had concluded that the only reason he knew anything was that "I think, therefore I am" *(Cogito, ergo sum).* He tried to apply scientific and mathematical principles to philosophy and questioned whether there was any objective reality. James Hanink, with Cantin, points out the basic, crucial difference in the starting point of the two philosophers. Instead of Descartes's famous *cogito,* "I think, therefore I am," Mounier has it, "I love, therefore I am."[8] This takes the onus from knowing to loving.

Personalism is not enlightened self-interest or "life-and-death struggle," but self-gift. When people asked Mounier about the difference between personalism and existentialism, he framed the answer in terms of the generosity and self-bestowal at the heart of personalism: "The vitality of the personal impulse is to be found neither in self-defense (as in petty [sic]-bourgeois individualism) nor in life-and-death struggle (as with existentialism) but in generosity or self-bestowal—ultimately, in giving without measure and without hope of reward."[9]

It is to Mounier and other personalists that we owe Peter and Dorothy's emphasis on personal responsibility in history (as opposed to withdrawal from the world). Peter Maurin's French roots and language helped him to keep abreast of all that was happening in the vital renaissance in the Catholic Church in France, of which personalism was so much a part. He was able to bring to the Catholic Worker what Henri Bergson called the *élan vital* (creative impulse) and to make the religious revival of France immediately present in the United States.

France played an important role in revitalizing the Catholic Church in the twentieth century. In his foreword to Mounier's *Be Not Afraid*, Leslie Paul describes the many blows that had fallen on France since the revolution of 1789, and how within this history a Catholic revival began which was unequalled anywhere else. He speaks of the influence and the greatness of the other thinkers and writers who were a part of the personalist movement with Mounier as well as those came before them:

> Indeed, the dread events of the 20th century which produced in Germany a Spengler, a Rosenberg and a Streicher as the authentic prophetic voices, in France produced quite another group of men who began the most vigorous exploration of social and spiritual problems and initiated a full-blooded Catholic revival distinguished especially in the person of Jacques Maritain by the most exhaustive intellectual and spiritual efforts. One thinks immediately of Bloy, Péguy, Claudel, Bernanos—and of Berdyaev too, for though he was a Russian, his mature life was spent in the Parisian circles for which Esprit was the proper spokesman—each of whom brought an Old Testament vigour of language to the task of exposing the intellectual cheats, pious frauds and confidential political tricksters of the age. They revealed an inflexibility of purpose and an inability to compromise that is the mark of genius. No other nation can boast of such a hierarchy; and if there is today a new Christian humanism we owe it to them. Emmanuel Mounier is one of them, in direct descent from Charles Péguy about whom he wrote his first work, and upon whose life he formed his own.[10]

The French renewal is fascinating, because it took place at a time when in England and the United States Maisie Ward was speaking of "France pagan," where the working class was being lost to the church through the despair brought on by the excesses and terrible treatment of workers during the Industrial Revolution, preparing the way for the workers to turn to Marxism. The great writers of the Catholic revival recognized this situation and were very much encouraged in their work by papal encyclicals that addressed the problem of workers and the whole social question, beginning in 1891 with Leo XIII's *Rerum novarum*.

In 1932 Mounier left his post as professor of philosophy and founded the personalist journal *Esprit*, where he, as editor, launched the principles of personalism, and writers of succeeding years and decades published their ideas on the subject. Bergson and Péguy especially influenced Mounier's thought in rejecting the scientism and determinism that controlled the content of classes at the Sorbonne at the time and thus his decision to leave university teaching.[11] Although it was a daring venture for Mounier to leave the security and respect of his position as a university professor, he had come to believe that it was his task to take philosophy beyond the academic establishment, to make it alive, engaged with the world. It was certainly not because he lacked intellectual acumen that he left his professorship. Michael Kelly has pointed out that Mounier scored above all his competitors save one on the examination that was the highest academic competition in the French education system, an exam that Jean-Paul Sartre, the future father of existentialism, took for the first time in the same year and, "against all expectations, failed."[12]

Esprit grew out of a movement, of conferences and discussions in every part of France around spirituality and faith in relation to analyses of the social problems and burning controversies of the time. Among the many Catholic and Orthodox intellectuals involved in the personalist movement with Mounier were Jacques Maritain, Nicholas Berdyaev, Jacques Ellul, and a young Jesuit seminarian named Jean Daniélou who later became a cardinal (and whom Dorothy Day met in New York through Helene Iswolsky[13]). Mounier participated in the monthly gatherings the

Maritains held at their home in the Paris suburb of Meudon that included these creative thinkers. Many who attended these gatherings joined Mounier in his new venture with *Esprit*. It was Maritain, along with some "friendly clerics," who later, when *Esprit* came into some question with the archbishop of Paris, helped to explain and defend it.[14] *Esprit*, however, was not only for Catholics; from the first, articles were published by others who shared the personalist communitarian vision.

Mounier and the others who gathered to discuss and to try to implement the ideas of personalism saw the crisis of the century as one of civilization and culture, manifested dramatically in the Wall Street crash in 1929. Mounier expressed the challenge to personalists as one so profound as to "patiently, cooperatively *remake the Renaissance* after four centuries of error."[15] They perceived the task on a grand scale: "Contrary to what takes place with many petty reformers, our program must be cut in a pattern of large dimension. Historically, the crisis that presses upon us is more than a simple political crisis or even than a profound economic crisis."[16]

Mounier was not only a philosopher. He had participated in the St. Vincent de Paul Society, begun by Frederick Ozanam in the nineteenth century. Mounier's involvement in its activities "gave him some experience of poverty in the working-class areas of Grenoble, and helped him to understand the intolerable social conditions in which much of the working class lived."[17]

Writing after Mounier's death about his perspective on civilization, ethics, and morality, philosopher Paul Ricoeur noted that Mounier's whole enterprise could have been called moral, "if Mounier had not rejected with horror the mind of the moralist." To Mounier the moralist always seemed to be lost "in generalities and rhetoric, restricted to the dimension of the individual without a foothold on history, and tainted with hypocrisy." According to Ricoeur, "through his criticism of 'the doctrinaire or moralist error,' Mounier helped restore the reputation of ethics, making it traverse the whole sphere of technics, social structures, and ideas and undermining the force of determinisms and ideological apathy. He has made ethics real and truthful."[18]

The same was true of the Catholic Worker movement in the United States. Personalism infused first *The Catholic Worker* newspaper and the movement, and ultimately a much wider group of people, with a new and broader ethical ideal. The fresh approach to living the gospel and the creative, daring, demanding ethics of the Catholic Worker has inspired generations of young people.

When the Catholic Worker movement began in 1933 with its newspaper, discussions, and hospitality, it brought people together in the United States in the way *Esprit* did in France. The phrase "clarification of thought," so well known from presentations and discussions at the Catholic Worker, was also used by Mounier.[19]

In order to make Mounier's writings available in the United States, Peter first translated them himself at the Worker and then convinced the Benedictine monks at Saint John's Abbey to translate and publish *The Personalist Manifesto*. The monks' translation that Dorothy mentioned in her columns is the English translation available to this day in libraries: *The Personalist Manifesto*, Longmans Green and Co., 1938. *The Catholic Worker* took the same stand (neutrality) as that of Mounier and *Esprit* during the Spanish Civil War (unpopular in both France and the United States) and published an article by Mounier himself about it in 1936.

Like the personalism featured in *Esprit*, the Catholic Worker is a movement, not a system, a movement engaged in a positive way in the world. As Mounier put it, "What makes personalism very difficult for some to understand is that they are trying to find a system, whereas personalism is perspective, method, exigency."[20] And again: "Personal man is not desolate, he is a man surrounded, on the move, under summons."[21]

He understood that misrepresentations or distortions of Christianity often made it difficult, if not impossible, for people to believe. When living saints who embodied "generosity, freedom, suffering and creation" were absent, when religion was gloomy or used to support and reassure its followers in a bourgeois lifestyle, the faith itself became unrecognizable. Mounier wrote in response to Nietzsche, who ridiculed Christianity, angry not at Nietzsche, but at those who had created the caricature:

> L'Affrontement chrétien, another of Mounier's works...manifests a sense of outrage at the distortions of Christianity which had moved Nietzsche to ridicule it. His anger was not directed at Nietzsche, but at those Christians who had so adulterated the strength and joy of the Good News, that it could not but become the object of scorn....Nietzsche's scorn becomes Mounier's exhortation:
> "Better songs would they have to sing for me to believe in that Savior; more like saved ones would his disciples have to appear unto me!"[22]

Mounier, Maurin, and Day wrote extensively against bourgeois individualism and industrial capitalism. They decried the coercion of Communism and fascism, but also saw the evils of speculation, usury, and capital disconnected from labor as even more strongly entrenched in society and the cause of great harm. With Mounier they warned: "Modern Christianity is dangerously allied to capitalist and bourgeois Liberalism."[23] Mounier could not accept the ethos of seeking security and comfort strictly for oneself and one's own family in the midst of the worldwide depression, the economic and spiritual crisis of his time. One of the earliest influential issues of *Esprit* carried articles on the problems of Christianity in the modern world: "Mounier's own article set the tone. Pointing out the massive desertion of spiritual values by Christian people, he denounced the extent to which the Church had compromised itself with the temporal forces of the world....Catholic doctrine, he continued, required obedience to temporal powers only so long as they did not constitute a tyranny. Western capitalism did constitute a tyranny, he insisted, and only the possibility of a worse, Communist, tyranny should deter Catholics from entering into revolution." In that first issue Mounier critiqued the bourgeois who "sought the order and tranquility necessary to procure a mediocre contentment based on possessions." He went so far as to describe this phenomenon, which he called a moral rather than an economic category, as a subtle representative of the Anti-christ.[24]

The personalists were outspokenly critical about the ever-growing and expanding, powerful modern state, so closely tied to industrial capitalism.

William Griffin points out that in his early article, "The Communitarian Revolution," Mounier warns about the "increasing centralization of economic and political power," noting that "both sides of the…spectrum, Left and Right, are corrupted by this concentration of power." Griffin reflects that he was "prophetic in his denunciations in 1935, of the tremendous political power that became an instrument for the spiritual and physical oppression of so many," in Nazi Germany and in the Nazi occupation of France, among other countries. Mounier maintained that "only pluralism in political life and decentralization of the economic structures can defend the person from the relentless concentration of power which is an inexorable trend in every form of modern political ideology."[25]

Cantin addresses the question of private property in Mounier's writing, emphasizing the creative idea of even property facilitating self-donation. Noting that Mounier's "*De la propriété capitaliste à la propriété humaine,* has been called one of the best treatises on Christian property in any language" she provides a brief summary of its content:

> In this treatise, Mounier reiterates the classic view that property is a man's extension of himself. He notes that through the acquisition of property, the capitalist extends the sphere of his control. However, it is only a physical and not a personal extension of himself that occurs through his acquisition of property. He uses his property like a protective shell to make himself less vulnerable to the intrusion of a world which makes demands on the unprotected. By means of property the capitalist arranges for himself a spacious solipsism and becomes unavailable to the outside world.
>
> On the other hand, true personal possession involves the use of goods not for self-protection, but for self-exposure. As an extension of the person, and not simply of the body, it facilitates communication and the possibility of making oneself present to others. Personal property is the extension of one's being, not

simply of his having. It facilitates the personal act of self-donation and generosity.[26]

Mounier criticized the economics of the business world that
tries to ignore the dignity of the person and to organize itself only
for profit. He wrote that the system of factories under capitalism,
where the ownership of property is in the hands of the few, "is
based on contempt, conscious or implicit, of the laborer." As an
example, Mounier quoted Frederick Winslow Taylor, who like
Henry Ford propagandized for the assembly line in factory work,
in which the worker spent all day repetitively doing some small
task: "We don't ask you to think. There are others who have been
paid to do that."[27]

Mounier believed that the biggest problem of modern capitalism has been proclaiming the primacy of economics over history, over the life of the people, over community, over living out
one's faith and one's values. His blueprint for that economy asks
everyone to lay aside greed and materialism. He emphasized that
in any ethical approach to economics, profits do not have rights,
but workers do. For Mounier the priority of profit flawed the capitalist system, since in it the person is subordinated to consumption, consumption in turn is subordinated to production, and
production to speculative profit. He critiqued basing everything
on a profit motive unrelated to the good of the human person,
especially the worker. He went so far as to say that "the extreme
importance attaching today to the economic problem among
human preoccupations is a sign of social disease," explaining that
this distorted view was related to the lack of a philosophy of life:

> The economic organism underwent a sudden proliferation at
> the close of the 18th century and like a cancer it has upset or
> even eaten away the rest of the human organism. Through lack
> of a reaction thereto or of a philosophy of life, the majority of
> critics and of men of action accepted the accident as the normal
> state of affairs. They proclaimed the primacy of economics over
> history and regulated their actions according to this primacy—
> after the manner of a cancer quack who would decide that a
> patient thinks with his cancerous growths! A more correct view

of the proper requirements of the person...demands a revolt from this deformed perspective.[28]

In articulating the difference between individualism and personalism, Mounier described bourgeois capitalists as those who had refused the Mystery. "Individualism proclaimed the self-sufficiency of the demanding citizen, it refused mystery and the call of spiritual presences....Everything became a race for money and a quiet life...."[29]

Mounier argued that it is inconceivable to base one's life on comfort, accumulation, and consumerism. He knew that the meaning of life, and specifically Christian life, was much more profound. He contrasted the attitude in which comfort is made into a transcendental and everything becomes a commodity or a business, with that of other historical periods, even with the beginnings of individualism:

> We are indeed far from the hero. The rich man of the classical period is himself fast disappearing. On the altar of this sad world there is but one god, smiling and hideous: the Bourgeois. He has lost the true sense of being, he moves only among things, and things that are practical and that have been denuded of their mystery. He is a man without love, a Christian without conscience, an unbeliever without passion. He has deflected the universe of virtues from its supposedly senseless course towards the infinite and made it center about a petty system of social and psychological tranquility. For him there is only prosperity, health, common sense, balance, sweetness of life, comfort. Comfort is to the bourgeois world what heroism was to the Renaissance and sanctity to mediaeval Christianity—the ultimate value, the ultimate motive for all action.[30]

Mounier, with Péguy, affirmed that the crisis of the twentieth century was *both* economic and spiritual. He was not satisfied with the explanation of the crisis by Marxists, who said it was a classic example of economic crisis, a crisis of structure. He knew there was a spiritual problem as well. Mounier not only adopted Péguy's famous phrase, "The revolution will be moral, or there will be no revolution," but defined it more closely: "The moral revolution will be economic or there will be no revolution. The economic revolution will be moral or nothing."[31] In one of his Easy Essays Peter Maurin captured the profundity of Péguy and Mounier's thought:

> Charles Péguy once said:
> "There are two things
> in the world:
> politics and mysticism."
> For Charles Péguy
> as well as Mounier
> politics is the struggle for power
> while mysticism
> is the realism
> of the spirit.

By contrast to the almost exclusive emphasis on economics in most people's lives and in practical philosophy, Mounier emphasized the primacy of the spiritual. His primacy of the spiritual, however, was not separate from the world. He, like Peter and Dorothy, insisted that the personalist revolution could not be simply enshrined in academia and in theory. The communitarian personalist "revolution" required action. Personalist action would begin with a change of heart and a sense of one's destiny. Mounier placed personalist action in the context of vocation: "Every person is responsible for incarnating and living out the values of his or her vocation....First, the values of one's vocation form a person, form the habits of being. Therefore, Mounier says of personalists, 'we will act through what we are as much as we will act through what we do and say.' Secondly, the quality of personalist action will not resemble the frenetically externalized activism of fascist and communist ideologues."[32]

Mounier emphasized engagement in the world for the Christian, making it clear that a Christian has a responsibility to act in the world, to be available to respond. This engagement in the world makes life unpredictable. Mounier reminded his readers: "Availability is as essential as loyalty, the test of history as much as intellectual analysis." Anyone who has ever been a Catholic Worker or worked in the service of the poor knows how demanding availability can be. Mounier wrote even about sin in this perspective, emphasizing that sin is not just an individual affair, but includes taking personal responsibility and creative thought and action. He elaborated on the traditional concept of sins of omission: "Modern narcissism has reduced sin to an individual preoccupation. It has placed the stress on the tarnishing of one's image of oneself...which disguises its [sin's] basic perspectives, revolt against God and desertion from one's post. But the parable of the talents is the very kernel of the Gospels. That talent was not given to you to be polished and re-polished but to be turned into two talents."[33]

Mounier presented the importance of the will in one's engagement with others, in making one's contribution to the world, and insisted on the connection between love and will and action. The influential philosophy of Kant, for example, while emphasizing the human will, did not require personal engagement for the common good. Mounier insisted: "To will, it is first necessary to love." He pointed out the error in Kant's understanding in this regard: "Without love, without reason, without truth, the 'autonomous will' can be mistaken." Mounier here quoted Péguy: "'Kantian philosophy has kept its hands clean,' said Péguy. 'Yes, but it hasn't any hands.'"[34]

Mounier described the inadequacies of the approach of moralizers and others who, while interested in the spiritual, "are strangers to the living reality which is history...who do not try to influence living history by means of a strong spiritual structure which could give rise to a program of definite action through a profound knowledge of the needs and the techniques of the present day." Mounier suggested that some of these folks might be naïve in relation to what Pope John Paul II later called structures of sin: "They properly exhort individuals to cultivate the virtues which give strength to social life. But they forget that historical forces, freed from submission to the spiritual, have created collective structures and material necessities that we must inevitably reckon with insofar as 'the spiritual itself is embodied in flesh.' Such men are a constant source of danger, since they tend to lead the spiritual forces, which we should like to inject into history, above or around the historical happenings without coming to grips with them."[35]

In the Catholic Worker, as for Mounier, faith, thought, and engagement in the world could not be separated. Miller noted, "The theme of the personalist idea held commonly by Mounier, Maritain, and the Catholic Worker, was that the primacy of Christian love should be brought from its position of limbo where human affairs are concerned and infused into the process of history."[36] In the May 1955 *Catholic Worker* Dorothy described what personalist action in history meant in Peter's thought and program. It was not socialism, but the personalism of the gospel:

> His whole message was that everything began with oneself. He termed his message a personalist one, and was much averse to the word socialist, since it had always been associated with the idea of political action, the action of the city or the state. He wanted us all to be what we wanted the other fellow to be. If every man became poor there would not be any destitute, he said. If everyone became better, everyone would be better off. He wanted us all "to quit passing the buck," and trying to pass on the work to George to do....
>
> He had taken to himself that new constitution, that new rule of the Sermon on the Mount, and truly loved his enemies and wanted to do good to all men, including those who injured him or tried to enslave him. He literally believed in overcoming evil with good, hatred with love. He loved the rich as well as the poor, and he wanted to make the rich envy the poor who were so close to Christ, and to try to become closer to them by giving of their means....

For personalists it is unthinkable that life, freedom, and economics could be separated from responsibility, ethics, and spiritual values. Love, rather than individualism, is the key. In *The Personalist Manifesto* Mounier described what a personalist community (thus the "communitarian" aspect) would be like, a description which sounds remarkably like the doctrine of the common good:

> If we were to describe its ideal realization, we should describe it as a community in which each person would at all times be able

to achieve his fruitful vocation in the totality and in which the communion of all in the totality would be the living outcome of the efforts of each one. Each one would have a place of his own in the whole which no one else could fill, but which would harmonize well with the whole. Love would be the primary tie and not any constraint or any economic or "vital" interest or any extrinsic apparatus. Each person would there find, in the common values transcending each one's own limitations of place and time, the tie that binds all members in the whole.[37]

Mounier, like Peter and Dorothy, did not expect the complete realization of such a community in time and on earth, but believed that "the fullness of community—the Kingdom of God—has some kind of limited existence during this life." Cantin points out that Mounier does not have a "two-world metaphysics"; he uses the word *beyond*, rather than *after*, to describe the Christian view of the relationship of the reign of God now and in eternity: "It exists now as the very beyond which inspires movement, development, personalization, and history."[38]

Peter expressed the personalist's starting point in building such a community in unforgettable words in one of his Easy Essays:

People say:
"They don't do this,
they don't do that,
they ought to do this,
they ought to do that."
Always "They"
and never "I."
The Communitarian Revolution
is basically
a personal revolution.
It starts with I,
not with They.
One I plus one I
makes two I's
and two I's make a we.
We is a community,
while "they" is a crowd.

Catholic Workers did not wait for the government or other agency structures to ponderously begin to do something, but tried to act personally as Jesus asks his followers to do in the Sermon on the Mount and Matthew 25. While Catholic Worker personalism drew from the French version, it was lived out in a unique way in the Catholic Worker movement, reflecting Peter Maurin's synthesis of philosophical ideas and the richness of Church tradition. Harry Murray described the way personalism has evolved with later Catholic Workers. It became *the* Catholic Worker philosophy, but not exactly on the European model: "Although the Worker has clearly appropriated the European personalists' emphasis on the value of the person, the central concept of Worker personalism is personal responsibility. When asked what they mean by personalism, most contemporary Catholic Workers reply that it means assuming personal responsibility for one's brothers and sisters—that it means not leaving the poor to the tender mercies of the state welfare bureaucracy."[39]

Peter Maurin described with deceptive simplicity the personalist vision of the Catholic Worker:

A personalist
is a go-giver,
not a go-getter.
He tries to give
what he has,
and does not
try to get
what the other fellow has.
He tries to be good
by doing good
to the other fellow.
He is altro-centered,
not self-centered.
He has a social doctrine
of the common good.

In Catholic Worker Houses of Hospitality the emphasis on personal responsibility and voluntary poverty means doing the work oneself. There are, for example, no janitors in Catholic

Worker houses. Scholars and workers alike were and are expected to take personal responsibility: "This interpretation of personal responsibility is applied to daily routine, as when one Worker complained to another about some overflowing garbage bags, evoking the response, 'If you see something that needs done, do it. Take personal responsibility.'"[40]

Some asked whether the city or federal government or the Archdiocese of New York helped the Catholic Workers and why they were carrying the burden of doing the work themselves with what seemed to be little help. They depended on donations and were obviously poor. Dorothy Day answered by describing the personalist base for the very practical work in which she and the others were involved:

> No one asked us to do this work. The mayor of the city did not come along and ask us to run a bread line or a hospice to supplement the municipal lodging house. Nor did the Bishop or Cardinal ask that we help out Catholic Charities in their endeavor to help the poor. No one asked us to start an agency or institution of any kind. On our responsibility, because we are our brothers' keeper, we began to try to see Christ in each one that came to us. If a man came in hungry, there was always something in the icebox. If he needed a bed and we were crowded, there was always a quarter around to buy a bed on the Bowery. If he needed clothes, there were our friends to be appealed to, after we had taken the extra coat out of the closet first, of course. It might be someone else's coat but that was all right too.[41]

The person who attempts to live out the philosophy of personalism in receptivity to the Mystery not only may have an impact on the world in which he or she lives, but also be personally changed. Mounier said, "Action is not judged primarily by the accomplishment of an external work but by the edification of the agent, the development of his ability, of his virtues, of his personal integrity."[42] Observing the human condition in various projects, personalist followers of Jesus can keep from despair through Jesus' reminder that the weeds survive with the good plants in the midst of living out the gospel: "The parable of the tares and the wheat is the truest symbol of the Christian vision of History. An accursed harvest springs up throughout the years to make all human Utopias ineffectual and to shatter the dream of a world which shall become innocent from the moment it is so decreed: such is the role of 'Christian pessimism.' But growing tirelessly amidst these unhallowed fields is the kingdom of God, named and unnamed, with slow irresistible force."[43]

In the obituary of Emmanuel Mounier in *The Catholic Worker* in April 1950, Dorothy memorialized one who had so helped to shape the vision of the movement:

> It was a great shock to us to hear of the death, by heart attack, in Paris of Emmanuel Mounier, at forty-five. Mounier was the guiding spirit in the French personalist movement, and founder and director of *Esprit*, the magazine which is the organ of the movement. Mounier, who was the child of peasants, was a brilliant scholar at the Sorbonne.
>
> Peter Maurin used to say wherever he went, "There is a man in France called Emmanuel Mounier. He wrote a book called *The Personalist Manifesto*. You should read that book."
>
> Mounier himself was a pilgrim of the Absolute, and now he has gone to that God who is a person, three Persons in one God.

Mounier continues to inspire the Catholic Worker movement to this day.

Francis of Assisi: Saint of Voluntary Poverty and Nonviolence

St. Francis of Assisi (1182–1226) was an important model for the Catholic Worker movement. Peter Maurin shared the joy and excitement of Francis in living the gospel in poverty and freedom. Like Francis, Peter gave up any ideas of power, domination, or expediency as means to accomplish his goals, but rather inspired others with the idea of their vocation. Dorothy Day wrote in the September 1945 *Catholic Worker* that Peter Maurin not only brought the ideas of St. Francis to the Catholic Worker movement, but also lived in many ways like Francis himself:

> Peter is always getting back to St. Francis of Assisi, who was most truly the "great personalist." In his poverty, rich; in renouncing all, possessing all; generous, giving out of his heart, sowing generously and reaping generously, humble and asking when in need, possessing freedom and all joy.
>
> Without doubt, Peter is a free and joyous person. And it is the freedom and joyousness that comes from a clear heart and soul. There are those who might say it comes because of his anarchistic nature, his refusal to enter into political controversy, his refusal to use worldly means to change the social order. He does not indeed refuse to use mystical means, physical means, secular means, the means that are at hand. But the means of expediency that men have turned to for so many ages, he disdains.

Others compared Dorothy herself to St. Francis. Kenneth Woodward assessed the impact of her life and work in exactly those terms: "Dorothy Day did for her era what St. Francis of

Assisi did for his: recall a complacent Christianity to its radical roots."[1]

Peter and Dorothy brought Francis's message to the twentieth century, teaching by their example that the way to rebuild church and society is the way of Francis. Like Francis, Peter and Dorothy made a decision not to start a sect, but to remain in the framework of the church, modeling a unique way of transforming the church and world by calling people more deeply to the gospel. The bond with the church allowed Francis and the Catholic Workers to maintain their radicalism in following the gospel without losing perspective or seeking self-aggrandizement. Their critique of the church and the secular world was their very lives.

The attraction of the Catholic Worker to the life and methods of Francis was not unrelated to the amazing effect he had on the practices of economics, war, and the social structure of his time. Pragmatists wonder that the methods of Francis could even be considered. Remember, they might say, this is the real world. Catholic Workers, however, saw through their study of history that the methods of Francis had profound practical effects.

Dorothy and Peter and the early Catholic Workers read *The Little Flowers of St. Francis*, a fourteenth-century classic, and G. K. Chesterton's book, *St. Francis of Assisi*. They studied Francis especially in Pope Pius XI's encyclical *Rite expiatis* (known in English as *St. Francis, Herald of the Great King*), in Johannes Jorgensen's biography of the saint, and in Father Cuthbert's book. They had good taste: Theodore Maynard has pointed out that perhaps the best examination of textual criticism of the early sources regarding Francis "is to be found in Johannes Jorgensen's St. Francis of Assisi and Father Cuthbert's book of the same title."[2]

Francis, the son of a wealthy cloth merchant, had spent his early years as a pleasure-seeking leader of youth in Assisi, became a knight, and fought in war. He later experienced a profound conversion, rejected his father's wealth and the use of force and violence, and embraced poverty. He had had wealth in the home of his father; he found much greater wealth in the freedom of voluntary poverty.

In seeking to understand his vocation, Francis spent many hours in prayer. At first, when the Lord asked him to rebuild his church, Francis thought he meant a church building, and he did that with his own hands at San Damiano. It became clear, however, that his mission was even greater—to renew the heart of the whole church in his time.

When Francis had twelve followers, he went to Rome (or some say marched to Rome) to ask permission of the pope to found his Franciscan order. At first he was rebuffed, but soon a friendly cardinal paved the way for him, and his new order was approved. Chesterton tells the story that upon their return journey home, many clamored to join the friars: "In one place in particular, it is said, the whole population of a town, men, women and children, turned out, leaving their work and wealth and homes exactly as they stood and begging to be taken into the army of God on the spot."[3]

The world flocked to Francis. He had become the new person in Christ described by St. Paul. His love for the crucified Christ transformed him and made the Lord visible to those who knew him. Upon meeting him, many laypeople and clergy who had begun with little faith (and fewer faith-deeds), and who had been leading superficial lives, gave up what they had to follow Jesus. Francis's followers included brothers and priests, the women's order started by Francis and Clare (known as the Poor Clares), and the huge membership of the Third Order of laypeople. The little brothers and sisters who followed Francis abandoned all seeking of power (Francis relentlessly hunted them down if they didn't). Their radical commitment to the gospel overcame power and corruption and, ironically, they became in a unique way the most powerful people on earth. They didn't need guns—in fact, Francis forbade them to be soldiers. Theirs was a different kind of power.

With his conversion, Francis said he married Lady Poverty. Not only did he embrace poverty, but the poor as well. Peter Maurin described his perspective in an Easy Essay:

St. Francis thought
that to choose to be poor
is just as good

as if one should marry
the most beautiful girl in the world.
We seem to think
that poor people are social nuisances
and not the Ambassadors of God.
We seem to think
that Lady Poverty
is an ugly girl
and not the beautiful girl
that St. Francis of Assisi
says she is.

Francis's love for the poor and the outcast is dramatically illustrated by his work with lepers, who were completely shunned in his world. Having met and kissed the diseased leper in the name of Jesus, Francis was never the same:

> Nothing was in sight but a leper who dragged himself along, coming slowly toward Francis. For a moment disgust and horror rose in him and by force of habit his hand began to lift itself toward his nose to shut off a stench that had not yet come to him. Then he told himself, "You are not a knight of Christ if you are unable to conquer yourself." He knew that this was somehow a great moment, the crisis of a battle, when one man's cowardice may imperil the entire issue. No, he would be loyal and true....
>
> As he drew level with the poor putrefying wretch, Francis leaped from his horse. His first intention had been to do as he had formerly done and toss the man a coin; instead he ran to him and took the diseased body in his arms. A face eaten away and swollen into the aspect of a lion gazed at him; in the eyes was a look of astonishment. He put a kiss upon the hands, upon which there were only stumps of fingers, pressing into them all the money he had in the wallet at his girdle. And upon that shapeless mouth he put a kiss....
>
> When he had ridden a hundred paces, something made Francis swing his body round in the saddle and look back. There was the dusty road, and the fields were open on either side. But there was no leper in sight.[4]

With this experience Francis began to serve the leper community through the Works of Mercy and gradually others joined him in his work. He had been totally changed by his encounter with the Jesus of the gospels and Jesus in the poor, and insisted that the gospel must become flesh where the Lord became flesh, among the poor.

Francis lived at a time when the faith of the people was not strong and their knowledge of their beliefs limited. Ignorance and corruption added up to the need for change and improvement—a church and society in need of reform. Francis was there to write the book on reform and nonviolent revolution. He knew how to reform without destroying, calling his followers to abandon everything to become disciples of Jesus and to love especially the poor and afflicted. He began the reform with himself. His methods were faith, contemplation, living the gospel, and sacrificial nonviolent love in unity with the church. He led a tremendous campaign to bring the spirituality of the gospel to the people, and in doing so changed the face of Europe without firing a single shot, insisting that his followers not seek riches, not make oaths (to feudal lords), and not bear arms. In the book the Catholic Workers studied, Father Cuthbert described the reform of Francis and his followers:

> Wherever they were received by the people, the spirit of faction and heresy was lessened: men forgot their discontent and shook off their quarrels; a new sense of life sprang up amongst them, beside which political programmes and party feuds were of little concern. Of those who had hitherto thought of reform as something to set their neighbors right, many now began to take it as something primarily concerning themselves: and that was the beginning of peace....Very swiftly the people recognized that the brethren saw in the Church, above and beyond the petty contentions of men, a Divine presence amidst the things of earth: and this simple uncontentious faith did more to revive the loyalty of a people whose faith was strong in spite of discontent, than all the controversy could have done.[5]

In the June 1934 *Catholic Worker* Dorothy addressed the terrible social situation of her own age, quoting from a pamphlet by Father Cuthbert on how the perspective of St. Francis could not only bring about changes in the social order but also provide a witness of faith and action for the world:

> Father Cuthbert of England in a pamphlet entitled *St. Francis and You*, published in 1905, wrote: St. Francis laid the foundation of a new social order of things within the Church. This was his special work, and the work of his order—to induce Christian society to live by Christian principles; to be Christians in very deed as well as by profession. St. Francis by laying upon his Tertiaries the precept never to bear arms except in defense of the Church, struck a fatal blow at the entire (feudal) system....
>
> These words are as true now as they were in 1905. We call upon the comfortable people to recognize and to fight the industrial evils that are dragging the people down and making them in their blind and perverse human hopelessness to turn from their Mother the Church.

At the time of Francis the Christian perspective on avarice had become dim and the drive toward wealth defined the lives of many; those who had it often considered the poor undeserving, lousy creatures. Pius XI described in *Rite expiatis* (no. 8) the realities Francis faced when he spoke of nonviolence and love for the poor, naming extortion and usury as two of the sinful methods used by the greedy to build up huge fortunes at the expense of the poor:

> Those who did not belong to that most unfortunate class of human beings, the proletariat, allowed themselves to be overcome by egotism and greed for possessions and were driven by an insatiable desire for riches. These men, regardless of the laws which had been promulgated in many places against vice, ostentatiously paraded their riches in a wild orgy of clothes, banquets, and feasts of every kind. They looked on poverty and the poor as something vile. They abhorred from the depths of their souls the lepers and neglected these outcasts completely in their segregation from society....The custom, too, was prevalent of monopolizing wealth and piling up large fortunes. These fortunes were often acquired in divers and sinful manners, sometimes by the violent extortion of money and other times by usury.

In *Rite expiatis*, Catholic Workers found a model for their work in building a new and just social order in the midst of difficult times. The Holy Father insisted that Francis was to be imitated in his radical adherence to Christ and the gospel, not just admired.

Often the "hard sayings" and teachings of Francis have been ignored or marginalized as impractical. Brigid Merriman points out that this encyclical made all the difference for Catholic Workers in taking seriously the challenge of St. Francis: "*Rite expiatis* provided Dorothy with a different understanding of Francis than that of the popular media, giving her a strong foundation for understanding the active dimension of the Franciscan charism. It was clearly one that moved beyond the pious sentiments of Franciscan birdbaths, which was a part of popular devotion to Francis."[6]

The challenge of the encyclical for the Catholic Worker movement was highlighted by Dorothy as she wrote in the paper as early as April 1934: "We continue to cling to the *ideal* as held up in the Gospel and the encyclical on St. Francis of Assisi. *We* shall not reach it, we know. But that does not mean that there is no use trying." In the October 1944 *Catholic Worker,* Dorothy recalled the way in which Peter had introduced her to *Rite expiatis* and Francis: "It was not with the social encyclicals of the Popes that Peter began my indoctrination. It was with the prophets of Israel and the Fathers of the Church. It was also with Pius XI's encyclical on St. Francis of Assisi. 'Here is the way,' he seemed to shout, but, sadly, 'since men are what they are, and want a plan, all right, here are plans' and then out came the social encyclicals of Leo XIII, Pius XI, and now latterly, Pius XII."

In the May 1953 *Catholic Worker,* she again told how from the beginning Peter had emphasized *Rite expiatis* as a method as well as a spirituality. His approach was that of Francis: "He always aimed at the best, and to him voluntary poverty, manual labor, was the beginning of all true reform, which was to begin with one's self."

It was not only Pius XI who recommended the methods of St. Francis as the best way to respond to the problems of any age. In his Easy Essays Peter quoted from three other popes who had recommended his way to laypeople in responding to problems in the social order:

"We are perfectly certain
that the Third Order of St. Francis
is the most powerful antidote
against the evils that harass
the present age."
   –Leo XIII

"Oh, how many benefits
would not the Third Order of St. Francis
have conferred on the Church
if it had been everywhere organized
according to his wishes."
   –Pius X

"We believe that the spirit of the Third Order,
thoroughly redolent of Gospel wisdom,
will do very much
to reform public and private morals."
   –Benedict XV

Dorothy wrote about how in the face of materialism and corruption the witness of love in voluntary poverty could change people's hearts, both within and without the church. In 1966 she put into historical perspective the thorny issue of wealth in the church, with a similar theme of that of *Rite expiatis*, in which the pope had regretted that "even greed for wealth and pleasure was not absent among the clergy":

> I am thinking of how many leave the Church because of the scandal of the wealth of the Church, the luxury of the Church which began in the very earliest day, even perhaps when the Apostles debated on which should be highest in the kingdom and when the poor began quarreling as to who were receiving the most from the common table....St. Paul commented on the lack of esteem for the poor, and the kowtowing to the rich, and St. John in the Apocalypse spoke of the scandal of the churches, "where charity had grown cold."
>   It has always been this way in the Church...,the struggle for detachment, to grow in the supernatural life which seems so unnatural at times, when the vision is dim.[7]

The secret of Francis was his commitment to the gospel. Books were hard to come by, so in order to share the Word, he actually took pages out of the New Testament and gave them to people. Chesterton tells the story of how Francis found inspiration from the scriptures for starting his order and for his spirituality. The three gospel passages he found when he opened the Bible at random three times were guides for him throughout his life:

> According to one story, he merely made the sign of the cross over the volume of the Gospel and opened it at three places reading three texts. The first was the tale of the rich young man whose refusal to sell all his goods was the occasion of the great paradox about the camel and the needle. The second was the commandment to the disciples to take nothing with them on their journey, neither script nor staff nor any money. The third was that saying, literally to be called crucial, that the follower of Christ must also carry his cross.[8]

Dorothy, who also loved the Bible, imitated Francis in his approach to the scriptures on that occasion, seeking direction through simply opening the Bible and reflecting on what she found on the page that fell open: "She found herself randomly opening the Bible three times in conscious imitation of Francis of Assisi, a saint whom she greatly admired and whose life of voluntary poverty and peacemaking she strove to emulate. Although a minor incident, it indicates nonetheless that Dorothy sought direction from the sacred text as much as did the medieval Francis."[9]

Throughout her life, Dorothy continued to reflect on the life and work of St. Francis. When considering whether she should take another trip to start yet another Catholic Worker house in another city, she wondered in the December 1971 *Catholic Worker* what St. Francis would do. She said that she found inspiration in an ancient book about St. Francis:

> [I] sat in the chapel at Tivoli one evening after Compline reading the *Little Flowers of St. Francis*. I'd been asking myself, "Should I continue my pilgrimages or stay home?" And opening the book the answer came. St. Francis was asking the same question. A Brother said, "Keep wandering and spreading the news." So I went to Wheaton, Ill., where 250 Franciscans were meeting from coast to coast and the call of the assembly was:

"The Lord spoke to Francis and told him to be another kind of fool, the kind of fool such as the world has never seen."

When she shared the teachings of the Sermon on the Mount with others, Dorothy, like Peter, tried to find a way to win people over without seeming to pass judgment on them. In the July–August 1964 *Catholic Worker*, she said that Francis was her model in this: "If we could strive for the spirit of a St. Francis, and it would be good to read his life and struggles, we would be taking a first step, but it is only God himself who can make a Saint, can send the grace necessary to enable him to suffer the consequences of following his conscience and to do it in such a way as not to seem to be passing judgment on another, but rather win him to another point of view, with love and with respect." In that article Dorothy reprinted part of the text of the Sermon on the Mount, hoping that by the nonpreachy example of Francis, people would be inspired to follow the challenging words of Jesus.

In his rule for the laypeople who followed him, the Third Order Franciscans, Francis incorporated his understanding of the Sermon on the Mount, especially the instruction to love enemies and how it should be lived out. He asked his followers to give up fighting. Eileen Egan points out that the influence and importance of Francis "does not lie simply in the fact that he attracted thousands of followers who committed themselves to living according to the Gospel, owning nothing, and supporting themselves by manual labor, or failing that, by begging. Of greatest importance…was his opening of lay people to the option of nonviolence." Francis provided specific rules "that made for nonviolent living by lay Christians" and changed the social structure of the time:

> They are to be reconciled with their neighbors, and to restore what belongs to others. They are not to take up lethal weapons, or bear them about, against anybody. All are to refrain from formal oaths unless where necessity compels in the cases excepted by the Sovereign Pontiff in his indult, that is for peace, for the faith, under calumny and in bearing witness.
>
> These rules, innocent-sounding though they may be, undercut the whole basis of the feudal system, a pyramid of mutual obligations. At the peak of the pyramid was the nobility,

essentially a military class, and each nobleman with his comple-
ment of knights. The upkeep of the warrior-knights called for
support from vassals and underlings. Oaths recognized by the
noble, generally the landowner, bound the vassal to fulfill his
obligations, which included service in military campaigns....

The refusal to bear arms was a condition of membership in
the Franciscan Third Order.[10]

St. Francis, and later the Catholic Workers, responded to the
challenge of the Beatitudes. They understood that the gospel
meant a whole new way of life, different from the dominant culture; it meant freedom from the constraints of the pressure of
conformity to bourgeois or consumer society, where following
one's vocation was inhibited by constant preoccupation with
appearances of success and security. Peter spoke of something that
Francis knew, that "detachment from material things is the mys-
terious key to spiritual freedom," the key to joy, and to the ability
to possess things as God wishes us to possess them, on loan, as it
were, for this life.[11] In the April 1934 *Catholic Worker*, Peter,
opposed to the wage system, quoted Johannes Jorgensen's biography of St. Francis,[12] who taught that one's work should be given
away as a gift:

> According to Johannes Jorgensen
> a Danish convert living in Assisi
> St. Francis desired
> that men should give
> up superfluous possessions.
> St. Francis desired
> that men should work with their hands.
> St. Francis desired
> that men should offer their services
> as a gift.
> St. Francis desired
> that men should ask other people for help
> when work failed them.
> St. Francis desired
> that men should go through life
> giving thanks to God for his gifts.

This idea of offering their services as a gift, working without wages, was sometimes the one that readers of *The Catholic Worker* found most difficult to accept. As Dorothy said in the May 1953 issue, "To work without wages! Here was the saying that made people turn away, shrugging their shoulders. How hard this was to take!" Dorothy described how this extraordinary approach worked when practically applied in the Catholic Worker movement: "Young people gave their services and unemployed workers gave their skills, and readers of *The Catholic Worker* sent in materials goods and money, so...that we have kept going on this basis of voluntary poverty and 'abolition of the wage system,' for those who preferred to give their services rather than go out and earn a wage for them."

People often asked Dorothy about the keynote of Peter's message. She answered in the May 1947 *Catholic Worker*: "One could say at once, without hesitation, poverty. It is what sets him apart, it is what distinguishes him from the great mass of the teachers of the day. In a time when we are living in an acquisitive society, Peter Maurin is the poor man." Catholic Worker John Cort agreed; in describing the meaning of poverty for both St. Francis and the Catholic Worker. Dorothy quoted him as saying that poverty was the "most significant message we had for the world."[13]

Francis understood the Sermon on the Mount to mean that poverty is the basis of all the other gospel virtues: "In his Sermon on the Mount of Beatitudes Christ the Master-Model as a matter of fact grounds all the seven other gospel virtues squarely on the foundation of poverty: 'Blessed are the poor in spirit, for theirs is the kingdom of heaven....' Where other saints would root the three evangelical counsels—poverty, chastity, obedience—in radical obedience, Francis would ground them in root poverty."[14]

The voluntary poverty adopted by the Catholic Worker movement, following Francis, meant a certain precarity. Dorothy sent out *The Catholic Worker* across the country to everyone she or friends of the movement knew and appealed for assistance for the Houses of Hospitality. Each year, one or two appeals were sent to the rapidly growing numbers of readers of the paper to assist financially in the work. Dorothy did not set up a foundation or amass savings. The Worker survived from year to year and day to day with the generosity of those who were drawn to the work and the spirituality of the movement. Dorothy responded to questions about whether the official church or Catholic Charities or the government helped them:

> We do not ask church or State for help, but we ask individuals, those who have subscribed to *The Catholic Worker* and so are evidently interested in what we are doing, presumably willing and able to help. Many a priest and bishop sends help year after year. Somehow the dollars that come in cover current bills, help us to catch up with payments on back debts, and make it possible for us to keep on going. There is never anything left over, and we always have a few debts to keep us worrying, to make us more like the very poor we are trying to help. The wolf is not at the door, but he is trotting along beside us. We make friends with him, too, as St. Francis said. We pray for the help we need, and it comes.[15]

The Catholic Workers discovered that freedom from wage and hour restraints allowed a better use of one's skills and creative resources in simplicity, without the inhibition of government regulation and the albatross of bureaucracy always and ever raising its ugly head, lurking in the background. Their lives were not controlled by having to tailor the work to the demands of a particular rich sponsor (in Francis's time or later) or to spend 30 percent of the time counting and creating statistics in order to insure further funding. The Works of Mercy were performed freely without grantsmanship, fund-raisers, the edifice complex (focus on fancy buildings to guarantee funding), public relations efforts and charity balls, a board of directors made up of rich and influential people, or building up an endowment. The Catholic Workers did not look to the government or later the Community Chest or the United Way for support.

Peter Maurin showed that voluntary poverty provides the freedom to do the Works of Mercy without having one's life controlled by the economic factor, which is so often the case. It allows people to avoid professionalism, the pitfall of those who approach being a professional with emphasis on the latest style in clothing, fancy offices, receptionists, and credentials on the wall.

Professionalism believes the superprofessional, the expert, knows better than any other person how to teach people how to live—without the richness of a great philosophy or the clear message of Jesus and often without great respect for the person. This was not the way of Francis or of the Catholic Worker. The service of voluntary poverty is service, unadulterated.

Voluntary poverty was not always easy. It required faith. There were no salaries at the Worker; they survived through donations or through an occasional fee from Dorothy's writings. The talks she gave in parishes or Newman centers as she traveled around the country were financed by those who invited her to speak. The Catholic Workers distinguished between voluntary poverty and destitution, the difficult situation of those who are involuntarily poor, which the Worker emphatically did not recommend. However, often the Workers' poverty was very real poverty. Dorothy graphically described it in the September 1939 *Catholic Worker* in one of her appeals for funds:

> We have always pointed out that poverty is with us as a means to an end, not an end in itself. Also, we distinguish between decent poverty and destitution....
>
> Our poverty is not a stark and dreary poverty, because we have the security which living together brings. But it is that very living together that is often hard. Beds crowded together, much coming and going, people sleeping on the floor, no bathing facilities, only cold water. These are the hardships. Poverty means lack of paint, it means bedbugs, cockroaches and rats and the constant war against these. Poverty means lack of soap and Lysol and cleansing powders. (How to provide soap, for instance, for two hundred and fifty men, such as the Pittsburgh house takes care of? Or even for the forty-five or so we have here?)

Voluntary poverty did not mean not working. It really meant much work, without all the amenities and labor saving devices. With voluntary poverty one has the freedom to work many extra hours and some Workers did and do, trying to creatively live out the Beatitudes. They would not do the work for money.

When the War on Poverty was presented as a solution to problems in society by Lyndon Johnson, an interviewer asked

Dorothy, "How do you think the Church can best assist the War on Poverty?" She responded, "By teaching Holy Poverty—a philosophy of poverty and a philosophy of work."[16]

Peter and Dorothy knew that the inspiration for Francis's commitment to voluntary poverty came from the gospel and they shared relevant gospel passages with readers and visitors to the Catholic Worker. Dorothy wrote of the poverty of Jesus in *The Long Loneliness*:

> The great mystery of the Incarnation, which meant that God became man that man might become God, was a joy that made us want to kiss the earth in worship, because His feet once trod that same earth. It was a mystery that we as Catholics accepted, but there were also the facts of Christ's life, that He was born in a stable, that He did not come to be temporal King, that He worked with His hands, spent the first years of His life in exile, and the rest of His early manhood in a crude carpenter shop in Nazareth....He trod the roads in His public life and the first men He called were fishermen, small owners of boats and nets. He was familiar with the migrant worker and the proletariat, and some of His parables dealt with them. He spoke of the living wage, not equal pay for equal work, in the parable of those who came at the first and the eleventh hour.
>
> He died between two thieves because He would not be made an earthly King....And He directed His sublime words to the poorest of the poor, to the people who thronged the towns and followed after John the Baptist, who hung around, sick and poverty-stricken at the doors of rich men.[17]

The ideal was to imitate Jesus in his poverty. In the April 1950 *Catholic Worker*, in an article called "Poverty without Tears," Dorothy noted that while many speak of poverty of spirit, the world also needs as a witness those committed to voluntary material poverty: "We must admit the possibility of detachment in the midst of obvious luxury of house and equipage and table, but just the same, what we need today in the face of materialist America and Russia, is the glorious poverty of St Francis, of St. John Marie Vianney, of Charles de Foucauld, of St. Benedict Joseph Labré—whose poverty was the destitution of our skid rows and boweries."

In the same article, however, Dorothy added a caution to those who would begin to embrace poverty, knowing that many who seek to imitate the abandonment to Divine Providence of a Francis often have many practical difficulties and may abandon the whole idea. She suggested starting gradually: "I learned about vocations to poverty, about presumption and pride in poverty, about the extremists who went to the depths in practicing poverty...and after a few years left work and settled down to bourgeois and individualistic comfort. It is good to accept one's limitations, not to race ahead farther than God wants us to go, not to put on sackcloth and stand on the street corners."

Dorothy reflected in *The Catholic Worker* in April 1953 that Francis himself did not embrace poverty in one single instant, but that "it seemed to grow on him":

> St. Francis was the little poor man and none was more joyful than he. But he began with fear and trembling, with tears, hiding out in a cave from his irate father, expropriating some of his goods (which he considered his inheritance) in order to repair a church and rectory where he meant to live. It was only later, that he came to love Lady Poverty. He took it little by little; it seemed to grow on him. Perhaps kissing the leper was one great step that freed him from attachment to worldly goods, of his fastidiousness, or fear of disease.

In *Loaves and Fishes* Dorothy again wrote about how for most people voluntary poverty is not embraced all at once. "Sometimes, as in St. Francis's case, freedom from fastidiousness and detachment from worldly things, can be attained in only one step. We would like to think that this is often so. And yet the older I get the more I see that life is made up of many steps, and they are very small ones, not giant strides." She commented on kissing lepers twice herself, and finding herself not immediately the better for it:

> The first time was early one morning on the steps of Precious Blood Church. A woman with cancer of the face was begging (beggars are only allowed in slums) and when I gave her money—which was no sacrifice on my part but merely passing on alms someone had given me—she tried to kiss my hand. The

only thing I could do was to kiss her dirty old face with the gap-ing hole in it where an eye and a nose had been. It sounds like a heroic deed, but it was not. We get used to ugliness so quickly. What we avert our eyes from today can be borne tomorrow when we have learned a little more about love....

The second time I was refusing a bed to a drunken prosti-tute with a huge, toothless, rouged mouth, a nightmare of a mouth. She had been raising a disturbance in the house. I kept remembering how St. Therese said that when you had to say no, when you had to refuse anyone anything, you could at least do it so that the person went away a bit happier. I had to deny this woman a bed, but when she asked me to kiss her, I did, and it was a loathsome thing, the way she did it. It was scarcely a human, normal mark of affection.

We suffer these things and they fade from memory. But daily, hourly, to give up our own possessions, and especially to subordinate our own impulses and wishes to others—these are hard, hard things; and I don't think they ever get any easier.[18]

In spite of their commitment to poverty, the Catholic Workers were given enough help to continue their work for many years. In the February 1974 *Catholic Worker,* writing about her acceptance of an award from the Paulist Fathers, a statue of St. Francis, Dorothy described this paradox: "*Abandonment to Divine Providence* was a favorite book of Isaac Hecker, founder of the Paulist Fathers, whose award I received when I spoke in Boston. The award was a beautiful little desk statue of St. Francis and reminded me of our attempts to practice voluntary poverty....The Lord keeps putting into our hands the means to carry on our work and the people to do it."

As she recommended that others do, Dorothy herself prayed to be poor, to love poverty. In the February 1953 *Catholic Worker,* she recounted that before she began a journey she visited a church, asking Francis to help her: "When I left New York, October first, I put in the hands of the statue of St. Francis, in the courtyard of the church at 32nd St., a bright red rose, and begged that he teach me ever more about poverty...."

Catholic Workers found inspiration in the maxim of Francis to rejoice even in times of tribulation. He taught his followers to find even joy in love of enemy, in persecution, in the painful experiences of life, because this is the way the Lord was treated. In the October 1963 issue of the paper Dorothy wrote, "One of my favorite stories in the *Fioretti* [Little Flowers of St. Francis, part 1, chapter 8] is 'This, then, is perfect joy.'" Dorothy brought up the phrase again in the *Catholic Worker* of May 1976: "How often that has been used around the Catholic Worker, making us laugh for joy at the sudden light and perspective given to our problems."

As has been the case with Francis, the temptation might be to simply admire Dorothy Day and Peter Maurin rather than follow in their footsteps. As Georges Bernanos, whose books Dorothy read and recommended, wrote:

> My dear brothers! I'll repeat now what I've already said, because it's always the same thing: If you had followed this saint instead of cheering him, Europe would never have known the Reformation, or the Wars of Religion, or the terrible Spanish repression. For it's you this saint was calling. But death was not partial: it struck everyone equally. And today we're facing a similar danger."[19]

*The Common Good
vs. Individualism*

Dorothy Day's and Peter Maurin's views on economics and on the
social order flowed from church teaching on the common good,
the universal destination of goods, the dignity of the human person, and the responsibility for God's creation held in trust for
future generations articulated by the fathers of the church and St.
Thomas Aquinas. The very name Catholic Worker reflected their
understanding that the concept of the common good must include
the good of the masses who worked. Dorothy told how Peter
explained to everyone who would listen about the doctrine of the
common good: "Among the books he was carrying one day was
The Thomistic Doctrine of the Common Good. A cheerful well-man-
nered woman who appeared interested in his ideas and eager to
learn dropped in to make a call and a small contribution to the
work. Peter immediately gave her the book." (That particular
woman, unfortunately, returned the book much later without having had time to read it.)[1]

Peter believed with church tradition that faith, ethics, and
economics could not be separated. He wrote in one of his Easy
Essays:

> According to St. Thomas Aquinas
> man is more
> than an individual
> with individual rights;
> he is a person
> with personal duties
> toward God,
> himself,
> and his fellow man.

As a person
man cannot serve God
without serving
the common good.

Peter was aware of the currents of thought of individualism of the past several centuries that had moved away from the concept of the common good. His background in philosophy and theology and his commitment to the gospel made him very capable of refuting those who tried to convince him that enlightened self-interest was not only not wrong as a motivation for one's life, but would actually help everyone. Peter believed in trying to become better rather than trying to be "better off."

Peter's sources for his synthesis of ideas regarding faith, the common good, the life of the community and its practical application in economics included not only Aquinas and the fathers of the church, but the prophets of Israel and twentieth-century thinkers such as R. H. Tawney, A. J. Penty, G. K. Chesterton, Hilaire Belloc, Christopher Dawson, and Thorstein Veblen. As a part of what he called her "Catholic education," Peter introduced Dorothy to the papal encyclicals *Rerum novarum* and *Quadragesimo anno*, great documents of the social teaching of the church that, in response to terrible working conditions and child labor in industrialized countries in the nineteenth century, emphasized the dignity of labor and insisted that employers treat workers more justly. Aware that relatively few Catholics had read the encyclicals, Peter said he wanted to make the encyclicals "click."

Peter criticized the materialism of both capitalism and socialism. He had read Marx and believed that socialism would not have existed if not for the excesses of capitalism. His experience and studies had shown him that neither capitalism nor Marxism was based on working toward the common good or respected the true dignity of the person. He called the two systems "The Two Bourgeois." Peter proposed instead communitarian personalism that included the commitment to actively work toward the common good:

The personalist
spreads the social doctrine
of the common good.
He spreads the social doctrine
of the common good
through words and deeds.
He speaks through deeds
as well as words,
for he knows that deeds
speak louder than words.
Through words and deeds
he brings into existence
a common unity,
the common unity
of a community.

The work toward the common good described by Peter included the idea he so often expressed that Christians and all people of good will should work towards a world where it was "easier for people to be good." The definition the Second Vatican Council later gave to the common good in *Gaudium et spes* (no. 26) as "the sum total of social conditions which allow people, either as groups or as individuals, to reach their fulfillment more fully and more easily" was very similar to Peter's words.

The father of modern capitalism, Adam Smith, had taught his followers to base their decisions in economics on "enlightened" self-interest and individualism. In *The Wealth of Nations* Smith contended, as his followers do today, that pursuing one's own economic interest would ultimately benefit the many. Machiavelli (and Max Weber[2] centuries later) argued that an expediency that bent moral concepts as needed was not only allowable in economics as well as politics, but to be recommended. The authors whom Peter recommended argued that Christians should take a different approach to society than individualism, expediency, or state-run collectivism.

English historian A. J. Penty, whose books were recommended by Peter Maurin, argued that the individualism of Smith and his followers was nothing new. Individualism and avarice had flourished long before the coming of Christ in the ancient Greek and Roman world and had allowed the rich to become richer and the poor poorer. This had divided their societies "into two distinct and hostile classes—the prosperous landowners, the merchants and the money-lending class on the one hand and the peasantry and the debt slaves on the other," in a new phenomenon in history up to that time.[3] The reality in Rome was worse, where wealth was concentrated in the hands of a few. The Romans already had what is now touted as a "global market" through their conquest of the world and they spoke of "free trade." When it came upon the scene, Christianity presented a distinctly different perspective. That is not to say that avarice, the accumulation of wealth, and selfishness were erased (avarice continued to be a reality and was named a cardinal sin), but attitudes toward it were shaped in the light of eternity.

Penty (and later R. H. Tawney) showed that those such as Adam Smith who once again advocated unfettered individual competition and making money by foreign trade had to turn the ethics of economics upside down to make it acceptable. They had to throw off centuries of church teaching on economics and ethics. Smith and his followers formed what Penty called the "pernicious habit of viewing social and industrial activities primarily from the point of view of the profit accruing from them rather than from that of the well-being of the community as a whole...."[4] Smith, however, was actually less harsh than those who later claimed his mantle in economics, in that he allowed for some restraints on self-interest.

Ancient Rome had managed to find legal methods to enforce wealth for the few and poverty for the many. Penty argued that what later came to be touted as "enlightened" Roman law was developed to protect the interests of these "economic vampires." Roman law included the "infamous Statute of Limitations," on property rights, by which after a certain period of time a person who had stolen another's land became the permanent owner.[5] It was Penty's contention, as well as Peter Maurin's, that the economics of Christian civilization was corrupted when Roman law was brought back to Europe. Peter wrote Easy Essays about the devastating effects of the replacement of the canons of the church regarding ethical social practices by Roman law, recommending Penty's book on the subject.

Penty described what happened historically in regard to concepts of property ownership, beginning with the early church when all was held in common, through later development of doctrine, and then the abandonment by society of church teaching on property that came with the Reformation:

> What happened with regard to usury happened also in respect to the institution of property....The Church came to recognize the institution of private property....Still the Church did not regard possession as absolute but as conditional, and dependent upon the fulfillment of certain duties. Such as failed in their duties might be called upon to surrender it. They had no legal or moral claims. "Private property and common use"—the formula which Aquinas borrowed from Aristotle—became the official attitude of the Church. The Roman lawyers sought to reintroduce into society the old Pagan idea of absolute property rights in the interests of the territorial princes. But the Church would have none of it, and did all in its power to resist the encroachments of the Roman Code. The Reformation changed all this by removing opposition to the inroads of Roman Law. The rights of property, from being objective and dependent upon the fulfillment of duties, became subjective and absolute.[6]

Dorothy quoted Peter on property and responsibility in the *Catholic Worker* in June–July 1933, where he presented a very different view from that of Roman law: "I am not opposed to private property with responsibility. But those who own private property should never forget that it is a trust." When he said this, Peter was following the tradition of the church on the universal destination of goods, that the right of private property does not mean the right to destroy it or to use it completely selfishly. Peter spoke about acceptance of the responsibility ownership entailed.

Penty argued that Catholic monasteries had provided an alternative to economic individualism. The many monasteries followed church tradition, in which private property was not meant to be strictly for individualistic use. When the reintroduction of Roman law began to change the economic framework, the monasteries did not change in their approach to the community. In the late medieval economy, monks worked to sustain themselves, but monasteries (as was true from the beginning of monasticism) were also centers of charity, hospitality, and assistance to the local community. Not only did their prayer help to sustain the Body of Christ, but practical help was given as well. Penty researched the archives of the British Museum and found evidence that the monasteries were the source not only of charity, but also of consistent assistance toward independence to the community. In England, for example, they provided not only food, but seeds for planting and other basics so that farmers could be independent.[7]

The monasteries were the object of vilification and destruction during and after the Reformation. Their property was confiscated, the monks and nuns evicted, and all the land given to rich noblemen who were politicians. Penty showed that the destruction of the monasteries left the poor without defense. After Henry VIII sent Oliver Cromwell and his men to "plunder, sack, gut" and raze to the ground all the monasteries of England, the assistance they had given to the poor and to the communities surrounding them was sorely missed. Penty recounted that landlords, upon the suppression of the monasteries, "speedily raised the rents and enclosed the commons. In other cases the peasantry were simply turned out of their holdings...." While there was poverty in the Middle Ages, he argues, "the monasteries must on the whole have relieved it, for one of the charges brought against them is that they were too indiscriminate in their charity and that many beggars had become dependent on them." Penty answered the age-old question regarding beggars and whether they took too much advantage of the generosity of others: "It is not necessary to deny the truth of such statements, but to point out that if the monasteries supported beggars they were created by the landlords who, with the help of the Roman lawyers, had dispossessed the peasants and turned them adrift."[8] Penty showed what happened to the people when support from the monasteries no longer existed:

After the suppression [of the monasteries], the poor were deprived at one fell swoop of alms, shelter and schooling. The consequence was that great numbers, left entirely destitute of the means of existence, took to begging and thieving. Henry VIII is said to have put 72,000 thieves to death after he destroyed the monasteries. When she became queen, Elizabeth complained bitterly that she could not get the laws enforced against them: Such was the degree of beggary, of vagabondage, and of thievishness and robbery, that she resorted particularly in London and its neighbourhood to martial law. But it was all of no avail. The people had been rendered destitute and there were only two possible policies for dealing with them if economic injustices were to be maintained—extermination or legal pauperism. Shrinking from the former, resort at last was made to the latter, and some general permanent and solid provision was made for them. In the forty-third year of her reign there was passed the measure which we know to-day as the Elizabethan Poor Law, from which our Poor Law derives.[9]

G. K. Chesterton, frequently quoted by Catholic Workers, described in similar terms what happened when the monasteries were destroyed, and individualism and commercialism accelerated. Chesterton's critique presented briefly what R. H. Tawney would later develop into a major study, the impact of Calvinism and the concept of predestination on economics and especially on the average or poor person. Chesterton contrasted in ironic terms the generous role of the abbey guesthouse in the community with the so-called progress imposed by the destruction of a way of life, to be replaced by Puritanism, Calvinism, and industrial capitalism. Chesterton argued that the new system of wage slavery, in which so many workers who had been uprooted from the country owned nothing and depended on the whim of employers, could not be the way to civilization.[10]

Penty and Chesterton contended that the guilds of craftsmen of the medieval cities had been better than industrial capitalism with its assembly lines and pricing according to whatever the market would bear. Peter Maurin agreed. He believed that something on this model could again be an alternative to individualistic economics. Dorothy quoted a talk Peter had given on economics and the encyclicals in the February 1947 *Catholic Worker*: "The original guilds had the idea. There is a pamphlet, 'The Sound Old Guilds,' the Paulist Press publishes it." Some argue that not everyone belonged to the guilds; Peter did not argue the point. He noted, however, that while the guilds had existed basically in the cities, and there were no guilds in the rural districts, what they had in the country was simply an ideology, "the ideology of the Gospel." In other words, not the survival of the fittest in harsh competition. Christopher Dawson's works provide details about the way in which the guilds functioned. He emphasizes the unity of religious, ethical, and economic practices in the guilds (or gilds in the medieval spelling), and their fraternal and religious character, contrasting the liberty of free association and the emphasis on mutual aid in the guilds with later individualism.[11]

The books of R. H. Tawney were a major source for Peter Maurin in understanding what had happened to the positive connection between faith and economics, such as that in the guilds. In a book recommended by both Peter and Dorothy, he explained the difference between what had developed over centuries into an acquisitive society and what should rather be a functional one.[12] The Catholic Workers agreed with Tawney that the acquisition of wealth was no basis for a meaningful life. Peter's pithy Easy Essays showed the futility of the acquisitive attitude:

> On the Cross of Calvary
> Christ gave His life to redeem the world.
> The life of Christ was a life of sacrifice.
> We cannot imitate the sacrifice of Christ on Calvary
> by trying to get all we can.
> We can only imitate the sacrifice of Christ on Calvary
> by trying to give all we can.
> What we give to the poor
> for Christ's sake
> is what we carry with us
> when we die.

Peter and Dorothy especially quoted Tawney's *Religion and the Rise of Modern Capitalism*, which shows the dramatic changes in concepts away from the common good. Tawney contended that what happened in the historical process generated by the Reformation was the movement of the focus of exchange from the social solidarity group (common good) to the individual. He argued that the social character of wealth that had been the essence of medieval doctrine was lost through the unexpected development of economic individualism that sprang to a large extent from the notion of private interpretation of Sacred Scripture. In their eagerness to rid the world of the corruption of the Catholic Church at the time, the reformers replaced the church teaching of solidarity with the teaching of individual salvation without good works. As Tawney put it, "Individualism in religion led insensibly, if not quite logically, to an individualist morality, and an individualist morality to a disparagement of the significance of the social fabric as compared with personal character."[13]

In England and in the young United States, with time and pressure from merchants, Puritanism (the outgrowth of Calvinism) added a "halo of ethical sanctification to the appeal of economic expediency, and offered a moral creed in which the duties of religion and the calls of business ended their long estrangement in an unanticipated reconciliation." Gradually, the Reformation idea that individual conscience decides led to the practical conclusion that might be thought of as whatever works, whatever is comfortable, whatever makes a profit. Those in trade argued that "business affairs should be left to be settled by businessmen, unhampered by the intrusions of an antiquated morality or by misconceived arguments of public policy." Economics became separated from ethics. The contrast with earlier Christian teaching on the sin of avarice is striking. The church had always taught that greed, the implementation of the desire to gain more and more wealth, was one of the capital sins, and the idea of acquiring wealth was limited by a body of moral rules imposed under the sanction of religious authority.[14]

Even more surprising, however, is that what had been considered natural frailty (the inclination to amass wealth) and had been condemned by the fathers of the church was converted by this reasoning to be resounding virtue. As Tawney pointed out, this naturally, if unintentionally, modified the traditional attitude towards social obligations. The Puritans published many books about business as a calling, including *The Tradesman's Calling*, *Husbandry Spiritualized*, *Navigation Spiritualized*, *The Religious Weaver*. Tawney noted that these books went very "lightly over

traditional scruples" over profit making and prices, and even concluded that trade itself is a kind of religion.[15]

While economic abuses sprang slowly, if unexpectedly, from
Reformation individualism, they had their roots in the attitude of
some of the reformers towards the poor. What might be called the
mission statement of the early Calvinists institutionalized St.
Paul's dictum, "If a man does not want to work, neither let him
eat." In his theocracy at Geneva, Calvin himself laid down strict
rules about the poor, forbidding begging. Tawney described them:
Calvin "urged that the ecclesiastical authorities should regularly
visit every family to ascertain whether its members were idle, or
drunken, or otherwise undesirable....In the assault on pauperism,
moral and economic motives were not distinguished. The idleness
of the mendicant was both a sin against God and a social evil."[16]

The general rule also in England became to whip and punish
wandering beggars. There had been protest against indiscriminate
almsgiving by "Papists," and Luther had denounced the demands
of beggars as blackmail. The Puritan attitude was that idleness was
a great evil and that the poor are "victims not of circumstances,"
but of their own "idle, irregular and wicked courses." There was
no questioning of the economic system and its contribution to
poverty. "Practical success was at once the sign and the reward of
ethical superiority....A society which reverences the attainment of
riches as the supreme felicity will naturally be disposed to regard
the poor as damned in the next world, if only to justify itself for
making their life a hell in this."[17]

To contrast the Calvinist view towards the poor with the
Catholic tradition, Peter Maurin told of how in his parents'
Catholic village in France, the poor were received as the ambassadors of God, whereas in a Huguenot village the beggar received
malediction and rejection. He also recounted that he had wit-
nessed a bishop from Cleveland, Ohio, appropriately reprimand a
priest for chasing a beggar from the cathedral steps, saying,
"Where there is no beggar, there is no cathedral."[18]

The mixture of the doctrine of predestination of Calvinism with
commerce encouraged the supposedly secular view that economics
should be allowed to be guided by the "invisible hand of the market"

in a deterministic way, which gave justification to viewing the poor as poor through their own fault. Dorothy and Peter, with Tawney, disagreed with this attitude. Interpreting the Judgment Day scene of the twenty-fifth chapter of Matthew to require Christians to work to create a more just social order, Peter and Dorothy recommended Tawney's books to readers for an appreciation of the task before them. The Last Judgment would condemn those who abandoned the poor, those who allowed dreadful working conditions. As Dorothy phrased it in an article in *The Catholic Worker* of May 1936: "Inasmuch as we do not concern ourselves with such conditions, we are responsible for them. 'Inasmuch as ye have done it unto the least of them Ye have done it unto Me,' Christ said."

St. John Chrysostom, one of the great fathers of the early church who was frequently quoted in *The Catholic Worker*, presented the authentic Christian view toward the poor in his sermon on almsgiving and hospitality:

> Regrettably, there are persons who have come to such an advanced point of harshness that not only do they fail to show mercy or weep for or bring consolation to those who are in misery, but they frequently heap insults on the unfortunate and say that the catastrophes of those unhappy ones were after all merited by their victims.
>
> In what respect, please tell me, do they suffer deservedly in wanting to eat rather than to starve? Oh no, someone says, you miss the point! What we mean is that the poor will not work. Well, then, are you not taking a holiday when you live luxuriously? Do you not perform a work that is far worse than any idleness, when you seize property, and treat your victims violently, and amass an excess of goods?...
>
> How could it not be strange that you, with your belly conveniently full and your frame duly fattened, quaffing your drink late into the evening, consume your life deep in the folds of the pillows of a delicately padded couch, and fail to direct your gaze to this poor person who is naked and trembling and starving?...[19]

As Penty pointed out, the changing concepts in economics included not only those toward property and the poor but also, very significantly, toward usury. Peter did not hesitate to present his view that a key factor in the inadequacy and injustice of the economic system was the acceptance of money lending at interest. With the prophets of Israel and the fathers of the church, he condemned what he called living off the "sweat of another person's brow," instead of one's own labor:

> The Prophets of Israel
> and the Fathers of the Church
> forbid lending money at
>   interest.
> Lending money at interest
> is called usury
> by the Prophets of Israel
> and the Fathers of the Church.
> When people used to listen
> to the Prophets of Israel
> and the Fathers of the Church
> they could not see anything
>   gentle
> in trying to live
> on the sweat of somebody else's
>   brow
> by lending money at interest.

An example of the early church condemnation of usury of which Peter spoke so often is that of St. Gregory of Nyssa in his homily, "Against the Usurers." Gregory listed some of the scripture passages referred to by Peter:

> Have you not noticed that the very need for a loan is a movingly expressive plea addressed to your compassion? This is the reason for which the law, that letter which leads us to the era of the true faith, forbids on every page the taking of usurious gain (See Exod 22:24, Lev 25:36–37, Deut 23:20, Is 14:5 in LXX, Ezek 18:7–8, Neh 5:7–11, Prov 28:8). If you loan money to your brother, do not oppress him (cf. Exod 22:24–25)....
>
> And grace, springing abundantly from the very fount of goodness, legislates that we forgive the debts which are owed us, using the words, "If you lend to those from whom you expect repayment" (Luke 6:34)..."And forgive us our debts as we forgive those who are our debtors" (Matt 6:12).

Gregory excoriated the usurers, contrasting their hard-heartedness with the mercy of God: "How, then, can you presume to pray, you who engage in usurious practices? With what sort of conscience do you appeal to God—you who take everything and have never learned to give?...What value is there in your affording relief to one person, when you make many poor? If there were not a superfluity of usurers, there would not be a plethora of the impoverished. Release the tribe of your debtors, and all of us will have a sufficiency of goods."[20]

Originally, the reformers had no plan to undermine the rules of good conscience that control economic transactions and social relations, even though with John Calvin, the centuries-old consistent Christian teaching against the taking of interest on loans changed. Calvin's relaxing of the ancient condemnation was key in the development of new attitudes towards economics. Tawney noted that Calvin "dismisses the oft-quoted passages from the Old Testament and the Fathers as irrelevant, because designed for conditions which no longer exist...."[21] Calvin's acceptance of usury gradually fostered acceptance of it by the churches. While he had limited the circumstances under which interest could ethically be taken, in later centuries Calvin's authority was invoked by those who insisted that to take remuneration for the loan of money was never sinful.

A. J. Penty wisely noted that arguments about private property obscured the larger issues of speculation and control of money. While possession of land is terribly important, the stock market and speculation and currency and its regulation control much of the economy.[22] Chesterton, with the Catholic Workers, questioned the basic idea of lending money at interest. He described in *G. K.'s Weekly* of February 7, 1935, the potentially devastating ethical effects of putting one's money in stocks or engaging in speculation, when one could not then take responsibility for what another did with the money: "As modern investments are made, almost anybody may have his money in some sense in an armament firm, or a business financing an assassination firm, for all the individual investor generally knows about it.

Now this sort of anonymity and anarchy...is obviously nothing more than one vast dishonourable muddle."

Dorothy Day raised these issues in the May 1974 *Catholic Worker*, on the matter of not knowing to what diabolical use one's invested money is being put and how the interest in the purchase of homes unjustly increases the cost: "Can I talk about people living on usury, on the interest accruing from stocks and bonds, living on the interest, 'never touch the principal,' not knowing in what ways the infertile money had bred more money by wise investment in God knows what devilish nerve gases, drugs, napalms, missiles, or vanities, when housing and employment, honest employment for the poor were needed, and money could have been invested there? What houses the employed have been able to buy double in cost, what with interest and insurance added on."

Dorothy told the story of how the saints distinguished between philanthropy, which might be built on the backs of the poor, and Christian charity. The story raises the question of whether Catholic Workers or others who help the poor might even be able to accept money from philanthropists whose money comes from oppression of the poor:

> Here is a story of St. Ignatius of Sardinia, a Capuchin recently canonized. Ignatius used to go out from his monastery with a sack to beg from the people of the town, but he would never go to a certain merchant who had built his fortune by defrauding the poor. Franchine, the rich man, fumed every time the saint passed his door. His concern, however, was not the loss of the opportunity to give alms but fear of public opinion. He complained at the friary, whereupon the Father Guardian ordered St. Ignatius to beg from the merchant the next time he went out.
>
> "Very well," said Ignatius obediently. "If you wish it, Father, I will go, but I would not have the Capuchins dine on the blood of the poor."
>
> The merchant received Ignatius with great flattery and gave him generous alms, asking him to come again in the future. But, as Ignatius was leaving the house with his sack on his shoulder, drops of blood began oozing from the sack. They trickled down on Franchine's doorstep and ran down through the street to the monastery. Everywhere Ignatius went a trail of blood followed

him. When he arrived at the friary, he laid the sack at the Father Guardian's feet. "Here," Ignatius said, "is the blood of the poor."[23]

Dorothy wrote about the economic system from the point of view of the Catholic Workers, those who knew the poor. She knew that what was later called the trickle-down theory did not raise all boats: "The merchant, counting his profits in pennies, the millionaire with his efficiency experts, have both learned how to amass wealth. By following their example, and given health of mind and body, there is no necessity for anyone, so they say, to be poor nowadays. But the fact remains that every House of Hospitality is full, and we wish we had room for more. Families write us pitifully for help."[24]

At the same time as Dorothy and Peter received the poor in Houses of Hospitality, they believed that the social and economic system, what Dorothy sometimes called "the filthy, rotten system," needed to be rebuilt, to be changed. They knew that many business executives did not treat persons, the workers, with the dignity with which God had endowed them. In the 1947 *Catholic Worker*, Dorothy wrote of the injustice of building up excess profits while poor workers suffered: "On the one hand, the capitalist-industrialist robber baron weeps that if he paid a living wage industry would go broke and all the workers would be out of jobs. On the other hand, they have such huge surpluses of property and money and goods, and the worker remains in his pauper, proletariat, destitute state."

Dorothy and Peter objected strongly to the materialistic lifestyle dominating American culture, the consumerism fomented by large corporations with incessant advertising. Personal vocation was being replaced by a materialistic quest. They saw that unthinking conformity in keeping up appearances and in wasteful consumption dictated by style imprisoned people, taking away their freedom.

With social and economic critic Thorstein Veblen, whose books they recommended to their readers, the Catholic Workers inveighed against the "conspicuous waste" demanded by a consumer culture. Using the constant purchase of clothing to maintain standards of fashion and respectability as an example, Veblen showed the superficiality of giving extraordinary importance to outward signs of success: "Probably at no other point is the sense of shabbiness so keenly felt as it is if we fall short of the standard set by social usage in the matter of dress. It is true of dress in even a higher degree than of most other items of consumption, that people will undergo a very considerable degree of privation in the comforts or the necessities of life in order to afford what is considered a decent amount of wasteful consumption."[25]

Dorothy spoke about the need for a revolution—a revolution of the heart—to break away from the grip of materialism that tries to replace our values and take possession of our souls. For her, to tempt people constantly and to barrage them with advertisement is immoral and unethical. She wrote in the April 1953 *Catholic Worker* that to entice people into materialism is contrary to the law of God: "There have been many sins against the poor which cry out to high heaven for vengeance. The one listed as one of the seven deadly sins, is depriving the laborer of his share. There is another one, that is, instilling in him the paltry desires to satisfy that for which he must sell his liberty and his honor....Newspapers, radio, TV and battalions of advertising people (woe to that generation!) deliberately stimulate his desires, the satisfaction of which mean the degradation of the family."

Always remembering the Catholic Worker commitment to "pure means," Dorothy wrote that some jobs should be given up if they did not contribute to the common good; she asked people to pray for the grace to do so. The questions were "Have they to do with shelter, food, and clothing? Have they to do with the Works of Mercy?" She excoriated banks, insurance companies, loan and finance companies for expropriating property from the working poor, suggesting that a person discerning a vocation should consider before engaging in certain work: "This would exclude jobs in advertising, which only increases people's useless desires. In insurance companies and banks, which are known to exploit the poor of this country and of others. Banks and insurance companies have taken over land, built up farms, ranches, plantations of 30,000, 100,000 acres, and have dispossessed the poor. Loan and finance companies have further defrauded him. Movies, radio have further enslaved him....Whatever has contributed to his misery and degradation may be considered a bad job."[26]

Dorothy quoted Ed Willock's well known "jingle" from the first issue of *Integrity* magazine about the ethical hazards one might encounter in work. Her commentary included the problem of working in preparations for war:

> John Smith puts on his hat and
> goes to Church on Sunday.
> And John Smith goes to hell for
> what he did on Monday.

> Not Saturday night, mind you, when he may be taking surcease from care in some tavern, but for the work he engages in, whether it is the advertising business, or a fat job in the Rubber Company or Cooper or Nickel Mines, or a Steamship company. We participate in the sin of others, we are all helping to make the kind of a world that makes for war.

Peter taught people instead to adapt their current jobs to reflect their faith, to use their skills to create a better world. Dorothy recounted his asking a successful lawyer to go and help the poor:

> I remember a lawyer who came up to me one time when I was speaking at the Cleveland House of Hospitality and said, "Peter tells me I should give up my practice here and go down to the heart of Arkansas, where there is segregation on the books and where they are proposing to sterilize the 'feeble-minded as part of the solution to that problem.'" It might have been Mississippi or Alabama, but the fact that the lawyer was so terribly disturbed by this suggestion showed me what power Peter had over others. He not only made them think, but he even made them question their motives, their vocations. I felt this visitor was trying to say to me, "Am I practicing law to get rich or to serve my fellow man?"[27]

Those who were searching for and had not been able to find their vocation often went to the Catholic Worker. In the May 1955 *Catholic Worker*, Dorothy recalled Peter's advice to those who were trying to determine their life's work, beginning with not depending on usury: "Peter would tell them, 'first of all, earn a living by the sweat of your own brow, not someone else's. Choose a work that can be considered honorable, and can be classed under the heading of a Work of Mercy, serving your brothers, not exploiting them. Man's work is as important to him as bread, and by it he gains his bread. And by it he gains love too, because he serves his brother.'"

As Dorothy said, "Peter was no dreamer, but knew men as they were. That is why he spoke so much of the need for a philosophy of work. Once they had that, once their desires were changed, half the battle was won."[28] Peter defended the dignity of labor against the frequently held idea that manual labor is menial, to be despised, that those who engage in manual labor are less as persons than white-collar workers. Veblen described this attitude:

> Labour comes to be associated in men's habits of thought with weakness and subjection to a master. It is therefore a mark of inferiority, and therefore comes to be accounted unworthy of man in his best estate. By virtue of this tradition labour is felt to be debasing, and this tradition has never died out. On the contrary, with the advance of social differentiation it has acquired the axiomatic force due to ancient and unquestioned prescription....
>
> Conspicuous abstention from labour therefore becomes the conventional mark of superior pecuniary achievement and the conventional index of reputability; and conversely, since application to productive labour is a mark of poverty and subjection, it becomes inconsistent with a reputable standing in the community.[29]

It is perhaps this attitude toward manual labor that has allowed those who engineer the economy to believe themselves justified in paying less than a living wage and in imposing working conditions that have ignored the dignity of the laborer. The Catholic Worker, with its identification with monasticism, was very aware of the dignity of manual labor.

Dorothy often pointed out that modern economics ignored the concept that depriving the laborer of his share was one of the seven deadly sins. As they worked toward the betterment of the economy, Catholic Workers supported workers in their struggles to form unions as one way to address unjust conditions under the existing one. When the Catholic Worker movement began, unions were not legal in the United States. Catholic Workers supported those who were trying to organize and picketed with them. They met with labor leaders and heads of steel companies and with priests and bishops interested in labor issues.

The early Catholic Workers picketed a New York department store notorious for underpaying employees and making them work long hours. New York's finest—the police—were arresting and carrying the picketers off to jail, until Dorothy and the Catholic high school students accompanying her showed up with picket signs quoting the popes on just wages. The police, mostly Catholic, were dumbstruck: "When we entered the dispute with our slogans drawn from the writings of the Popes regarding the condition of labor, the police around Union Square were taken aback and did not know what to do. It was as though they were arresting the Holy Father himself, one of them said, were they to load our pickets and their signs into their patrol wagons."[30]

The Catholic Worker concern for workers already in the factory system and the desire to create a better social order was often misunderstood and misinterpreted. Their support of unions cost *The Catholic Worker* subscriptions and financial help. Dorothy wrote of 3,000 copies of the paper being cancelled at a Catholic high school in New York after the students picketed with Catholic Workers in supporting striking workers and tried to organize a boycott. Dorothy Day explained the Catholic Worker involvement in support of workers to readers in the January 1939 *Catholic Worker*:

> Nobody seems to understand that when we are out at strike meetings or picket lines or demonstrations distributing the paper, we are trying to bring the social teachings of the Church to the man in the street. They also insist upon believing that we are participating in the strike or endorsing one faction against another. We do not know the least thing about factions in the various unions. How could we keep up on them all? The great job that *The Catholic Worker* has to do is to try to reach the workers, bring to

them a philosophy of labor, speak to them of Christian solidarity, and point out the need of a long-range program....

The Association of Catholic Trade Unionists was started at the Catholic Worker by John Cort as a response to the recommendations in *Rerum novarum* and *Quadragesimo anno*. It was not a union per se. "The association," Cort said, "will not be a rival union. It will not seek to divide the working class. It will serve as a teaching unit that would attempt to teach Catholic men and women their rights and duties." Stanley Vishnewski recalled that the Catholic Worker pledged its support to John in his attempt to form such an association and encouraged him to write out his ideas for the paper.[31] The ACTU met at the Catholic Worker, but it was soon recognized that it would be best if it became independent. The response was so great that soon there was no space for the ever-growing membership and the Catholic Workers wanted to be sure it did not take over the whole Catholic Worker.

Peter Maurin, who was not so sure about unions, often said, "Strikes don't strike me!" He was concerned about the potential for violence when strikes took place. When the sit-down strike was introduced, he was able to endorse this unequivocally as a method of nonviolent action. He related the sit-down strike to the philosophy and methods of Mahatma Gandhi, who developed his nonviolent methods in response to the deplorable working and economic conditions under what was called "free trade" in India under English colonial rule. Maurin insisted, with Gandhi, that the sit-down strike be conducted according to the doctrine of pure means toward good ends.

Dorothy wrote in the January 1954 *Catholic Worker* about Peter's concerns about union organizing: "He hated mass action and pressure groups and feared unions deteriorating into political action. He hated class war and wanted us to love the enemy, the capitalist and industrialist and munitions maker, even while trying to 'put business out of business.'" Stanley also wrote about Peter's perspective on union organizing and the need to also relate to employers: "Peter advocated that an Association of Catholic Employers be formed to work in conjunction with the Association of Catholic Trade Unionists. Peter thought that this would bring about harmony rather than a class struggle."[32]

When unions became legal and gradually more established, the Catholic Workers de-emphasized this aspect of their work. Much later, however, when a ragged band of migrant farm workers drove across the country with Cesar Chavez to ask her help, Dorothy immediately responded. The paper supported the formation of a union for the poorest workers and in 1973 Dorothy was arrested with other supporters of the United Farm Workers and briefly jailed.

The Catholic Worker movement had a larger, different vision than labor unions. They supported workers in their struggle for better working conditions and a wage on which to support a family, but the movement and its newspaper advocated another kind of economics where these problems would not exist. In her early book, *House of Hospitality*, Dorothy had written regarding the support of the Catholic Worker for those trying to form unions, noting that unions were not the end solution: "Let us be honest, let us say that fundamentally, the stand we are taking is not on the ground of wages and hours and conditions of labor, but on the fundamental truth that men should be treated not as chattels, but as human beings, as 'temples of the Holy Ghost.' Let us be honest and confess that it is the social order which we wish to change."[33]

In the society envisioned by Catholic Workers, workers would be treated with dignity and neither employers nor workers would begin by appealing to enlightened self-interest, "a phrase reeking with selfishness and containing a warning and threat." The new order would treat workers as human beings: "The Popes have hit the nail on the head. No man may outrage with impunity that human dignity which God Himself treats with reverence....Religion teaches the rich man and employer that their work people are not their slaves; that they must respect in every man his dignity as a man and as a Christian; that labor is an honorable employment; and that it is shameful and inhuman to treat men like chattels to make money by, or to look upon them merely as so much muscle or physical power."[34]

Dorothy described the long, difficult task facing those who would work to build a communion of love in a social order based on the common good and the gospel: "We can do much to change the face of the earth, in that I have hope and faith. But these pains and sufferings are the price we have to pay....If we love enough, we are going to light that fire in the hearts of others. And it is love that will burn out the sins and hatreds that sadden us. It is love that will make us want to do great things for each other. No sacrifice and no suffering will then seem too much."[35]

9

Economics Worthy of the Human Person

As personalists, Peter Maurin and Dorothy Day believed there had to be a better system than one in which the majority of workers could not earn enough to support their families and the conditions under which they worked violated the dignity of the person. They advocated instead the economics of distributism—an economics the Catholic Workers considered worthy of the human person made in the image and likeness of God.

The word *distributism* comes from the idea that a just social order can be achieved through a much more widespread distribution of property. Distributism means a society of owners. It values the work of artisans and of handcrafts as opposed to the assembly line. It is related to the idea of subsidiarity and decentralization emphasized in papal encyclicals on Catholic social teaching and economics. In his encyclical *Quadragesimo anno* Pius XI, who was a contemporary of Dorothy and Peter, defined and advocated subsidiarity: "It is an injustice and at the same time a great evil and disturbance of right order to assign to a greater and higher association what lesser and subordinate organizations can do. For every social activity ought of its very nature to furnish help to the members of the body social and never destroy and absorb them" (no. 203). Dorothy made reference in the December 1963 *Catholic Worker* to Pope John XXIII's emphasis on the importance of subsidiarity in his encyclical *Mater et magistra*.

In the July–August 1948 *Catholic Worker*, Dorothy presented the Catholic Worker position on distributism: "The alternatives are not capitalism or socialism....We must take into consideration the nature of man and his needs, not just cash—commodities, food and clothing, but a home, a bit of land, and the tools with which to work, part ownership in workshops and stores and factories." Dorothy and Peter knew that owners would benefit and business would benefit if workers had a sense of responsibility and ownership of the work they did. Worker ownership not only respected the dignity of the person, but paid off with good production and better quality.

Peter Maurin had investigated alternative economic models in France before emigrating to Canada and the United States. There he discovered that it was possible to have just policies towards workers and still run a successful business. He had learned of the story of Léon Harmel, an industrialist who introduced many constructive changes in the spinning mills owned by his family, having been inspired by the "high Christian ideals and good labor practices of his father." Peter knew that Harmel had been assisted in his approach by priests of the Sacred Heart especially dedicated to helping workers, and that "he had worked out some solutions to the ever-present problems of old age, sickness, poverty, and hunger" that were ahead of their time, including profit sharing and groups of employees working together on solving problems.[1] He later wrote an Easy Essay about Harmel and his ideas and practice. In the January 1947 *Catholic Worker*, Dorothy described Harmel's life work as an employer who brought his policies in harmony with the teachings of the gospel. She mentioned how he had inspired Pope Leo XIII in his writing of the encyclical *Rerum novarum*, so important to Catholic social teaching.

Maurin also visited the cooperatives and small enterprises in the south of France that were developed from the economic ideas of Prince Peter Kropotkin. Interestingly, both Dorothy and Peter had studied Kropotkin's books even before they met. Dorothy Day said on several occasions in her writings (for example, in the February 1974 *Catholic Worker*) that Peter came to her with St. Francis in one hand and Kropotkin in the other. In one of the early chapters of *The Long Loneliness*, Dorothy mentioned four of Kropotkin's books of which she was aware before she met Peter: *Fields, Factories and Workshops; Mutual Aid; The Conquest of Bread; Memoirs of a Revolutionist.* These books had come out while Peter was still in France. Dorothy described Kropotkin's economic vision: "Kropotkin looked back to the guilds and cities of the Middle Ages, and thought of the new society as made up of federated associations, co-operating in the same way as the railway companies of Europe or the postal departments of various countries co-operate now."[2]

Kropotkin began to develop his social theories by studying the medieval village communes of Russia. Dorothy said of Kropotkin: "He lived and worked so closely with peasants and artisans that his writings are practical handbooks."[3] After the Russian revolution Kropotkin had to leave the country because he disagreed with the violent, totalitarian methods implemented there.

Before her conversion to Catholicism, Dorothy explored not only Kropotkin's economic ideas, but his anarchism as well. Having read Tolstoy in her youth, she was attracted by the idealism of nonviolent anarchism, which he embraced. *Anarchism* is a word that has many interpretations and often evokes negative responses. The Catholic Worker did not mean by it that anything goes, nor did it promote chaos. In the December 1949 *Catholic Worker*, Dorothy summed up the Catholic Worker's understanding of the word: "The word anarchist is deliberately and repeatedly used in order to awaken our readers to the necessity of combating the 'all-encroaching state,' as our Bishops have termed it, and to shock serious students into looking into the possibility of another society, an order made up of associations, guilds, unions, communes, parishes—voluntary associations of men, on regional vs. national lines, where there is a possibility of liberty and responsibility for all men."

Knowing that the word *anarchism* upset people and that often those who heard it thought it meant violence, Dorothy described various forms of it in *The Long Loneliness*, discussing questions of authority and freedom. The definition she preferred came from the *American Encyclopedia*; it emphasized the establishment of "a new order based on free and spontaneous cooperation among individuals, groups, regions and nations."[4] This was the type of anarchism that has been associated with the Catholic Worker movement.

Kropotkin scathingly criticized the consequences of the idea of the division of labor championed by Adam Smith. The assembly line separated white-collar or business owners from workers to such an extreme that Kropotkin called it a caste system: "The division and subdivision—the permanent subdivision of functions has been pushed so far as to divide humanity into castes which are almost as firmly established as those of old India."[5]

As Kropotkin brought out the evils of the assembly line and the precarious situation of what he called wage slaves, he lamented the uprooting of the agricultural laborer who, instead of working on the family farm he loved, was forced to become a migrant worker:

> Nay, even the agricultural labourer, who formerly used to find a relief from the hardships of his life in the home of his ancestors—the future home of his children—in his love of the field and in a keen intercourse with nature, even he has been doomed to disappear for the sake of the division of labour. He is an anachronism, we are told; he must be substituted, in a Bonanza farm by an occasional servant hired for the summer, and discharged as the autumn comes: a tramp who will never again see the field he has harvested once in his life.[6]

Kropotkin, a scientist, had faith in the human person and believed that at heart, people were open to working together in a spirit of cooperation. His book *Mutual Aid* refuted the Darwinian and Malthusian idea that the nature of humanity allowed only the approach of the "survival of the fittest." Kropotkin gave many examples of cooperation even in the animal kingdom to show that Darwin's basic premise was mistaken. Writing about the influence of Kropotkin on the Catholic Worker movement, William Miller points out that Kropotkin believed that more could be accomplished through cooperation among small groups than most people imagined: "'Woe to the weak' was the new doctrine....By the beginning of the twentieth century the idea of the endless good of 'competition' had ramifications in all aspects of human association. It was this new dogma of science that Kropotkin attacked....Opposed to struggle and survival as the evolutionary vehicle, he found another principle—cooperation—more profound and pervasive than the Malthusian principle."[7]

Peter Maurin, convinced of the basic goodness of the human person even though wounded by original sin, was interested in Kropotkin's alternative to Darwinism and cutthroat competition. Kropotkin's emphasis on the participation of each person in some aspect of manual labor or crafts work related well to the Benedictine tradition on work and prayer so much a part of the Catholic Worker program.

Kropotkin's economic ideas were very like those of the English distributists, whose ideas the Catholic Workers followed closely. Dorothy and Peter read and recommended to their readers the writings of G. K. Chesterton, Hilaire Belloc, and Father Vincent McNabb, OP, who advocated decentralization and small ownership as the basis for the economic system: "We have advised our readers to begin with four books, Chesterton's *What's Wrong with the World?*, *The Outline of Sanity*, and Belloc's *The Servile State* and *The Restoration of Property*...."[8] These writers insisted that people should not be treated like cogs in a machine or made to work twelve hours a day in backbreaking work in coal mines or factories while the directors and stockholders of the corporations became fabulously wealthy.

Dorothy noted the similarities between Kropotkin and the distributists: "Kropotkin wanted much the same type of social order as Eric Gill, the artist, Father Vincent McNabb, the Dominican street preacher, G.K. Chesterton, Hilaire Belloc and other distributists advocated, though they would have revolted at the word anarchist, thinking it synonymous with chaos, not 'self-government' as Proudhon defined it."[9]

Wealthy industrialists spoke against socialism and defended private property. Their understanding of the right to private property, however, was quite different from that of the tradition of the church. The Catholic Workers pointed out the difference, quoting St. Thomas Aquinas on property—that each person should be able to have some. Frequently, when Dorothy quoted Thomas, in the next sentence she emphasized St. Gertrude's maxim: "Property, the more common it is, the more holy it is" (for example, May 1972 *Catholic Worker*). Father McNabb, often quoted in *The Catholic Worker*, said, "The Divine Right of Property means not that some men shall have all property, but that all men shall have some property."[10]

Chesterton said that the popular image of capitalism was something quite different from the reality of a few people controlling everything. He could have been in agreement with what many small businesspeople considered capitalism, especially in a world where everyone owned some capital or property. Criticizing an unbridled capitalism that put the majority of money and resources in the hands of a few big corporations and individuals, he declared: "To say that I do not like the present state of wealth and poverty is merely to say that I am not the devil in human form. No one but Satan or Beelzebub could like the present state of wealth and poverty."[11]

When distributists criticized the excesses of capitalism, they made it quite clear that they did not advocate socialism. Chesterton cuttingly illustrated the fallacies in the idea of private property in both capitalism and Communism: "A pickpocket is obviously a champion of private enterprise. But it would perhaps be an exaggeration to say that a pickpocket is a champion of private property....Capitalism and Commercialism...have at best tried to disguise the pickpocket with some of the virtues of the pirate. The point about Communism is that it only reforms the pickpocket by forbidding pockets."[12] Addressing the fear of Communism, he said, "It is all very well to repeat distractedly, 'What are we coming to, with all this Bolshevism?' It is equally relevant to add, 'What are we coming to, even without Bolshevism?' The obvious answer is—Monopoly. It is certainly not private enterprise."[13]

Chesterton, like Kropotkin, criticized the division of labor in industrialism that pigeonholed workers into a mind-dulling, repetitive labor. He knew that the opinions of Henry Ford were against Catholic teaching on the dignity of the human person. Ford made it clear that in his opinion most people were not smart enough to do anything except repetitious work, that most people preferred the mechanical action of the assembly line and were only fitted for it. As Chesterton put it, "It will be noted that Mr. Ford does not say that *he* is only fitted to mind machines; he confesses frankly that he is too fine and free and fastidious a being for such tasks."[14]

Critics accused distributists of trying to return to a dreamy past. Chesterton responded that the critics were the real reactionaries, that their economic ideas were in no way new: "They are always telling us that we think we can bring back the past, or the barbarous simplicity and superstition of the past; apparently under the impression that we want to bring back the nineteenth century. But they really do think they can bring back the nineteenth century....They call us reactionaries if we talk about a Revival of Faith or a Revival of Catholicism. But they go on calmly plastering their papers with the headline of a Revival of Trade. What a cry out of the distant past! What a voice from the tomb!"[15] The nineteenth-century economics to which Chesterton referred was Liberalism with a capital L or simply Trade, especially Free Trade. Its proponents promised it would lead to prosperity and the wealth of nations. This economic Liberalism did lead to prosperity and wealth—but for the few—and was at the heart of colonialism.

Dorothy cited Chesterton's sharp response to those who criticized distributism as being visionary and utopian in the December 1948 *Catholic Worker* (quoting from *What's Wrong with the World*). Her account of the "refugees from ruthless industrialism" who came to stay at the Houses of Hospitality or receive food at the Catholic Worker lent authenticity to the critique:

Here is what Chesterton said about such a criticism:

"They say it (the peasant society) is Utopian, and they are right. They say it is idealistic, and they are right. They say it is quixotic, and they are right. It deserves every name that will indicate how completely they have driven justice out of the world; every name that measures how remote from them and their sort is the standard of honorable living; every name that will emphasize and repeat the fact that property and liberty are sundered from them and theirs, by an abyss between heaven and hell."

This sounds pretty harsh from the gentle Chesterton, but we, who witness the thousands of refugees from our ruthless industrialism, year after year, the homeless, the hungry, the

crippled, the maimed, and see the lack of sympathy and understanding, the lack of Christian charity accorded them (to most
they represent the loafers and the bums, and our critics shrink
in horror to hear them compared to Christ, as our Lord Himself
compared them) to us, I say, who daily suffer the ugly reality of
industrial capitalism and its fruits—these words of Chesterton
ring strong.

Belloc, like the other English distributists and the Catholic
Workers, based his economics in the social encyclicals, beginning
with *Rerum novarum*. He was also in accord with the Catholic
Workers on the question of usury. Dorothy mentioned in the
July–August 1945 issue of the paper that when in New York,
Belloc visited the Catholic Worker and she and John Cort went
out to dinner with him. In the December 1948 *Catholic Worker*
Dorothy recommended his ideas on local economies: "Hilaire
Belloc, in his *Restoration of Property*, gives a good blueprint for
action. He talks about large-scale machinery, what must come
under common ownership (and he endorses communal as against
state ownership) and what can be broken up into smaller units."

Belloc, like Penty, Dawson, and Tawney, saw the destruction of
the monasteries across England described in the previous chapter
and the subsequent development of an oligarchy as the root of the
economic injustices following in the wake of the Industrial
Revolution. He vehemently disagreed with those who contended
that the excesses of monopoly capitalism, however unfortunate,
necessarily flowed from the development of new methods of production and new machinery. Belloc insisted that the terrible social
conditions of the Industrial Revolution need not have existed, that
it was not economic determinism that created them, but an already
existing control by the few of wealth and the means of production:

> Under the effect of such false arguments as these we have been
> taught to believe that the horrors of the Industrial System were
> a blind and necessary product of material and impersonal forces,
> and that wherever the steam engine, the power loom, the blast
> furnace and the rest were introduced, there fatally would soon
> appear a little group of owners exploiting a vast majority of the
> dispossessed.

It is astonishing that a statement so unhistorical should have gained so general a credence. Indeed, were the main truths of English history taught in our schools and universities today, were educated men familiar with the determining and major facts of the national past, such follies could never have taken root.[16]

Dorothy later wrote several pages in the October 1946 *Catholic Worker* criticizing the approach of Cardinal Cardijn, who organized a movement among factory workers. She analyzed at length a pamphlet written by the cardinal called, "The Spirit of the Young Christian Workers." While she agreed with his concern for factory workers, Dorothy disagreed with the idea of sanctifying one's work on an assembly line, insisting that the work itself must be changed so that workers could be treated as human beings. She could not accept that workers who were laboring under inhuman conditions should simply be told that the way to holiness was to pray while they were working. She cried out: "What is the great disaster is that priests and laity alike have lost the concept of work, they have lost a philosophy of labor.... Those who do not know what work in the factory is, have romanticized both it and the workers, and in emphasizing the dignity of the worker, have perhaps unconsciously emphasized the dignity of work which is slavery, and which degrades and dehumanizes man."

In his encyclical *Rerum novarum* Pope Leo XIII had said: "Workers are not to be treated as slaves; justice demands that the dignity of human personality be respected in them, ennobled as it has been through what we call the Christian character....It is shameful and inhuman, however, to use men as things for gain and to put no more value on them than what they are worth in muscle and energy" (no. 31). Dorothy's passionate writing echoed the Holy Father's words: "Can one sanctify a saloon, a house of ill fame? When one is in the occasion of sin, is it not necessary to remove oneself from it?...In the great clean shining factories, with good lights and air and the most sanitary conditions, an eight-hour day, five-day week, with the worker chained to the belt, to the machine, there is no opportunity for sinning as the outsider thinks of sin. No, it is far more subtle than that, it is submitting oneself to a process which degrades, dehumanizes."

Those who work to rebuild the social order may become discouraged when they see others, even priests or laypeople of the church, lined up with the tyranny of giant corporations, seemingly oblivious to the plight of workers. In that column Dorothy recalled Catholics to the church's social teaching:

> Are the priests on the side of the worker, to change his life, so that he can lead a good life, with his little community, the family? Or are they on the side of big business, in their acceptance of the status quo? Are they on the side of St. Thomas who believed that a certain amount of goods was necessary to lead a good life? On the side of the popes who believe that those goods consist not in electric ice boxes, inlaid linoleum, radios, cars, but in property "which is proper to man," a piece of earth to cultivate, room for a goodly sized family, privacy, work for all, opportunity for education, not in schools of business, such as our colleges have now become?...

Addressing the question of the destruction of the environment and the emphasis on preparations for war in the only places where many could find work, Dorothy questioned how these surroundings could possibly be sanctified: "Should the worker sanctify his surroundings in the lumber camps where huge forests are being denuded all over the country, for profit?...Do we just 'adapt ourselves' to this evil of destruction and waste, not only of men but of raw materials? We can no more bless it, 'sanctify it' than the priest can bless the scrap iron which he sprinkles with holy water in the church yard before it sets off to kill Japanese or Germans."

Dorothy insisted that too much was being asked of the workers and their families. She held up papal teaching and the words of the saints and decried the lack of perception of those who did not understand what was at stake:

> It is not right that heroic sanctity be demanded of the worker and the women of his family. We are all called to be saints, St. Paul says, and Pope Pius XI has repeated in his encyclical on St. Francis de Sales. It should be an ordinary thing, not a heroic thing. What is being done to make it possible for the worker to be a saint, a good ordinary saint, following the Little Way?

Maybe the worker's life is a Way of the Cross, but it is a continuation of the mission of Christ the Worker....

I am tired of hearing our Lord compared to a modern factory worker.

In spite of her criticisms of the Young Christian Workers pamphlet, in her characteristic style Dorothy later welcomed members of the Young Christian Workers to the Catholic Worker in New York as fellow workers in the apostolate of Christ.

One of the keystones of the three-point program that Peter presented to Dorothy when they met in 1932, in addition to cult and culture, was cultivation. On a small or communal farm, the whole experience of work could be different from the assembly line or that of the migrant laborer, and the unemployed might find a new life on the land. Dorothy described the economics of the Catholic Worker program, including the agrarian aspect: "Ours was a long-range program, looking for ownership by the workers of the means of production, the abolition of the assembly line, decentralized factories, the restoration of crafts and ownership of property. This meant, of course, an accent on the agrarian and rural aspects of our economy and a changing emphasis from the city to the land."[17]

Dorothy described Peter's vision of the land: "Every talk of Peter's about the social order led to the land. He spoke always as a peasant, but as a practical one. He knew the craving of the human heart for a toehold on the land, for a home of one's own, but he also knew how impossible it was to attain it except through community."[18]

Peter recommended that farms (not huge agribusinesses, but family farms or farming communes) be as self-sufficient as possible, avoiding dependence on exports from faraway places. Then, as now, the importation of food in large quantities involved enormous corporations, frequent exploitation of poor workers, and the destruction of family farms and the environment. Dorothy recounted how Peter's philosophy was implemented in his big family in France: "Once as we sat around the table at dinner Peter was giving us slogans and he proposed this one: 'Eat what you raise and raise what you eat.' We asked him what they ate in his family when he was a boy. 'We did not eat the calves, we sold them,' he said. 'We ate salt pork every day. We raised no hops, and there was no beer. We raised no grapes, so no wine. We had very little meat. We had plenty of bread—there was a communal oven. We had plenty of butter; we had eggs. We had codfish from the Brittany fishermen....We had vegetable soups, salads and cheese."[19]

This was the local economy with practical implications: "Eat what you raise and raise what you eat meant that you ate the things indigenous to New York climate, such as tomatoes, not oranges; honey, not sugar, etc. We used to tease him because he drank coffee, chocolate or tea, but 'he ate what was set before him.'"[20]

Father McNabb, like Peter, believed that things should be produced locally. He phrased his insights in economic terms that were the opposite of the current slogans: "The area of production should be as far as possible coterminous with the area of consumption. The utilitarians were wrong in saying that 'things should be produced where they can be most economically produced.' The true principle is: *things should be produced where they can be most economically consumed.*"[21]

Peter related the idea of farming communes and agronomic universities to his whole program and spoke often of the importance of workers and scholars enlightening each other. Arthur Sheehan said that when Peter spoke of the Green Revolution, he was contrasting it to the Communist one: "Peter called these hopeful ideas the Green Revolution, a peaceful one, opposed in spirit and theory to the Red Revolution advocated by Karl Marx."[22] Pointing out that Peter did not agree with Marx that classes were inevitably involved in a violent struggle against each other, Sheehan reminded readers of Peter's study of history and economics and his conclusions that contrasted so much with those of Marx:

Marx has based much of his theory of revolution on a belief in irreconcilable war between the 'haves' and 'have-nots,' those possessing wealth and others with only their daily labor to support them. He documented his ideas from a study of the revolutionary Paris Commune of 1848 with its terrible violence.

Peter went back to the peaceful communes of France for his inspiration. He often wondered why historians gave so much attention to the violent Paris story and so little to the peaceful fruitful life of the other ninety French communes.[23]

While through the newspaper the Catholic Workers presented the theology of the common good, a just understanding of the concept of property and ownership, and the ideas and examples of a local economy, Catholic Worker ideas on distributism were not based purely on theory and theology. They tried to put them into practice.

The Catholic Worker recommended setting up farms and many were started. The experience of families on the farms was often difficult because of lack of knowledge of farming, and of money and equipment. There were, at times, tensions between the workers and the scholars on the farms. While the scholars were discussing ideas, the workers were working. The workers did not always appreciate the distinction. It also was not easy to finance the beginning of family farms or communal farms. Dorothy explained Peter's ideas on beginning a farm: "Peter's plan was that groups should borrow from mutual-aid credit unions in the parish to start what he first liked to call agronomic universities, where the worker could become a scholar and the scholar a worker. Or he wanted people to give the land and money. He always spoke of giving. Those who had land and tools should give. Those who had capital should give. Those who had labor should give that. 'Love is an exchange of gifts,' St. Ignatius had said."[24]

In the January 1939 *Catholic Worker*, Dorothy gave readers a chance to implement this exchange of their gifts, to help out with the farming communes, framed in a letter that she addressed to Peter Maurin:

> If you meet anybody in your travels that wishes to contribute to the Catholic Worker Farming Commune Building Fund, please tell them that we must build a house for Arthur and his son, and Frank Mamano, our barber, not to speak of a new roof for the barn and the new roof for the lean-to on the house, a large-sized pig pen to take care of the 150 pigs we expect by next year and the assembly room on the top of the hill where you can lecture undisturbed until two o'clock in the morning. When it comes to the little houses, just a few hundred dollars would pay for the

lumber. Perhaps somebody will make themselves responsible for one or another of these projects. Another thing that we need is a new horse or rather two new horses.

Dorothy explained in the July–August 1948 *Catholic Worker*, however, that while distributism had an agrarian emphasis, that "does not mean that everyone must be a farmer." In *House of Hospitality*, she had written: "While we stress the back-to-the-land movement so that the worker may be 'deproletarianized,' we are not going to leave the city to the Communists."[25] However, the farms were an important part of the attempt to live out the principles of distributism and a voice against the corporate and government policies that have destroyed so many small farms in favor of agribusiness. Some Catholic Worker farms continue today.

Studying the cooperative movement in Antigonish, Arthur Sheehan had begun to read *The Catholic Worker* with the second issue and was interested in its advocacy of distributist economics. He visited Peter Maurin, spoke with him, became a Catholic Worker, and a good friend of Peter. He told in his book about Peter's writing in the paper and about his own reaction when he discovered it, noting the connection with English distributists:

> I remember the shock I felt on first reading his ideas in the second issue of the paper. I was in a hospital bed in Antigonish, Nova Scotia, Canada, recuperating from a long illness with plenty of time to read and think. Peter's view seemed to integrate with those of G. K. Chesterton and Hilaire Belloc and the English distributist movement leaders. Each week, I was reading *G. K.'s Weekly* and thought it the best of all Catholic publications. Peter seemed to me to be the American voice of those ideas. Chesterton and he were studying the bad effects of industrialism and showing the way toward a better society. Both agreed on a return to land, crafts, and small ownership.[26]

Fathers Moses Coady and J. J. Tompkins had established a center of the cooperative movement in Antigonish, where Sheehan had first discovered the *Worker*. Dorothy visited these co-ops in Nova Scotia, where she met Father Coady, and wrote about her visit in the September 1938 *Catholic Worker*. As the

Antigonish experience showed, one antidote to monopoly was credit unions and cooperatives, where the members had some control over their money and production. Dorothy wrote about the Catholic Worker interest in cooperatives in her early book, *House of Hospitality*: "The cooperative movement is a good one because it offers an opportunity to rebuild within the shell of the old with a new philosophy, which is a philosophy so old that it seems like new. And in the cooperative movement there is a chance for a real united front and for a peaceful and ethical accomplishment of our aims."[27]

Cooperatives and distributist principles were recommended in *The Catholic Worker* in the development of credit unions and maternity guilds to help families. From the earliest years *The Catholic Worker* supported church teaching while at the same time critiquing the economic system for making it difficult for families to survive. Peter Maurin included maternity guilds in his Easy Essays, recommending: "Maternity Guilds for the welfare of needy mothers bringing young children into the world." Examples of cooperatives for couples and families were featured in the pages of *The Catholic Worker*. In November 1936, there was an article on a "Co-op Hospital," where the services included births of children, dental care, and surgery.

In the July–August 1962 issue of the paper, Dorothy spoke of the Catholic Worker theme of the use of spiritual weapons instead of violence, extending this spirituality to include church teaching on the family. Dorothy believed that this profound spirituality was as necessary in order to follow church teaching on birth control as it was to respond in love to enemies of any kind. She recommended again that guilds and credit unions in the parish help families:

> Over and over again we hear that such a technique as nonviolence, voluntary poverty, suffering, and prayer and fasting are too heroic weapons to expect the laity to use. And yet in our time they are compelled to use them, and without the training and preparation necessary to such heroism. In the life of the family heroic virtue is expected, in accepting from the hand of God each child sent or accepting continence or celibacy within marriage. The teaching of the Church in regard to marriage and

its indissolubility demands over and over again heroic sanctity. And in both cases without the help of the teaching of voluntary poverty and the mutual aid which maternity guilds and credit unions in the parish could give.

The Catholic Workers, like Chesterton and Belloc, did not stop with their advocacy of ownership for all in the field of economics, but also advocated decentralization in politics. The distributists believed that the modern state was encroaching on the person's freedom and responsibility. They believed in democracy; they did not believe in what is presented as democracy but does not give the ordinary person an authentic role or trust the person's judgment. Chesterton argued that every human being was worth saving in the eyes of God and should be respected. He believed that just having the vote, when all was controlled by the powerful, did not emancipate the average person.

The English distributists and the Catholic Workers saw the modern state tied up with monopoly capitalism as a religion with strict doctrines, demanding absolute obedience from all its members. Chesterton, following Belloc, spoke of the "Church of the Servile State." Dorothy often referred to the irony of so many people granting unquestioning obedience to what she called Holy Mother the State while criticizing the idea of the leadership of Holy Mother the Church. She and Peter Maurin saw that what was presented as freedom and democracy could easily become totalitarian, and that what was recommended by press and politicians or mass movements might have little to do with truth, charity, and justice.

Contrary to the impression given in the film *Entertaining Angels* about her and the Catholic Worker movement, Dorothy did not have a great interest in women getting the vote. She, who did not look to the state even before her conversion to Catholicism for solutions to the world's problems, had sympathized with the National Women's Party when they marched for voting rights because they, like other protesters, were being mistreated and jailed: "It was mainly because my friend Peggy Baird was going that I decided one evening to accompany her. The women's party who had been picketing and serving jail sentences had been given very brutal treatment, and a committee to uphold the rights of political prisoners had been formed....The suffragists in Washington had been treated as ordinary prisoners, deprived of their own clothing, put in shops to work, and starved on the meager food of the prison."[28]

Dorothy reflected on the experience of being jailed with the suffragists in the story of her conversion, emphasizing that suffrage was not a priority for her: "The cause for which we were in jail seemed utterly unimportant. I had not much interest in the vote, and it seemed to me our protest should have been not for ourselves but for all those thousands of prisoners throughout the country, victims of a materialistic system. They were enduring punishment which would not cure them nor deter them from future crimes, and they were being punished by men not much better than themselves, indeed, far worse in some cases."[29]

Anne Klejment points out that when Dorothy was arrested with the other women, "the jaunt had potential for furnishing the confirmed social realist with new material for freelance articles," and notes that only "one story, a mediocre and moralistic description of degrading jail conditions for women, resulted from the trip, but it said nothing about suffrage or wartime." Klejment describes the meaning of Dorothy's participation with the suffragists at a time long before she became Catholic or met Peter Maurin: "Although she picketed the White House and was arrested, Day had no interest in promoting women's suffrage....Day thought that voting, with its limited choices, and parliamentary politics rife with deal making, stifled genuine change. She trusted only in the direct action of the masses to result in social revolution and would *never* vote in an election."[30] In the May 1974 *Catholic Worker*, Dorothy wrote that she had never voted. Miller's biography also provides a quote about her views on politics and voting. "It was a matter of principle, yes, and also because I did not know any candidates, and also because of discouragement with the prevailing political system. Yet we are to rebuild society within the shell of the old, to use the I.W.W. jargon."[31]

When asked about election politics in an interview for the *Bill Moyers Journal*, Dorothy gave an answer closely related to distributism, subsidiarity, and the theology of the Mystical Body of Christ: "If I stayed long enough in one place...I would be more interested in local politics and I think that's very necessary....Martin Buber had the right idea when he said, 'the state should be a community of communities....'"[32]

In the May 1972 *Catholic Worker* article, "Catholic Worker Positions," Dorothy reaffirmed the Catholic Worker position on reforming economics and the social order—not government takeover, nor huge corporations, but a nonviolent revolution from below: "We believe in worker-ownership of the means of production and distribution, as distinguished from nationalization. This is to be accomplished by decentralized co-operatives and the elimination of a distinct employer class. It is revolution from below and not (as political revolutions are) from above."

Criticism of Catholic Worker advocacy of distributism came from both right and left. Critics insisted it was impractical. In the July–August 1956 *Catholic Worker*, in an article called "Distributism Is Not Dead," responding to those who dismissed it as a theory from the '30s, Dorothy restated the relevance and importance of this approach to economics: "The very fact that people are always burying distributism is evidence of the fact that it is not dead as a solution. John Stanley buried it last year in the *Commonweal* and *Social Justice* of the Central Verein in St. Louis some months ago buried it. But it is an issue that won't be buried, because distributism is a system conformable to the need of man and his nature."

The publication of E. F. Schumacher's book *Small Is Beautiful* revived the whole idea of distributism. Dorothy recommended the book in the February 1974 issue as part of the tradition of "organic and decentralist economics," relating it also to the philosophy of work of which Peter Maurin spoke: "We need a new economics with a strong emphasis on institutions on the land, decentralization, more study as well as more laboring at meaningful work. Small industries and hospices on the land mean more employment. There is no unemployment on the land, Peter used to say."

In his study of English converts, Joseph Pearce points out what many who read *Small Is Beautiful* had not known, that not only did Schumacher have excellent economic credentials, but like Chesterton's and Belloc's, his economic theories were "underpinned by solid religious and philosophical foundations, the fruits of a lifetime of searching. In 1971, two years before the publication of *Small Is Beautiful*, Schumacher had become a Roman Catholic, the final destination of his philosophical journey."[33] His economics is the fruit of his study of the social encyclicals of the church.

Distributists made practical recommendations for the implementation of the ideas of decentralization and a local economy (similar to what is today called sustainable development minus the Malthusian and New Age aspects). Schumacher's book presented many. Chesterton had presented his own. When anyone asked Chesterton what they could do immediately in order to begin to transform the economics of the world, he said:

> Do anything, however small, that will prevent the completion of the work of capitalist combination. Do anything that will even delay that completion. Save one shop out of a hundred shops. Save one croft out of a hundred crofts. Keep open one door out of a hundred doors; for so long as one door is open, we are not in prison....A hundred tales of human history are there to show that tendencies can be turned back, and that one stumbling block can be the turning point. The sands of time are simply dotted with single stakes that have thus marked the turn of the tide.[34]

Chesterton had specific recommendations for legislation that would help to create a society of owners instead of laws to create monopoly. They included the "taxation of contracts in order to discourage the sale of small property to big proprietors and to encourage the break-up of big property among small proprietors...the establishment of 'free law for the poor,' so that small property could always be defended against great...the deliberate protection of experiments in small property, if necessary, by tariffs and even local tariffs, and subsidies to foster the starting of such experiments."[35]

Readers of *The Catholic Worker* sometimes asked for more clarification on the meaning of distributism. They wondered how it could ever work or be accomplished. Catholic Workers argued, with Chesterton, that laws must be changed from those that favor enormous corporations to those that help the small farmer or entrepreneur. On this point Dorothy quoted a pamphlet by S. Sagar, made up of a collection of articles which had run in *The Weekly Review*, adding her own commentary in brackets:

> The principle from which the law can start is that all its subjects should exercise control of land and capital by means of direct family ownership of these things. This, of course, is the principle from which, until yesterday, our own law started. It was the theory of capitalism under which all were free to own, none compelled by law to labor....Unfortunately, in practice, under capitalism the many had not the opportunity of obtaining land and capital in any useful amount and were compelled by physical necessity to labor for the fortunate few who possessed these things. But the theory was all right. Distributists want to save the theory by bringing the practice in conformity with it.[36]

Dorothy, with Peter Maurin, knew that a change in economics must begin with a change in hearts and minds. She described his vision:

> Peter rejoiced to see men do great things and dream great dreams. He wanted them to stretch out their arms to their brothers, because he knew that the surest way to find God, to find the good, was through one's brothers. Peter wanted this striving to result in a better physical life in which all men would be able to fulfill themselves, develop their capacities for love and worship, expressed in all the arts. He wanted them to be able to produce what was needed in the way of homes, food, clothing, so that there was enough of these necessities for everyone.
>
> It was hard for me to understand what he meant, thinking as I always had in terms of cities and immediate need of men for their weekly paycheck. Now I can see clearly what he was talking about, but I am faced with the problem of making others see it. I can well recognize the fact that people remaining as they are, Peter's program is impossible. But it would become actual, given a people changed in heart and mind, so that they would observe the new commandment of love, or desire to.[37]

Even with support from society, Dorothy and Peter knew that the change from centuries of individualism and massive corporations would not come easily. It would have to spring from a revolution of the heart. Dorothy often said, "All is grace." In the

July-August 1943 *Catholic Worker*, reflecting on her participation in one of the retreats that had become so much a part of the Catholic Worker, she applied the retreat teaching to Catholic Worker efforts to change the social order, to build an economics that reflected human dignity: "Here in the Catholic Worker, in Houses of Hospitality and on farming communes, speaking and writing and working, I have been trying to change the social order. Now I realize that I must go further, go deeper, and work to make those means available for people to change themselves, so that they can change the social order. In order to have a Christian social order we must first have Christians."

Pure Means from a Converted Heart: Jacques and Raïssa Maritain

Jacques (1882–1973) and Raïssa (1883–1960) Maritain of France were friends of Peter Maurin, Dorothy Day, and the Catholic Worker movement in its earliest years. Peter, a French immigrant, introduced the Maritains to the Workers and served as translator during their visits to the New York house. Peter was able to translate Jacques's writings for *The Catholic Worker* and the world before most of them became available or popular in English. From the first year of its publication, *The Catholic Worker* recommended Jacques Maritain's books to its readers. Later, Dorothy wrote about Raïssa's books in her columns as she read them.

As young university students, Jacques from a Protestant background and Raïssa from a Russian Jewish émigré family, the Maritains had been in despair over answers to the metaphysical questions and had made a pact to commit suicide together if they didn't find meaning in life. When they met, Jacques already had a master's degree in philosophy and was continuing his studies, and Raïssa was studying science at the Sorbonne in an atmosphere at that time in which questions of faith or wisdom were rejected and deemed inappropriate, in favor of only natural science, empiricism, mechanism, and materialism. The two of them were searching for something to justify existence, "in order that human life be not a thing absurd and cruel."[1]

The Maritains joined the Catholic Church, especially under the influence of Léon Bloy, who provoked them into believing that life was worth living. Bloy wrote and spoke with a sword instead of a pen, almost shouting at people through his writing: "Wake up, do something with your life, for God's sake!" He introduced them to Catholicism and became their godfather when they were baptized. The journey to conversion was not easy for the Maritains in an intellectual climate in which Catholicism was totally rejected. Raïssa spoke of "preparing ourselves to enter among those whom the world hates as it hates Christ." Jacques thought that in becoming a Catholic he would have to "utterly forswear the intellectual life."[2] In their search for truth, as they studied Catholic doctrine and tried to reconcile it with the rationalism of their university, Bloy, instead of using apologetics, presented them with the model of the saints, which changed their lives forever: "He placed before us the fact of sanctity. Simply, and because he loved them, because their experience was near his own—so much so that he could not read them without weeping—he brought us to know the saints and mystics.…We were shown heroic Catholicism—sanctity in its terrible trials, in its humility and its divine charity, in its asceticism, in the beatitude wherein it reaches its fulfillment, in its pure harmony, in its power, in its beauty."[3]

Dorothy Day wrote several times in *The Catholic Worker* (and as late as the May 1947 issue) about how Peter Maurin had introduced the Catholic Workers to the story of the Maritains and to the ideas of Léon Bloy, the pilgrim of the Absolute, and "that great and terrible line of his, which converted the Maritains, '*There is only one unhappiness*, and that is—NOT TO BE ONE OF THE SAINTS'" (Dorothy's emphasis).

Jacques later studied Catholic philosophy and became one of the twentieth century's best-known philosophers. He was involved in the renewal of the thought of St. Thomas Aquinas; he was also a Christian personalist communitarian.

Maritain pointed out that Aquinas's idea of the common good, even in an economic and political reality, is based on the uncreated common good of the Trinity. Both Thomas and Maritain believed that action to create a better world must be rooted in contemplation, from which work toward the common good would flow. Maritain, with Thomas, asserted that a commitment to the common good was not simply an option, but characteristic of the life of the Trinity itself, of the very heart of God, and thus for each person made in his image and likeness. As he put it in philosophical language, "at each degree of the analogy of being, the primacy of the common good" is affirmed.[4] Maritain argued that selfishness and addiction to consumerism and power could be overcome through prayer and contemplation. An economic system that depends on masses of workers laboring long hours in sweatshops could be seen in its terrible reality. A Christian approach to the social order, rooted in love and the communion of saints, could be seen, not as something impossible to contemplate, but the natural fruit of prayer. His theology presented work toward the common good as participation in and flowing from the mystery of God.

Maritain contrasted his personalism and a true conception of the common good with the counterfeits of the materialistic philosophy of society in its three principal forms: bourgeois individualism, Communist anti-individualism, and totalitarian or dictatorial anti-Communism and anti-individualism. He was convinced that all three of these "disregard the human *person* in one way or another, and, in its place, consider, willingly or not, the *material individual* alone."[5] Some in the 1930s, as now, went so far as to try to claim the mantle of Christian personalism and even of St. Thomas Aquinas himself in support of economic individualism. In a masterful understatement that there is sometimes an "intellectual exactitude" in the use of the term, Maritain distinguished a personalism centered in the dignity of the person and the common good from "every social philosophy centered in the primacy of the individual and the private good."[6]

Maritain, like Peter and Dorothy, linked the concept of the common good to that of the Mystical Body of Christ, in which all the members and potential members had responsibility for one another within the grace of their union with God. Maritain later did so with Pius XII's reaffirmation of this unity, noting that the encyclical *Mystici corporis* is "truly the charter of the Christian doctrine on the person." The encyclical insisted that every moral association of persons, if we look to its ultimate usefulness, must in the end be "directed to the advancement of all and of every single member. For they are persons."[7]

The Maritains invited leading French intellectuals to Sunday afternoon gatherings at their home in Paris to share and discuss ideas. Emmanuel Mounier and Nicholas Berdyaev were among those who attended regularly, as well as Helene Iswolsky, who later became a good friend of Dorothy Day. Maritain was often a mentor for the younger people in their exploration of Christian communitarian personalism and defended them and their ideas in Rome. He encouraged the publication of the personalist journal, *Esprit*.

The Maritains came to visit the Catholic Worker on several occasions, Jacques first in 1934 and Raïssa soon after. Jacques wrote to Peter Maurin after his first visit: "'Tell Dorothy Day...how very happy I was to visit her, and how touched at the reception given me by your friends. I wish I could have said all that was in my heart—never was I more vexed by my inability to speak fluent English. It seemed as if I had found again in the Catholic Worker a little of the atmosphere of Péguy's office in the Rue de le Sorbonne. And so much good will, such courage, such generosity....'"[8]

The Catholic Worker announced another visit by Maritain in the January 1936 issue, with the headline "Jacques Maritain, Noted Philosopher, Is Guest of Catholic Worker Paper." Dorothy was proud of the relationship of the Catholic Worker movement with the Maritains. *The Catholic Worker* of June 1945 announced that Jacques was giving some copies of the paper to the pope: "With great boldness, I decided to ask him to present some issues of the *Catholic Worker* to Pope Pius XII....He promised, with his usual gentle cordiality, to make selections from the papers and give them to the Holy Father."

One of the most important things Maurin translated for *The Catholic Worker* (in January 1935) was "Pure Means," a free translation in Easy Essay format of a chapter of Jacques Maritain's *Freedom in the Modern World*. "Pure Means" stressed the importance of achieving one's goal in the world without using sinful means. Maritain articulated in a new way this concept for the twentieth century and shared it with the Catholic Workers. Examples of the principle of pure means would be that to make peace is a good thing, but one cannot achieve it by bombing innocent civilians; it is not moral to become fabulously wealthy while one's workers toil under deplorable conditions or at slave labor.

Stanley Vishnewski, who spent his life at the Catholic Worker collaborating with Dorothy Day, wrote about Maritain's visits and presence and the adoption of this teaching at the Catholic Worker. He included Jacques's defense of the Catholic Worker:

> The philosopher and thinker who had the greatest appeal for the early Catholic Worker was Jacques Maritain. His teaching on the use of 'Pure Means' was one of the cornerstones of the philosophy of the Catholic Worker. His maxim: 'Victory or defeat with pure means is always victory' was imbedded in our way of thinking and our activities....
>
> When Maritain came to the Worker to give a lecture he attracted one of the largest crowds we ever had at a meeting. The place was packed with people and many had to stay outdoors. Maritain talked in French and Peter translated for him. Maritain was a soft-spoken man and his eyes had a dreamy quality to them. One felt that he was in tune with the Infinite. He looked even shorter than he normally did when he stood next to Peter the peasant. Maritain would speak for a few minutes in his soft voice and then would wait for Peter, who would translate in a booming voice that I am sure the people on the outside heard....
>
> A critic of the Catholic Worker told Maritain that he thought the weakness of the Catholic Worker Movement lay in the fact that it neglected political action.
>
> Maritain thought for a brief second, and then spoke in French, which Peter translated. Maritain stated that on the contrary, the Catholic Workers dealt with matters politic in the true Aristotelian sense, and that there was a great need for such a work as the Catholic Workers were doing.
>
> It made me happy when Maritain concluded his talk by saying that the principles set forth by the Catholic Worker were thoroughly sound and met with his greatest admiration and approbation.[9]

Some "scholars" who have attempted to resurrect Machiavelli and present him as a model, even though, or perhaps because, he allowed suspension of church teaching at times in the interest of expediency, also claim Maritain. The ethics of pure means, expounded by Maritain, however, made the Machiavellian politics of expediency totally unacceptable. Peter Maurin immortalized Maritain's critique in one of his Easy Essays: "Jacques Maritain told us that Machiavellism is the modern heresy."

Reflections in *The Catholic Worker* over the years reemphasized the question of ends and means, the necessity of pure means to achieve good ends that Jacques Maritain had introduced to the Workers in the '30s. For example, Dorothy understood that the use of impure means to achieve desired ends undermined all the original good intentions of Communist government leaders. In the May 1951 *Catholic Worker,* she analyzed what had happened to Mao Tse Tung, who began by reading the great Chinese classic, *All Men Are Brothers,* "a Robin Hood tale of bandits who afflicted the rich and took care of the poor." He had employed the ancient phrases from the book of Confucius, where unity, sincerity, friendship, and love were emphasized so much. Dorothy recognized that the very serious problem that subsequently caused so much suffering in China was that of using the wrong means to try to achieve this goal: "It is a question of means and ends. We cannot quarrel with the end." She insisted that the actions of the United States also be evaluated on the use of pure means—she wanted her country to use moral means to achieve its ends. In the same article, she critiqued U. S. policy: "We, too, have used force in a way so gigantic that in its very magnitude it outdoes the compulsion of the enemy....We did a clean job of wiping out whole cities, by obliteration bombing, flame throwers, making human torches of countless numbers of human beings."

Dorothy reminisced in her May 1976 *Catholic Worker* column about how "Peter also kept in touch with such thinkers as Jacques Maritain, who visited us in our store front at 15th Street and who gave us his book, *Freedom in the Modern World,* calling special attention to the chapter on the 'Use of Pure Means.'" Peter Maurin believed that the great freedom of the human person brought with it tremendous responsibility to do good in the world, to be exercised with purified means. He encouraged readers of *The Catholic Worker* to study Maritain's philosophy on this topic: "If you want to know what to do with freedom, read

Freedom in the Modern World by Jacques Maritain." For Maritain, as for Peter, freedom flowed from contemplation and one's vocation: "The pursuit of the highest contemplation and the pursuit of the highest freedom are two aspects of the same pursuit."[10]

Peter recommended Maritain's books in *The Catholic Worker* during the 1930s, especially *The Things That Are Not Caesar's* and *Integral Humanism*, in addition to *Freedom in the Modern World*. Dorothy also included them in a small reading list she made, saying, "Peter is always making lists of books for people to read so I shall give my own list herewith." On that list were two of Maritain's books, *True Humanism* and *Freedom in the Modern World*.[11]

Peter and Dorothy related not only to Jacques Maritain, but also his wife, Raïssa. Dorothy mentioned her book, *We Have Been Friends Together*, in the December 1938 issue of the paper in the context of the personalist communitarian movement in France. In the February 1942 *Catholic Worker*, Dorothy wrote: "*We Have Been Friends Together* is a book which I must keep talking about, it is so lovely, so stimulating. It is the story of Raïssa Maritain's life, first in Russia and then in France, her early schooldays, her meeting with Jacques, who became her husband, and their friends, Charles Péguy and Léon Bloy. The story takes one up to their conversion and I will await with happy expectancy the continuation of this account."

Credit must be given to the Maritains, as well as to Mounier, for promoting the concept of the primacy of the spiritual, which became a key concept at the Catholic Worker. Raïssa was a contemplative and a poet, and Jacques, who wrote many volumes about Christians relating to the world, was also a deeply spiritual person. While famous as a Thomist, Maritain's philosophy was integrated with life and prayer. Spirituality was the core of their lives; the Maritains had the Blessed Sacrament in their home. "Everything in Jacques' work we have first lived in the form of a vital difficulty, in the form of experience—problems of art and morality, of philosophy, of faith, of prayer, of contemplation," Raïssa wrote in her *Journal*.[12]

Brigid Merriman points out how Raïssa's reflections in *Adventures in Grace* spoke to Dorothy "at a time when the Lacouture retreat[13] occupied the forefront of her mind" and how the retreat "addressed the relationship between God's grace and human effort in personal sanctification; so, too, did *Adventures in Grace*."[14] In the July–August 1945 *Catholic Worker*, Dorothy made the connection with that book of Raïssa and the themes of St. John of the Cross in the retreat:

> Reading Raïssa Maritain's Adventures in Grace and was much interested in her account of Pere Clerrisac's spiritual direction....Jacques and Raïssa were reading St. John of the Cross at the time and were intensely desirous of sanctity, and conscious of the need for effort to attain it. Pere Clerrisac emphasized God's grace rather than personal effort. A point which I well understand. It interests me much to see this struggle of two points of view which goes on still, and I do not see why there should be any opposition between emphasizing the need for effort toward personal sanctification and at the same time the calm faith that God can do all things. "Love God and do what you will." I love the Maritains for their love for St. John of the Cross.

Merriman reminds us that for Jacques the primacy of the spiritual was to be "achieved in this life through engagement in the present world rather than through withdrawal and separation," always accompanied by an interior conversion. This was very much in harmony with the social commitments of the Catholic Worker movement. Maritain wrote of the unity of action and contemplation, best exemplified in the gift of self:[15]

> It is through love that the knowledge of divine things becomes experimental and fruitful. And precisely because this knowledge is the work of love in act, it also passes into action by virtue of the very generosity and abundance of love, which is gift of self. Then action proceeds from the superabundance of contemplation, and that is why, far from suppressing action or being opposed to it, contemplation vivifies it.[16]

Jacques distinguished the contemplation of a Christian from the way it was understood in the ancient world, where it was considered to be for a select few. He emphasized the importance of contemplative prayer and growth in the spiritual life for every person. The Maritains, like the Catholic Workers, wanted to help to incorporate the primacy of the spiritual into the lives of lay people by encouraging a retreat movement for laity and priests alike. Dorothy referred to Maritain's endorsement of the idea in the July–August 1954 *Catholic Worker* as she wrote about her reflections on a retreat she had just made: "It was Father Casey's third annual retreat with us, though he would rather call it a little school of spirituality, recalling an article of Jacques Maritain from an old *Commonweal* in which he pointed out a need for Houses of Hospitality on the land where schools of the spiritual life could be conducted for the laity."

Maritain's recommendation of having Houses of Hospitality for retreats included the hospitality part for those most in need. His interest in the Catholic Worker movement flowed from his philosophical and theological understanding of the Gospel passage from Matthew 25, so central to the Catholic Worker. Maritain carried the idea of serving Jesus in the poor further than many interpreters of the text, tying it to another frequently quoted verse from the Bible on the poor:

> The Gospel text: "The poor you will always have with you"…means on the contrary: Christ himself will not always be among you, but you will recognize Him in the poor, whom you must love and serve as Him. It is not a social class that is designated here; it is the men who have need of others in order to subsist, whatever may be the nature, the origin, and the cause of their indigence. So long as there are oppressed castes or classes, there love will go first to seek them; if one day there are no longer any of these, it will find them still wherever they may appear. And because it loves them, it wishes that one day there will be no more oppressed classes or castes.[17]

Dorothy wrote of how much the Workers shared with Jacques on the centrality of scripture, how he spoke of the need to study the scriptures in order to find Christ: "'Read the Gospel prayerfully,' he said, 'searching for the truth, not just to find something with which to back up your own arguments.'"[18]

Jacques, like *The Catholic Worker*, took a position of neutrality during the Spanish Civil War. In November 1937, the paper published his article criticizing that war, showing his "dismay at the atrocities that were cloaked under the guise of a religious war" on both sides, often against innocent noncombatants. Maritain wrote during the Spanish Civil War that it was blasphemous to kill in the name of Christ or religion. He argued that it was bad enough to kill in a just war, but Christians were obliged to remove any religious element from military conflict. Like the Workers, Maritain was heavily criticized for his stance.

Both the Maritains and Catholic Workers worked against anti-Semitism before World War II. In January 1939, the *Catholic Worker* carried an article noting Maritain's radio address directed against anti-Semitic propaganda. In the November 1939 issue, Dorothy wrote a lengthy review of Jacques's book, *A Christian Looks at the Jewish Question*, in which she, like Maritain in the book, did not mince words on the racism of anti-Semitism. Referring to a statement of Pius XI, in that book Maritain had written that all Christians "are converts to the God of Israel who is the true God, to the Father whom Israel recognized." Dorothy added the words of Pius XI to which Maritain had referred: "When he commented upon the words of the Canon of the Mass, *sacrificium Patriarchae nostri Abrahai*, 'Notice that Abraham is called our patriarch, our ancestor. Anti-Semitism is incompatible with the thought and sublime reality expressed in this text. It is a movement in which we Christians can have no part whatsoever. Anti-Semitism is unacceptable. Spiritually we are Semites.'"

Catholic Workers had been actively working against anti-Semitism and especially the situation in Germany throughout the 1930s. The paper carried articles about the dangers of fascism and attacked Hitler's policies towards the Jews, and the Workers picketed the German consulate. Years later, in her "On Pilgrimage" column in the February 1979 *Catholic Worker*, Dorothy answered the criticisms of Elie Wiesel who spoke on the radio about the holocaust and no one crying out. Dorothy reminded him that they did cry out, they actively protested: "*The Catholic Worker* and *Commonweal*, and Doctors Chapman and Pollock—both, I believe, graduates of the Institute of Medieval Studies at Toronto (much esteemed as a center of learning by Peter Maurin)—all protested—Bill Gauchat, head of the Cleveland Catholic Worker group, too."

Merriman recounts that in the ensuing years Dorothy Day continued to mention Maritain and his books, including reviews of several books in the paper:

> Though Maurin introduced the Catholic Worker movement to Maritain, it was Dorothy who was instrumental in keeping Maritain's later works before the minds of the paper's readers. To this end Dorothy commissioned and approved a number of book reviews. Each of these in its own way underscored Maritain's insights revolving around the dignity of the human person, socially responsible and firmly rooted in this world's realities, who at the same time is destined for union with God, both in this life and the next.[19]

In time, Jacques Maritain left the Bowery and the Catholic Workers to preside at America's great secular universities. He was already a frequent visitor to North America and, since 1932, had come each year to the Institute of Mediaeval Studies in Toronto to give courses of lectures. With the outbreak of war at the end of 1939, Maritain decided not to return to France. Following his lectures in Toronto at the beginning of 1940, he moved to the United States and taught at Princeton and Columbia universities.

In later years Jacques did not always agree with Dorothy Day; an example is World War II. However, Dorothy used his principles in judging both war and economics. Maritain had pointed out years before that to insist on the pure means inspired by the gospel in one's work in the world would not be easy, but might bring criticism from all sides, might even isolate the person to some degree: "The Christian has to look to a very high plane for the laws that govern his life and action and that segregate him in the social order alike from the apostles of a revolution born of hate and from the representatives of an order based on avarice."[20] Dorothy had to be prophetic during World War II and take great risks while so many others in the church in the United States supported the war, even Maritain.

Dorothy was not confused, as were so many others, by those who proposed situation ethics in the 1960s. She was convinced of objective truth and of the need for pure means. In the May 1975 *Catholic Worker*, she credited both Jacques Maritain and Peter Maurin in teaching Catholic Workers about pure means toward the ends they wanted to achieve, applauding the commentators on the Vietnam War for at least discussing these issues: "I am happy to hear news commentators, almost all of them, talking of means and ends. Jacques Maritain, philosopher, and Peter Maurin, poor peasant and teacher, both taught us since 1933 that we must work towards 'the purification of our means.'"

For Dorothy the pure means of love taught in the New Testament was the answer. She mentioned the question of means and ends in many columns throughout the years, always insisting that one could not use immoral means (that is, assassinations, obliteration bombing) to achieve good ends. She taught, however, that to insist on pure means did not mean sitting idly by while injustice raged; for her it was crucial to confront evil in the world through the power of love. This meant fasting, prayer, love of enemies, protesting injustice, transforming the world in Christ—the weapons of the Spirit. The response of the Christian to the world was not separation from the world, not a weak response to be overshadowed by the great commitment of those who found heroism in war, but the way of the gospel. In her article, "Love Is the Measure," in the June 1946 *Catholic Worker*, Dorothy wrote:

> We confess to being fools and wish that we were more so...there is nothing that we can do but love, and dear God—please enlarge our hearts to love each other, to love our neighbor, to love our enemy as well as our friend....What does the modern world know of love?...It has never reached down into the depths, to the misery and pain and glory of love which endures to death and beyond it. We have not yet begun to learn about love. Now is the time to begin, to start afresh, to use this divine weapon.

Dorothy and Peter shared with the Maritains the belief that a revolution must come, but that it must be one that begins with a revolution in one's heart. The question of methods to transform society was one of means and ends, the commitment to pure means that the Workers so enthusiastically adopted in their first years. As Maritain had said:

> The purity or sincerity of an attempt to renew the temporal order on Christian principles excludes all ways and means that are not sincere and pure.
>
> A Christian revolution can succeed only by the use of just those means which are beyond the ability of others to use. If Faith is able to move mountains, is it powerless to shift the mighty from their seats? If Christians, who live by Faith in their private lives, lay aside their faith when they approach the things of political and social life, they must be content to be towed like slaves in the wake of history.[21]

For Dorothy, the commitment to pure means meant nonviolence. No matter how bad the system was, or how badly they wanted to change it, Catholic Workers could not use or advocate violence. In the May 1972 *Catholic Worker*, she reiterated again the methods of the movement, pointing out that to use impure means is to determine the end, which will not be the desired result:

> We believe...that the revolution that is to be pursued in ourselves and in society must be pacifist. Otherwise it will proceed by force and use means that are evil and which will never be outgrown, so that they will determine the END of the revolution and that end will again be tyranny....
>
> We believe that success, as the world determines it, is not the criterion by which a movement should be judged. We must be prepared and ready to face seeming failure. The most important thing is that we adhere to these values which transcend time and for which we will be asked a personal accounting, not as to whether they succeeded (though we should hope that they do), but as to whether we remained true to them even though the whole world go otherwise.

The spirituality of church and world of the Maritains extended to the world of art. Their interest in poetry and art found an echo in the spirituality of the woman (Dorothy) who frequently quoted the line from Dostoevsky: "The world will be saved by beauty." Merriman made the connection that "Maritain had argued that art is a fundamental necessity in human life, its beauty teaching persons the pleasures of the spirit and preparing them for contemplation as the end of all human activities." Dorothy's column in the January 1936 *Catholic Worker* mentioned Maritain's *Art and Scholasticism*, demonstrating the necessity for art as a preparation for contemplation."[22] In that book Jacques wrote of the life and work of the Christian artist:

> A Christian work would have the artist, as artist, free.
> But it will be Christian, it will reveal in its beauty the interior reflection of the brilliance of grace, only on condition that it overflows from a heart possessed by grace....Art demands tranquility, said Fra Angelico, *and to paint the things of Christ, the artist must live with Christ.*[23]

While in his book Maritain was not only speaking of the visual arts, but writers and others involved in creative work, it was especially applied to that field. The work of two artists in the pages of *The Catholic Worker* reflected the interest and appreciation of both Peter Maurin and Dorothy Day for art and its unique possibility of communicating the incarnation and the lives of the saints, together with the text of articles in the paper. The Workers' understanding of the relationship between spirituality, manual labor, and the Works of Mercy was depicted in the work of Ade Bethune, which from the early years appeared in the *Catholic Worker*. The young artist and her mother were present at the Catholic Worker during some of Maritain's visits in the 1930s. William Miller speaks of her art work as making a "personalist statement" and gives Peter credit for the idea of depicting the saints in manual labor, which he also called "menial" labor:

> Its woodcuts [and drawings] depicting Christ and the saints as workers have helped to fuse a sense of the divine in the performance of menial labor. Christ was shown working in a carpenter shop; Mary was a housemaid who swept the floor; and St. Joseph worked at his sawbench. It was an artwork that gave the feeling of the humanity of Christ and the community of man, signified in the performance of those menial tasks that represented the foundation on which men could reach for higher things.

The artist who did this work, Ade Bethune, came to Dorothy Day and Peter Maurin in January 1934. A recent graduate of New York's Cathedral High School for girls, looking for an outlet for her talent, she was sent to the Worker by the editor of *Liturgical Arts* magazine. It was Maurin who told her to depict Christ and the saints as workers. In the March 1934 issue, Dorothy Day editorially expressed her thanks to St. Joseph (who was taken as the patron of the movement) for sending them an artist.[24]

The other artist who from 1950 on distinguished the pages of the paper was Fritz Eichenberg.[25] Miller said of Eichenberg's work:

> [To] many who have come to know *The Catholic Worker*, no one person, excepting Dorothy Day, stands out as having given the paper its characteristic mark during this era as does the Quaker artist Fritz Eichenberg. His woodcuts began appearing in the Worker in 1950, and it was not long before they became the paper's most arresting feature. One required no schooling or sensitivity to the hidden nuances of art to comprehend the peace and joy that the presence of the Christ child brought to man and nature as depicted in a Christmastime, full-front-page reproduction of the infant Jesus among the animals.[26]

Twenty years after Dorothy Day's death, in the October–November 2000 issue of *The Catholic Worker*, Daniel Mauk reminisced about Fritz Eichenberg, his art, and his relationship to the Catholic Worker movement: "One of the major events in Fritz's life took place in 1949 when his friend, Gilbert Kilpack, arranged for Fritz to sit next to Dorothy Day at a conference on religious publishing at Pendle Hill, a Quaker Retreat Center." Quoting an interview Eichenberg gave to Robert Ellsberg, Mauk tells how "Dorothy asked Fritz for something emotional, something that would touch people through images, as she was trying to do through words, and something that would communicate the spirit of the Catholic Worker to people who, perhaps, could not read the articles." Eichenberg told Ellsberg, "Dorothy stood for everything I thought would make this world a better place. She cared for the underdog, the oppressed, the poor, the ones who were easily discarded....I never knew, thirty years ago, that my humble work for *The Catholic Worker* would become almost an identification for me."

After Raïssa's death, Jacques went to live with the Little Brothers of Jesus in France. In the last book he wrote, when he was eighty-five, he mentioned the "founding of the personalist journal *Esprit* in 1932 and *The Catholic Worker* at nearly the same period," calling those events the "point of rupture" which announced the end of the confusion over what he called a "Manicheanlike aberration" about the meaning of the world and the Christian response to it, over the previous two centuries. Here Maritain included what had been the "spiritual impoverishment of a Christian laity, who continued in general to imagine that the call to the perfection of charity, with what it implies of life of prayer and, as much as possible, of contemplative recollection, was the exclusive school of monks."[27]

In the July–August 1973 *Catholic Worker*, Dorothy added a little section on prayer to her column and mentioned the Maritains as powerful friends in heaven: "I pray not only for those who have died, but **to** them also. In our November issue, I hope to write about our own dear departed, and about the lowliest and the highest among them. Right now, I am praying to Jacques and Raïssa Maritain."

St. Teresa of Avila

Dorothy recounted in *The Long Loneliness* that she had read about Teresa of Avila (1515–1582) in William James's book, *The Varieties of Religious Experience*, and had read Teresa's autobiography even before becoming interested in Catholicism.[1] Although James was skeptical about religion, he had presented Teresa as one of the "ablest women on record"—though he felt it was "a pity that so much vitality of soul should have found such poor employment." Brigid Merriman told how this description of Teresa's ability, along with her emphasis on "the correlation between prayer and personal life and action" drew Dorothy to her, and called Dorothy's predilection for Teresa "outstanding."[2] Dorothy told of reading Teresa's *Foundations*, a description of the nun's establishment of two monasteries and fifteen convents in her Carmelite reform within a period of twenty years. Dorothy mentioned in her column in the May 1967 *Catholic Worker* that when she first met Peter Maurin, he noticed in her library the story of St. Teresa's life and her writings.

Teresa de Ahumada y Cepeda was born in Avila, Spain, in 1515. With her father's wealth Teresa lived a life of luxury. Even after she entered the convent at age twenty, laxity in regard to convent discipline allowed her to continue a life of concern for prestige, reputation, and family honor, and even carry on an active social life. Many years later she underwent a profound conversion.

Preferential treatment of those with better family ties continued into the religious life at that time, even though incompatible with the very idea of religious vocation. It was many years before Teresa, a person of tremendous depth, could make the break from a gossipy social life within convent walls to the spiritual greatness for which she later became famous.

St. Teresa went through a second conversion after she had spent her first twenty years as a Carmelite at the convent called La Encarnación in this distracting atmosphere. After years of what she later considered a very shallow existence, Teresa discovered the profound aspects of the spiritual life and attempted to live a life of continued recollection and prayer. Dorothy related Teresa's struggle with mediocrity over the course of many years to a fear of total dedication to God. In *From Union Square to Rome*, Dorothy wrote:

> St. Teresa knew that she was far from leading the life she wished to lead when she entered the convent. She wished to give herself up wholly to God. She wished everything she did, every word she said, to tend to that end....
>
> She tells how she was kept from prayer. "The sadness I felt on entering the oratory was so great that it required all the courage I had to force myself in. They say of me that my courage is not slight, and it is known that God has given me a courage beyond that of a woman; but I have made a bad use of it."
>
> She told, too, of watching the hourglass, of how she was filled with distractions, of what a constant hard struggle it was to force herself to prayer and spiritual reading. And these struggles went on for twenty years!
>
> "I wished to live," she wrote, "but I saw clearly that I was not living, but rather wrestling with the shadow of death; there was no one to give me life, and I was not able to take it."[3]

This is the fear of conversion and its consequences that Dorothy, like Teresa, had to face. As Dorothy said in the same passage, "As a convert I can say these things, knowing how many times I turned away, almost in disgust, from the idea of God and giving myself up to Him." Society often depicts those who go through a conversion as choosing a life of narrowness and boredom, when as a matter of fact, once they have made the leap of faith, converts like Dorothy Day and Teresa seem to have more full, exciting and joyful lives than anyone—although the paschal mystery always includes both cross and resurrection.

Her conversion experience led Teresa to be interested in the reform of her Carmelite order and she began that enormous task.

However, her first object of reform was herself. This was accomplished by powerful spiritual experiences that reinforced her total commitment to the service of God. Dorothy, a convert to Catholicism, identified with this conversion.

Teresa had lived a life of boredom and mediocrity even while a nun, thanks to the advice of what would now be considered "politically correct" confessors and spiritual directors, who kept telling her she was doing fine. Teresa blamed half-learned confessors who allowed her to wallow in this lightweight existence of gossip and frivolous pursuits for so long. "What was venial sin," she said, "they said was no sin at all, and what was serious mortal sin, they said was venial."[4]

Dorothy, wanting to dedicate herself completely to God and to grow in the spiritual life, similarly wrote about her own sins and about confessors who dismissed them as not sins at all. Following great spiritual writers, she wanted every moment and every desire to be lived in the presence of God. She wrote several times about making a confession and receiving the response that she was being too scrupulous, that she should not be concerned about those small things she had mentioned. Dorothy brought in Teresa's writing to support her view: "No one needs to be afraid of our committing excesses here, by any chance—for as soon as we do any penances, our confessors begin to fear that we shall kill ourselves with them."[5]

Being, as James described her, one of the "ablest women on record," Teresa used all of her skills, wit, and wisdom to reform her order and to establish a number of new monasteries with stricter rules. She was a gifted organizer, but even more a wise mentor to the many nuns, new and old, who came to join her new monasteries. Teresa desired that other Carmelite nuns be helped to grow in the spiritual life without wasting as much time as she had. She not only called them to a very serious religious commitment and life of prayer, but also understood the spiritual and psychological needs of the nuns and took these into account. Teresa had been one of the wealthy nuns and had been known in her convent as Doña Teresa de Ahumada; in her reformed convent she was known simply as Teresa of Jesus.

Teresa ran into resistance with her reforms, which included a return to the original Carmelite spirit of the monasteries, different from the one closely tied to the values of honor, blood, and family in the Spain of the time. Her reform included voluntary poverty and asceticism for all the nuns, limitation on opportunities for receiving visitors at the convents to counteract distractions, an intense sense of mission, and an emphasis on mental prayer rather than many repeated vocal prayers. The nobility resented her reforms and the city tried to close down her first convent.

It was through the help of a respected Franciscan priest, Peter of Alcántara, and contacts that he had made for Teresa in the hierarchy that she was able to continue her work of renewing her order during a very turbulent period of history.[6] With the encouragement and model of this priest who had initiated a reform of his order to be more based on Francis's own life, Teresa changed the financial basis of the convents she founded to one of voluntary poverty. Her reformed Discalced Carmelite convents were maintained by alms and the work of the nun's own hands. Teresa wrote extensively about voluntary poverty in her book, *The Way of Perfection*.

Dorothy identified with Teresa's organizational abilities in her founding of many new convents and bringing them to the original vision of her order. Like Teresa and Francis, the Catholic Worker movement made voluntary poverty a central concept in the foundation of houses. When the Catholic Worker movement faced practical challenges and decisions and shortage of money, Dorothy turned to Teresa's book of the founding of her monasteries for inspiration: "Reading St. Teresa's *Foundations* last night gave me much courage to proceed. If our surroundings are cold, desolate and dirty with the dirt of poverty which is so hard to combat, it is the more suited to us. Our debts are now one thousand five hundred and thirty dollars. We are most completely dependent on God."[7]

Dorothy turned again to Teresa for inspiration in 1950 when the Catholic Workers were dispossessed of the house at 115 Mott Street and were having difficulty finding a suitable replacement. She commented in the June 1950 *Catholic Worker* on the terrible condition of so many of the buildings, which made their purchase impractical. Dorothy told how, while other Workers roamed the streets looking for places, she sat down and read *The Foundations* of St. Teresa and thought about how different the times were when Teresa was alive:

> We are hemmed in by regulations that are made to protect the poor from grasping landlords, as well as from disaster....We would like to tackle that building next door in the same spirit, doing it floor by floor, moving in apartment by apartment, but it cannot be done. We would not be permitted and we cannot even contemplate trying it, because there is the business of water, gas and electric. There is no chance of our sneaking in, in the dead of the night as St. Teresa did with her nuns, and taking possession. It would be a matter of fifty thousand dollars worth of repairs.

Dorothy's devotion to St. Joseph originally came from her reading of Teresa, who counted on his prayer for practical help. Teresa's first reformed convent was called San José. Dorothy told how she, like Teresa, relied on St. Joseph as her banker and householder, and similarly Dorothy and the Catholic Workers asked his help in all kinds of practical situations.[8] Stanley Vishnewski recounted how, when funds were low, Dorothy would remind the Catholic Workers that "it was time to start picketing St. Joseph and to implore him to send us the necessary money to keep the work going." New Workers and guests of the Houses of Hospitality sometimes didn't understand what this meant, but Stanley recalled Dorothy's explanation:

> It was St. Joseph, Dorothy told us, who managed to get the money and the means to keep his small family going when they lived on earth....
>
> Beatrice, who lived in the Hospice, asked Dorothy with a worried expression on her face if "we will have to carry picket signs in church?"
>
> Dorothy smiled: "The only picket signs that we will take to church will be our Rosary beads. We will all try to spend an hour in church before the Blessed Sacrament...."
>
> "St. Joseph will take care of our bills," Dorothy would write to our creditors. "And who is this St. Joseph?" the printer

phoned up to ask. "Tell him that the bill is getting too high and that we won't be able to extend him any more credit."[9]

While Dorothy quoted Teresa frequently over the years and relied upon her methods, she did not hesitate to criticize or point out her errors. Teresa's brothers were among those who, as Dorothy said in the May 1954 *Catholic Worker*, "went to the new world, piously to bring the faith, but also to make their fortune, very frankly expressed." Dorothy continued, "It is hard to see things with a pure heart, with a single eye, as a Christian should....All men seek that which is good, love, fame and fortune, and often these two aims cross, as in the case of the French who went to Indo-China to civilize, to convert, and to develop it." In the context of criticizing the French colonization of Indo-China years before the Vietnam War, Dorothy raised issues about Teresa's acceptance of money from her "colonizing" brothers for her new convents. In her unique style, in the same paragraph, Dorothy critiqued Marxists for their use also of the wrong means to try to achieve good ends:

> It is a story familiar to those who have read the letters of St. Teresa of Avila, who wrote to her colonizing brothers who went to the new world....The great St. Teresa was only too thankful for the money her brothers gave her when she was setting up her new foundations. One can well see how the Marxists would read this history, and the kind of emphasis they would place on it. And in so many ways their criticism is true. It is their means to attain their ends of brotherhood that are wrong. Just as our means too, are often wrong.

Teresa had her lighter side, what Dorothy called delightful. Dorothy's account in *The Long Loneliness* about her included a number of little stories that she later used throughout the years in her columns in *The Catholic Worker* to lighten and illumine the experiences and struggles of life in the Houses of Hospitality: "She was a mystic and a practical woman, a recluse and a traveler, a cloistered nun and yet most active. She liked to read novels when she was a young girl, and she wore a bright red dress when she entered the convent."[10] Dorothy retold one of Teresa's famous stories: "Once when she was traveling from one part of Spain to another with some other nuns and a priest to start a convent, and their way took them over a stream, she was thrown from her donkey. The story goes that our Lord said to her, 'That is how I treat my friends.' And she replied, 'And that is why You have so few of them.'"[11]

Dorothy sprinkled her writings with other stories that helped to explain her attraction from her earliest reading of Teresa to the model of this great saint:

> [Teresa] called life a "night spent at an uncomfortable inn." Once when she was trying to avoid that recreation hour which is set aside in convents for nuns to be together, the others insisted on her joining them, and she took castanets and danced. When some older nuns professed themselves shocked, she retorted, "One must do things sometimes to make life more bearable." After she was a superior she gave directions when the nuns became melancholy, "to feed them steak," and there were other delightful little touches to the story of her life which made me love her and feel close to her. I have since heard a priest friend of ours remark gloomily that one could go to hell imitating the imperfections of the saints, but these little incidents brought out in her biography made her delightfully near to me. So I decided to name my daughter after her.[12]

Dorothy recommended Teresa as a model, a saint "who was not content to be like those people who proceeded with the pace of hens about God's business, but like those people who on their own account were greatly daring in what they wished to do for God."[13] In a commentary in the December 1933 *Catholic Worker* on the enormity of the good work that could be done, including publishing *The Catholic Worker* newspaper, Dorothy quoted Teresa: "Never rest, never rest, there's no peace on earth, we say cheerfully with our patron saint, St. Teresa of Avila."

Dorothy, who spent so much of her time in writing and understood her vocation as that of a journalist, identified with Teresa's writing. Like Dorothy's, Teresa's writing took place in the midst of a very busy schedule in the work of founding convents and traveling all over Spain. It is amazing that Dorothy was able to write as much as she did in the midst of her travel on speaking engagements and founding Houses of Hospitality, not to mention living in busy Houses of Hospitality, and the quantity of letters she often spoke of answering. As she wrote of combining writing with babysitting (her daughter's children) Dorothy remembered in the October 1953 *Catholic Worker* that "St. Teresa of Avila always used to write by night rather than interrupt the work of her houses and foundations during the day."

With their personalist approach and the models of the saints, the Catholic Workers did not let themselves become discouraged by what often seemed insurmountable problems in the world, including war and the economic system and so much suffering that the guests in the Houses of Hospitality experienced. Dorothy quoted Teresa on the possibilities in life in cooperation with God's grace, no matter how difficult the times: "Let people 'not lay the blame on the times, for all times are times in which God will give His graces to those who serve Him in earnest.'" Dorothy recalled there Teresa's theme that the only way we can show our love for God is by our love for our fellows—adding, "And not an abstract love either....It is not by editing a paper or by writing and speaking that I am going to do penance and achieve sanctity. But by being truly loving and gentle and peaceful in the midst of trouble."[14]

Teresa's life was a union of contemplation and action, with love of neighbor and the building of communities flowing out of prayer. A central theme of her writings is that all are called to the summit of the mountain in prayer, that the mercy of God is reaching out to every soul, even though it may take a long time for a person to respond. What is required of each is a change of heart, a change so profound that a person will be able to perceive and follow the voice of God. Teresa, however, like so many great saints, did not allow the search for union with God in prayer to be separate from the love of neighbor: "The Lord asks of us only two things: love of His Majesty and love of our neighbor....We cannot know whether or not we love God, although there are strong indications for recognizing that we do love Him; but we can know whether we love our neighbor."[15]

Dorothy picked up especially on Teresa's theme of the incarnation, on the importance of meditating on the person of Jesus as the way to understand God. As she wrote in the September 1934 *Catholic Worker*, "St. Teresa of Avila said that we should meditate more on the love of God for us, rather than our love for Him. And she emphasizes His sacred Humanity and says that by never losing sight of that it is easier for us to realize that love." Dorothy, like Teresa, emphasized the humanity of Jesus and treasured the Blessed Sacrament. In that same article, addressed as "Another Letter to an Agnostic," Dorothy wrote about the importance of the Blessed Sacrament, the sacrament of the humanity of Jesus: "It took me a long time as a convert to realize the presence of Christ as *Man* in the Sacrament. He is the same Jesus who walked on earth, who slept in the boat as the tempest arose, who hungered in the desert, who prayed in the garden, who conversed with the woman by the well, who rested at the house of Martha and Mary, who wandered through the cornfields, picking the ears of corn to eat."

Dorothy concentrated on Teresa's practical approach and her teachings regarding the love of God and neighbor and the fruits of prayer, rather than on the mystic's famous visions and extraordinary experiences. Her response to a visitor to the Catholic Worker illustrates this: "The first time she came down she stood at the door dramatically and said to me abruptly, 'Do you have ecstasies and visions?' Poor dear, so hungry for mystical experience, even if secondhand, after a long life of faith. I was taken aback. 'Visions of unpaid bills,' I said abruptly."[16]

Dorothy read Teresa carefully on prayer. Merriman's research of Dorothy's unpublished writings confirms that at the very least by 1965 her reading had included *The Way of Perfection* and *The Interior Castle*.[17] In the March–April 1975 *Catholic Worker*, five years before her death, at a time when Dorothy was trying to gradually withdraw from her very active life and spend more time in contemplation, she again quoted Teresa in her reflections on prayer and on the stages of a person's life: "St. Teresa wrote of the three interior senses, the memory, the understanding and the will, so even if one withdraws, as I am trying to do from active work, these senses remain active....I am convinced that the life of prayer, to pray without ceasing, is one of prime importance."

In Teresa's day, reputable church people recognized the profundity of her spiritual life and defended her, and so the church authorities of New York recognized the spiritual depth and gifts of Dorothy Day. People asked why Cardinal Spellman, who was far from a pacifist, didn't close Dorothy Day down during World War II when she so strongly opposed the war. Apparently, the cardinal didn't want to take his chances in confronting a saint. The reflections that Dorothy shared in July-August 1964 with readers of *The Catholic Worker* and in other writings showed that criticisms and reports to the chancery actually brought her closer to the church because church officials invited her to have coffee and discuss complaints, without censuring her.

Both of these great women were active, strong, independent leaders—but what Teresa and Dorothy challenged most was the mediocrity in the lives of women and men. They saw the church not as an obstacle for women, but the source of their freedom and strength in a society that did not always value women's capabilities. They were powerful women who did not seek power for its own sake, but for service. While they recognized the humanness of church members, they never forgot that the church was instituted by Christ for the salvation of saints and sinners, even though the tremendous profundity of their lives overshadowed many of their contemporary church representatives. The choice made by Teresa and by Dorothy to direct their lives to God inspired lives of dedication and loving service in so many others, which had a powerful impact on the church and society. The depth of their commitment and their influence was rooted in the profundity of their spiritual lives.

Raymundo Panikkar reflected that it is difficult to categorize St. Teresa—perhaps in the same way that it is difficult to categorize Dorothy Day or Peter Maurin:

> Some saints reflect the perfections of God by their hidden and silent lives; some others are leaders, some are heroes of sacrifice and some victims of love; some have a rather weak human nature and some are real *genii* if we look at them from a human point of view. Sanctity is as manifold as man and his nature.

There is, however, not a little difficulty in classifying Teresa of Avila. If we class her as contemplative because she reached the highest degree of fruition of God and union with Him, we forget that she led an extremely active life. If we rank her among the teachers, we overlook the fact that she was also a reformer in the active field as well as a poet.[18]

St. Catherine of Siena, a Woman Who Influenced Her Times

In their early meetings Peter Maurin told Dorothy Day about the role of St. Catherine of Siena (1347–1380) in history and his hope that Dorothy would imitate her. As he described the way Catherine intervened with politicians and with the pope to try to resolve the thorny problems of the day, Peter exclaimed, "Ah, there was a saint who had an influence on her times!" Dorothy conjectured in *Loaves and Fishes* that it was perhaps because he noticed a life of St. Catherine of Siena in Dorothy's library that he began to speak of her.[1] Dorothy said, "Before he knew me well, Peter went about comparing me to a Catherine of Siena who would move mountains and have influence on governments, temporal and spiritual. He was a man of enthusiasm and always saw great talents in people."[2]

Reflecting much later, Dorothy wrote in the May 1973 *Catholic Worker* that she didn't rush into the public role that Peter described: "He would have liked to see in me another Catherine of Siena who would boldly confront bishops and Wall Street magnates. I disappointed him in that, preferring the second step in his program, reaching the poor through the works of feeding, clothing and sheltering, in what he called 'Houses of Hospitality,' where the Works of Mercy could be carried out."

Later on, however, Dorothy did at times play such a role, confronting officials over building-inspection problems for the Houses of Hospitality, air-raid drills, war, the proliferation of arms. Ultimately, she did, indeed, influence governments, temporal and spiritual. She had friendly discussions with Catholic bishops to address great questions of the time. One memorable example of her calling attention to an archbishop's failings was the picketing during the cemetery strike in New York when Cardinal Spellman had brought in seminarians as strikebreakers.

Dorothy frequently quoted Catherine of Siena in her writings over many years, especially emphasizing one particular saying: "All the way to heaven is heaven because He said 'I am the Way.'" This short quote was full of significance for Dorothy, as it was for Catherine. It relates to the ancient tradition of Jesus as the Way—the way to redemption and eternal life, the way to life rather than death, the way to love, the way to God. Catherine's quote about the Way provided the perspective for daily life at the Worker. Her emphasis on the joy of living in the present with Jesus as the Way gave spiritual and theological support to the personalist Catholic Worker ideals of not only hoping and praying for heaven some day, but working to create a world "where it is easier for people to be good," where life would be easier and more joyful for others. In the December 1971 *Catholic Worker*, Dorothy related Catherine's theology in their implementation of the spiritual as well as the corporal Works of Mercy: "Peter Maurin told us to reach the workers by the Works of Mercy. Counseling, consoling, comforting, holding out hope that 'all the way to heaven is heaven,' as St. Catherine of Siena said, go with the work of feeding, sheltering and clothing. Getting out a paper is part of this direct action—which is also to make people think."

Merriman has pointed out in her study of Dorothy's spirituality that Catherine's saying has a deep spiritual meaning: "It is based on John's gospel (14:6) and adapted from *The Dialogue*, in which the saint uses as her central image, Christ as the bridge between heaven and earth," by reason of his having joined himself with our humanity. In Catherine's imagery, there are three stairs, which are the three spiritual stages. The Son of God is the Way, in the image of a bridge.[3]

Dorothy, reticent about her own spiritual life, did not write in Catherine's extravagant language, but the great number of times she quoted the saint about "all the way to heaven is heaven" indicates that for her the phrase also held this kind of significance. As Merriman has said of Dorothy's interpretation of it, "The application was contemporary, yet intense, as was Catherine's."[4]

Dorothy used the phrase to simply describe the joy of the beauty of a day and God's creation in the April 1954 *Catholic Worker:* "All the way to heaven is heaven on a day like this." In the December 1947 *Catholic Worker* she wrote of St. Bernard's monastery in Latrobe, Pennsylvania, which she visited, describing life there in the joy of the Way: "It is a happy place, such a monastery, with its atmosphere of work and study and prayer. It reminds you of that saying of St. Catherine of Siena, "All the way to Heaven is Heaven, for He said, 'I am the Way.'"

The frequent quotation of this passage is understood by Merriman as a sign of Dorothy's "realized eschatology."[5] Dorothy was concerned about the kingdom of heaven, but also emphasized that eternal life begins now and that Christians are to help to bring it about. For example, Catherine's quote appeared in Dorothy's chapter on distributism and economics:

> We are not expecting utopia here on this earth. But God meant things to be much easier than we have made them. A man has a natural right to food, clothing and shelter. A certain amount of goods is necessary to lead a good life. A family needs work as well as bread. Property is proper to man. We must keep repeating these things. Eternal life begins now. "All the way to heaven is heaven, because He said, 'I am the Way.'" The Cross is there, of course, but "in the cross is joy of spirit." And love makes all things easy.[6]

For Miller, "All the way to heaven..." illustrated Dorothy's concept of time and eternity. He argues that for Dorothy the phrase is closely related to Berdyaev's thought, which influenced the Catholic Worker so much: "How many times she had quoted St. Catherine of Siena: 'All the way to Heaven is Heaven'; how many times she had emphasized 'now' in the building of the new earth, and how unconcerned she had always been about the time-made judgments of success or failure where the Catholic Worker movement was concerned."[7]

Dorothy applied Catherine's phrase to many situations in daily life in a practical theology that anticipated the *ressourcement* of the concept of the paschal mystery—the death *and* resurrection of Christ in the theology leading up to and predominating in the documents of the Second Vatican Council. Dorothy pointed out that while we are taught to suffer and embrace the cross, nevertheless, "All the way to heaven is heaven...."

Catherine, a very powerful woman in the church, had a great following of disciples that included many men, among them outstanding theologians. She lived at a time when papal leadership was at a low. The Papal States had armies and were in conflict with the various city-states in Italy. Pope Gregory XI had actually left Rome to stay in Avignon. Catherine's mission was to convince the pope to return to Rome, to reform the clergy and the administration of the Vatican. After Gregory's death there was a schism in the church, and there were actually two popes, each claiming to be the real one. Catherine supported the Roman claimant, Pope Urban VI, and helped to bring unity and peace between the pope and Florence, Italy, which had been under a papal interdict and had suffered economically because of it.

In spite of the human weaknesses of the popes and the deteriorated situation that existed at that time, Catherine, in describing the Holy Father, called him, "Our Dear Sweet Christ on Earth." She understood that theologically he was that, the Lord's representative on earth, even though he did not appear to be in any way a tower of strength. She also may have used the phrase to give him support in a difficult political situation. One of the issues of *The Catholic Worker* borrowed Catherine's use of this phrase in a banner headline on the front page referring to the death in 1939 of Pope Pius XI as the death of "Our Dear Sweet Christ on Earth." Dorothy, inspired by Catherine, was obviously not embarrassed to use such language.

Dorothy, who worked toward publication of more realistic lives of the saints, shared down-to-earth stories of saints with her readers. One example of her frankness in writing about them is her comment in the May 1947 *Catholic Worker:* "St. Catherine of Siena, it is said, talked until she put people to sleep and then woke them up to listen some more." Miller gave more details in his biography of Dorothy: "There is a story told of her [Catherine] that she could talk for twelve hours at a stretch, and when the listener, whether he was a priest or bishop, fell asleep under the barrage, used to wake him up and insist upon his continuing to listen."[8] Dorothy compared her with Peter Maurin, whose discussions would often go on all night.

Catherine became a Dominican sister when she was eighteen, but did not live in a convent. As part of a group known as the *Mantellate* (most of whom were widows), she lived in her own home and it was expected that she would care for the poor and the sick in the community. After she first received the habit, she spent three years in her room in solitude, silence, and prayer, only going out to Mass at the parish church in the mornings. At the end of three years she had an intense mystical experience, and at the Lord's request, left her room of solitude to cook and help her family, as well as the poor and sick of the community, but her contemplation continued in the midst of activity.

Catherine, like Peter Maurin and Dorothy Day, had a tremendous sense of the interdependence of the members of the Body of Christ. Her prayer was centered on Christ and his love, but also on the other members of the Body of Christ, those neighbors in whom she could serve the Lord. While the understanding of the Mystical Body of Christ was somewhat different in Catherine's time, it had then a social meaning that was also the way the Catholic Worker movement understood it: that a person's attitude and actions affected the church, the Body of Christ, and other people profoundly. Catherine quoted from her *Dialogue* with God:

> I have told you how every sin is done by means of your neighbors, because it deprives them of your loving charity, and it is charity that gives life to all virtue. So that selfish love which deprives your neighbors of your charity and affection is the principle and foundation of all evil.
>
> Every scandal, hatred, cruelty, and everything unbecoming springs from this root of selfish love. It has poisoned the whole

world and sickened the mystic body of holy Church and the universal body of Christianity.[9]

Catherine of Siena was declared a doctor of the church by Pope Paul VI. Suzanne Noffke emphasizes that while she had no formal schooling, St. Catherine was nevertheless "completely immersed in the main current of Catholic teaching, and she is impeccably orthodox even in subtle distinctions where one might expect her, untrained as she was in formal theology, to have slipped up at least occasionally."[10] Although Catherine's ideas were not new, but from the tradition, what was original with Catherine was "her capacity for fresh and vivid expression of that tradition."[11] This phrase could describe Peter Maurin and Dorothy Day as well as Catherine.

Dorothy printed various passages from *The Dialogue* of St. Catherine in *The Catholic Worker*, each bearing "the essential message that love for God is shown through love of neighbor." Dorothy's understanding of active love through Matthew 25, meeting Christ in contemporary guise in the poor, was confirmed for her by Catherine's example.[12] Dorothy, contemplative in action, identified with this contemplative in action from many centuries earlier. An example of her references to Catherine and love for God and neighbor over the years is the following quotation in the May 1941 issue of the paper:

> St. Catherine of Siena records our Lord as speaking to her thus:
> "I require of you that you love Me with that love wherewith I
> love you. This you cannot do to Me, because I have loved you
> without being loved....You cannot then, render to Me the love
> that I require of you; and therefore I have set you in the midst
> of others, in order that you may do to them what you cannot do
> to Me; that is, love them freely and without reserve, and with-
> out expecting any return from it; and then I consider done to
> Me whatever you do to them."

Catherine not only wrote that one's love for God must be expressed through love for neighbor. She personally cared for the sick and dying even during the outbreaks of the plague. Berdyaev later commented about her: "St. Catherine of Siena...attaches great importance to her ability to overcome her repulsion for the smells associated with sickness and sick people." He placed her care for the sick and suffering within the Catholic spirituality that "propounded the remarkable and profound doctrine of man's participation in the matter of expiation," associating her care for plague victims with "the intense experience of Calvary and of suffering in Christian mysticism, with the importance attached by Catholic saints and mystics to the care of the sick."[13]

The Catholic Worker not only featured articles about the saints, but illustrations as well. Dorothy's first conversation with Ade Bethune, whose art later filled the pages of *The Catholic Worker*, included depicting St. Catherine of Siena and Don Bosco in practical situations:

> She flipped through pages of the Missal. "In April we have the feast of Saint Catherine of Siena. She was the twenty-first child of a dyer and, rather than going to church to say prayers, she had to cook for her father's workmen. So she made the kitchen her temple. Catherine also visited a prisoner, who was to be executed, and helped him to repent."
>
> Could I make pictures of these great stories? Yes, I could. "Then, there is also John Bosco. He will be canonized this year and his day will come in April. He made a home for street boys. He taught them trades so they could earn an honest living by the work of their hands."
>
> A great program opened up before me. In the lives of two actual holy people of the fourteenth and nineteenth centuries, this energetic woman had sketched a lifetime plan for me....
>
> The March 1934 issue included all four of the pictures I had sent in. In the April issue, Dorothy printed two pictures of St. Catherine of Siena and one of St. John Bosco, all three accompanied by a little story she wrote.[14]

In the May 1970 *Catholic Worker*, Dorothy took the opportunity to reaffirm what she called her belief in the evangelical counsels as her means and methods in bringing about a better world, putting all in the perspective of Catherine's theology: "I'd like to reaffirm my belief in the nonviolence of poverty, chastity, and obedience as a means of achieving our ends as far as we can achieve them in this world. Of course I believe in working for the here and now, and not a pie in the sky. St. Catherine of Siena said, 'All the way to heaven is heaven, since Jesus said, I am the Way.'"

In describing the politics of the Catholic Worker in the October 1950 *Catholic Worker*, Dorothy went so far as to say that the real representatives of Christians are the saints, rather than elected representatives who may be distracted by power politics. She framed her argument in Catherine's famous phrase:

> Our representatives are the saints, the thinkers, uniting us in a community of interest, in a human relationship in this world and the next. And we have to work hard **in this world,** to begin our heaven now, to make a heaven for others...because this is the teaching of the saints.
>
> All the way to heaven is heaven, because Christ said, I am the Way. St. Catherine of Siena said this. We are to be Christ to each other, and see Christ in each other, and so we will love one another. "And for these there is no law," in the legal worldly sense, but only "the liberty of Christ."

What Merriman called Dorothy's realized eschatology was related to what Dorothy and Peter, along with Mounier and Berdyaev, called a correlation of the material and the spiritual. When Dorothy explained in the November 1962 *Catholic Worker* that human work was a key part of this correlation, she employed again Catherine's quote about showing one's love for Jesus by showing love for those around you, along with the famous, "All the way...":

> Man is a creature of body and soul, and he must work to live, he must work to be co-creator with God, taking raw materials and producing for man's needs. He becomes God-like, he is divinized not only through the sacrament but by his work, in which he imitates his Creator, in which he is truly "putting on Christ and putting off the old man, who is fearful and alienated from his material surrounding." He must be taught those words of Catherine of Siena, "I have left myself in the midst of you," Jesus said to her, "so that what you cannot do for me, you can do for those around you." And "All the way to Heaven is heaven, for He said, 'I am the Way.'"

When Dorothy wrote about a philosophy of work or about terrible conditions under which laborers had to work, she brought in Catherine's phrase to illustrate that one's daily work should not be a hell. The social order should be changed so that working conditions were not so dreadful. In the December 1946 *Catholic Worker*, using the example of the terrible darkness in which miners worked, month after month, she wrote, "All the way to heaven is heaven, because Christ said, 'I am the Way.' And work should be part of heaven, not part of hell."

Catherine's image of the way over the bridge as the way to heaven is contrasted in her *Dialogue* with the river that flows underneath it. The way over the bridge is Christ and the Christian way of perfection and the river below is the way of the devil, or as Merriman described it, following Catherine, nominal Christianity.[15] Merriman related this for Dorothy to the Lacouture/Hugo retreat,[16] to which she returned year after year in order to have the faith and strength to continue her work in the world. The retreat asked for "maximal" rather than minimal Christianity. In describing the retreat, which some critics had described as too rigorous, Dorothy defended it in Catherine's words, describing it as a time not only of rigor but of delight, including the phrase: "All the way to heaven is heaven, since He said, I am the Way."[17]

While Dorothy emphasized that much of the suffering in the world is caused by human beings, she believed that it also often held a deeper meaning in the spiritual life. Her reflections on the meaning of suffering resonated with Catherine's experience and teaching, employing the image of pruning. In the gospel and in the retreat, suffering is related to the image of the vine and the branches, drawing from the natural reality that plants and trees are cut back and pruned, appearing ugly and bare, only to blossom forth in their beauty. Dorothy wrote:

> Some suffering is more visible, some hidden. If we long for beauty, the more our faith is tried, as though by fire, by ugliness. The more we long for love, the more all human love will be pruned, and the more we will see the venom of hatred about us. It is a pruning, a cutting away of love so that it will grow strong and bear

much fruit. The more we long for power, the more we will destroy and tear down until we recognize our own weakness.[18]

Similarly, Catherine reported God's teaching on pruning in her *Dialogue:* "Just as the gardener prunes the branch that is joined to the vine so that it will yield more and better wine, but cuts off and throws into the fire the branch that is barren, so do I the true gardener act."[19]

For Dorothy the mystery of suffering was inseparable from the theology of the Mystical Body of Christ in which it is understood that one's faith, one's love, but also one's sins affect the other members. Facing daily the suffering of so many who came to the Houses of Hospitality, she found hope in St. Paul's teaching that "in my flesh I am completing what is lacking in Christ's afflictions" (Col 1:24), and that if we bear one another's burdens, suffering will be lightened:

> The stink of the world's injustice, and the world's indifference is all around us. The smell of the dead rat, the smell of acrid oil from the engines of the Pennsylvania railroad, the smell of boiled bones from Swift's. The smell of dying human beings....
>
> Compassion—it is a word meaning "to suffer with." If we all carry a little of the burden, it will be lightened. If we share in the suffering of the world, then some will not have to endure so heavy an affliction. It evens out. What you do here in New York, in Harrisburg, helps those in China, India, South Africa, Europe and Russia, as well as in the oasis where you are. You may think you are alone. But we are members one of another. We are children of God together....But still, suffering is a mystery as well as a penalty which we pay for others as well as ourselves.[20]

Catherine expressed this mystery succinctly: "The sufferings you endure will, through the power of charity, suffice to win both atonement and reward for you and others."[21]

Many of the things that were said of Catherine could be said equally well of Dorothy. For example, Giuliana Cavallini said of Catherine: "Faith was no abstraction to her, but a living tie with her Beloved. Her love of truth and her straightforward language aiming at the core of things come to us as a joyful relief from the many compromises and falsehoods weighing in on us in our daily life."[22]

Noffke calls Catherine a "mystic activist." In describing Catherine's balance of contemplation and action, Noffke brings out what is also so true of Dorothy, her "absolute refusal to compromise Truth as she experienced it in God," even in the face of much criticism:

> It was precisely what she experienced in contemplation that impelled her into action. And all that she touched or was touched by in her activity was present in her prayer....
>
> Her absolute refusal to compromise Truth as she experienced it in God, the urgency she felt to reverse every falsification she saw, made her look the naïve fool more than once....She was indeed a social mystic—but even more properly a mystic activist.[23]

Dorothy, who made a holy hour each day in the presence of the Blessed Sacrament, spent time in spiritual reading, practiced the presence of God, prayed the Liturgy of the Hours, and attended daily Mass, did not pray simply to refuel herself for further activity. Her prayer was integral to her daily life. She faced much criticism for her refusal to compromise the truth, especially in the Catholic Worker stand against the use of force and violence as incompatible with the gospel. In the face of so much tragedy and war in the world, Dorothy maintained hope through the words of the fathers of the church and of the saints, especially Catherine, who said, "All the way to Heaven is Heaven, because Jesus said 'I am the Way.'" In the September 1967 *Catholic Worker*, Dorothy wrote:

> One of the early Fathers of the Church once wrote that if we could stand on a mountain top and see all the misery and tragedy of the world, we could not survive the horror of it. Now we have television and can indeed see what is happening, can witness the murder of Lee Harvey Oswald, the torture of prisoners in Vietnam, the death of our own soldiers—horror upon horror, until the mind and soul are blunted, sated with blood,

blood which cries out to heaven. Indeed Jesus is in agony until the end of the world.

Juliana of Norwich said, and it is for our comfort, "the worst has already happened and been remedied." The worst being the Fall, and the remedy is still with us, "the same yesterday and today and forever." Even today, there are samplings of heaven, in love expressed, in peace maintained. "All the way to heaven is heaven, because He said, 'I am the Way.'" (All the way to hell can be hell too.)

Dostoevsky and Other Russian Writers

References to the works of Russian writers, especially Dostoevsky, appeared frequently in the writings of Dorothy Day. In *The Long Loneliness*, Dorothy described her early reading of the Russian writers and their impact on her search for faith. She longed to find living examples of the Christianity about which she had been reading: "The Russian writers appealed to me too, and I read everything of Dostoevsky, as well as the stories of Gorki and Tolstoy. Both Dostoevsky and Tolstoy made me cling to a faith in God, and yet I could not endure feeling an alien in it. I felt that my faith had nothing in common with that of Christians around me."[1]

In the July–August 1971 *Catholic Worker*, Dorothy wrote of the effect of this reading in her search for understanding in the midst of the harsh realities of sin, injustice, and destitution. These great works depicted beauty and joy in faith even in the midst of suffering and humiliation, related to the sufferings of Christ:

> From my high school years, I have been fascinated by Russia, and it was the books of Tolstoy, Dostoevsky, Turgenev and Chekhov which did much to bring about my conversion. I was haunted by Levin's struggle for faith in *Anna Karenina*, by the reminiscences of Fr. Zossima in *The Brothers Karamazov*, Raskolnikov's in *Crime and Punishment*, turning to the Gospels in Siberia, Turgenev's story of the crippled yet radiant peasant girl in one of his Sportman's Sketches, etc. There is a fascinating book, *The Humiliated [Face of] Christ in Russian Thought* by Gorodetzky...which brings out what I mean.

Dostoevsky was the Russian novelist who had the greatest impact on Dorothy. Miller stressed his influence: "She would, in

fact, throughout her life, be a passionate devotee of Russian literature, and in time the genius of Dostoevsky recommended itself
to her so strongly that his effect on her was oracular and remained
so all of her life."[2]

One of the passages from Dostoevsky that Dorothy frequently
quoted was, "All my life I have been haunted by God." Those who
have seen the play written and presented about her called *Haunted
by God* may not know that the quote comes from the character
Kirilloff in Dostoevsky's *The Possessed*. As Dorothy said in the
story of her conversion, "'All my life I have been tormented by
God' a character in one of Dostoevsky's books says. And that is the
way it was with me. You will notice that I quote the Russian
author a good deal....I quote him often because he had a profound
influence on my life, on my way of thinking."[3]

Stanley Vishnewski remembered that Dorothy once told
another Worker that "the only way he would ever understand the
Catholic Worker was by reading Dostoevsky."[4] As late as May
1973, Dorothy wrote in the paper of the significance of the great
writer on her life with the poor in the Houses of Hospitality: "I
do not think I could have carried on with a loving heart all these
years without Dostoevsky's understanding of poverty, suffering,
and drunkenness."

Dorothy and Peter Maurin, influenced very much by monastic
spirituality, could not embrace the way of consumerism and materialism that inhibits the freedom to follow the teachings and example of Jesus. The tradition of asceticism in living out the gospels in
the church, what they and Dostoevsky called the monastic way, was
much more attractive to them. In its second-anniversary issue, *The
Catholic Worker* published Maurin's Easy Essay presenting
Dostoevsky's wisdom on the monastic way in a paraphrase of the
words of Father Zossima from *The Brothers Karamazov:*

> Look at the worldly
> and all who set themselves up
> above the temple of God.
> Has not God's image and His
>   truth
>   been distorted in them?...

The world has proclaimed the
    reign of freedom
    but what do we see in this
    freedom of theirs?
Nothing but slavery
    and self-destruction.
The monastic way
    is very different.
Obedience, fasting and prayer,
    are laughed at,
    yet only through them
    lies the way
    to real, true freedom.

Before the advent of the Catholic Worker, during her time in Greenwich Village Dorothy had continued her reading of Dostoevsky. The bohemian life she was leading brought her disappointment and great suffering and in her search for meaning she turned to the Russian writer: "The characters, Alyosha and the Idiot, testified to Christ in us. I was moved to the depths of my being by the reading of these books during my early twenties when I, too, was tasting the bitterness and the dregs of life and shuddered at its hardness and cruelty."[5]

Dorothy's writing brought out her passionate response to Dostoevsky. She identified with some of the characters in his books in their spiritual experiences and learned from others whose pride and defiance kept them from the light of faith: "I could not hear of Sonya's reading the Gospel to Raskolnikov in *Crime and Punishment* without turning to it myself with love. I could not read Ippolyte's rejection of his ebbing life and defiance of God in *The Idiot* without being filled with an immense sense of gratitude to God for life and a desire to make some return."[6] Dorothy was especially touched by the sign of hope in *Crime and Punishment* when Raskolnikov took the New Testament that Sonya gave him to Siberia as he began his time of penal servitude. Her own identification as a writer with Dostoevsky is apparent in Dorothy's *Loaves and Fishes:*

Last week, stopping to browse as I passed a second-hand book-store on Fourth Avenue I came across a battered old copy of Dostoevsky's *The Insulted and the Injured....*

It is the story of a young author—it might be Dostoevsky himself—of the success of his first book, and of how he read it aloud to his foster father. The father said, "It's simply a little story, but it wrings your heart. What's happening all around you grows easier to understand and to remember, and you learn that the most downtrodden, humblest man is a man, too, and a brother." I thought as I read these words, "That is why *I* write."[7]

Dorothy not only read and reread Dostoevsky, but sought out the best studies of his works and integrated their ideas into her own commentaries about the great author. One of these books was Nicholas Berdyaev's *Dostoievsky*, in which Berdyaev describes the reading of the great writer as a profound spiritual experience. As she compared characters in the different novels, she referred to Berdyaev's insights and complained about her copy of his book: "Many of the ideas of *The Possessed* and *The Brothers [Karamozov]* are in that early novel. Versiloff a more mature Stavragin, Berdyaev said. I wish I had his book on Dostoevsky. I have only a defective copy with 50 pages missing."[8]

In her October 1953 "On Pilgrimage" column, Dorothy brought to her readers' attention Henri de Lubac's book, *The Drama of Atheist Humanism*. She told readers that the book "treats of the writings of Feuerbach, Marx, Nietzsche, Comte and the answer which Dostoevsky gives to their disbelief." De Lubac presents Dostoevsky as the alternative to the atheism, rationalism and positivism of the nineteenth century and as the one who had already responded to the profound questions raised especially by Nietzsche, who came after him: "He overcame the temptation to which Nietzsche was to succumb. That is what gives his work its extraordinary scope. Whoever plunges into it comes out immunized against the Nietzschean poison while aware of the greatness of Nietzsche." Both Dostoevsky and Nietzsche saw the profound problems of their time, and rejected the philosophies and ideologies that had developed to respond to them. However, the two thinkers had very different responses to what they perceived as a crisis of mores in civilization and two millennia of Christianity: "Nietzsche, in cursing our age, sees in it the heritage of the Gospel, while Dostoevsky, cursing it just as vigorously, sees in it the result of a denial of the Gospel."[9] The men took opposite paths to understanding the mysteries of life and eternity: "[W]hile one yielded to the lure of the path ostensibly leading to man who has become a god—to the 'overman'—the other took the way that leads to God who has been made man."[10]

Many who never read Dostoevsky became familiar with the themes and passages of Dostoevsky's writings through Dorothy. His phrase about the practice of love in *The Brothers Karamazov* became closely associated with Dorothy because she quoted it so often: "Love in practice is a harsh and dreadful thing compared to love in dreams." This phrase was so frequently used at the Worker that Miller's first book about the movement was entitled *A Harsh and Dreadful Love.* Miller recounted in that book Dostoevsky's story of the society lady who came to the monk to seek advice on faith and immortality and received these words as the monk's response:

> She is worried about immortality. It is such a problem; no one can prove it, "and I say to myself, 'What if I've been believing all my life, and when I come to die there's nothing but the burdocks growing on my grave? as I read in some author. It's awful. How can I prove it? How can I convince myself?'" Father Zossima responds with the Worker's radical answer, the one that Dorothy Day has repeatedly given as the substance of the Worker philosophy. To the woman's final demand of how, the monk replies: "By the experience of active love....In as far as you advance in love you will grow surer of the reality of God and of the immortality of your soul."
>
> And what was meant by "active love," the woman asked. She loved humanity. Often she dreamed of a life of service to the unfortunate that filled her with warmth. She could nurse the afflicted; she would be ready to kiss their wounds. But sometimes she wondered how she would react if she were not repaid in gratitude for her service. What if the patient "began abusing you and rudely commanding you, and complaining to the superior authorities of you (which often happens when people are in great suffering)—what then?" She could not bear ingratitude. "I

expect my payment at once—that is praise, and the repayment of love with love. Otherwise I am incapable of loving anyone."

Miller told how much Dostoevsky's response in these words of Father Zossima had meant for Dorothy Day and the Catholic Worker movement. In the day-to-day reality of loving the poor, the broken, who came to the Catholic Worker and the often-difficult stand for nonviolence and love of enemy, there was seldom an immediate response of gratitude. Dorothy frequently recalled Father Zossima's words to the woman:

"Love in action is a harsh and dreadful thing compared to love in dreams. Love in dreams is greedy for immediate action, rapidly performed and in the sight of all. Men will even give their lives if only the ordeal does not last long but is soon over, with all looking and applauding as though on the stage. But active love is labor and fortitude, and for some people, too, perhaps a complete science. But I predict that as you are getting further from your goal instead of nearer to it—at that very moment you will reach and behold clearly the miraculous power of the Lord, who has been all the time loving and mysteriously guiding you."[11]

In the July–August 1971 *Catholic Worker*, Dorothy noted that she, rather than Dostoevsky, was sometimes given credit for the phrase about love in practice being harsh and dreadful. She insisted on credit being given to the true author: "In my little brochure, printed by the Paulist Press, called *Meditations*, the publisher, or blurb writer, gave no credit to Dostoevsky's Fr. Zossima, but attributed the words to me in a paragraph on the back cover."

This phrase sustained Catholic Workers through difficult moments in the Houses of Hospitality when problems were overwhelming and guests were often anything but grateful. The rush of romantic emotion often associated with helping the poor faded after a few days or weeks of immersion in the work of hospitality, and Workers had to be sustained by something much deeper. Writing late in her life in the May Day 1976 issue of *The Catholic Worker*, Dorothy reflected on the history of the Catholic Worker movement, bringing in the famous statement from *The Brothers Karamazov* that helped the Catholic Workers keep a better perspective in difficult times: "Sometimes life is so hard, we foolishly look upon ourselves as martyrs, because it is almost as though we were literally sharing in the sufferings of those we serve. It is good to remember—to clutch to our aching hearts those sayings of Fr. Zossima—'Love in practice is a harsh and dreadful thing compared to love in dreams.'"

In the Worker movement the expression of love in practical terms did not mean that one must take the whole world on one's shoulders or that everything must be a grand gesture. Workers would not have survived long in Houses of Hospitality without the belief that small acts performed in love mattered. Dorothy retold another story from Dostoevsky that dramatically illustrated the practicality and importance of love for neighbor and its role in the Final Judgment, even though expressed in little things:

> Do you remember that little story that Grushenka tells in *The Brothers Karamazov?* "Once upon a time there was a peasant woman, and a very wicked woman she was. And she died and did not leave a single good deed behind. The devils caught her and plunged her into a lake of fire. So her guardian angel stood and wondered what good deed of hers he could remember to tell God. 'She once pulled up an onion in her garden,' said he, 'and gave it to a beggar woman.' And God answered: 'You take that onion then, hold it out to her on the lake, and let her take hold and be pulled out. And if you pull her out of the lake, let her come to Paradise, but if the onion breaks, then the woman must stay where she is.' The angel ran to the woman and held out the onion to her. 'Come,' said he, 'catch hold and I'll pull you out.' And he began cautiously pulling her out. He had just pulled her out when the other sinners in the lake, seeing how she was being drawn out, began catching hold of her so as to be pulled out with her. But she was a very wicked woman and she began kicking them. 'I'm to be pulled out, not you. It's my onion, not yours.' As soon as she said that, the onion broke. And the woman fell into the lake and she is burning there to this day. So the angel wept and went away."[12]

Dorothy added her own reflection to Dostoevsky's onion story, a commentary on her life and spirituality: "Sometimes in thinking and wondering at God's goodness to me, I have thought that it was because I gave away an onion. Because I sincerely loved His poor, He taught me to know Him. And when I think of the little I ever did, I am filled with hope and love for all those others devoted to the cause of social justice."[13]

A person might be considered foolish in giving away onions or in radically following the gospel in other ways. Dorothy referred in the May 1974 *Catholic Worker* to the character of Myshkin, especially as described by the term *holy fool*, which she said had a "special significance in Russian literature and is used to describe Myshkin in *The Idiot*, a truly Christ-like figure." She noted here as she did on other occasions that so many at the Catholic Worker were considered "holy fools in the eyes of our friends and readers." She especially identified Myshkin with Peter Maurin when he was beginning to become ill in the years before his death and the noise in the house, the constant talking by guests with their problems, was overwhelming to him. He was unable to think, but he never complained: "Thinking of Peter, Dorothy then thought of Dostoevsky's Prince Myshkin, who, like Maurin, 'is described as entirely passive, willingly accepts suffering, is easily put upon, answers offense by begging forgiveness, and exaggerates the good in others while constantly overlooking evil.' Dostoevsky, she said, described this 'submissiveness' as 'the most fearful force that can exist in the world.'"[14]

Another of Dostoevsky's lines that has sometimes been attributed to Dorothy instead of to the Russian author is: "The world will be saved by beauty." Her January 1973 "On Pilgrimage" column explained why she quoted it so frequently:

> "Beauty will save the world," Dostoevsky wrote. I just looked up this quotation in Konstantin Mochulsky's *Dostoevsky, His Life and Work*....In a paragraph on page 224, in speaking of art, Dostoevsky is quoted as saying, "It has its own integral organic life and it answers man's innate need of beauty without which, perhaps he might not want to live upon earth...."
>
> It was Jack English who, in one of his letters from the Trappist Monastery in Georgia, wrote to me that line from Dostoevsky's notebook, "Beauty will save the world."

Miller's commentary on what beauty meant to Dorothy brought together the words of St. John of the Cross she often quoted, "At the end of life we shall be judged on love." Noting that the words *love* and *beauty* have often come to have different meanings than their original, he described the beauty meant by Dorothy and by Dostoevsky: "In this era when even the word 'love' means something that has lost all harmony with an ideal of beauty and of the eternal, Dorothy has lived for love and suffered for love in a way that is a striking example of how beauty can be restored. When Dostoevsky's doddering old professor says that 'beauty will save the world,' he is referring to the beauty that is built on love."[15]

In the midst of busy Houses of Hospitality, Dorothy sometimes found time to listen to beautiful music on the radio and even on occasion to attend the opera when someone was kind enough to donate tickets. She was also sometimes able to create beauty in simplicity and even poverty and appreciated the gift of others who did so. She told the story of what happened when one family joined a Catholic Worker farm and destroyed the beauty in the name of appearing to be poor:

> Another family moving in with us, on one of our Catholic Worker farms, felt that the beautifying which had made the farmhouse and its surroundings a charming spot was not consistent with a profession of poverty. They broke up the rustic benches and fence, built by one of the men from the Bowery who had stayed with us, and used them for firewood. The garden surrounding the statue of the Blessed Virgin, where we used to say the rosary, was trampled down and made into a wood yard filled with chips and scraps left from the axe that chopped the family wood. It was the same with the house: the curtains were taken down, the floor remained bare, there were no pictures— the place became a scene of stark poverty, and a visiting bishop was appalled at the "poverty." It had looked quite comfortable before, and one did not think of the crowded bedrooms or the outhouse down the hill, or the outdoor cistern and well where water had to be pumped and put on the wood stove in the kitchen to heat. Not all *these* hardships were evident.[16]

Dorothy wrote a reflection on how beauty does not have to be expensive, but can be found in poor neighborhoods in her "On

Pilgrimage" column in the February 1955 *Catholic Worker*. She had been traveling in Minnesota: "There is a poor little church down in that section, a frame building and painted a bright swampy green. It was light and warm inside and had the feeling of a much-loved place. There was a shrine to Our Lady of Guadalupe and no matter how garish the decorations, this presentation of Our Lady is always of unutterable beauty. She is the patroness of the Americas and I love to visit her in the shrines, and make special requests there. They are usually in the neighborhoods of the poor."

Dorothy's reflections on beauty and Dostoevsky's phrase included her appreciation of the beauty of nature and her ability to see beauty even in those who were suffering and poor—perhaps especially in the faces of the suffering and poor, because like the Russian authors she recognized the humiliated face of Christ in the poor.

Many aspects of the active life of the Catholic Worker were considered foolish or rash by some observers. Admirers of the Works of Mercy, for example, often could not understand protests that led to jail. However, Dorothy wrote about her jail experiences as a part of the reality of her living of the gospel. Having been jailed on several occasions for her principles, Dorothy understood the despair and suffering of prisoners and the difficulty of maintaining one's faith and hope in prison. She told how even before she became a Catholic she had agreed with Tolstoy's view of prisons, that those who were locked away often represented a failed social and economic system as much as criminality: "Before I had merely read about prison life and had agreed with Tolstoy that such punishment of criminals was futile when we were guilty for permitting such a system as ours to exist and that we, too, should bear the penalty for the crimes committed by those unfortunate ones. We all formed part of one body, a social body, and how could any limb of that body commit a crime alone?"[17]

Dorothy, who knew so well activists who work heroically for various causes, appreciated Tolstoy's commentary on the irony of a situation in which sometimes those who talk so much about love, universal love, and brotherhood are not willing to speak to each other: "[Tolstoy] tells of political prisoners in a long prison train, enduring chains and persecution for their love for their brothers, ignoring those same brothers on the long trek to Siberia."[18]

Dorothy quoted Dostoevsky on prisons numerous times. His own experience as a prisoner in Siberia lent authenticity to his writings. In the September 1940 *Catholic Worker*, she mentioned that several of his books give the message that "it is possible for a man to lead a perfect life even in jail." In the January 1974 issue, she said she had a "goodly selection of books about prisons and prisoners, beginning with Dostoevsky's *House of the Dead*," where he wrote about his experience in prison in Siberia.

In the October–November 1974 *Catholic Worker*, Dorothy wrote of Dostoevsky's experience at forced labor, relating it to the need for a philosophy of work, a theme frequently explored in the movement. In that article Dostoevsky's words about the devastating effects of having to do meaningless work supported Dorothy's critique of the assembly line in factory work. Manual labor is not to be despised unless the tasks are meaningless and useless: "Our Maggie, when she was saving money towards settling in West Virginia, had a job in a neighboring village from eleven at night until seven in the morning, on an assembly line where a few motions glued a Timex watch box together, which box is discarded of course as soon as the watch is taken out. Small factory work in the country would not be so bad if something useful were being turned out. But what a torture to do such useless work! I am reminded of the words of Dostoevsky, in *The House of the Dead*."

As he did in his writings on prisons, Dostoevsky explored in other characters and situations the questions of freedom or the lack of freedom for the human person and its consequences for those who exercise it. In difficult times, facing the practical consequences of freedom within the Catholic Worker movement, Dorothy remembered the scene of the Grand Inquisitor in *The Brothers Karamazov*. She included that scene in a recommended reading list in her early book, *House of Hospitality*, where she described feeling low and oppressed about discouraged Catholic Workers who were weary of the idea of freedom and personal responsibility: "Today I just happened to light on Dostoevsky's 'Grand Inquisitor' which was most apropos. Freedom—how men hate and chafe under it, how unhappy they are with it."[19]

In addition to her own extensive reading of Dostoevsky's books, Berdyaev's commentary was one of Dorothy's sources for understanding his profound view of freedom. Berdyaev pointed out that it was often not understood that freedom was the greatest theme in Dostoevsky's writing, a freedom that often brought suffering and tragedy. Berdyaev outlined the fundamental question of freedom and Christianity posed in the Grand Inquisitor passage:

> For Dostoevsky the theme of man and his destiny is in the first place the theme of freedom, that freedom is the centre of his conception of the world, that his hidden pathos is a pathos of freedom....What has been called his "cruelty" is directly associated with this. He was "cruel" because he would not relieve man of his burden of freedom, he would not deliver him from suffering at the price of such a loss, he insisted that man must accept an enormous responsibility corresponding to his dignity as a free being.[20]

Not only does the Inquisitor not believe in God, he has lost faith in the human person. In his commentary on the Grand Inquisitor scene, Berdyaev noted that the words of the Inquisitor would actually take away freedom because he cleverly does away with the concept of sin and evil:

> [The Grand Inquisitor] has a secret: he does not believe in God or in any meaning of life which alone could give sense to people's suffering in his name, and, having lost this belief, he sees that large numbers of persons have not the strength to bear the burden of freedom conferred by Christ. Not believing in God, the Grand Inquisitor also ceases to believe in man, for they are two aspects of the same faith; Christianity is the religion of the God-man and therefore demands belief in both God and man. But the idea of the God-man, the uniting of the divine and human principles in one freedom, is precisely the idea that the Grand Inquisitor will not have....He must escape from

Christian freedom and its burden of discriminating and choosing between good and evil.[21]

Berdyaev pointed out that the choice is between freedom with all its risks and suffering or "contentment without freedom." The Grand Inquisitor does not believe that most people can handle freedom and that therefore only a few should make the decisions. Christianity, on the contrary, respects the great destiny of humankind, made in the image and likeness of God, and therefore free: "A man can bear neither his own sufferings nor those of other people, yet without suffering there can be no liberty of choice, so we are faced with a dilemma: on the one side, freedom; on the other, contentment, well-being, rationalized organization of life; either freedom with suffering or contentment without freedom. An overwhelming majority of people choose the last."[22] For Dostoevsky, however, it is in Christ that liberty and divine harmony are brought together and that one can find meaning and hope. The freedom of God and the freedom of human persons are "reconciled in the grace of freely-given love."[23]

Struggling with questions of freedom and seeking to alleviate suffering, loneliness, meaninglessness, people often turn to community, to friends, and attempt to anticipate in the here and now the communion that can only be fully realized in God and in the communion of saints. The Grand Inquisitor not only spoke of bread as a temptation, but of community. Miller noted that Peter and Dorothy recognized that the temptation is to try to build community only within time, without the perspective of the eternal, a community that may be illusory:

> Community, as the Inquisitor declares, is the ultimate quest of every person, more powerful than the need for bread, although the two are curiously and inextricably interwoven. Of community, there are two visions. There is the vision of a community of eternity that has been sustained by hope over much of the history of humankind by the belief in immortality. The other vision, which has arisen in this recent moment of history, is one of a community that can be achieved in time as the only community that can be had because there is no eternity. Since the Inquisitor is "wise," he knows that there can be no community

in time because time destroys all that it touches. Thus, says the Inquisitor, all that can be done for people to satisfy this—the main "craving" of every soul—is to give them illusions of community: rallies, parades, stirring exhortations, games, and "innocent dances."[24]

Community and friendship in the perspective of the eternal was a goal of the Catholic Worker—to counteract the "long loneliness." Dorothy's friendship of many years with Helene Iswolsky is an example. Iswolsky, who in her retirement eventually came to live at the Catholic Worker farm at Tivoli, gave talks at the Worker on the Russian writers both she and Dorothy loved. Dorothy summarized one of Helene's lectures at the Catholic Worker on three great Russian authors in the October 1949 *Catholic Worker*, where Dorothy tantalizingly hinted at some of the great themes of their writings: "The first week in September we had Helene Iswolsky at the farm at Newburgh, giving a course on Dostoevsky, Tolstoy and Soloviev, the three great Russians....She spoke of Soloviev who told of the glories of the Incarnation, and is the link between the East and the West. She spoke of the three great men who emphasized the dignity of the human person....These three men wrote of the struggle of man towards God and to all of them the golden key which opened the doors of prisons and led out of darkness was the key of love."

Dorothy's commentary on one of Helene's lectures emphasized the need for people to have the will to change the economic system, not to be "escapists," not accept a state of the world in which people might well say, "Why bring children into the world, the world being what it is?" Writing of Iswolsky's talk on Dostoevsky's love for life, Dorothy emphasized that fighting for a cause such as a better economic system was part of "the zest for life, that appreciation of the value of life, the gift of life," which Dostoevsky had never lost after his experience of almost being executed by a firing squad.

Dorothy and Helene shared not only a love for the Russian writers, but also for the Eastern liturgy of the Catholic Church and ecumenism with the Orthodox Church. Iswolsky's life work of ecumenism between Christian East and West was first inspired by

Soloviev, whom she later called her "great master" and that "great pioneer of ecumenism."

Helene brought the thought of Soloviev to the *Catholic Worker* when much of his work was not available in English. Dorothy mentioned Soloviev in her reflections in the November 1971 *Catholic Worker*, describing him as "that philosopher of ecumenism, who so influenced Dostoevsky's thinking," and noted that Helene Iswolsky was speaking to her as she wrote.

Because she was interested in ecumenism and also because of her love for the Russian liturgy, Dorothy appreciated very much Soloviev's ecumenism. She read Soloviev on love and sexuality and quoted from his book, *The Meaning of Love*. Convinced that the expression of sexuality in marriage had to do with the imagery of God's love for each person and the Body of Christ, Dorothy did not accept so-called studies of sexuality which defended sexual experiences not related to marriage (such as pedophilia) on the basis that they were common phenomena. When the Kinsey Report was published, for example, her comment was scathing: "'All the way to heaven is heaven,' said St. Catherine of Siena, 'because He said, I am the Way.' We have too many samples of hell, and the Kinsey report is one of them."[25] Dorothy presented Soloviev as a beautiful alternative to Kinsey.

Not only did Soloviev insist that sexuality had a much deeper meaning than what was reflected in something like the Kinsey Report, but he also argued that love is real, as well as profound. Dorothy wrote, "Recently I have been reading *The Meaning of Love* by Soloviev, and he refuses to accept the idea, so universally accepted, that love is an illusion, a lure, succumbed to so that the purpose of procreation is fulfilled, and then vanishing."[26] Love, argued Soloviev, was the restoration of the image of God in the world of matter, in the incarnation. Reflecting on the difficulty of continuing to love when the first special emotion and idealization of the loved one has passed, Dorothy looked to Soloviev for insight and shared a passage from his writing:

> It is well known to everyone that in love there inevitably exists a special idealization of the beloved object, which presents itself

to the lover in an entirely different light from that in which out-
siders see it....

Each man comprises in himself the image of God.
Theoretically and in the abstract, this Divine image is known to
us in mind and through mind, but in love it is known in the concrete and in life. And if this revelation of the ideal nature, ordi-
narily concealed by its material manifestation, is not confined in
love to an inward feeling, but at times becomes noticeable also
in the sphere of external feelings, then so much greater is the
significance we are bound to acknowledge for love as being
from the very first the visible restoration of the Divine image in
the world of matter....[27]

Soloviev spoke of abiding faith in conjugal love, so difficult in
a materialistic, deterministic society:

But, in order for the faith to be a living faith, it must set itself
steadfastly against that existing society where meaningless
chance builds its dominion upon the play of animal passions
and, still worse, human passions. Against these hostile powers,
believing faith has only one defensive weapon—endurance to
the end. To earn its bliss, it must take up its cross. In our materialistic society it is impossible to preserve true love, unless we
understand and accept it as a moral achievement. Not without
reason does the Orthodox Church in her *marriage* ceremony
make mention of holy *martyrs* and compare their crowns to the
bridal crowns.[28]

In an article entitled "To Die for Love" in the September
1948 *Catholic Worker*, Dorothy wrote that the problem of love and
fidelity, of considering real love an unlasting illusion, affected
most people. Reflecting there on *The Meaning of Love*, she insisted
on "the need to study this problem, to seek the growth of this
love, so that the force of love may be set loose in the world today,
to combat the terrible force of violence that we have unloosed."

It was not only Iswolsky who linked Dostoevsky and Soloviev.
Theologian Hans Urs von Balthasar contended that their writings
reflect their friendship so closely that it is difficult to know which of
them conceived some of the characters in Dostoevsky's novels:
"Between Soloviev and Dostoevsky there was the closest friendship

and the most intimate commerce of soul and mind, so that (for instance) we do not know which of them first conceived the figure of the Grand Inquisitor...."[29] Balthasar also described the oneness of their thought by noting that one of Dorothy's most often quoted themes from Dostoevsky, the one on beauty, was also used by Soloviev, who "prefaced his essay on natural aesthetics with Dostoevsky's dictum that 'beauty will save the world.'"[30]

Marina Kostalevsky notes that although Dostoevsky is very widely read and that books of criticism of his works abound, one aspect that especially has not been studied enough is the key role and influence of Soloviev in Dostoevsky's life and writing, and vice versa.[31] (As usual, the Catholic Worker was on the cutting edge of ideas in making these connections, in this case through the insights of Helene Iswolsky.) Kostalevsky describes Soloviev's series of lectures on the God-man, Christ, which Dostoevsky "attended conscientiously," and which attracted large numbers of young people in an age of rationalism when few spoke of faith. She analyzes Dostoevsky's novels around this theme, making the contrast between the God-man of the incarnation and the man-god, the superman of anti-theists like Nietzsche, which appealed so much to Hitler.

The ethics of Dostoevsky and Soloviev, which flowed from their understanding of the incarnation, was dramatically expressed in Dostoevsky's greatest novels, where he confronted the consequences of the philosophy of utilitarianism and the exaggerated idea making a god out of oneself. One example is the student who said in *Crime and Punishment:* "Kill her, take her money and with the help of it devote oneself to the service of humanity and the good of all. What do you think, would not one tiny crime be wiped out by thousands of good deeds?...One death, and a hundred lives in exchange—it's simple arithmetic!" Other characters present the commercial enlightened self-interest view: "Science now tells us, love yourself before all men, for everything in the world rests on self-interest." The philosophical arguments were placed in the character's mouth: "Here's a theory of a sort, the same one by which I for instance consider that a single misdeed is permissible if the principal aim is right."[32]

Berdyaev had profoundly addressed Dostoevsky's treatment of these questions in his book that Dorothy studied. What is ethical? What is allowable? Everything? To what lengths can expediency and utilitarianism justify the most terrible actions? If not, why not?

It is a question that always troubled Dostoevsky, and he was always putting it in one form or another: it is behind *Crime and Punishment* and, to a considerable extent, *The Possessed* and *The Brothers Karamazov*. Free man is faced with this dilemma. Are there moral norms and limits in my nature or may I venture to do anything? When freedom has degenerated into self-will it recognizes nothing as sacred or forbidden, for if there be no god but man then everything is allowable and man can try himself out at will....

All things are not allowable because, as immanent experience proves, human nature is created in the image of God and every man has an absolute value in himself and as such. The spiritual nature of man forbids the arbitrary killing of the least and most harmful of men....Our neighbor is more precious than an abstract notion, any human life and person is worth more here and now than some future bettering of society. That is the Christian conception, and it is Dostoevsky's.[33]

Through many of his characters Dostoevsky explored the mystery of suffering and evil and tragedy. His dramatic presentations repudiating the idea of killing a human being for whatever supposed "higher end" affirmed for Dorothy her stand against killing. Reflecting on the worst violence of war, Dorothy turned again to the Grand Inquisitor scene in the March 1966 *Catholic Worker* when she wrote,

Of course, there were, and always will be, great gaps in my understanding of such questions as the problem of evil in the world and God's permission of it. I cringe still at Ivan Karamazov's portrayal of "a God that permits" the torture of children, such torture as is going on today in the burning alive of babies in Vietnam. Theologians debate situation ethics and the new morality (leaving out of account the problem of means and ends) while the screams of the flaming human torches, civilians and soldiers, rise high to heaven. The only conclusion I have ever been able to reach is that we must pray to God to increase our faith, a faith without which one cannot love or hope. "Lord, I believe, help thou my unbelief."

Berdyaev argued that Dostoevsky's novels brought a very profound light to a confused world often filled with darkness, the light of Christ himself:

> He showed that the light in our darkness is Christ, that the most abandoned individual still retains God's image and likeness, that we must love such an one as our neighbour and respect his freedom. Dostoevsky takes us into very dark places but he does not let darkness have the last word; his books do not leave us with an impression of sombre and despairing pessimism, because with the darkness there goes a great light. Christ is victorious over the world and irradiates all. Dostoevsky's Christianity was light-bearing, the Christianity of St. John.[34]

Dostoevsky's books were first published and Soloviev gave his first lectures during an age of rationalism. Their ideas were not in vogue. Literary critics were very hard on Dostoevsky. Perhaps it took a profoundly spiritual person to understand him. As Berdyaev said: "The fact is that really to 'get inside' Dostoevsky it is necessary to have a certain sort of soul—one in some way akin to his own—and we had to wait for the spiritual and intellectual movement which marked the beginning of the twentieth century before such souls could be found."[35]

One of those souls was Dorothy Day.

The Famous Retreat

When Father Onesimus Lacouture, SJ, died in 1951, Dorothy Day attended his funeral and wrote his obituary in the December 12, 1951, *Catholic Worker.* She declared then that Peter Maurin and Father Lacouture were the two men who had had the most influence on her life and so, in a way, on the life of the Catholic Worker.

Dorothy had known Lacouture first only through the priests who gave the retreat he founded, especially Josephite Father Pacifique Roy and Father John J. Hugo, a diocesan priest from Pittsburgh who spread the retreat throughout the United States. Later she went to visit him in Canada. In the obituary she referred to her visit: "The last time I had seen Fr. Lacouture was at Sudbury, Canada, where I had gone to speak. He was procurator of the college there and we talked all one day of the spiritual life and of the retreats which we had been having since we met Father Pacifique Roy, another Canadian, in 1940, when he had introduced us to the work of Fr. Lacouture." Dorothy's obituary spoke of Father Lacouture, who taught us "how to die to ourselves, to live in Christ," and the folly of the cross. "I should like to see on his gravestone the words, 'He made all things new,'" she said, "because his teaching of the love of God so aroused our love in turn, that a sense of the sacramentality of life was restored for us, and a new meaning and vigor was given to our lives."

Dorothy was so overwhelmed with the beauty of the retreat and its message of the gospel that she encouraged others to make it and made it herself over twenty times. Hoping that the spirituality of the retreat would become rooted in all those associated with the Catholic Worker movement, she arranged for the retreats to be given at the Worker, especially the farms. Dorothy's efforts to promulgate the retreat soon included not only Catholic Workers and readers of the paper in general, but also other friends, priests, and bishops, and especially the poor. She called the retreat "the bread of the strong": "To us the retreat was the good news. We made it as often as we could, and refreshed ourselves with days of recollection....It is not only for others that I must have these retreats....I too must nourish myself to do the work I have undertaken; I too must drink at these good springs so that I may not be an empty cistern and unable to help others."[1]

The retreat consisted of a week of silence (one could bring only the Bible and a writing pad) and several conferences a day given by the retreat master. Based on the scriptures, the spirituality of St. John of the Cross, and the first week (of four weeks) of the Ignatian Exercises, it was a liberating spiritual experience for Dorothy. "This is what I was looking for in the way of an explanation of the Christian life," she exulted during a retreat with Father Hugo. "I saw things as a whole for the first time with a delight, a joy, an excitement which is hard to describe. This is what I expected when I became a Catholic."[2]

Dorothy believed that the retreat was crucial to the development of sanctity meant for all Christians. She could not accept minimalist Christianity. "So little is expected of lay people," she said, quoting a Benedictine friend. "The moral theology we are taught is to get us into heaven with scorched behinds. What kind of an unwilling, ungenerous love of God is this," she continued. "We do little enough, and when we try to do more we are lectured on Jansenism! I don't even know what it is. I only know that I am self-indulgent."[3]

Like those who gave the retreat, Dorothy was sometimes criticized for holding up the gospel call to give up all to follow Jesus and his command, "Be perfect, as your heavenly Father is perfect," as norms of conduct for laypeople. In *House of Hospitality*, before she made the retreat, she had already written about what it meant to seek perfection, to grow in holiness, to live the gospel. She presented the challenge to young people who came to the Worker from schools and colleges talking about security, a weekly wage:

Christ told Peter to put aside his nets and follow Him. He told the rich young man to sell what he had and give to the poor and follow Him. He said that those who lost their lives for His sake should find them. He told people to take no thought for the morrow. He told His followers that if anyone begged for their coats to give up their cloaks too. He spoke of feeding the poor, sheltering the homeless, of visiting those in prison and the sick and also of instructing the ignorant. He said, "Inasmuch as ye have done it unto the least of these, ye have done it unto Me." He said: "Be ye therefore perfect as your heavenly Father is perfect."[4]

Dorothy recounted in the May 1947 *Catholic Worker* that it was Peter Maurin who had introduced her and the other Catholic Workers to Léon Bloy and his insistence that all Christians must strive to be saints; that it was Peter who had shared with them Pope Pius XI's encyclical on St. Francis de Sales in which he emphasized that all are called to be saints, laymen and religious, that this is our goal, union with God:

"Be perfect
as your Heavenly Father
is perfect."
"If you want
to be perfect
sell all you have,
give it to the poor
and follow Me."
–*New Testament.*
The law of holiness
embraces all men
and admits
of no exception.

Dorothy came to the Lacouture retreat with a great deal of spiritual formation and familiarity with the great classics on the spiritual life. William Portier describes in the September–October 2002 *Houston Catholic Worker* the influence of Dorothy's first spiritual director and the roots of the spirituality he shared with her:

Day found [Paulist Father] McSorley at a time in her life when she needed spiritual "solid food" (Heb 5:14; 1 Cor 3:2) and he did not hesitate to give it to her. He drew upon the [Isaac] Hecker tradition he received from Walter Elliott. In Hecker's own practice of spiritual direction, Louis Lallemant (1587–1635) and Jean Pierre de Caussade (1675–1751) figured prominently. During the 1860's, Hecker gave Lallemant's *Spiritual Doctrine* (especially the section on "Purity of Heart") to those under his direction. In another century, McSorley gave it to Day. "Now reading Father Louis Lallemant's *Spiritual Teaching*," she wrote in 1939, "recommended by Father McSorley." In a 1966 column, she recalled that McSorley had also given her Caussade's *Abandonment to Divine Providence*. "We who are such activists, need more of this teaching." Alluding to the controversy that led Caussade to publish under another Jesuit's name, she assured readers: "No danger of Quietism with Catholic Worker enthusiasts."

The retreat became known in the Catholic Worker movement as "The Retreat." Its purpose was conversion, *metanoia*, a radical change of heart and mind, such as John the Baptist and Jesus demanded as they began to preach. The retreat teaching was that Christians are saved by love, a love that goes way beyond keeping rules. Those who gave the retreat taught that every word, every thought and prayer, every action should be infused with God's love. Retreat masters cautioned about not becoming stuck on the "samples" of God's glory here on earth, but relinquishing them in order to obtain the pearl of great price. They reminded retreatants of a line from St. Augustine that Dorothy often quoted from the retreat: "He who says he has done enough has already perished."

Dorothy's first contact with the retreat came from Father Roy, a Josephite priest from Quebec, who later visited the Catholic Worker frequently and spent time there as a carpenter. She described his first visit to the Catholic Worker when he talked for many hours about the ideas from the retreat:

> We were sitting in the dining room having our morning coffee when Father Roy started to talk to us about the love of God and what it should mean in our lives. He began with the Sermon on the Mount, holding us spellbound, so glowing was his talk, so

heartfelt. People came and went, we were called to the telephone again and again, but still Father Roy went on talking to all who would listen. The men came in from the soup kettles in the kitchen which were being prepared for the soup line and stayed to listen, tables were set around us and the people came in and were fed and went out again, and still Father talked, and so the day went....

Father Roy talked to us of nature and the supernatural, how God became man that man might become God, how we were under the obligation of putting off the old man and putting on Christ, how we had been made the sons of God, by the seed of supernatural life planted in us at our baptism, and of the necessity we were under to see that the seed grew and flourished. We had to aim at perfection; we had to be guided by the folly of the Cross.[5]

Dorothy compared the impact of the experience of the retreat to that of those who met the Lord in the gospels on the way to Emmaus: "They knew Him then in the breaking of bread. They said to each other, 'Was not our heart burning within us, whilst He spoke to us on the way?'"[6]

"Love is the measure by which we shall be judged," Father Roy, like the other retreat masters, said repeatedly, quoting St. John of the Cross. This saying—"Love is the measure"—became a byword to Dorothy. And again from St. John of the Cross, "Where there is no love, put love and you will take out love."

"To give and not to take," Peter Maurin often said, "that is what makes man human." Love, Father Roy said, is what makes us want to give. Giving is the essence of religious life:...giving space in one's life and home, giving a welcome, giving forgiveness, giving love, even giving one's life. Don't save. Don't store up "treasure which moth and rust attack." Live by the rule of giving.[7]

Another theme of the retreat was sowing. As St. Paul said, "The point is this: the one who sows sparingly will also reap sparingly, and the one who sows bountifully will also reap bountifully" (2 Cor 9:6). Father Roy challenged Christians:

Suppose you want to go to California and it costs a hundred dollars. You have fifteen. It is not enough. So give it away. Give it to the poor. Then you suddenly have twenty-five, and that is not enough and so the only thing to do is to give it away too. Even seventy-five. That is not enough. Tell the Lord you need more. Throw it away recklessly. You will get it back a hundredfold....Maybe it will cover your spiritual needs, and not just your physical. But sow, sow! And as you sow, so shall you reap. He who sows sparingly, reaps sparingly.[8]

It was Father Roy who sent Dorothy and the Catholic Workers to Father John Hugo. In her obituary of Father Roy in the November 1954 *Catholic Worker*, Dorothy quoted him as saying, "The man who can really give the retreat is Father Hugo."

Dorothy made the retreat many times with Father Hugo, who came to be a tremendous influence in her life. His presence and spiritual direction at the retreats was a great encouragement to Dorothy in the radical and courageous stands she took, especially in regard to economics and war. Father Hugo's book *Applied Christianity*, a first collection of retreat conferences, was issued in 1944 by the Catholic Worker Press, with Dorothy herself encouraging and supervising. It was published under the imprimatur of Cardinal Francis J. Spellman.[9]

In the seminaries in the time before the Second Vatican Council, when what Father Hugo called a somewhat "impoverished and naturalistic" version of the theology of St. Thomas Aquinas was taught, the New Testament emphasis on growth in holiness and love for all Christians was not given much emphasis. In writing about the retreat Hugo noted, "In my own four years of theology, I never heard even once in the classroom that all are called to holiness. That call, we were led to believe, was reserved for religious; for whom it was also often mistakenly regarded as only a counsel." His first introduction to the radical call of the gospel came from Jacques Maritain, in his book, *Prayer and Intelligence*. He said he "did not meet the doctrine again until I heard it expounded by Father Lacouture."[10]

When Father Hugo made the retreat with Lacouture, the call was unmistakable to him. He embraced it, began to give the retreat himself, and made it central to his life's work. He continued to be a diocesan priest, giving the retreat as he had time and permission to priests and laypeople and at the Catholic Worker at Dorothy's request.

In his retreat Father Hugo, like Father Lacouture, brought those who attended to embrace the paschal mystery. He presented the theme of sowing, emphasizing the integration into one's life of the gospel image of the grain of wheat that must fall into the ground and die in order to bear fruit, as well as another illustration from nature in the gospel, the "pruning" which takes place in the spiritual life. He emphasized the weapons of the Spirit and the need for Christians to forgive. He suggested that retreatants (Christians) forgive seventy times seven. He taught what Peter Maurin called the "shock maxims" of the gospel: the love of enemies (even in war), giving away your second cloak, turning the other cheek, going the second mile, being poor as Christ was poor. He stressed with Matthew 25 that Christ is hidden in the poor, the hungry, the thirsty, the naked, the homeless. As Dorothy had quoted Father Lacouture in the April 1942 *Catholic Worker*, "If we cannot see Jesus in the poor man, we surely cannot see Him under the poverty-stricken veils of bread."

Dorothy's acquaintance with the de Montfort Fathers came through the retreat, which recommended devotion to Mary according to the writings of Louis de Montfort. Dorothy published an article by Father Hugo in *The Catholic Worker* of July–August 1942 on "Our Lady, Queen of Apostles," in which he mentioned Louis Grignon de Montfort and a pamphlet by him on "True Devotion" to Mary.[11]

Since the retreat demanded so much, it was bound to have its critics. Giving up things to find a person, Jesus Christ, did not always appeal, even though the gospel makes it clear that one must give up all and follow him. The criticism of the retreat fell on Father Lacouture, who had given it to over six thousand priests; it also fell on Father Hugo. It is understandable that Hugo would have been very unpopular with some. He not only called a spade a spade. He called a cross a cross:

Radical Christianity is discovered only at the cross, but who desires to be crucified? Like Peter and the other apostles—before the coming of the Holy Spirit!—we all tend to prefer a Christianity without the cross, "air-foam Christianity," as it was satirized by Ed Willock [in *Integrity* magazine] in an outrageous cartoon showing a contented Catholic snuggled down on a cross spread with that seductive cushioning. Many attempt a life of vigorous and dedicated action, while failing to realize that such action is authentically Christian and efficacious only when grafted to the Tree of Life on Calvary.[12]

Those who gave the retreat, like the great saints and spiritual writers over the centuries, pointed out that detachment is required to hear the voice of God. One might have to turn off the radio (now television). Those who lived the retreat, especially priests, gave up both listening to car radios and smoking. It is not clear why such an issue was made of the call to give up these things, although it seemed that it was the spelling out of specific things to give up that created some of the conflict. Not smoking and not having a car radio became an outward sign of an inward change, so much so that those who didn't like the retreat accused the converted of being unorthodox and borderline Catholics, almost like a sect. Never before in the history of the church had orthodoxy required smoking and having a car radio. Dorothy tried to explain the ideas of the retreat on detachment to her readers:

> How shall we have the means to help our brother who is in need? We can do without those unnecessary things which become habits, cigarettes, liquor, coffee, tea, candy, sodas, soft drinks and those foods at meals which only titillate the palate. We all have these habits, the youngest and the oldest. And we have to die to ourselves in order to live, we have to put off the old man and put on Christ. That it is so hard, that it arouses so much opposition, serves to show what an accumulation there is in all of us of unnecessary desires.[13]

Father Hugo remembered that after she gave up smoking (which was so difficult for her), Dorothy "liked to recall how Father Zossima, in Dostoevsky's *The Brothers Karamazov*, asserted that he had known revolutionaries who had betrayed their cause out of an attachment for tobacco."[14]

In reflecting on voluntary poverty and giving up luxuries and unnecessary things, or even things considered necessary by many, Dorothy reminded people that the saints used to walk from one end of Europe and Russia to the other. She commented, "Of course, we are not all given the grace to do such things. But it is good to call to mind the *vision*. It is true, indeed, that until we begin to develop a few apostles along these lines we will have no mass conversions, no justice, no peace. We need saints. God, give us saints!"[15]

The retreat, however, was not all renunciation. It was filled with the revelation of God's love—and also good food and beautiful surroundings. When some wondered why there were nice meals at some of the retreats, held in beautiful surroundings, Dorothy answered in the November 1957 *Catholic Worker* that in the light of the demands of the retreat, it was very helpful to have them: "We needed the comfort of those meals, the beauty of those surroundings, because in that great silence which descended upon us, many of us faced the life of the spirit for the first time, and in the resulting conversion of heart were terrified at the prospect of what God might demand of us."

Dorothy never wavered in her defense and support of the retreat and Fathers Lacouture and Hugo. She reminded critics of the retreat that its theology was very much in the spirit of St. John of the Cross: "The Christian life is certainly a paradox. The teaching of St. John of the Cross...is of the necessity for detachment from creatures, of the need of traveling light through the dark night. Most of us have not the courage to set out on this path wholeheartedly, so God arranges it for us."[16]

The retreat challenged people, introduced them to a solid spirituality, and those who embraced it changed their lives. People began to pray and meditate for the first time in their lives. Classical authors came into the hands of those who made the retreat, for example, St. John of the Cross, Lallemant and De Caussade, Chautard, Marmion, Teresa of Avila, Thérèse of Lisieux, Newman, Faber, Thomas à Kempis.

Retreat leaders insisted on spiritual direction for retreatants so they would not do inappropriate things in their newfound pursuit of holiness. They quoted Teresa of Avila, who said, "He who directs himself is directed by the Devil."

Controversy about the retreat helped to encourage those who gave it, as well as Dorothy, to study further its theology in order to assure that it had a solid theological foundation. Dorothy's citations in her writings of the works of Henri de Lubac, SJ, on nature and grace, as well as other theologians, are indications of this study:

> It was the old controversy of nature and grace, and not being a theologian I cannot write about it. I had heard some lay theologians talk about the dangerous teaching in the *Imitation of Christ* in Book Three, Chapter Fifty-three, on the "divers motions of Nature and Grace," and yet on the other hand, Pope Pius XI called it that "incomparable work."
>
> On this side of the Atlantic controversy began and spread through articles in the *Ecclesiastical Review* attacking Father Hugo's teaching. In France there was controversy about the teaching of another Jesuit, Father de Lubac, whom we had read with enthusiasm as a biographer of Proudhon, *The UnMarxian Socialist*, and as the author of *The Drama of Atheist Humanism*. It seemed a wonderful thing to me that priests and laity could still become excited about points of doctrine, about nature and the supernatural, nature and grace, about forces, spiritual capacities far more powerful than the atom bomb.[17]

William Miller shows how Father Hugo responded to those who raised questions about the retreat and nature and grace, explaining Lacouture's understanding of this theological concept. It was that of St. John of the Cross, who had also been misunderstood and assaulted by his Carmelite brethren and then cited by the Inquisition, but later became a doctor of the church: "Father Lacouture had not placed nature in opposition to grace; he had made nature the model from which ascended the path to heaven."[18]

It is worthy of note here that neither Henri de Lubac nor the retreat accepted a dualism between one's life as a Christian and life in the world. Like Father de Lubac, the retreat taught that there must not be a cleavage between what one believed and read in the New Testament and what one lived. The abstract categories of neo-scholastic theology were not sufficient; the gospel must be lived. The idea was not abandoning the world, but calling the world itself to a whole new set of values and way of life, that of the gospel.

The retreat taught priests to teach from the New Testament, not just the theological manuals. Any attempt to reject the neo-scholasticism of the manuals at that time would put one in serious trouble, as was the case with Father de Lubac, who was forbidden to teach for a long period until shortly before the Second Vatican Council. The retreat was rejected in Canada and Father Lacouture was forbidden by the Jesuits to preach or hear confessions. It was when he was at a very low point in his life that Dorothy visited him. They both came disenfranchised, as it were, to the meeting—he being forbidden to preach the retreat and she in a state of discouragement over the Catholic Worker movement being devastated by its stand on pacifism during World War II.

Father Lacouture died years before the Second Vatican Council began and was never restored by the Jesuits to teaching. In his last years he was able to work with Native Americans under a very sympathetic bishop, Alfred Langlois, who would have liked to have him give retreats to all the priests and seminarians in the diocese, but the Jesuit superiors would not allow it.[19] Father Hugo, however, whose life was filled with controversy in his younger days, was later totally vindicated by Bishop John Dearden, who had been sent to Pittsburgh to censure him, and by Bishop Dearden's successor, Cardinal John Wright, who appointed him chair of the Diocesan Theological Commission. Dorothy celebrated these vindications in her writings.

Within the Catholic Worker movement itself, there were critics of the retreat and some who rejected it completely. Some former Catholic Workers who are now editors of Catholic magazines and publishing houses still are very uncomfortable with the retreat and Dorothy's insistence on the importance of its spirituality for herself and for the movement. Criticism within the movement focused on the difficult challenge of the retreat. Critics believed that the retreat demanded too much from people. They gave the impression that the retreat asked people to give up art and beauty—rather, the retreat asked that all done be for the glory of God and for the poor. Father Hugo wondered if the rejection of the theology of the retreat might be a "practical denial of the paschal mystery."[20]

It was Father Hugo himself who wrote to Dorothy cautioning against rigorism and those who were too rigorous in the retreats:

> First of all, it appears that a spirit of rigorism is creeping in among some of our friends in an excessive emphasis on external penance....We should preach love rather than penance, penance simply as a means of progressing in love. And we should treat penance as secondary and supplementary....
>
> This rigorism shows itself in certain doctrinal exaggerations. For example: in the statement that all will be damned who do not *achieve* the degree of perfection to which they are predestined. Such a statement is erroneous and has no theological foundation....I hope that you will be most careful in stating theological truths and will not betray yourself into any exaggerations by a temptation to startle or impress. The truth is startling enough.
>
> Rigorism shows itself in a tendency to impose certain singularities of dress, of manner, of devotion....It shows that they [retreatants] are confusing the shadow with the substance. Also, they are putting themselves in the proximate danger of spiritual pride, since they tend to regard all who do not adopt their singularities as imperfect or damned.[21]

In Dorothy's later evaluation of the retreat, Father Hugo fared better with Dorothy than did some other retreat masters. She felt, for example, that although Father Roy was a great carpenter, "his joyous spirit was shadowed by an austerity which he tended to impose on the group."[22] But Father Hugo was considered the best of retreat masters and confirmed again as "a very old and precious friend who used to give us the famous retreat," as late as the January 1970 *Catholic Worker*. That same issue included a review of Father Hugo's book on St. Augustine as well as paragraphs of Dorothy's own, describing his presentations at the retreat:

I say I am reminded of Fr. Hugo when I write...about death because he used to end his delightful, stimulating and provocative retreats with a little dissertation about death. "When your friend comes to you to tempt you to waste your time,—'come and let us drink at the neighboring tavern,' tell him, Go away, I am dead and my life is hid with Christ in God" (famous words of St. Paul).

As he preached his retreats it was often with enjoyment and humor, but with a deep sense, you felt, of the strong conflict in which we were engaged in our attempts to lead a spiritual life. All that we did, work or play, eating or drinking, should be done in the name of the Lord Jesus. Work was creative, expiatory, redemptive, and certainly a sharing in the suffering of the world.

In her "Fall Appeal" in the October–November 1973 *Catholic Worker*, Dorothy referred again to Father Hugo, the teachings of the retreat, and how much they meant for Catholic Workers in continuing to be able to love the poorest, even the unlovable, in Houses of Hospitality: "Among us at St. Joseph's House, as with every family, there are those easy to love, and others hard to love. And 'we love God as much as the one we love least!' as Fr. Hugo once said, thinking no doubt of Christ's words—'Whatever you do to the least, you do to Me.'"

Some who have written and continue to write about Dorothy Day attempt to explain her life and witness without mentioning the retreat and its profound spirituality. They applaud Dorothy's activism, her life with the poor, her amazing stand for truth in the face of criticism on all sides in regard to pacifism, but do not recognize its spiritual base. As Father Hugo reflected on Dorothy's life, "There would be later friends and co-workers who would be ignorant of this history of the retreat, would pass it by, speak slightingly of it, or even deny it. But Dorothy continued to make this same retreat all through the 1960s and up until 1976." It is a mystery that this important aspect of her life and spirituality can be almost erased by its simple omission or by the stroke of a pen, when she herself declared so many times how important it was to her. Hugo said: "Such critics prefer to see her through the secular mystique of activism rather than rooted in the authentic mysticism of prayer and love. As Sister Peter Claver put it accurately, 'They won't give God the credit.'"[23]

Father Hugo, who knew Dorothy so personally and provided spiritual direction to her during retreats, gave a homily on November 5, 1981, at a Dorothy Day Memorial Mass offered as part of a centennial celebration at Marquette University, in which he said, "The impact of the lives of Dorothy Day and Peter Maurin on all who have known and admired and loved them can be nothing less than laboring with them with all our hearts, even at this late day, as fellow workers in the Kingdom." He described Dorothy's impact on his own life:

> While I served, within the range described, as Dorothy Day's teacher and counselor, I also went to her for counsel....Perhaps the most important lesson I learned from Dorothy, from her own manner of life, was how widely and deeply the conventional Christianity in which I grew up—"the religion of common sense"—is permeated by the bourgeois spirit, i.e., that preoccupation with "the comforts of life," which Newman says, tend to "choke up all the avenues of the soul through which the light and breadth of heaven might come to us." To meet Dorothy, and to see her in her own chosen surroundings of abject poverty...was to step out of the seductive atmosphere of our affluent consumer society and see a world of stark reality, the only place where the Gospel seems at home because it offers hope for all.[24]

Father Hugo wrote of Dorothy as a "contemplative in action, an authentic mystic in the Catholic tradition." He called her a saint of the paschal mystery, "a mystic in the Pauline sense, loving to the limit, in utter death to self, and persevering in this dying life for fifty years until her actual death and, as we confidently believe, her passage to glory." He described the application of her understanding of death and resurrection in her life and work: "Dorothy understood the paschal mystery existentially. She lived it daily, perseveringly amid outcasts, 'sowing' pleasure, convenience, amenities, leisure, doing this all her life into old age....She has made the paschal mystery alive for us. And she was enabled to do this quietly, with equanimity, although not without pain and occasional spluttering, by what she had learned about 'sowing' and 'pruning' from the teaching of Father Onesimus Lacouture, SJ."[25]

Father Hugo concluded that there was "no need to hunt for miracles in Dorothy's life. Her whole life was the miracle. She has been in our time a luminous example of the twofold love of God and neighbor fused into one in the furnace of divine love."

Dorothy Day: Spiritual Leader of American Catholic Pacifism

One of Dorothy Day's great gifts to the Catholic Church and to the United States was her drawing together of biblical and theological resources to establish pacifism and conscientious objection as a legitimate stance for Catholics and for Americans. The *ressourcement* accomplished by Dorothy and Peter Maurin, along with priest-theologians and other Catholic Workers who assisted them, made available teachings from the fathers of the church and biblical reflection and exegesis against participation in war. Difficult positions taken by the Catholic Worker on war were based on faith, the scriptures, Catholic tradition and theology, and the history of saints who practiced nonviolence. *The Catholic Worker* facilitated the formation of conscience for many people on war and peace and developed the moral and intellectual tradition of nonviolence within Catholicism.

An example of this retrieval of the pacifist tradition from the early church was Dorothy's quote from St. John Chrysostom regarding Christians who resort to violence: "St. John Chrysostom says in regard to our Lord's sending us out as sheep among wolves, that if we become wolves ourselves, He is no longer with us." Chrysostom's words appeared a number of times in the paper, during World War II, and again as late as the March 1966 *Catholic Worker.* The newspaper retold the stories of saints who had refused to participate in violence.

As Dorothy articulated the position of Catholic pacifism in the pages of *The Catholic Worker,* she had Peter Maurin's support in her stand against war. Peter had been forced to participate in the reserves after military service in France, even as a Christian Brother, and had been very uncomfortable doing so:

> Then came a shock, an interruption in his religious life by the call to military service....The rough, coarse banter, the never-ending raw humor of the barracks room hardly appealed to him. He had dedicated his life to elevating the hearts and minds of the children of God. Now he found himself in an atmosphere that seemed completely alien to his aims. He hated the whole thing, the discipline for killing, the loss of individual dignity, the general lowering of standards. Peter observed closely the grad-ual loss of manners, the bitterness in men's eyes, the slow devel-opment of the impersonal human machine demanded by the high command. To obey quickly and efficiently—that was all that counted.
>
> Discipline and hard work were not new to Peter. He was used to both. It was the misdirection of all this activity that dis-mayed him. Over and over he asked himself the question: Why am I, a religious dedicated to winning souls for Christ, caught up in this militaristic system?[1]

Dorothy wrote in the April 1948 *Catholic Worker* about the kinds of destructive things that Peter had described from his expe-rience in the military, contending that those who justified war were perhaps unaware of the psychological damage done to those who participated in military training: "A defense of Jesus Christ by bombs, a blood-soaked earth, quick death, hate. A hate that always exists in war despite the unreal and pedantic distinctions of theologians whose love of refinements is equaled only by their ignorance of psychology, of what happens to a man to get him prepared to murder." Because of the constant interruption of his life and vocation by required participation in the military, Peter left France to go to Canada.[2] By going to Canada to escape forced military service, he was part of the tradition later continued dur-ing the Vietnam War. In the February 1954 *Catholic Worker*, Dorothy clarified Peter's position on pacifism and anarchism and his rejection of labels: "The greatest message which Peter Maurin had for us was this reminder of man's freedom. That is why he never used the word pacifist or anarchist. Privately he admitted to both positions and letters from his brother in France tell us that he always considered himself a pacifist."

Prior to her conversion to Catholicism, Dorothy Day was very much a part of the antiwar movement. She participated in demonstrations against U.S. involvement in World War I and was clubbed, albeit accidentally, by police. The socialist paper, *The Masses*, for which Dorothy was assistant managing editor, took a pacifist stand. The local postmaster, by refusing to mail it, to "send anything through the mail that he considered treasonous," closed down *The Masses*. Dorothy saw her hopes for impacting the government or the war dashed.[3]

During and after World War I, many progressives became political activists; Dorothy did not throw in her lot with them. Anne Klejment and Nancy Roberts recount that as a young secular radical, Day was "overwhelmed by the failure of the Left to make a difference." She was seeking a more profound way of life. Her opposition to war and her determination to construct a more just social order were not stifled by embracing Catholicism, but strengthened by her new faith. After Dorothy's conversion, "as a Catholic radical, the many spiritual gifts she received from her rekindled faith encouraged perseverance and boldness in her opposition to war....."[4]

Dorothy incorporated ideas from Catholic teaching into her pacifist stand. Klejment suggests that she remembered lines from *The Baltimore Catechism* (so recently studied for her conversion), such as "all human beings who share in God's grace are 'temples of the Holy Ghost.'"[5] Reflecting on the theology of the Mystical Body of Christ, with its beautiful teaching about the bonds of unity between the actual and potential members made in the image and likeness of God, Dorothy concluded that these members should not have bombs dropped on them. An article in the October 1934 *Catholic Worker* entitled "The Mystical Body of Christ" began with a quote from St. Clement of Rome: "Why do the members of Christ tear one another, why do we rise up against our own body in such madness; have we forgotten that we are all members of one another?" War was described in that article as an illness that weakens the whole body. "All men are our neighbors and Christ told us that we should love our neighbors, whether they be friend or enemy....If a man hates his neighbor, he is hating Christ." The stand of the Catholic Worker against force and war was not an isolated idea; it was a part of a way of life based in personalism, voluntary poverty, and the practice of the Works of Mercy as an alternative to the works of war. Catholic Worker opposition to violence in all its forms was not a quietistic pacifism, but the active nonviolence of love, a love that fights for justice. Their stand came from the teachings of Christ. As Dorothy wrote in the May 1949 paper: "We believe that Christ went beyond natural ethics and the Old Dispensation in this matter of force and war and taught nonviolence as a way of life." Dorothy articulated pacifism in these terms in the November 1949 *Catholic Worker*: "If we spend the rest of our lives in slums, as I hope we will who work for and read *The Catholic Worker*, if we are truly living with the poor, working side by side with the poor, helping the poor, we will inevitably be forced to be on their side, physically speaking. But when it comes to activity, we will be pacifists, I hope and pray, nonviolent resisters of aggression, from whomever it comes, resisters to repression, coercion, from whatever side it comes, and our activity will be the Works of Mercy. Our arms will be the love of God and our brother."

When the Catholic Worker began, there was another Catholic voice already present in the United States that addressed the issue of war and peace. The Catholic Association for International Peace (CAIP) had been started in 1927 by Monsignor John A. Ryan and was given space at the National Catholic Welfare Conference headquarters in Washington, D.C. While it claimed to be the "official" organization on peace for the Catholic Church in the United States, the CAIP held positions very different from those of the Catholic Worker. The CAIP later used the just war doctrine to justify support for the Roosevelt administration in entering World War II and criticized the pacifist position. The CAIP "supported the war effort and did not help any individual who objected to World War II, whether they registered their dissent within the law or were resisters." This "peace organization" did not address the moral questions of obliteration bombing and supported

Truman's decision to use the atomic bomb, despite Pius XII's condemnation of it because of the killing of civilians involved.[6]

In contrast, Dorothy spoke and wrote against Americanism, a concept in which American democracy, tied to manifest destiny/capitalism, is presented as the best way of expressing the faith, rather than the church influencing American culture. Dorothy brought her faith to critique her country's actions in the light of the gospel. *The Catholic Worker* challenged the belief that the United States has a special providential role in history that allows it to dominate other countries and that the use of violence was and is justified in pursuing this "manifest destiny." Stephen Krupa, SJ, points out that "the Catholic Worker was the only group in the history of the American Catholic Church that refused to view the nation's wars as the moral crusade of Christianity against the evil forces of tyranny," or to identify with a blind patriotism that included the "entrenched myths that have structured life and social consciousness for most Americans."[7]

Catholics in the United States eventually absorbed these myths that had come with the Puritans. Given the history of anti-Catholicism and the accusation that loyalty to the pope was treasonous, it had been difficult for Catholics, many of whom were immigrants, to go against the American mainstream, even if it meant going to war. The desire for acceptance created an almost superpatriotism in American Catholics to prove their allegiance to the United States.

Dorothy believed that one's attitudes toward war and peace and a host of other issues must come first from the gospel of love and the rich tradition of the church, rather than politics or even patriotism. Critics of religion who contend that it not only may support violence and war, but actually cause it, have not discovered the way to practice religion presented by Dorothy Day in the April 1948 *Catholic Worker*:

> Why is *The Catholic Worker* opposed to [Universal Military Training] and to war? Because we are Communists? No! For we were opposed to World War II when the Communists were for it. Because we are indifferent to the fate of the Church? No! For she is our Mother, the Bridegroom of Jesus Christ. But she is

more than real estate, she is more than temporal power, her spirit is not the spirit of the world and she has no need to be defended by the arms of the world. No more than her Divine Master who refused such defense.

We are against war because it is contrary to the Spirit of Jesus Christ, and the only important thing is that we abide in His Spirit. It is more important than being American, more important than being respectable, more important than obedience to the State. It is the only thing that matters. We are against Universal Military Training because it is preparation for sin, for the sin that is war. That it is better that the United States be liquidated than that she survive by war.

For Dorothy, as for Peter Maurin, the difficult questions of freedom, authority, and love of country were complicated by what they called the "ever-encroaching" modern state with its military emphasis. They believed that even within what are called modern democracies, there is evidence of totalitarianism and infringements on conscience, and that the ordinary person is implicated in war making, like it or not. It was what Dorothy called one of the greatest problems of the day. She posed the fundamental questions in an article in the February 1954 *Catholic Worker*, emphasizing her belief that the command not to kill was to be taken seriously by Christians:

How obey the laws of a state when they run counter to man's conscience? "Thou shalt not kill," divine law states. "A new precept I give unto you that you love your brother as I have loved you." St. Peter disobeyed the law of men and stated that he had to obey God rather than men. Wars today involve total destruction, obliteration bombing, killing of the innocent, the stockpiling of atom and hydrogen bombs. When one is drafted for such war, when one registers for the draft for such a war, when one pays income tax, eighty per cent of which goes to support such war, or works where armaments are made, one is participating in this war. We are all involved in war these days. War means hatred and fear. Love casts out fear....

The modern States which built up a Hitler, which did not depopulate concentration camps and gas chambers by providing living space, giving asylum or by imposing economic sanctions, are monstrosities. When they are driven to force finally, they fail to accomplish that peace which they set out for. It is a greater blood bath than ever, with threat of more to come.

The Catholic Worker and Pacifism

From the beginning, *The Catholic Worker* published articles on the ethical issues involved in modern war. During World War I, Catholic conscientious objection to war was not recognized. At that time, the few Catholics in the United States who resisted the military draft because of questions of conscience were jailed for long periods. In 1933, Dorothy announced in the paper that delegates of the Catholic Worker movement would attend the United States Congress Against War, and that they would represent "Catholic Pacifism." One might say that with this announcement, Catholic pacifism existed in the United States for the first time.[8]

In April 1934, the paper published a review of pacifist Franziskus Stratmann's book, *The Church and War*, which condemned modern war on the basis of the just war theory. Father Stratmann, a German Dominican, had become convinced during World War I that war could not be the solution to the world's problems; he became a key figure in the German peace movement, later going to jail and exile under Hitler. Dorothy often referred to his book in her writings, and published articles by Stratmann over the years. Her inclusion of his writings is an example of how, rather than abandon the just war theory, Dorothy used it to condemn all modern war in the light of the technology of mass destruction.

Articles in the paper quoted the popes on the rights of conscience in the modern nation-state, as well as the words of priests, bishops, and cardinals who raised issues about conscription and war. *The Catholic Worker* carried articles throughout the 1930s by Pope Pius XI, who vigorously attacked nationalism as a source of war.

Tom Cornell, one of two Catholic Workers who first publicly burned their draft cards as a protest against the draft during the Vietnam War, has pointed out that two voices emerged in the pages of the paper: "One is based in just war tradition and speaks of conscientious objection, arguing for a 'just war pacifism.' The other ignores just war categories and emphasizes the Mystical Body, the example of Jesus and the demands of love met in the corporal and spiritual Works of Mercy...although there is never any open contradiction between the two..., there is a significant difference of tone and emphasis."[9]

Along with well-known writers such as Jacques Maritain, Georges Bernanos, and Emmanuel Mounier, the newspaper took a neutral stance in regard to the Spanish Civil War. Because the anti-Franco forces indiscriminately slaughtered so many priests and religious sisters, there was a tremendous backlash among Catholics in the United States against the forces of the Left in Spain. For many, the Catholic Worker position of neutrality in that war was difficult to understand. In order to help people grasp the deeper issues involved, Dorothy printed the commentary of French personalist Emmanuel Mounier in the December 1936 *Catholic Worker*. Mounier insisted that even in a situation like that occurring in Spain, a Christian approach to the remaking of the social order be grounded in Christians "who will set themselves to live their Christianity by a sort of re-conversion." He placed the roots of the tragedy of Spain in the problem of Catholics compromising "the Church by binding it to a political cause which is not hers, while in revenge furious hordes pillage, burn and kill all that in their eyes represents religion," referring, perhaps, as Dorothy later did, to Franco's acceptance of the aid of fascist Mussolini and his son. Dorothy responded to heavy criticism of the paper's position on the Spanish war in the September 1938 *Catholic Worker*, trying to help readers understand:

> We all know that there is a frightful persecution of religion in Spain. Churches have been destroyed and desecrated, priests and nuns have been tortured and murdered in great numbers.
>
> In the light of this fact it is inconceivably difficult to write as we do. It is folly—it seems madness—to say as we do—"we are opposed to the use of force as a means of settling personal, national, or international disputes." As a newspaper trying to effect public opinion, we take this stand....
>
> We pray those martyrs of Spain to help us, to pray for us, to guide us in the stand we take. We speak in their name. Their blood cries out against the shedding of more blood, against a

spirit of hatred and savagery which aims towards a peace founded upon victory, at the price of resentment and hatred enduring for years to come. Do you suppose they died, saying grimly—"Alright—we accept martyrdom—we will not lift the sword to defend ourselves but the lay troops will avenge us!" This would be martyrdom wasted. Blood spilled in vain. Or rather did they say with St. Stephen, "Father, forgive them," and pray with love for their conversion? And did they not rather pray, when the light of Christ burst upon them, that love would overcome hatred, that men *dying* for their faith, rather than *killing* for their faith, would save the world?...

St. Peter drew the sword and our Lord rebuked him. They asked our Lord to prove His Divinity and come down from the cross. But He suffered the "failure" of the cross. His apostles kept asking for a temporal Kingdom, even with Christ Himself to guide and enlighten them they did not see the primacy of the spiritual. Only when the Holy Ghost descended on them did they see....

We are praying for the Spanish people—all of them our brothers in Christ—all of them Temples of the Holy Ghost, all of them members or potential members of the Mystical Body of Christ.

World War II

Catholic Workers did not wait until World War II had begun to analyze the problems that caused it. They did not consider World War II an aberration or simply a reaction to the evils of Nazism, but a part of an historical reality that included what had happened to Germany when it was almost destroyed economically and politically after World War I. They described the roots of war in terms of capitalists "eager to turn a profit from the armaments business." In Dorothy's September 1939 editorial in *The Catholic Worker*, "We are to Blame for New War in Europe," she related the policies before World War II to "materialism," "greed," and "idolatrous nationalism...for their ruthless subjection of another country." The editorial reflected the Catholic Worker call for a fundamental transformation of the world economic and social order.

Jim Forest points out that long before World War II, and throughout the '30s, *The Catholic Worker* condemned and actively opposed anti-Semitism and Nazism. Catholic Workers made an appeal for the United States to accept those who were trying to escape what was daily becoming a more dangerous situation. Unfortunately, their appeal was not heeded. Forest wrote:

> Opposition to Hitler led the New York Catholic Worker community to the docks on the Upper West Side in 1935 to join in picketing the German liner Bremen....On other occasions the Catholic Worker joined in picketing the German embassy. An appeal published in *The Catholic Worker* called on the nation to open its doors to "all Jews who wish free access to American hospitality." Similar appeals came from many quarters, but went largely unheeded. Only the exceptional and the fortunate were allowed in. The majority were turned away. Most of them died in the Nazi concentration camps.[10]

The argument that World War II was fought to save the Jews and therefore was a good war did not hold water with Dorothy Day, who simply responded that it didn't save the Jews, as was clear by the numbers of people incinerated. As Forest pointed out, before and during the war the United States rejected many Jews who wanted to enter the country as refugees. The U.S. government refused to accept even those who were legal refugees (90 percent of quotas went unfulfilled), for fear of overloading the labor market, sending those who arrived in boats seeking entrance to the United States back to concentration camps.[11]

The Catholic Worker critique of the war included recommendations that might have saved many from the Holocaust. The paper advocated working toward the release of all Jews in Nazi camps before an all-out military campaign took place: In the May 1943 issue the *Worker* featured a talk by Jessie Hugham, secretary of the War Resisters League, in which the point was made that if the war continued to be pressed unconditionally "we shall be signing the death sentence of the remnant of the Jews still alive. If, on the contrary, we demand the release of all Jews from the ghettos of occupied Europe and work for a peace without victory...there is a chance of saving the Jews."[12]

When the United States entered the war, Dorothy's stand against war became even more controversial. World War I had been fought as "the war to end all wars." Popular opinion in the United States in the '20s and '30s had been against U.S. involvement in war, especially another world war—that is, until the bombing of Pearl Harbor. Then, many who had been against war changed, and they found Dorothy's opposition to World War II not only unfathomable, but also unforgivable. This included some Catholic Workers. Even Peter Maurin sadly said to Dorothy, "Perhaps silence would be better for a time than to continue our opposition to war. Men are not ready to listen."[13] Dorothy, however, continued her stand. The circulation of *The Catholic Worker* dropped, and many houses closed. Dorothy sent a letter to all Catholic Worker groups, insisting that at least each Catholic Worker house accept and distribute the paper, even if they could not adopt her strict pacifist ethic. The criticism, even within the movement, was surprising to Dorothy, since from the beginning *The Catholic Worker* had declared its pacifism: "It struck me then how strange a thing it was; here we had been writing about pacifism for fifteen years and members of two of our groups were just beginning to realize what it meant."[14]

To deal with the crisis Dorothy's letter precipitated, pacifist Father Paul Hanly Furfey led a 1940 Labor Day weekend retreat at the Easton farm for seventy-five Catholic Workers from around the country. Father Roy was there, giving a Lacouture retreat within a retreat. Dorothy's letter of invitation to the retreat was an introduction to the spirituality she hoped would become rooted in all those associated with the Catholic Worker movement. However, no one there changed position on the major question. Many young men involved with the Catholic Worker joined the military in the following year.

One of the most pressing and immediate concerns for the Catholic Worker before and during the outbreak of World War II was the protection of those who because of their conscience did not believe they could participate in war. For this reason, *The Catholic Worker* editorialized against the military draft. As early as September 1939, the paper took a stand against universal conscription, acknowledging the risk to its very existence for taking such a position during wartime. The decision in the Congress was imminent and it would affect all the young men in the United States if such a law were passed. The testimony that Dorothy gave before the U.S. Senate Committee on Military Affairs against conscription was published in the July–August 1940 *Catholic Worker,* along with that of Monsignor G. Barry O'Toole, professor of philosophy at the Catholic University of America. Dorothy spoke there not only against conscription, quoting priests and bishops, but also against the arms buildup, "the expenditure of billions when millions of our citizens are in need and hunger." The arguments against conscription centered on the totalitarian nature of the military draft, imperiling a person's sacred and inalienable rights to vocation, to free choice of work, to liberty of action.

The Catholic Worker ran articles by Father John J. Hugo and other theologians who were developing a sound theology of peace. Hugo, who had helped Dorothy deepen in many areas of spirituality, was also influenced by her. When World War II began, Father Hugo had considered becoming a military chaplain, but it was at this point that he encountered Dorothy's "intransigent" pacifism. Dorothy introduced him to priest-pacifists like William Orchard and to the writings of Franziskus Stratmann. Because of Dorothy's counsel, Hugo did not volunteer as a chaplain for soldiers, but began instead to write articles for *The Catholic Worker* on Catholic pacifism and especially the immorality of the military draft.[15] In those articles he recommended trust in the power and love of Christ, which could truly transform the world, and, following scripture, the use of the weapons of the Spirit to overcome evil.

Hugo's "The Immorality of Conscription" was published as a supplement to the November 1944 issue of *The Catholic Worker* and reprinted in the April 1945 issue. Hugo's expression of the dignity of the human person made in the image and likeness of God touched a chord during a time of total military mobilization in the country and was very popular. There was so much demand for it that the article was published again in the April 1948 issue, along with another 75,000 extra copies for distribution.

Father Hugo joined the efforts of Catholic Workers in retrieving the sources from the early church in support of nonviolence. In his book *The Gospel of Peace* (given an imprimatur by

Cardinal Spellman, no less), he included an appendix on "Patristics and Peace," filled with quotes from the fathers of the church in support of nonviolence. He addressed there the question of how Christians could possibly participate as soldiers in the early church—a question frequently written about by the fathers of the church, who allowed those recently converted to Christianity to remain as soldiers as long as they didn't kill anyone. The concept of *tranquillitas ordinis* (an army preserving peace) from this period is often used to justify war. Hugo quoted Father Victor White, OP, on how this concept, developed during the Roman Empire when the army resembled more a police force, could not be applied to a totally different international context.

Hugo shared Dorothy's conviction that wars were fought not just for the lofty reasons presented by leaders of nations for their justification, but that the causes of war were very frequently, at bottom, economic. Making the connection between economics and war, Dorothy entitled one of the chapters of *The Long Loneliness*, "War is the Health of the State." Father Hugo wrote that war based on greed for power and material things was not just: "God put the goods of the material world here, not for the aggrandizement of nations greedy for power, but for all men, that they might have the material goods required for virtuous living. When great nations use their strength to despoil the world, like pirates fighting one another for loot, they make impossible from the very beginning the realization of that law by which all men are to be joined to one another in mutual love."[16]

The retreat that Hugo and Roy had given at the Catholic Worker and that Dorothy had attended so often gave a deepening theological and spiritual basis for her pacifism. Sandra Yocum Mize argues that the retreat gave her a "special lens" through which she could see the difficulties and trials of life in Catholic Worker Houses of Hospitality, problems of economic destitution and preparations for war in so many parts of the world. This lens was "a life defined through the Paschal Mystery," the possibility of living a life that truly reflected the love relationship between God and each human person within a community of believers. The retreat emphasized the importance of making choices between good and better, rather than simply between good and evil, and in this context, "absolute pacifism seemed better than any compromise in cooperating with the military."[17]

The methods of protesting war of the Catholic Worker were the spiritual weapons: prayer and penance, fasting, receiving the sacraments, prayer vigils, voluntary poverty, suffering, marches and demonstrations preceded by prayer, picketing, and noncooperation with preparations for war. The penitential quality of the pacifism of the Catholic Worker distinguished it from the religious pacifism of the Fellowship of Reconciliation (of which she was a member), and the American Friends Service Committee, which were more rooted in the Social Gospel notion of corporate responsibility.[18] In the January 1941 *Catholic Worker*, Dorothy wrote an article entitled "Pacifism Is Dangerous, So Is Christianity," in which she went so far as to say, "If we are not going to use our spiritual weapons, let us by all means arm and prepare." In the July–August 1956 *Catholic Worker*, she again emphasized this theme, noting that prayer should be the first, and not the last, resort: "Just as daily or frequent communion had become rare since the days of the early Christians, until the days of St. Pius X, so also the use of spiritual weapons ceased to be put first. For many centuries the tradition has been to fight first and when all other weapons have been used, then to trust in prayer. We need to reverse this practice, and with faith and love, overcome the enemy...."

During the whole of 1942, the paper carried theological articles on what the response of the gospel and even the just war theory might be to the war. In the February issue, Dorothy outlined what the response of Christian love to violence should be, no matter how terrible the situation:

Perhaps we are called sentimental because we speak of love. We say we love our president, our country. We say that we love our enemies, too. "Hell," Bernanos said, "is not to love any more."

"Greater love hath no man than this," Christ said, "that he should lay down his life for his friend."

"Love is the measure by which we shall be judged," St. John of the Cross said....

"Love is an exchange of gifts," St. Ignatius said.
Love is a breaking of the bread....
Love is not the starving of whole populations. Love is not
the bombardment of open cities. Love is not killing, it is the lay-
ing down of one's life for one's friend.

Speaking of the unique witness of the Catholic Worker during World War II, William Cavanaugh gives special insight into
the theology of the Mystical Body of Christ of the movement:
"While most saw the Mystical Body as that which united
Christians in spirit above the battle lines which pitted Christians
in Europe against one another, Dorothy interpreted the Mystical
Body as that which made Christian participation in the conflict
simply inconceivable. The Mystical Body of Christ does not hover
above the national borders which divide us; it dissolves them."[19]
Dorothy knew well that there was evil in the world. Her
approach, though, was not to demonize one person or nation, but
to point out that the struggle is with principalities and powers, not
flesh and blood, that "we are all members or potential members of
the Body of Christ." Cavanaugh describes Dorothy's profound
understanding of the concept:

> Although Dorothy Day was one with the Catholics of her age in
> speaking of the Church as the Mystical Body of Christ, she in fact
> was closer to the patristic and early medieval theologians who saw
> the Church as the *corpus verum*, the true body of Christ. Here was
> a sacramental sensibility which felt the Body of Christ as an
> almost physical reality. The strained sinews, the open wounds, the
> contorted face, the purplish blood of the crucifixes adorning
> Catholic churches were reflected and manifested in a very real
> sense in the broken and torn bodies which were appearing both
> on the doorsteps of the Catholic Worker houses, and in far
> greater magnitude on the battlefields of Europe.[20]

Dorothy critiqued actions of her country during World War
II on ethical grounds. As she had done as a muckraking journalist
in the years before her conversion to Catholicism, she went to see
with her own eyes what was happening, whenever possible. After
visiting the "concentration camps" on U.S. soil where the

Japanese in the United States were forcibly detained, she strongly criticized the destruction of people's lives in the "Grave Injustice Done to Japanese on West Coast" in the June 1942 *Catholic Worker:*

> I saw a bit of Germany on the West Coast. I saw some of the concentration camps where the Japanese men, women and children are being held before they are resettled in the Owens Valley or some other place, barren, windswept, inaccessible.
>
> The strange part of this wholesale imprisonment of an innocent people is that many of them are native-born citizens of this country. But that means nothing in wartime.
>
> Wholesale evacuation of areas in Los Angeles, San Francisco, Portland and Seattle have already been carried out and as I stopped in each city, there were still groups being moved. Whole areas had been vacated, houses empty. According to friends in Portland, business and property had to be sold at a loss and there were those who took advantage of this misfortune of the evacuees...

In the very next issue of the paper (July–August 1942), Dorothy wrote about having received letters from the U.S. government complaining about the publication of information on the concentration camps, as well as her critique against using Catholic property for war preparation. She pointed out that censorship was still voluntary, but that the pressure was on the *Worker* not to criticize: "Letters also came during the month from the Office of Censorship in Washington....Objection was made to our story on the Japanese...and to our calling attention to anti-aircraft nests on the West Coast. The exchange of letters was pleasant, we apologized for our indiscretion in naming locations such as cities and monastery gardens by name, and they thanked us. But we are forced to repeat our protest at the presence of anti-aircraft batteries or some kind of camps along our waterfront, on the property of Catholic institutions." In that article she pointed out that the issues that had come up in this case were some of the same ones involved in the Spanish Civil War. She was as opposed then as she had been in the '30s to using church property for the purpose of war.

The patriotic stance of many Catholics made it difficult for the government to understand the Catholic Worker movement. J. Edgar Hoover, the head of the FBI for many years, saw Dorothy as a threat to American military plans, and even before World War II he asked that she be placed in custodial detention (jail) in the event of a national emergency.[21] That order was never carried out. One can only conjecture that FBI officers, who were frequently Irish Catholics and even ex-seminarians, could not bring themselves to arrest someone opposed to war because she was a daily communicant. One can imagine the confusion of the FBI agents as they listened to Dorothy and Peter speak of being pacifists because of their Catholicism. Some were unable to resist giving contributions for the poor who came to the Catholic Worker. Dorothy Day told about FBI visits in the July–August 1942 *Catholic Worker*: "We have so many visits from FBI men who are making inquiries as to the sincerity of young Catholic men claiming the status of conscientious objectors that we all but wrote an editorial this month on 'Love and the FBI.' One government man acted as though he had never heard of the Sermon on the Mount and the idea of loving one's enemies is strange to many of them."

During the years after World War II, Dorothy continued to be investigated by the FBI because of her pacifism. She had the protection of Cardinal Spellman of New York, who never opposed or condemned her, even though she later criticized him in the paper for his support of U.S. policies in Vietnam. The FBI could easily have closed down the Catholic Worker in the '40s if the powerful church leader had spoken negatively about Dorothy.

After the military draft became the law of the land, in the November 1942 issue of *The Catholic Worker* Dorothy told of the beginning of two conscientious objectors' camps for Catholics that had been established and of the Association for Catholic Conscientious Objectors, "which we set up at 115 Mott Street." Gordon Zahn later said that the ACCO, this "impressive sounding organization," was simply a "front" for the Catholic Worker.[22] The historic peace churches had worked out an agreement with the U.S. government for Civilian Public Service for their members who were conscientious objectors. These churches—

Quakers, Mennonites, and the Church of the Brethren—accepted an agreement for no pay for civilian alternative service, which was expected to last only one year, during which the churches planned to support their own members. Instead, the program lasted throughout the war, and the Catholic Worker was unable to fund the Catholic camps for very long; thus, Catholics went into the camps set up by the peace churches. Only 162 Catholics participated. Because Catholics were known for just war reasoning, this is actually a surprisingly large number to have been approved by the government at the time. *The Catholic Worker* carried news about young men related to the movement who were making decisions of conscience in regard to participation in war. In the December 1942 issue, for example, Dorothy published information on individual Catholic Workers, young men who had developed a pacifist response to conscription. Some participated in noncombatant roles.

In the February 1942 issue, Dorothy responded to criticism of the Catholic Worker pacifist position, continuing the patristic theme from St. Clement of Rome, sounded in the early issues. Dorothy explained that she had to speak: "Many friends have counseled us...'Don't write about it. Don't mention it. Don't jeopardize the great work you are doing among the poor, among the workers. Just write about constructive things like Houses of Hospitality and Farming Communes.' But we cannot keep silent." In that article she not only presented the case for nonviolence from the gospel and from saints like St. John of the Cross, but took on those who accused her of sentimentality:

> "But we are at war," people say. "This is no time to talk of peace. It is demoralizing to the armed forces to protest, not to cheer them on in their fight for Christianity, for democracy, for civilization. Now that it is under way, it is too late to do anything about it."...Another Catholic newspaper says it sympathizes with our sentimentality. This is a charge always leveled against pacifists. We are supposed to be afraid of the suffering, of the hardships of war.
>
> But let those who talk of softness, of sentimentality, come to live with us in cold, unheated houses in the slums. Let them come to live with the criminal, the unbalanced, the drunken, the

degraded, the pervert. (It is not decent poor, it is not the decent sinner who was the recipient of Christ's love.) Let them live with rats, with vermin, bedbugs, roaches, lice (I could describe several kinds of body lice).

Let their flesh be mortified by cold, by dirt, by vermin; let their eyes be mortified by the sight of bodily excretions, diseased limbs, eyes, noses, mouths.

Let their noses be mortified by the smells of sewage, decay and rotten flesh. Yes, and the smell of the sweat, blood and tears spoken of so blithely by Mr. Churchill, and so widely and bravely quoted by comfortable people.

Let their ears be mortified by harsh and screaming voices, by the constant coming and going of people living herded together with no privacy. (There is no privacy in tenements just as there is none in concentration camps.)

Let their taste be mortified by the constant eating of insufficient food cooked in huge quantities for hundreds of people, the coarser foods, the cheaper foods, so that there will be enough to go around; and the smell of such cooking is often foul.

Then, when they have lived with these comrades, with these sights and sounds, let our critics talk of sentimentality.

"Love in practice is a harsh and dreadful thing compared to love in dreams."

As the war progressed, one of the key moral issues discussed in the pages of *The Catholic Worker* was obliteration bombing of cities. When the United States dropped bombs on German and Japanese cities, causing the death of untold numbers of civilians, *The Catholic Worker* could not be silent. In response to Hiroshima and Nagasaki, Dorothy Day wrote what Mel Piehl called "perhaps the most impassioned and eloquent public protest by any American writer in immediate response to the bomb."[23] In the September 1945 issue of *The Catholic Worker*, she fearlessly judged the atomic bomb in the light of the gospel:

Mr. Truman was jubilant. President Truman. True man; what a strange name, come to think of it. We refer to Jesus Christ as true God and true Man. Truman is a true man of his time in that he was jubilant. He was not a son of God, brother of Christ, brother of the Japanese, jubilating as he did. He went from table to table on the cruiser which was bringing him home from the Big Three conference, telling the great news; "jubilant" the newspapers said. *Jubilate Deo*. We have killed 318,000 Japanese.

That is, we hope we have killed them, the Associated Press, on page one, column one of the *Herald Tribune*, says. The effect is hoped for, not known. It is to be hoped they are vaporized, our Japanese brothers, scattered, men, women, and babies, to the four winds, over the seven seas. Perhaps we will breathe their dust into our nostrils, feel them in the fog of New York on our faces, feel them in the rain on the hills of Easton....

Our Lord Himself has already pronounced judgment on the atomic bomb. When James and John (John the beloved) wished to call down fire from heaven on their enemies, Jesus said: "You know not of what spirit you are. The Son of Man came not to destroy souls but to save." He said also, "What you do unto the least of these my brethren, you do unto Me."

In the same issue of the *Catholic Worker*, Father John Hugo also critiqued the attitude of manifest destiny that was used to justify obliteration bombing by the United States: "It was the peculiar conviction of democratic righteousness with which America had perpetrated the act, even more than its sheer physical destructiveness, that made the bomb so terrible....This was done, not by Nazis, or barbarian militarists, but by a nation that claimed to be acting in the very name of freedom, of moral justice, of civilization itself."

After the war, Dorothy welcomed back to the Catholic Worker the young men who had gone to fight, even though their position had been different from hers. She also helped any veterans who were in need, as she mentioned in her letter of appeal in *The Catholic Worker* in July–August 1947: "We know you have many calls made on you, from Europe, from Asia, from all over the world, but there are our own veterans, wounded morally, mentally, spiritually, and our veterans of the class war, with their ruptures, amputated fingers, legs,—sick brains, sick bodies, sick souls."

The end of World War II brought not the peace that had been hoped for, but the Cold War, and a nearly constant threat of nuclear war. During the 1950s, education and work for peace continued along with hospitality and the other facets of the Worker program. In the May 1950 *Catholic Worker*, Dorothy wrote about her participation in a fast for peace, a time of intense penance and prayer.

In the April 1953 *Catholic Worker*, as she had on many other occasions, Dorothy advocated voluntary poverty as a spiritual weapon as well as a practical means of avoiding participation in preparations for war. Voluntary poverty in this context meant taking jobs that were not part of the war industry; it meant earning little so that one would not have to pay war taxes, at that time related to the Korean War: "Our whole modern economy is based on preparation for war and that is one of the great modern arguments for poverty."

During the cold war, Catholic Workers resisted McCarthyism. Under the guise of fighting Communism, Senator Joe McCarthy labeled great numbers of Americans as Communists and ruined their reputations and careers. Dorothy courageously wrote about the harm these attacks had done in the June 1953 *Catholic Worker*, referring to Senator McCarthy and his investigations as a manifestation of evil: "Man's freedom stems from his free will, and he must respect the freedom of other men because they are made to the image and likeness of God and are temples of the Holy Spirit. To build up fear of other men is to build up hatred too. 'Perfect love casts out fear.' Such a witch hunt as has been set loose in the country today, serves to distract the mind from our growing materialism, and to set us in the self-righteous position of rooting out the evil in other men, paying no attention to the beam in our own eye...."

Following their principles, Dorothy and other Catholic Workers refused to participate in "preparedness for war," advocating instead the pure means of love. They were jailed for engaging in civil disobedience against compulsory nuclear civil-defense drills. As she had during previous jail stays, Dorothy used the time and the difficult circumstances when in jail for refusal to participate in air-raid drills as an opportunity to pray. William Miller told us, "The Psalms were her strong spiritual fare. In jail in the late 1950s for her refusal to take shelter during an air raid warning, she commented in notes to friends how some of her fellow inmates longed for a 'fix.' Her morning 'fix,' she said, was her reading of the Psalms."[24] Writing from prison, Dorothy expressed in the July–August 1957 *Catholic Worker* how difficult it continued to be to explain to others the Catholic Worker refusal to participate in those drills: "It is very hard to make it clear that we do not want to harass people who are only doing their duty and that although we break one law in order to make our point clear about our refusal to cooperate with psychological warfare, we bend over backward to show our respect for the desire for the common good which most laws are for. Certainly our very Works of Mercy are to show our sense of responsibility for our brothers and our desire to do our share and more than our share in a realm where the State is not supposed to function except in cases of crisis." The demonstrations against the air raid drills quickly grew to great numbers, and the drills were eventually stopped.

Vietnam War

The leadership of the Catholic Worker in opposing American involvement in Vietnam during the 1960s is legendary. From the beginning, Catholic Workers protested against the Vietnam War and supported conscientious objectors and those who resisted the draft. The paper covered what was happening in Vietnam as well as reporting on protests by Catholic Workers and others involved in the peace movement.

Dorothy Day was no stranger to the history of Indochina (Vietnam) prior to the participation of the United States in the Vietnam War. Long before the Vietnam War began, she was writing about the problems of French colonialism in the country. In researching her book on St. Thérèse of Lisieux, Dorothy had stumbled upon one of Thérèse's favorite missionaries, Théophane Vénard, who had been martyred in Indochina. (He was canonized in 1988.) Dorothy quoted Vénard in the pages of *The Catholic Worker* (May 1954) about the oppression of the Vietnamese by the French in the name of civilizing pagans and Christianizing them. Vénard criticized his countrymen for being godless, secular, and utilitarian in Vietnam, rather than witnesses to the gospel. Dorothy concluded that it was not Christianity and freedom that were being defended, but possessions.[25] Dorothy saw that the

United States had inherited the stained mantle from the French, who had failed in their attempt to pacify (read colonize) Indochina in the name of stopping what was called the Bamboo Curtain, and later, Communism. Vénard's writings encouraged Dorothy in her contention of the falsity of "a central premise of the cold war, namely, that the contest between the communist powers and the United States and its European allies was an ideological and religious struggle of such great consequence, that the governments of the Christian West could use any and all means to secure victory."[26]

During the Vietnam War as during World War II, Dorothy wrote of her consistent commitment to nonviolence from the gospel, but also published articles in *The Catholic Worker* by those who condemned modern war on just war principles. It was during this period also that both Dorothy and Thomas Merton questioned John Courtney Murray's application of the just war theory in the nuclear age—and received criticism from Catholics who disagreed.[27]

Dorothy's "On Pilgrimage" column in the June 1966 *Catholic Worker* presented the works of war, and especially the use of napalm in Vietnam, in the context of the second part of the Matthew 25 story—that what one does to these least ones may bring condemnation at the Last Judgment. Dorothy wrote this two years before the coverage of the My Lai massacre which brought the horror of what was going on in Vietnam to the American public so graphically. Dorothy challenged the belief that absolutely anything, however barbaric, could be justified in war in the effort to contain Communism:

> Communities fight for government contracts, even for the manufacture of napalm, gasoline jelly, for noxious gases, not to speak of bombs, planes, helicopters, trucks, and all the armaments that go into devastating wars. How many countries we arm—to keep the peace, as they say. What insanity!
>
> If we keep coming back to this subject always in these pages, it is not only because Peace is the most important cause of our time, but because too, I have found on my travels so many people who not only do not question the morality of war (any more than an Eichmann questioned the morality of the

extermination of a people) but do not even know that napalm is a fire that burns the flesh from the bone and that there is nothing that can put it out.

God did not forgive the sin of ignorance, as Father Paul Hanley Furfey pointed out once, recalling the 25th chapter of St. Matthew.

Lord, when did we see you burned with napalm? Inasmuch as ye did it to one of these my little ones you did it unto me.

Tom Cornell tells the story of his question to Dorothy about her pacifism during those years: "The story has been written many times of a brash young Catholic pacifist who asked Dorothy Day in 1965 to write a clear, theological, logical, pacifist manifesto, noting that none had so far appeared under her name. I confess. It was I. I'm glad I did it, even if I'm often embarrassed by being reminded. I'm glad because Dorothy answered, 'I can write no other than this: unless we use the weapons of the Spirit, denying ourselves and taking up the Cross and following Jesus, dying with Him and rising with Him, men will go on fighting, and often from the highest motives, believing that they are fighting defensive wars for justice and in self-defense against present or future aggression.'"[28]

Consistent Ethic of Life

Dorothy not only articulated Catholic pacifism in the pages of *The Catholic Worker*, she also opposed violence in all its forms, embracing what has come to be called the consistent ethic of life.

The Catholic Worker protested the death penalty, even for suspected spies. In her commentary on the execution of the Rosenbergs in the April 1952 issue, Dorothy affirmed her commitment to life, and took the opportunity to point out that she did not consider joining committees the most effective method of working against violence:

I forgot to mention that we filed a protest in the Rosenberg case (who were sentenced to death for treason), and I had been asked to serve on a Rosenberg Committee and a Woman's for Peace Committee, but had refused because the grandchildren were having mumps and I was more interested in washing diapers and minding babies than I was in serving on Committees. It was one thing to dash out into the fray and speak once in a while, or march on a picket line. It was another thing to serve on a committee.

Dorothy's conversation with a young man about the Rosenberg case at the time emphasizes that Catholic Workers saw the death penalty itself, independent of any particular case, as a life issue: "Tony Aratari...came in to lunch and I asked him, 'Tony, why did you sign that petition for the Rosenbergs? Do you know you will be charged with collaborating with Communists?' 'It is because I am against capital punishment,' he said. In other words, Tony, as the rest of us, is in favor of life."

In the March 1966 *Catholic Worker,* years after World War II had ended, Dorothy rejected the idea of taking human life, regardless of whether the victim was innocent or a terrible dictator. She was not in favor of a plot like that of Bonhoeffer to kill Hitler: "Assassinations, by whomsoever they are attempted or perpetrated, are murders and do not solve the problems, which are always deep-seated, going back into the past. Cut off the head of one tyrant and half a dozen others spring into place. Nor do removals by another means solve problems which will always be with us. The need is to change the minds and hearts of men."

Within the Houses of Hospitality, it was often a challenge to respond nonviolently to violent situations. Among guests who had suffered greatly or who had been on the streets for years it was not uncommon for violence to erupt. The challenge was for Catholic Workers to defuse situations nonviolently. Dorothy wrote in the March–April 1971 issue of the *Catholic Worker,* describing the Houses of Hospitality as schools of nonviolence:

The work is not without danger—this adventure of ours. We live on a warfront—class war, race war. Mental cases abound, drugged youth haunt our streets and doorsteps. We are, here at First Street, a school of nonviolence. Not a week passes when there have not been knives drawn, a fist up-raised, the naked face of hate shown and the silence of bitterness and despair shattered by the crash of breaking crockery or glass, a chair overthrown. But there are other days when suddenly there is laughter, scraps of conversation among the men, and one feels men have been wooed out of their misery for a moment by a sense of comradeship between the young people serving and those served.

Dorothy used the example of responding to violence in the houses to answer the questions and accusations of so many who believe that pacifists will stand by while their relatives are attacked, making it clear that she was not opposed to police action when necessary:

> What would you do if an armed maniac were to attack you, your child, your mother? How many times have we heard this. Restrain him, of course, but not kill him. Confine him if necessary. But perfect love casts our fear and love overcomes hatred. All this sounds trite but experience is not trite.
>
> On one occasion an armed maniac did try to kill Arthur Sheehan, one of our editors during the war. A victim of World War I, who had already assaulted several other men in the house and almost broken my wrist one day when I tried to turn off the radio in the kitchen, took a large breadknife and a crucifix and announced that he was going to kill Arthur. Another woman and I seized him, forcing him to drop the knife. We could not hold him, however, and after he had hurled a gallon can of vegetables at Arthur and smashed a hole in the wall, we restrained him long enough to allow Arthur to escape. We called the police and asked that Harry be confined to Bellevue for observation, but since we would not bring charges against him the hospital released him the next day. Later we persuaded them to keep him for a month in the psychiatric ward. He was returned to the hospital, but at the end of thirty days he was out again, and continued to eat on our breadline during the war. Some time later we heard that he had shipped out on an oil tanker.[29]

Writing in the July–August 1962 *Catholic Worker*, Dorothy tied together the questions regarding life that were addressed to her whenever she, famous for her pacifism, gave talks, quoting Dostoevsky as she so often did: "I seldom speak at state universities or non-Catholic colleges without the question of overpopulation, birth control, abortion, and euthanasia coming up. The entire question of man's control over the life of others, over the life forces within man, is one of the most profound importance today. Kirilloff debated the question—Did God create me or is my life my own, to do with as I choose? And as an absolute gesture of defiance, an assertion of independence, a denial of God's existence, he took his life."

Dorothy regretted forever her lack of nonviolence in regard to her unwanted pregnancy. She had had an abortion long before her conversion to Catholicism in order to hold onto the man with whom she lived at the time, Lionel Moise. Her effort to hold onto him was unsuccessful; he left her anyway. Her biographer describes the devastating effect the abortion had on Dorothy: "Finally it was over. A life that had begun an unwilled journey into time, a life that was guilty of nothing, had been assaulted and made to die because it stood in the self-willed course of others. Its destiny, for whatever meaning, had no further business with history. Now only a bloody and battered blob of tissue, it lay on the receiving towel to be wrapped, no doubt, in toilet paper, and flushed down the drain. It was the realization of this that became a part of Dorothy's person and, finally, changed her life."[30] After the abortion Dorothy thought she could never have a child. It was her joy in becoming pregnant that initially led her to take the step to receive instructions in the Catholic Church.

Daniel Berrigan, SJ, known for his dramatic actions in opposition to the Vietnam War and to weapons buildup, but not so well-known for his opposition to abortion, always acknowledged his debt to Dorothy Day. Committed to the consistent ethic of life, he spoke out against abortion during the earliest days of Roe v. Wade, before many pro-life activists were even aware of the issues. Father Berrigan connected the indiscriminate killing of modern war with that of abortion. In his introduction to the 1981 edition of *The Long Loneliness*, Berrigan expresses the debt of Catholics to Dorothy Day, who had said no to violence and war. He recounts his reading of Miller's book on the movement, *A Harsh and Dreadful Love:* "When William Miller's history of the Catholic Worker Movement was published, I had just come out of prison during the Vietnam years. I stayed up all night, unable to put the book aside. What held me in thrall was an absolutely stunning consistency. *No* to all killing.

Invasions, incursions, excusing causes, call of the blood, summons to the bloody flag, casuistic body counts, just wars, necessary wars, religious wars, needful wars, holy wars—into the fury of the murderous crosswinds went her simple word: *no*."[31]

Taking so many risks and often jailed for his opposition to war, Berrigan credits Dorothy as the inspiration for those who followed: "Without Dorothy, without that exemplary patience, courage, moral modesty, without this woman pounding at the locked door behind which the powerful mock the powerless with games of triage, without her, the resistance we offered would have been simply unthinkable. She urged our consciences off the beaten track; she made the impossible (in our case) probable, and then actual. She did this, first of all, by living as though the truth were true."[32]

Dorothy did not always agree with the actions of Dan Berrigan or his brother Phil and the others who concluded that in order to draw attention to the terrible weapons being built each day for the destruction of human beings, they would have to destroy the weapons themselves. She wrote about the philosophical and theological differences involved in *The Catholic Worker*, but also emphasized in the December 1970 *Catholic Worker* how she and other Catholic Workers were keeping all those who had participated in these actions, and were now suffering in jail, in their thoughts and prayers:

> In general the Catholic Worker takes the position of the War Resisters, Quakers and Fellowship of Reconciliation peace groups in not taking part in these actions, on the principle that, although it was only property which suffered destruction, we ourselves have suffered violence, vandalism by hostile right-wing groups, the beating of individuals, the destruction of mailing lists and records, the burning of houses and barns, etc. So we repeat the golden rule, "Do unto others what you would have them do unto you," and its contrary, "Do not do unto others what you would not have them do unto you."
>
> But we take this opportunity to tell the Fathers Berrigan, and all those who are suffering imprisonment now, that not a day goes by that we do not think of them....

Dorothy was invited to speak at the Eucharistic Congress on August 6, 1976, in Philadelphia, held to honor all the members of the armed forces. August 6 was not only the feast of the Transfiguration, but also the announcing of the dropping of the atom bomb on Hiroshima, which the organizers of the Eucharistic Congress apparently did not remember. She began by talking about Works of Mercy and how they are carried out in the Houses of Hospitality. Recalling the need to be reconciled before approaching the altar, she called for repentance, quoting the words of Jesus, "Unless you do penance, you shall likewise perish." Suddenly, she mentioned Hiroshima and other military massacres and how insensitive the organizers of this event were to neglect what had happened on this day: "Our Creator gave us life and the Eucharist to sustain our life. But we have given the world deadly instruments of inconceivable magnitude." Dorothy continued, "I plead in this short paper that we will regard this military Mass, and all our Masses today, as an act of penance, begging God to forgive us." She concluded by expressing her gratitude "for the tremendous liberty there is in Holy Mother Church to hear these words."[33]

Through her courageous stand against violence, Dorothy gave to Catholic men and women an option for peace they did not previously have. In the future, Catholic young people may not be pressured to give their lives in war to "make peace." They are supported by the church in taking a stand against war.

16

St. Thérèse: Dorothy Day and the Little Way

Dorothy Day's book, *Therese: A Life of Therese of Lisieux*, the fruit of much research and study on Dorothy's part, provides new insights into the message of St. Thérèse (1873–1897) and reveals the depth of Dorothy's own spirituality. At the time when Dorothy wrote about her, Thérèse was already known to the world as the Saint of the Little Way. In the April 1952 *Catholic Worker*, Dorothy also called her "the saint of the responsible." Dorothy reflected in her book that while St. Thérèse's popularity was great, the social implications of her teachings were yet to be written. Since that time, the Carmelite contemplative has become even better known and was named a doctor of the church by Pope John Paul II.

In retelling the story of Thérèse's family, her childhood, and her brief years at a convent in France before her death at age twenty-four, Dorothy was able to relate to the young nun's life the profound philosophical and theological concepts of the roots of the Catholic Worker movement outlined in previous chapters. She drew out the social implications of Thérèse's Little Way of love in a creative way, emphasizing that she wrote in order to overcome the "sense of futility in Catholics, men, women, and youth, married and single, who feel hopeless and useless, less than the dust, ineffectual, wasted, powerless."[1]

In the April 1952 issue of *The Catholic Worker*, Dorothy had shared with readers that she was writing a book about St. Thérèse. Reflecting on tragedies and suffering in the world and in daily life recorded in the newspapers, Dorothy noted in that issue that most people feel they can do nothing about these tragedies, that their role is already written for them: "We have a fatalistic sense of taking part in a gigantic tragedy, a fearful adventure. Our life is charged with drama about which we can do nothing." She declared that she was writing a life of the Little Flower because Thérèse was determined to respond to the drama of sin, evil, and redemption in the world, "even though she was imprisoned to all intents and purposes, in a small French convent in Normandy, unknown to all the world." Thérèse's unusual method for engagement with the world was receptivity to God's love, her willing acceptance to be just a little grain of sand while the power of God's love worked within her.

Dorothy shared with readers at the outset that *Therese* was written very much from her own point of view, emphasizing aspects that interested her particularly. It was the common person, the worker, the masses who had proclaimed her a saint, and it was for them that she had written the book. Thérèse had given her message to the world at a time, Dorothy said, when holiness was not the "ordinary thing in this day of post-war materialism, delinquency, and all those other words which indicate how dissatisfied the world of the West is with its economy of abundance while the world of the East [today we would say the South] sits like Lazarus at the gate of Dives."[2]

In her book Dorothy emphasized, as she had so often done, the problem of governments becoming stronger and more centralized, and "the whole world given over to preparations for war and the show of force." Dorothy presented Thérèse's message as a powerful, explosive alternative force, a way of love that "can transform our lives and the life of the world, once put into effect." Thérèse's Little Way would blow the dynamite of the Catholic Church, as Peter Maurin had said was so necessary, in a force for good more powerful than the atom bomb: "Is the atom a small thing? And yet what havoc it has wrought. Is her little way a small contribution to the life of the spirit? It has all the power of the spirit of Christianity behind it....We know that one impulse of grace is of infinitely more power than a cobalt bomb."[3]

Dorothy was able to focus on concerns and events in Thérèse's family life and her spirituality in this regard which other biographers may have overlooked. In what other book on St. Thérèse, for example, could one find Dorothy's description of Thérèse's mother's discomfort with the violence and destruction of the Franco-Prussian War, during which so many men of the village lost a limb, together with Dorothy's commentary on St. Thomas's conditions for a just war? For Dorothy, who spent a lifetime working for peace, the Little Way included good deeds and acts of love, but also was related to sins of omission, the little things left undone, the protests not made, the stands not taken, the small things which might have made a difference.

Dorothy's earliest acquaintance with the Little Flower had come in the hospital when her daughter, Tamar Teresa, was born. Dorothy had decided to name her baby Teresa for St. Teresa of Avila. When another woman in the hospital asked if the Teresa were for St. Thérèse of Lisieux and wanted to give her a St. Thérèse medal, Dorothy was not comfortable with the idea. After the other woman pressed her, however, she did accept the medal and a role for the other St. Teresa/Thérèse for her baby: "I decided that although I would name my child after the older saint, the new one would be my own Teresa's novice mistress, to train her in the spiritual life. I knew that I wanted to have the child baptized a Catholic and I wanted both saints to be taking care of her. One was not enough."[4]

When one of her first confessors gave Dorothy Thérèse's autobiography *The Story of a Soul* to read, her response was that she was not looking for anything so simple. She "felt slightly aggrieved at Father Zachary," thinking that the priest might be insulting her intelligence with "pious pap" because she was a woman: "I dutifully read *The Story of a Soul* and am ashamed to confess that I found it colorless, monotonous, too small in fact for my notice. What kind of a saint was this who felt that she had to practice heroic charity in eating what was put in front of her, in taking medicine, enduring cold and heat, restraint, enduring the society of mediocre souls, in following the strict regime of the convent of Carmelite nuns which she had joined at the age of fifteen?"[5]

Dorothy said that it took her years to appreciate the Little Flower: "I much preferred then to read about spectacular saints who were impossible to imitate. The message of Therese was too obviously meant for each one of us, confronting us with daily duties, simple and small, but constant."[6] And yet, after years of studying great literature, great philosophers, liturgy and economics, after so many years of living the gospel among the poor and taking a courageous stand against violence and war, Dorothy found many answers to the great questions in the life and spirituality of this young woman. Writing in the *Houston Catholic Worker* of May–June 1996, Jim Allaire described the change in Dorothy's attitude toward Thérèse over the years of her life at the Catholic Worker. Her many humble chores with the poor provided her with schooling in the Little Way:

> Dorothy didn't just read about the Little Way and then decide to adopt it as a spiritual practice or attitude from among other spiritual methods or outlooks. Rather she discovered the Little Way within her experience of Catholic Worker life.
> Simply put, the Little Way was active love, the "harsh and dreadful love" that Dorothy often spoke about, quoting Dostoevsky's character Fr. Zossima. And when Fr. Zossima spoke of active love becoming for some people "a whole science" it was Therese's Little Way that was that science.

Dorothy discovered that the sweet book about Thérèse that she had rejected had been doctored and adapted, that some of the strongest expressions had been removed, and even the photographs had been touched up to make her look less haggard upon her death. Scholars had eventually objected and gradually her real pictures and writings became more available. Dorothy told readers: "Father Martindale, the British Jesuit, spoke out with indignation about this tampering with the pictures. In view of the gigantic role she was to play in the life of the Church, one can understand this wrath. Even her writing, her autobiography, her *Story of a Soul* was worked over, her strong expressions toned down, and it is only recently that we have had an authentic translation of her manuscript."[7]

Dorothy had always been interested in better hagiography, writing about the saints that was more realistic. She achieved this task herself in writing about Thérèse, applying her teaching to the most challenging issues. As Peter Casarella has pointed out: "Dorothy wanted to lift the veil of desiccated piety from the familiar image of the Catholic saints. Moreover, she was convinced that responding to the call to sanctity at the very center of one's daily life was the *only way* to confront widespread global injustices without exacerbating the cycle of violence and despair in the world."[8]

The Little Way is the way of faithfulness and love in the small things of every day. The deeper concept of spiritual childhood also underlies Thérèse's message. Dorothy explained in her book how it was through this spirituality that Thérèse received her nickname: "Therese called 'flowers' her little sacrifices of every day cast before God in what she called the way of spiritual childhood; it is from this idea that she received the nickname of so many who loved her, the Little Flower." By the time she endorsed Thérèse's Little Way, Dorothy had understood the concept of "little" as being profound. She described it in Thérèse's own words:

> There has been so much discussion of the diminutive "little" which Therese used constantly that it is good to remember her words of explanation…."To be little…is…not to attribute to ourselves the virtues we practice, nor to believe ourselves capable of practicing virtue at all. It is rather to recognize the fact that God puts treasures of virtue into the hands of his little children to make use of them in time of need, but they remain always treasures of the good God. Finally, to be little means that we must never be discouraged over our faults, for children often fall but they are too small to harm themselves very much."[9]

Dorothy noted Thérèse's connection with the Benedictine spirituality that so influenced the Catholic Worker, pointing out that before she went to the convent, Thérèse went to a Benedictine school. The importance of the Divine Office in Thérèse's life is emphasized over and over by Dorothy, as the *opus Dei* (work of God) of the Benedictine Rule. Both liturgy, including the Divine

Office, and manual labor, with their Benedictine roots as important components of monastic life (as in the Catholic Worker), are explored here. Thérèse, who was inexperienced at manual labor, at housework and yard work and not very good at it, embraced it nonetheless.

Dorothy, who read *The Imitation of Christ* over many years of her life, must have identified with Thérèse's frequent reading of that text so much that she memorized it. Thérèse said of the classic book: "Much to everybody's amusement, I always used to have it with me and my aunt would often open it at random and make me say by heart the first chapter she came to."[10]

Dorothy wrote of Thérèse, "Later she was to say that she could read nothing but the Gospels, and was so nourished by them, she loved them, that she wore them under her clothes, pinned next to her heart." Several times over the years in her columns in *The Catholic Worker,* Dorothy mentioned this endearing habit of Thérèse. Dorothy explained that she got this idea from St. Cecilia: "She made Cecilia her patroness. It was not because she was a patroness of musicians, but because she sang in her heart during trials and had unbounded confidence....Therese began to wear the Gospels next to her heart because it is said of St. Cecilia, 'the Holy Gospels lay ever on her breast.'"[11]

Thérèse had chosen the cloistered life at age fifteen, at a convent where two of her sisters had already entered. Dorothy observed that although she was raised in what would have been considered a working- or middle-class family with one servant (her father was a watchmaker and her mother made fine lace) and later lived in the Carmel, Thérèse's spirituality was not individualistic; she was not unaware of poverty and suffering in the world. As a child she had often been designated by her family as the one to help the poor, giving them things with her own hands or inviting poor families to the Martin family table.

Thérèse wanted to be a missionary to foreign lands, and through her prayer she actually became one. She had wanted to go to the Carmelite convent in Hanoi, but was unable to because of her health. She is now the patroness of the missions. Reference is made in Thérèse's writing to Father Théophane Vénard in

Vietnam, about whom Dorothy also wrote in her columns in *The Catholic Worker*, and whose insights into the situation in Vietnam during the time the French were there gave her an early understanding of the Vietnam War.

Dorothy's own faith had matured with years of reading and prayer and through her participation in the famous retreat. It is logical that references to themes from the retreat would appear in *Therese*, because Thérèse read scripture and St. John of the Cross so much and the retreat has its basis in the Bible and the spirituality of John of the Cross. Dorothy alluded to Thérèse's words from St. John of the Cross: "Love was the measure by which she wished to be judged." Thérèse, like Dorothy, read John of the Cross as a teenager, although perhaps more exclusively. "It was later, during her convent life, that she read all of St. John of the Cross and the works of St. Teresa of Avila. She was still in her teens when she read these great masterpieces of the spiritual life, the work of two of the greatest mystics the world has known....Between the ages of sixteen and eighteen, Thérèse wrote, she read no one but St. John of the Cross, and over and over again in her autobiography she quotes from him, especially from his poetry."[12]

When Dorothy read in Thérèse's writings that all are called to holiness, this was not new to her. It was one of the great themes of Peter Maurin's teaching and of Dorothy's life. When she read of pruning, of stripping oneself to put off the old man and put on the new person in Christ, she recognized the words. She had been reading about this in St. Paul in the scriptures for many years and hearing it each year in the retreat. She repeats the idea in *Therese*: "All natural love is pruned in order that a supernatural love may grow."[13]

Thérèse insisted that everyone could be a saint, that it was through saints that the world could be transformed—a theme Dorothy herself had promoted. While she believed that she had a special vocation, that her vocation was to be a saint—and a special kind of saint for our times—Thérèse emphasized that her way really was for everyone, a most ordinary way.

Thérèse uses the language of the nuptial relationship from the Canticle of Canticles to describe the relationship of Christian to

Christ, another theme from the Lacouture/Hugo retreat that Dorothy often mentioned in her writings. The language of Thérèse and of the retreat, as Dorothy expresses it in her writings, is the language of lovers. It was also Dorothy's language when she admitted as she was coming to the decision to enter the church that she understood her common-law husband Forster Batterham's jealousy of her relationship with God: "Like all women in love, I wanted to be united to my love. Why should not Forster be jealous? Any man who did not participate in this love would, of course, realize my infidelity, my adultery. In the eyes of God, any turning toward creatures to the exclusion of Him is adultery and so it is termed over and over again in Scripture."[14]

Upon reading Thérèse's reflections in nuptial language on her first communion, Hans Urs von Balthasar suggested that perhaps being so young and without experience, Thérèse might not have known the depth of which she was speaking when she used this language.[15] Dorothy disagreed with the eminent theologian on this point. She wrote later: "In the convent of Carmel she [Thérèse] became the Spouse of Christ, and she did not hesitate to say that 'He had kissed her with the kiss of His mouth' and to apply the glowing and sensuous words of the Canticle of Canticles to her relationship with Him." Dorothy answered Balthasar: "What did she know of men, this sheltered and cloistered girl, loved only by family and Sisters in religion? She had been an observant child, and had heard many things she was not meant to hear, on visits away from home, on holidays at Trouville and Deauville, on those days when she went to the home of a friend of the family to be tutored and on their pilgrimage to Rome...."[16] Dorothy defended Thérèse's use of nuptial language, drawing from Berdyaev:

> Some have called attention to the sexual element in such lan-
> guage. It is the language of love, of course, and the only way to
> describe the love of God is in terms of the most intense human
> love, that between man and woman. One does not have to expe-
> rience it to know what it means. Nicholas Berdyaev states that
> the keenest and most intense love between man and woman is
> not dependent on sexual intercourse. This love which makes all

seem new is already described in the Old Testament as a wedding, and there has never been a greater song of love written than the Canticle of Canticles.[17]

The retreat had taught Dorothy that human nature is transfigured once the choice is made to respond to God with Mary's *Fiat*: "Be it done to me according to your Word." It is a choice that must be remade each day in order to respond to grace, to grow into the new person described in the scriptures. This was the abandonment to Divine Providence that allowed Thérèse to be daring in her desire to be a saint. She was responding to grace.

Dorothy's October 1949 *Catholic Worker* article pointed out that those who might see in Thérèse a sentimental piety perhaps were not well enough acquainted with her and her spirituality:

Either the Little Flower is looked upon (perhaps because of her nickname) with sentimentality, or, as one gets to know her better, with dread. On that frail battleground of her flesh was fought the wars of today. When she died her bones were piercing her body and she died in an agony of both flesh and spirit. She was tempted against faith and said that for the last years of her life she forced herself to believe with her indomitable will while a mocking voice cried in her ears that there was neither heaven nor hell, and she was flinging away her life for nothing. To her God was a consuming flame.

At the retreat Father Hugo spoke about the love of creatures often becoming such a distraction that God becomes very secondary in one's life. He called the good things of this life samples, meaning that they were a little sample of the great joy that is to be found in God. The samples, creatures, were just a shadow of what was to come. Thérèse also said, "But creatures! creatures!…It would be a mistake to look elsewhere for a shadow of beauty which [I] might take for Beauty itself."[18]

Dorothy told how Thérèse spoke of dying of love and how this became a reality for her. When she spoke in this way, however, neither Dorothy nor Thérèse was speaking of having visions and other extraordinary events, but seeking the truth in love: "It was not ecstasies of visions that Therese was talking about when she spoke of dying of love. 'All such fancies cannot help me; I can nourish myself only on the truth. That is the reason I have never wanted to have any visions. On earth we can never behold heaven and the angels as they really are. I much prefer to wait for that until after my death.'"[19]

Dorothy, who had suffered so much during World War II because of her pacifism, emphasized Thérèse's use of the weapons of the spirit in combating evil. As Dorothy said in the April 1952 *Catholic Worker:* "She [Thérèse] used the means at her disposal to participate in everything, to increase the sum total of the love of God in the world by every minute act, every suffering, every movement of her body and soul, done for the love of God and the love of souls. She used the spiritual weapons every one of us has at our disposal." An example of Thérèse's use of the spiritual weapons comes from her childhood. Thérèse had come to know that a man named Pranzini, who had murdered three people, was to be put to death by guillotine in France. Thérèse determined to try to save him through prayer:

> I heard talk of a great criminal just condemned to death for some horrible crimes; everything pointed to the fact that he would die impenitent....I felt in the depths of my heart *certain* that our desires would be granted, but to obtain courage to pray for sinners I told God I was sure He would pardon the poor, unfortunate Pranzini; that I'd believe this even if he went to his death without *any signs of repentance* or without having *gone to confession.* I was absolutely confident in the mercy of Jesus. But I was begging Him for a *"sign"* of repentance only for my own simple consolation.
>
> My prayer was answered to the letter! In spite of Papa's prohibition that we read no papers, I didn't think I was disobeying when reading passages pertaining to Pranzini. The day after the execution I found the newspaper *"La Croix."* I opened it quickly and what did I see? Ah! my tears betrayed my emotion and I was obliged to hide. Pranzini had not gone to confession. He had mounted the scaffold and was preparing to place his head in the formidable opening, when suddenly, seized by an inspiration, he turned, took hold of the *crucifix* the priest was holding out to him and *kissed* the *sacred wounds three times!* Then his soul went to receive the *merciful* sentence of Him who declares that in

heaven there will be more joy over one sinner who does penance than over ninety-nine just who have no need of repentance.

I had obtained the sign I requested....[20]

Dorothy's reflections on the Pranzini story emphasize Thérèse's use of the supernatural weapons on this occasion, but also focus on the primacy of conscience, exercising one's judgment at the same time as respecting authority.

Another incident in Thérèse's life illustrated the saint's way of working with earthly authority to implement what she understood to be the will of God. The young girl, discouraged by the local mother superior and the local bishop who had asked her to wait until she was older to enter the convent, traveled with her father to see Pope Leo XIII, himself, to ask permission to be admitted early. The priest who guided the group to Rome forbade anyone to speak at the papal audience. However, since speaking with him was the whole purpose of the trip, and her father and sisters had all told Thérèse she should speak, she ignored the order and spoke up: "This was the moment that Therese was living for, this was the time for her to make her request. Father Reverony had cried out loudly that 'he absolutely forbade anyone to speak,' and with her heart beating wildly, Therese turned to look at Celine. 'Speak,' her sister whispered, and the child spoke out bravely, 'Most Holy Father, I want to ask a great favor.'" Thérèse described the incident:

> The Pope bent his head at once, his face almost touching mine, while his piercing black eyes seemed to be gazing into my soul. I began again: "Most Holy Father, in honor of your Jubilee, let me enter Carmel at fifteen." The Vicar General of Bayeux was startled and far from pleased. "Your Holiness," he interrupted, "this is a child who wishes to enter Carmel; the superiors are already going into the question."
>
> "Very well, my child," said His Holiness, "do what the superiors decide." I clasped my hands and placed them on his knee, while I made the final effort. "Holy Father, if you said yes, everyone else would be willing." He gazed at me steadily, and said, stressing every syllable, "Well, well. You will enter if it is God's will."[21]

Dorothy's commentary on this episode emphasized Thérèse's confidence in the Holy Father, regarded as he was as Christ on earth, the head of the church, and also brought in the idea from St. Ignatius about the importance of working as though all depended on oneself and praying as though all depended on God—an idea often repeated in Catholic Worker circles.

It is not a surprise, somehow to find that Thérèse and her family, like Dorothy, studied the fathers of the desert and strove to imitate them. As Dorothy did as a child and when she first came into the church, Thérèse and her sisters longed to do great, heroic deeds for God. It took time to develop the "little" way. Thérèse, like Dorothy, read about the fathers of the desert and was attracted to their spirituality and their life. As children, Thérèse and her sisters played that they were hermits: "They read the *Lives of the Fathers of the Desert*, and they pretended they were hermits, she and her cousin Marie, who was her age; while one prayed, the other would be engaged in active work in the garden."[22] When Thérèse was finally given permission to enter Carmel at age fifteen, she described it as fulfilling her hopes for a desert experience: "Everything here delighted me, our little cell most of all; it was as though I had been transported to my faraway desert."[23]

Merriman points out that it was at the time of Dorothy's sabbatical during World War II (which turned out to be six months instead of the year she had planned) that Dorothy's understanding of the Little Flower deepened. It was her desert experience:

> I could see clearly the difference between the two Teresa's now and came to the conclusion that St. Therese of Lisieux was the loftier vocation, the harder and more intense life....
> From that "year" I spent away from my work, I began to understand the greatness of the Little Flower. By doing nothing, she did everything. She let loose powers, consolations, a stream of faith, hope and love that will never cease to flow. How much richer we are because of her.[24]

Even William James, the skeptic who wrote *The Varieties of Religious Experience*, which Dorothy had read as a teenager and where she discovered Teresa of Avila, also wrote of Thérèse of Lisieux. He followed her idea that everything significant happens through the Little Way in history, especially anything related to the eternal forces of truth: "The bigger the unit you deal with, the hollower, the more brutal, the more mendacious is the life displayed. So I am...against all big successes and big results; and in favor of the eternal forces of truth which always work in the individual and immediately unsuccessful way, underdogs always, till history comes, after they are long dead, and puts them on the top." Merriman points out this second connection with William James and writes: "Because of Thérèse, Dorothy found meaningful the excerpt from one of William James' letters to a friend. She remarked upon the connection herself, and reprinted it on many occasions." [25]

Dorothy's embrace of the Little Way was spiritual, but also extended to fields like economics and war and peace. Dorothy did not hesitate to connect the decentralization of distributism in economics with the spirituality of St. Thérèse of Lisieux. In the December 1965 *Catholic Worker*, Dorothy wrote that the Little Way could be applied to economics, that it was the way of the poor:

> Newman wrote: "Let us but raise the level of religion in our hearts, and it will rise in the world. He who attempts to set up God's kingdom in his heart, furthers it in the world." And this goes for the priest, too, wherever he is, whether he deals with the problem of war or with poverty. He may write and speak, but he needs to study the little way, which is all that is available to the poor, and the only alternative to the mass approach of the State. Missionaries throughout the world recognize this little way of cooperatives and credit unions, small industry, village commune and cottage economy. And not only missionaries.

Thérèse's approach to spirituality resonates with the philosophy of Christian personalism, which emphasizes putting into action one's belief in the gospel and the importance of taking personal responsibility. The gospels proclaim the freedom of the children of God, a freedom that might in this world almost be called anarchism, as it sometimes was in the Catholic Worker movement. Thérèse's Little Way is much more compatible with personalism than with bureaucracies and government agencies, and thus with the Catholic Worker movement.

In the 1938 *Catholic Worker*, Dorothy wrote about one of her visits to Canada where she studied cooperatives, holding them up to readers as an example of the Little Way: "We wish our readers to know of this power house which is Antigonish, which is sending light over the continent. They are in their beginnings after years of patient endurance and study. They are working the "little way" and little St. Therese whose statue stands over the altar in the Church on Scaterie Island must love them."

In the October–November 1972 *Catholic Worker*, Dorothy mentioned Thérèse as she spoke of the work in Houses of Hospitality and in the efforts to make a personalist response to the problems of the social order. In the context of what she referred to as the always more extreme power of the state, she advocated the Little Way and the folly of the cross as the best methods: "The work is hard. The struggle against the "all-encroaching State" is harder. But if God is with us who can be against us? In Him we can do all things. We do know that God has chosen the foolish of this world to confound the wise. So please help us to continue in our folly, in the 'Little Way' of St. Therese which attracts so many to participate in our work."

Dorothy found illustrated in Thérèse's life and words Matthew 25, a central scripture passage for the Catholic Worker movement. The heart of Thérèse's message through her Little Way is love, the love of God, which could be so well expressed in the Works of Mercy. Thérèse understood from Matthew 25 that one could not love God without loving other people. She wanted to be the one to care for the sick, to take the hardest jobs to relieve others: "How gladly would I have been Infirmarian to take care of that sister. Grace would have spoken louder than nature. Yes, I have a taste for that work. And with how much love I would have done it. Oh, how I should have made that sister happy, especially in calling to mind those words of Jesus: 'I was sick and you visited me.'"[26]

Thérèse's understanding of penance, even before she entered the convent, included her Little Way of doing things for others: "My mortification consisted in checking my self-will, keeping back an impatient word, doing little things for those around me without their knowing it, and countless things like that."[27] She wrote of the day-to-day challenges of living out her theology of the practice of love in her convent in her autobiography, especially with one sister who had the "faculty of displeasing me in everything, in her ways, her words, he character; everything seems very disagreeable to me":

> I took care to render her all the services possible, and when I was tempted to answer her back in a disagreeable manner, I was content with giving her my most friendly smile, and with changing the subject of the conversation....
>
> One day at recreation she asked in almost these words: "Would you tell me, Sister Therese of the Child Jesus, what attracts you so much toward me; every time you look at me I see you smile?" Ah! what attracted me was Jesus hidden in the depths of her soul; Jesus who makes sweet what is most bitter. I answered that I was smiling because I was happy to see her (it is understood that I did not add that this was from a spiritual standpoint).[28]

Thérèse and Dorothy were two women who at first glance most people would have considered exact opposites. Casarella has noted that the similarities between them are based not in an abstract system, but in the Works of Mercy and a refusal to accept a dualism between theology and daily life. He observes that like Dorothy, "To express the earnestness of her love for the bridegroom, she [Thérèse] chose the language least likely to be abstracted into a preconceived system":

> Both women witnessed to Christ in a world in which social and religious "idealism" was rampant but tragically detached from real problems in people's lives....Dorothy and Therese were both tireless seekers of the truth, but neither of them rested content with abstract formulae. The doing of the truth rested not on arid speculation or personal achievement but rather their virtual inversion. The more immersed these women became in the daily work of charity, the easier it became to write—itself a theological labor—the truth that all is grace.[29]

Both women understood in a profound way that love involved suffering. Dorothy said of Thérèse: "[She] knew, too, that to love is to suffer, and just as a mother brings forth her children with anguish, she offered herself to the suffering that would result from her desire for souls." Both women believed in joining their sacrifices and suffering to those of Christ. Dorothy spoke of Thérèse's "co-suffering with Christ in Carmel."[30]

Dorothy wrote on other occasions about sharing in the suffering of the world in order to lighten the burdens of others. Her reflections included the Little Flower's words:

> There is so much failure all about us. It is so hard to reconcile oneself to such suffering, such long, enduring suffering of body and soul, that the only thing one can do is to stand by and save the dying ones who have given up hope of reaching out for beauty, joy, ease, and pleasure in this life. For all their reaching, they got little of it. To see these things in the light of faith, God's mercy, God's justice. His devouring love!...
>
> Once when I suffered and sat in church in a misery while waves and billows passed over me, I suddenly thought, with exultation, "I am sharing suffering," and it was immediately lightened. But usually it is as the Little Flower said: "Let us suffer if need be with bitterness and without courage."[31]

Thérèse said her mission was "to make Love loved." By this she did not mean sentimentality or sweet feeling, but a self-giving, self-emptying love that involved suffering, united to that of Christ himself. She always emphasized the love and mercy of God.

Miller remarked that it had not been easy for Dorothy to come to her understanding, so like Thérèse's, that love is the answer to everything: "It is remarkable that Dorothy, in whose natural disposition were strong elements of self-assertiveness, contentiousness, and even combativeness, should be recognized as one of the eloquent voices of this era to speak for love as the ultimate reality in which all of the world's turbulence, pain, and hate could forever be resolved."[32]

17

The Legacy of the Catholic Worker in a Troubled World

The synthesis of faith, ideas, and practice of the Catholic Worker movement offers a unity of spiritual and social life to a fragmented, suffering world. The thought that shaped the movement, the deep roots from which it grew, are not outdated but needed more than ever today because of war and violence against life in a culture of death, terrorism and the fear of terrorism, the toil of the poor around the world in sweatshops or with no work at all, the desperate conditions that drive so many to migrate from their home countries in search of work, and the crises within the church itself.

In the Catholic Worker, love and justice are combined in one in the mystery of the incarnation. The movement does not accept a dualism between work for justice and charity, between public and private life, between theology and social theory or economics, between cross and resurrection, between the Jesus of history and the Christ of faith, between spirituality and religion, between the material and the spiritual, between body and soul—they are all inextricably interwoven in the best of Catholic tradition. The Catholic Worker is different from any ideology, whether libertarian, Marxist, feminist, neoconservative, or fascist. It does not follow Adam Smith, Machiavelli, Max Weber, Engels, Freud, Nietzsche, Kinsey, or any utilitarian philosopher. It does not deconstruct, but builds up, creating anew in the shell of the old through the practice of the fourteen Works of Mercy (broadly and practically understood). The movement is not liberal or conservative, said Peter, but radical. As he said (Dorothy's quote in the May 1977 *Catholic Worker*): "People are just beginning to realize how deep-seated the evil is. That is why we must be Catholic

Radicals, we must get down to the roots. That is what radicalism is—the word means getting down to the roots."

The dualism between faith and practice affecting many Christians when the Catholic Worker began appeared then as now to deny the possibilities of the radical Christianity of the saints or of the implementation of the teaching of the encyclicals. The Catholic Worker rejects the separation of the gospel from culture decried by modern popes. David L. Schindler, whose book, *Heart of the World, Center of the Church*, profoundly addresses this problem, included the reprinting of Dorothy's 1948 book, *On Pilgrimage*, in his series, "Ressourcement: Retrieval and Renewal in Catholic Thought," published by Eerdmans. Schindler, following John Paul II, describes the positive unity that should inform Catholic faith, life, and culture, the communion of love of the Trinitarian God and of the community of believers, at the service of the whole human family, the unity insisted on by the Catholic Worker movement: "Thus John Paul II in *Christifideles laici*:... 'There cannot be two parallel lives in their existence: on the one hand, the so-called "spiritual" life, with its values and demands; and on the other, the so-called "secular" life, that is, life in a family, at work, in social relationships, in the responsibility of public life and its culture....' This split between the faith which many profess and their daily lives deserves to be counted among the more serious errors of our age."[1] Accordingly, Christians cannot separate faith and life and ignore their brothers and sisters in need. Dorothy pointed out in the June 1935 *Catholic Worker* the problem with the perception of Christianity when this is true: "We have allowed our brothers and sisters, our fellow members in the Mystical Body to be degraded, to endure slavery to a machine, to live in rat-infested holes....And Wobblies could say—'Work and Pray—live on hay; you'll get pie in the sky when you die.'"

In a collection of essays on the Catholic Worker movement, Mel Piehl asked, "How has the Worker been able to combine its spiritual outlook with its political witness in a way that testifies to the autonomy and priority of faith, yet remains fully engaged with the most difficult and controversial issues of actual public life in the United States and elsewhere?" His answer was that the place to begin to understand this radical involvement was with the Worker's religious orthodoxy:

> Almost from its beginnings, the movement's adherence to traditional Catholicism has been misunderstood or dismissed as a curious anomaly. Secular radicals and many Protestants have often considered it a baffling or irrelevant hindrance to the movement's admirable social views. The historian Lawrence Veysey, for example, is one of those who have considered the movement's churchly orthodoxy a strange, marginal quirk: the Catholic Worker, he declares, "insisted on maintaining a tenuous tie with the Catholic Church."[2]

The tie was not tenuous. However, Piehl notes that even some who have recognized the importance of the Catholic faith to the life, spirituality, and work of Dorothy Day and Peter Maurin have not understand it as a strength:

> People who think of Catholicism as a kind of military hierarchy, in which superiors hand out orders to inferiors on all subjects, tend to see the freewheeling Catholic Worker's commitment to the church as incomprehensible or contradictory. Even some Catholics, depending on their point of view, have seen the Worker's traditionalism as either a calculated ploy for infiltrating radicalism into the church, or a clever camouflage to deflect conservative criticism.

Piehl concludes, "Anyone who looks very closely at the history of the Catholic Worker must eventually recognize the inadequacy of such interpretations."[3]

The founders of the movement believed that the powerful force of living the gospel is the way to counteract the dominance of evil, and they insisted that action be closely united with prayer and contemplation. Their theology was neither pie in the sky when you die, nor putting all of one's hope in human progress, but rather working in the world in cooperation with grace, the life and power of God. They profoundly understood the need for redemption. As Dorothy said, "I see around me sin, suffering, and unutterable destitution. There is misery, materialism, degradation, ugliness on every side. All I see some days is sin. The problem is gigantic. Throughout the world there is homelessness, famine, fear, and war, and the threat of war. We live in a time of gigantic evil. It is hopeless to think of combating it by any means than that of sanctity. To think of overcoming such evil by material means, by alleviations, by changes in the social order only—all this is utterly hopeless."[4]

Dorothy wrote strongly about the devastating effects of the economic system on the poor. Her words in the September 1956 *Catholic Worker* apply equally well today to the global market, in which so many have no jobs at all or work for a pittance in *maquiladoras*, factories far from the shores of wealthy nations who reap the profits from their work: "People always fall back on the phrase, 'It is the system.' We need to change the system. We need to overthrow, not the government, as the authorities are always accusing the Communists 'of conspiring to teach to do,' but this rotten, decadent, putrid, industrial capitalist system which breeds such suffering in the whited sepulcher of New York."

Believing that Christians should work to transform the social order in order to come to the biblical vision of a new heaven and a new earth, wherein justice dwells, they were trying to say with action, "Thy will be done on earth as it is in heaven." Peter and Dorothy were driven by the gospel and believed in striving together with others toward the common good—rather than by the invisible hand of the market or by imposing one's views by violence. People say this does not work, but it really worked for Francis of Assisi, who changed the face of the earth with the methods of the gospel.

Dorothy spelled out the unique contribution of the Catholic Worker: "Peter Maurin's vision of the City of God included Pacifism and Distributism. And that is what distinguishes us from much of the lay apostolate today. It is the talent Christ has given us, and we cannot bury it."[5]

Peter and Dorothy did not despair. They knew with Teresa of Avila that "all times are dangerous times," but also that "all times are times in which God will give His graces to those who serve Him in earnest."[6] It is still possible today, in spite of all, to know with Dorothy and Catherine of Siena that "All the Way to Heaven is Heaven because He said, I am the Way." It is not too late for every person to adopt Mounier's idea of vocation, following their destiny in the dynamism of personalism, the gift of self. This idea of self-donation became an important theme in the document of the Second Vatican Council, *Gaudium et spes*, so influenced by the Polish personalism of John Paul II. Berdyaev can provide a vision of great freedom to do good in God's providence without forgetting or denying Golgotha. A rereading of the twenty-fifth chapter of Matthew can remind Christians each day of responding to the poor as to the Lord himself. When the response to one's love seems to be harsh and dreadful, a reading of Dostoevsky can encourage perseverance in the Works of Mercy. The intense love of God, voluntary poverty, and pacifism of St. Francis can free the world from consumerism and war, as he cut through the mores and unquestioned practices of his time. The study of the lives of Jacques and Raïssa Maritain can lead Christians to a deeper conversion of heart, and to the courage and wisdom to use pure means for pure ends.

Some profound theologians and spiritual directors today affirm the teaching of the Catholic Worker. Capuchin Father Raniero Cantalamessa, preacher to the papal household, celebrates and affirms the Lord's presence in the poor of Matthew 25: "He who pronounced the words, 'This is my body,' over the bread has also spoken the same words about the poor. He spoke them when, talking about what people had done or failed to do for the hungry, the thirsty, prisoners, the naked and the stranger, He solemnly declared: 'You did it to me' and 'You neglected to do it to me.' This is the equivalent of saying: 'You remember that ragged person who needed a piece of bread, that poor person holding out his hand—it was me, it was me!'" According to Cantalamessa, Christ is not present in the poor person in the same way as he is in the Eucharist, but he is "really present in the least of the brethren," and he instituted this sign just as he did the Eucharist. Forgetting this, we can "trample on Christ in the poor," who are his bare feet with which he still walks this earth.[7]

Dorothy and Peter did not see themselves as left-wing Catholics, but as sons and daughters of the church. When

Dorothy became Catholic in 1927 there was no such thing as a liberal or conservative Catholic. Dorothy and Peter belonged to and identified with the church of the masses as well as intellectuals, assisting at daily Mass at the local parish church, and confessing their sins each week. They saw themselves as carrying out the gospel and the writings of the popes and the fathers of the church.

Recognizing the great gift she has to offer the church, Cardinal John O'Connor, known as a conservative churchman, led the way in the canonization process for Dorothy Day. In his letter to the Congregation for the Causes of the Saints initiating her canonization process, in spite of her having had an abortion in her youth, the cardinal described her conversion on the dramatic scale of that of St. Augustine:

> It has long been my contention that Dorothy Day is a saint—not a "gingerbread" saint or a "holy card" saint, but a modern day devoted daughter of the Church....
>
> To be sure, her life is a model for all in the third millennium, but especially for women who have had or are considering abortions. It is a well-known fact that Dorothy Day procured an abortion before her conversion to the Faith. She regretted it every day of her life. After her conversion from a life akin to that of the pre-converted Augustine of Hippo, she proved a stout defender of human life. The conversion of mind and heart that she exemplified speaks volumes to all women today on two fronts. First, it demonstrates the mercy of God, mercy in that a woman who sinned so gravely could find such unity with God upon conversion. Second, it demonstrates that one may turn from the ultimate act of violence against innocent life in the womb to a position of total holiness and pacifism. In short, I contend that her abortion should not preclude her cause, but intensifies it.

Cardinal O'Connor noted Dorothy's friendliness to radical groups hostile to the church, but explained that she never kept membership in these groups. She related to them because they were also concerned about the poor. It was her "complete commitment to pacifism in imitation of Christ" that separated her from these political ideologies: "She rejected all military force.

She rejected aid to force in any way." The Cardinal found what some had considered very radical in Dorothy to be with the heart of church teaching and tradition: "Much of what she spoke of in terms of social justice anticipated the teachings of Pope John Paul II and lends support to her cause."

An awareness of the influence of French personalism on the Catholic Worker movement helps to understand what O'Connor called her anticipation of the thought of John Paul II. Those involved in the Catholic Worker movement realize that the Works of Mercy not only benefit those served, but that the action of serving leaves traces, marks, on those serving in a way that impacts their future as well as those around them. Anyone who has ever spent a few months or even days at a Catholic Worker house, for example, is changed forever in some way. Mounier, French personalist, spoke of how a person becomes a person through acting. John Paul II, Polish personalist, called this the "intransitive." His "intransitivity thesis" tells us that "in acting we change the world around us, but more importantly we change and transcend ourselves." The intransitive dimension of our actions shapes our characters: "Human actions once performed," he observes, "do not vanish without trace: they leave their moral value, which constitutes an objective reality intrinsically cohesive with the person, and thus a reality also profoundly subjective."[8] James Hanink stresses that seeing the primacy of the intransitive is crucial even in a bare sketch of John Paul II's analysis.[9] The irony is that this truth is the opposite of the common belief that it is in the transitive production of objects that we become free.

The anticipation of the thought of John Paul II by Dorothy noted by Cardinal O'Connor in the area of social justice is especially evident in the Holy Father's writing on Catholic social teaching, the dignity of workers, and the common good. He comes close to being like Dorothy in his concern for world peace and his effort to stop war.

The most famous countercultural position of the Catholic Worker has been the refusal to participate in war or preparations for war. Today, pacifism and conscientious objection is recognized as a legitimate stance for Catholics. The Second Vatican Council declared that conscientious objection was an option for Catholics in the document, *Gaudium et spes* (79:3), and the same document condemned bombing of cities and civilians (80:3). The council concluded that within the context of the just war theory, modern nuclear war was immoral. These quotes were also included in the *Catechism of the Catholic Church* (nos. 2311 and 2314). When the United States Catholic Bishops affirmed pacifism and conscientious objection as an expression of Catholic faith in their 1983 pastoral, *The Challenge of Peace: God's Challenge and Our Response,* they credited Dorothy Day for her witness, acknowledging the legitimate use of nonviolent means for the defense of one's country.

Although he has not gone quite as far as Dorothy, the pope's writings on war have developed for the whole church the concerns and the theology of peace articulated in *The Catholic Worker.* In the encyclical *Evangelium vitae,* he raised doubts about war, as he did about the death penalty and an economics that hurts the poor. Using the symbolism of the prophet Isaiah of the lion and the lamb, the Holy Father has reasoned that the Commandments and the Beatitudes must lie down together. Theologian William Portier points out that John Paul II was able to take the theological discussion of war and peace beyond a disagreement between pacifism and just war doctrine. Portier notes that together with *Gaudium et spes* and the *Catechism of the Catholic Church,* if the pope is not actually saying "Just War no More," he has come very close: "While leaving the door open a crack for the serious possibility of 'humanitarian intervention,' the Pope seems possessed at the same time of a profound evangelical skepticism about using force as a means of securing justice. This skepticism is evident in both his opposition to the Gulf War and his extreme reluctance to urge international military intervention in Bosnia." Portier pointed out that between August 2, 1990, and March 4, 1991, John Paul II condemned the (first) Gulf War fifty-six times.[10]

Not all Catholics have accepted John Paul II's theology of peace, however. In the mid-1990s, George Weigel began publishing articles in the journal *First Things* recommending a new development of the just war theory to include a theology of a preventive war—attempting to give powerful nations the right to invade and attack others on the basis that these others were hostile and might possibly attack them. Weigel's idea was soundly rejected by the Vatican. When in 2002 and 2003 George W. Bush used this theory to insist on the right of the United States to act with a preemptive strike against Iraq in what he called a preventive war, John Paul II and Vatican officials spoke strongly and with one voice against the idea, insisting that "a preemptive strike is not in the *Catechism*" and cannot be included under just war theory. In the face of direct lobbying in favor of the U.S. position by neoconservative Catholics taken to Rome by President Bush's ambassador, the Vatican responded with a unanimity not seen before in their efforts toward peacemaking. Cardinal Joseph Ratzinger spoke of strengthening the section placing limits on the just war theory, as had been done regarding the death penalty, in a new, shorter edition of the *Catechism of the Catholic Church*. In opposition to the Vatican, Weigel has since forged ahead with his "development" of the just war theory.

The similarity that Cardinal O'Connor perceived in Dorothy Day's positions and the pope's teaching is evident in John Paul II's expression of the three key elements of Catholic social teaching in the Apostolic Exhortation from the Synod of Bishops on the occasion of his 25th anniversary in 2004, where he outlined what he called the three essential and concomitant points of reference in Catholic social teaching: the dignity of each person, solidarity, and subsidiarity.

The pope has insisted on giving love for the poor the first place in what he calls the preferential option for the poor. His trilogy of three encyclicals on Catholic social teaching, meant to be read together as his teaching on economics, asks employers to pay their workers justly and challenges those who have more material goods to change their lifestyles to make more available to those who have little. *Sollicitudo rei socialis* and *Centesimus annus* critique the development of a civilization of consumption, consumerism, and crass materialism with so much waste that destroys the environment, instead of a civilization of love (*SRI*, no. 28). It is not enough to give of one's surplus possessions, John Paul II has told us. "It requires above all a change of life-styles, of models of production and consumption, and of the established structures of power which today govern society" (*CA*, no. 58).

In *Laborem exercens*, John Paul II taught that the key to any economic system is the way workers are treated: "In every case a just wage is the concrete means of verifying the justice of the whole socioeconomic system and, in any case, of checking that it is functioning justly." He emphasized that this criteria relates to the "first principle of the whole ethical and social order, namely the principle of the common use of goods (no. 89). The Holy Father also argued there that private property (the philosophical justification for some of the excesses of capitalism) is not an absolute right, but is subordinated to the right to common use, to the fact that goods are meant for everyone" (no. 64). Profit, he said, cannot be the only criteria for business: The pope went to the heart of the matter when he decried the maximizing of profit by paying the workers as little as possible: "The attainment of the worker's rights cannot however be doomed to be merely a result of economic systems which on a larger or smaller scale are guided chiefly by the criterion of maximum profit" (nos. 79–80). This teaching is true even if the employers hide behind the idea of subcontractors who operate under sweatshop conditions.

The philosophy of economic Liberalism, that is, laissez-faire capitalism, is different from what is commonly referred to as liberalism with a small *l*. For several centuries, Liberalism has justified the practices of the robber barons who reaped enormous profits on the backs of badly paid workers who labored under dangerous conditions and worked incredibly long hours. This was justified in the name of the freedom of "democracy" and by utilitarian philosophers who put forward such theories as "the greatest good for the greatest number." The problem with this theory is that in reality the greatest good goes to the few.

The resurgence of this economics in today's world is called "neoliberalism," a "new" Liberalism that has created a global capitalism of such an enormous scale that it has left the poor nations and poor workers in desperate straits while adding to the pollution of the earth. In the United States neoliberalism goes by other names—neoconservatism, supply-side economics, free trade, or just economics. Neoliberal economics is applied to every field, even to what used to be vocations to professional service. No one in the United States is unaware, for example, of what making profit primary in the medical field has done to the availability of good medical care to the sick.

John Paul II sounded exactly like Dorothy Day and Peter Maurin when he condemned this economics:

> Various places are witnessing the resurgence of a certain capitalist neoliberalism which subordinates the human person to blind market forces and conditions the development of peoples to those forces. From its centers of power, such neoliberalism often places unbearable burdens upon less favored countries. Hence, at times unsustainable economic programmes are imposed on nations as a condition of further assistance. In the international community, we thus see a small number of countries growing exceedingly rich at the cost of the impoverishment of a great number of other countries; as a result, the wealthy grow even wealthier, while the poor grow even poorer.[11]

In the 1999 Exhortation of the Synod of America, *Ecclesia in America*, the Holy Father made the same condemnation: "More and more, in many countries of America, a system known as 'neoliberalism' prevails; based on a purely economic conception of the human person, this system considers profit and the law of the market as its only parameters, to the detriment of the dignity of and the respect due to individuals and peoples" (no. 56). The theme of the need for those who have more to change their lifestyles was confirmed and developed in *Ecclesia in America*.

Some influential Catholics disagree with the pope's assessment. In speaking around the world for the economics of neoliberalism in the name of the church, they have followed Adam Smith in placing the "invisible hand of the market" above traditional Catholic ethics and social teaching. Known in the United States as neoconservatives, these men have even tried to claim that Dorothy Day was in agreement with them, on the basis that she and Peter did not believe in big government. On the other hand, oddly enough, they accuse Catholic Workers of being socialists when they speak in defense of workers.

Tawney, Penty, and Maurin's analysis of the Calvinist influence in history can help us to understand what is happening today. Attitudes in the United States continue to be heavily influenced by the views of the Puritans as well as Smith. This especially includes the concepts that the poor around the world are poor through their own fault and are not blessed by God, and that the ownership of things is not only a sign of virtue, but even virtue itself. Those who do not make a profit or survive the system are perceived as not being clever or virtuous.

Cardinal Francis George of Chicago has said that Catholics in the United States are influenced by Calvinism, that even some who come from families where Catholicism has been practiced for generations are Catholic Calvinists. The extent of this influence on neoconservative/neoliberal Catholic economic thinking in the United States was evident in the description of the Synod of America by Father Richard Neuhaus, a convert to Catholicism. He presented the synod as a dialogue between Puritan minister Cotton Mather and Our Lady of Guadalupe, apparently placing them on the same level. Ultimately, his book came down on the side of Cotton Mather, with an insistence that Catholics in Latin America must adapt to Puritan values in economics and in evangelization.[12]

With Smith the "neocons" contend that in a free society each person must make a "personal definition" of the common good, and that it is impossible to know, given the invisible hand of the market, what might contribute to that good.[13] For example, Michael Novak has declared that not only is it impossible to work toward a common good, but that capitalism demands a new religion: "Not only a new theology, but a new type of religion" must be developed to make room for a wealth-creation "theology."[14]

Novak's *Este hemisferio de libertad*, a special Spanish-language version of his book, *This Hemisphere of Liberty*, published for Latin America in Mexico in 1994, upholds Chile under dictator Pinochet as the model for implementing the neoliberal economy. Novak there articulates a new morality—one, he says, that had been lacking in Catholic teaching. Quoting utilitarian philosophers, he teaches that self-interest and self-wealth-creation are the methods by which virtue is brought into society, order is brought into economics and into the whole of life, even in its moral and cultural aspects: "Pues sí, the pursuit of riches represents a fundamental improvement in human understanding of the way to virtue. Hume, Smith and others perceived correctly that wealth is a useful way to open to all...the way to virtue."[15] Neoliberalism does not admit avarice as one of the cardinal sins.

Novak has published a book of the kind popular among the Puritans, entitled *Business as a Calling.* Used as a vade mecum by some Catholic CEO's and professors of business administration, it features Andrew Carnegie as a hero because he created wealth and very late in life became a philanthropist.[16] Novak has apparently forgotten that the grandparents of so many in the United States, especially Catholic immigrants, worked for people like Carnegie under conditions one step up from slavery in steel mills and in coal mines, from dawn to dusk six days a week, never seeing their children from Sunday to Sunday. Carnegie's treatment of workers would have been considered sinful by the early church fathers or by medieval moralists, not the mark of a saint or hero, even if he repented and became a philanthropist, donating with much fanfare the money he made on the backs of so many workers. These great teachers, along with Dorothy Day and Peter Maurin, would have rejoiced in Carnegie's late change of attitude, but would never have presented his business practices as a model for others.

The primacy of the economic in daily and social life decried by Mounier and Berdyaev is no less a reality today. It exists in an exaggerated form in the tremendous pressure brought upon people to buy and possess things, live a certain lifestyle and reach for the highest level of comfort. Social consideration and display are priorities. Even among church people one must let the economic factor dominate or be considered odd.

Mounier denounced attempts to call spiritual values the affectations that sprang from the bourgeois moral code. The only major change in his reflections that Mounier would have to make today would be to include women with the men who had lost the Mystery in the pursuit of capitalism. Mounier predicted that some would later "adopt the formula of personalism for their own purposes." He cautioned later in his life that one of the most common temptations was to confuse personalism with "some late survival of individualism," and to cover individualism with a "mantle of personalism."[17]

The Acton Institute, a joint venture of Catholic and Calvinist libertarians on economics directed by Father Robert Sirico, has done exactly that. They have described the freedom of huge corporations to dominate and control all, while paying pitifully low wages to workers, as "economic personalism" and the epitome of a free and *virtuous* society. The Acton Institute, funded by corporations, provides free weekends in plush surroundings to seminarians, priests, and ministers to convince future church leaders that the way of wealth for the few is not harmful, but virtuous. Dorothy, who loved the Curé of Ars (St. John Vianney) and advocated voluntary poverty for priests as well as laypeople, would be scandalized. As she said in the February 1948 *Catholic Worker*: "If the priesthood studied distributism as a long-term movement and did not play two ends against the middle by endorsing the present capitalistic system, we would be ready for what the future would bring."

Peter Maurin took every opportunity to quote the prophets of Israel and the fathers of the church on the evils of usury, the practice of the taking of interest, which has been at the core of financial institutions for several centuries. He and Dorothy, like Chesterton, did not believe in giving proxies to huge corporations to do their work or depending on the practice of amassing money and the taking of interest to develop more and more financial security.

The destructive outcome of lifting the prohibition against usury over the centuries has been seen dramatically in recent years in the indebtedness of a world of poor countries to wealthier ones and to international economic institutions. Local economies have been destroyed in the attempt to repay external debts. In an article in the November 2000 *Houston Catholic Worker*, Gregorio Iriarte, OMI, showed how the economies of many countries were devastated when all their efforts, all their people's work, their whole economic system had to be dedicated to repaying loans to wealthy countries, the World Bank, and the International Monetary Fund. The poorer countries had just been freed from colonial control and needed help to get started on their own.

They had been raped of their resources and the labor of their people, and were pregnant with tremendous needs and hope in the face of terrible challenges. Those who lent money to them later continuously (Father Iriarte would say immorally) raised the interest rates on old loans. Iriarte explained what had happened and noted how Pope John Paul II raised the voice of conscience in a campaign for forgiveness of the debts:

> When money was plentiful, loans were made to dictators who did not have the good of their people at heart and did not use the money for the people's benefit. Those who made the loans were well aware of this; later the bankers irrationally raised the interest rates to astronomical levels, to the point where even though the poor nations have more than paid for their debts, none of the payments were applied to the principal and they are as indebted as they were before. Others raised their voices against this immoral activity, but it was with the leadership of the Church, in the person of John Paul II and his program for forgiveness of the debt for the Jubilee of the year 2000, that forgiveness of the foreign debt was taken seriously. However, at this writing, the people of most of those countries still labor under this immoral debt, a debt they never contracted and from which they did not benefit.

Neoconservatives, who claim a unique interpretation of the thought of John Paul II, did not join him in this effort, a rather glaring omission. The Acton Institute actually put a link on their Web site that calls the campaign for forgiveness of the debts morally questionable.

When Peter Maurin and distributists like Father McNabb insisted that one should eat what could be grown locally, they were prophetic about what would happen later in the twentieth century if the opposite plan were followed. Under the threat of cutting off loans, the international financial institutions have controlled in detail the economies and the lives of people in countries around the world. The International Monetary Fund and World Bank policies especially have affected agriculture, requiring poor countries to grow food for export to richer countries and import food for their own people. Local farmers cannot compete with products raised by agricultural conglomerates heavily subsidized by the U.S. or European governments. Poor countries are required to administer "structural adjustment," a program that includes privatization of their government services, including health services, education, and water supplies, and to "open their markets" to the United States. A further development has been the bizarre extreme of biopiracy, allowing multinational companies to patent seeds that had been developed in poor countries for centuries and to demand payment from those who had developed them to use their own seeds. The falsity of the claim that these programs will eventually make life better for the people has become clear, as the gap between a few rich and many poor has become greater and greater in each country. In 2003 even the International Monetary Fund admitted that its policies had led to more poverty in poor countries rather than less.

As Dorothy said in the September 1956 *Catholic Worker*, upon hearing about all of this, "Peter Maurin would give forth right now with an essay on money lending at interest, and the evils of the capitalist acquisitive society and how it is immoral to use money to make money." She herself would apply the second part of the Judgment scene in Matthew 25 to those who create these structures of sin, as she did in the January 1957 issue of *The Catholic Worker*:

We are the rich man of the world, and the poor man is at the gate, and we are afraid the day is coming when God will say, "Depart from me, accursed ones, into the everlasting fire which was prepared for the devil and his angels. For I was hungry and you polluted the earth with your mines and your bombs and wars which starved the poor; I was thirsty, and you contaminated even the ocean and the waters of the earth with your hydrogen bombs; I was a stranger, and you made agreements with former allies who now are enemies, to keep me in displaced persons' camps to this day, and daily you make more homeless; naked, and you make weapons and profits for the rich and the poor have not the clothes to cover them; I was sick and in prison, and my numbers ever increased."

Dorothy and Peter said that war had everything to do with economics. Canadian economist Michel Chossudovsky contends that it was the crushing of people economically in poor countries around the world through neoliberal economics imposed through the loans and the global cheap-labor economy, from Bosnia to Rwanda to India to Peru to Bolivia, that created a ground of desperation for urban and rural violence and increasing conflicts between ethnic groups in recent decades.[18]

Today's culture of sex could also use Dorothy's input on sexuality and marriage, about which she spoke positively and symbolically in regards to Christ and the church. Referencing Soloviev, she described sexuality in marriage as a way of discovering God—who is love. Dorothy's approach is a far cry from society's teaching on sexuality that abandons the relationship factor for more immediate gratification with the partner of the same or opposite sex, soon to be abandoned. Just as she critiqued Alfred Kinsey,[19] who skewed his research so badly that it is both useless and harmful, so now she still speaks to young people, the vast majority of whom want marriage despite its being undermined at every stage by the hedonistic approach of society.

Dorothy often criticized aggressive programs of birth control and abortion that targeted the poor and minorities as genocide. She didn't stop there, however, but insisted that Catholics help couples who were having children. Dorothy and Peter advocated just wages so a mother could stay home to care for a large family. They also critiqued the translation of the spirit of capitalism, with its emphasis on personal gain and profit, to modern-day sexuality. Today this is manifested not only in advertising, but also in the policies of multinational corporations that demand that their female employees in poor countries be sterilized or at least prove they are not pregnant. Decisions on loans from the international financial institutions are often tied to limiting the populations of poor countries, particularly those of races other than Caucasian.

In an interview in her eightieth year Dorothy repeated to church leaders the approach to economics she and Peter recommended. Her advice did not resemble in any way that of those who recommend that the bishops and pastors model their activities on business corporations:

> I had a chance twice to talk to the bishops. I said, "The first thing I would advise all bishops to do is to get rid of all their worldly advisers." I said, "this whole business of investing. It's usury, it's condemned in the catechism, in the same class as the seven deadly sins...money doesn't breed money." I said, "Don't invest money, except in the poor—there you might expect a return."
>
> We learn these things in the New Testament. There's a constant tension at the spiritual foundations; it's a matter of faith. The Lord will send you. If they want your coat, give up your coat.
>
> I mean, it just works. If it fails, well, that's because it should fail. It wouldn't matter.[20]

Dorothy's advice might have helped the bishops in responding to the terrible problem of pedophilia in the church. It was often the "worldly advisers," whether lawyers or psychologists, who advised the bishops to take actions that turned out to the detriment of all. New lay groups formed to address the pedophilia crisis may be helpful, but if they come forth with the same worldly advisers, things will be no better. They would have more credibility and be more successful if they began with Dorothy's advice of giving up all and following Jesus. They will have to reject trends that emerge in the dominant culture in order to have the least positive impact. It was the dominant culture and the press that accepted and promoted the libertine activity of the sexual revolution in the first place. Dorothy, speaking with the voice of experience, did not accept the sexual revolution.

For those who understand the deep roots and vision of the Catholic Worker, a special way of living in the world in integrity and truth opens up, a way that is so old it looks like new. It sometimes seems impossible to confront the monolithic problems and injustices in the world. Where can one begin? Peter and Dorothy recommended and demonstrated through their lives and witness the monastic way. They understood it, however, as a way of relating to the world rather than withdrawing from it. There is a growing awareness today of the possibilities of the monastic way as a creative, positive response to what Peter Maurin called a new Dark Age. Ecumenical conferences have been held, for example, among Mennonite and Catholic groups on the monastic way. Writers from varied backgrounds are recommending monasticism. Paula Hudson, a Benedictine lay oblate, has published *The Holy Way: Practices for a Simple Life* (Loyola, 2003). Morris Berman's *The Twilight of American Culture* extols the monastic "class" in the transformation of the chaos after the fall of the Roman Empire into the rise of a new Europe and recommends monasticism as the way to save American culture and civilization. By this Berman, not a Catholic, does not mean secluding oneself or necessarily going to a monastery, but living in a different way from the dominant commodity culture—what he calls the spiritual death of the late twentieth century.[21] The practical examples Berman gives of what the new monastic individual can do relate to subsidiarity, to the idea that "small is beautiful"—and to what Peter and Dorothy called the revolutionary technique of the monasteries.

As Dorothy said on several occasions, distributism, the idea of a local economy, is not dead. Practical examples exist and awareness of its importance is growing. The economics recommended by the Catholic Worker movement is presented today very effectively by Wendell Berry in his writings favoring a "local economy," in which each local community grows its own food and thus has food security. Berry critiques both global capitalism and Communism for their use of violent means. Like the Catholic Workers, he points out that in both systems economic determinism disallows the possibility of vocation and personal responsibility. Both systems promise that some day in the future all who are now poor will be helped by their economics in spite of the use of impure means. Berry says, "Communism and 'free market' capitalism both are modern versions of oligarchy. In their propaganda, both justify violent means by good ends, which are always put beyond reach by the violence of the means."[22]

Contemporary philosopher Alasdair MacIntyre shares Peter and Dorothy's ideas for an economics that will help to create a world where it is, as Peter put it, "easier for people to be good." Lamenting, like Maurin, a compartmentalized society that imposes a fragmented ethics, MacIntyre points out that political discussions and decisions regarding what would be good for society do not address the most basic questions of values and ethics.[23] MacIntyre, like Berry, advocates small-scale, local communities.

The most famous example of worker-ownership and management in a successful local business that is not agrarian and continues to exist and thrive is that of Mondragon in the Basque country in Spain. The inspiration for the Mondragon business(es) came from Don José María Arizmendiarietta, a priest who taught five young engineers about the social encyclicals and assisted them in putting the encyclicals into practice in setting up a small enterprise that became successful in a very short time. This enterprise, begun in 1956, is based on principles of cooperative ownership, democratic decision making, profit sharing, and community responsibility.[24]

A practical small business approach incorporating unusually good principles of economics flowing from the gospel is that of the Focolare movement, which operates over seven hundred small businesses in its Economy of Communion in different parts of the world. About one-third of the earnings of these businesses are retained, one-third goes to the development of the civilization of love, and one-third is given to the poor. The Economy of Communion "hopes to transform business structures from within by striving to establish all relations inside and outside the companies in the light of a lifestyle based on communion, that is, 'reciprocal gift' that the name implies."[25]

Joseph Pearce's 2001 book updating E. F. Schumacher's work provides examples of successful businesses on the distributism model and valuable insights into economics from the perspective of "small is beautiful."[26]

The key to the survival of Catholic Workers, despite failures to stop wars and injustice, is their rootedness in the daily practice of the Works of Mercy. When pressured to explain in detail what must be done to bring justice to the world, Dorothy answered in terms of local economics and concerns, a life more closely related to the gospel, and love for the poor through the Works of Mercy. Her answer might have surprised those who viewed her mostly as an activist: "I think we believe that it is in our everyday lives that God judges us, not in the positions we take on issues, the statements we sign, the political parties we join, the causes we advocate." She continued, "For me the heart of our work is just that, the daily pastoral responsibilities: making the soup and serving it, trying to help someone get to the hospital who otherwise might not get there, because he's confused, because she's not aware she even needs to go there...."[27]

The local scene of which Dorothy spoke now frequently includes people from very far away because of the massive migration that has been caused by what one might call the violence of the global market. Migrants today are those guests of the Houses of Hospitality whom she described years ago as refugees from ruthless industrialism.

The retreat Dorothy so often attended with Father Roy and Father Hugo presented the weapons of the spirit as the most important means of overcoming evil. Using the methods of the spiritual weapons has helped Catholic Workers to avoid becoming embittered or immobilized over injustice in society or because of church politics or failings. As Dorothy wrote in the June 1976 *Catholic Worker:* "Gregory the Great, who lived around the fifth or sixth century, wisely said that if we pour ourselves too fervently in Church or state affairs, or let ourselves be too upset, we are weakening, or even nullifying our most potent weapons—the weapons of the spirit."[28] This would include being swept up in the latest theme or scandal selected to be emphasized by the media to the point of losing perspective and all hope. Dorothy noted that whenever there is a problem in the Catholic Church, it is more heavily criticized and publicized than problems in other churches or institutions. She acknowledged, however, that the church as the bride and Mystical Body of Christ should be better than other groups.

Houses of Hospitality, work for justice, and resistance to violence continue today through the Catholic Worker movement in cities and on a few farms across the United States and in several other countries. Each Catholic Worker community responds to specific needs in its area and usually publishes a newsletter or newspaper to share ideas with those interested in the work. Some form of discussion or speakers for clarification of thought is also included. The communities are loosely connected as a movement; there is no structure or hierarchy, as should be expected from a movement based on personalism and the positive aspects of non-violent anarchism. The lack of formal leadership within the movement was not a problem during the lifetimes of Peter Maurin and Dorothy Day. They were the acknowledged leaders, visiting other Catholic Worker communities and approving leaders for new houses. After their deaths, however, there was the question of what would happen regarding leadership in the movement. At a national Catholic Worker gathering in the early 1980s, a number of Catholic Workers complained about the leadership vacuum and asked what should be done. The answer, of course, was obvious, "Continue feeding the hungry, clothing the naked, practicing hospitality until you drop! We still have the gospel!"

Neither the right nor the left really knows what to do with Dorothy Day and Peter Maurin. Some have not been able to understand the ideas because the Catholic Worker program was so different from the dominant culture. Peter was sometimes dismissed because of the poverty of his appearance, and because his writings were expressed simply so that everyone would understand. The misunderstandings about and even attacks on Peter and Dorothy and the movement, albeit subtle, have appeared in commentaries from seemingly opposite points of view, although both from the perspective of privatizing religion. Considered very liberal, Father Richard McBrien of Notre Dame suggested that Dorothy was like a founder of a "sect," and neoconservative Weigel placed her in his book *Tranquillitas Ordinis* (along with St. Francis) on the margin, outside mainstream Catholicism.

The Catholic Worker has never withdrawn from the world in a sectarian way. On the contrary, Peter Maurin's message is for all people of goodwill. Mark S. Massa argues that the Catholic Worker called both Catholics and Americans to their roots:

Day called American Catholics to keep their feet planted firmly "at the door" on the margins, in liminality, because it was precisely there, in the Little Way, that God was to be found. But in issuing such a radical call, ironically enough, Day stood not at the margins at all, but rather very much at the center of both the American and Catholic traditions: it was *because* Day was so committed an American and devout a Catholic that she demanded both traditions to make good on their promises about the poor and the marginalized, about feeding everyone at the table.[29]

Those who say that Dorothy was conservative on theological issues and progressive on social issues do not have it right. Those who try to co-opt Dorothy and the movement for politics or whatever ideology do not have it right. Those who complain about Dorothy's religious orthodoxy and seek a more secular answer through Peter Maurin definitely do not have it right. Peter's idea of blowing the dynamite of the church and practicing a model of Christian love in a divided world was for both Peter and Dorothy, as for the philosophers and saints who shaped the movement, simply being Catholic.

Dorothy and Peter have taught us to put our hope and faith in Christ and the community of his Mystical Body rather than to give our best allegiance to the secular, encroaching modern state. They taught us that mysticism is better than politics and that there is a better guide for our lives than mass psychology and opinion polls. They envisioned a world where workers and scholars might respect each other and work together, where artisans and artists and small businesses might replace assembly lines. They taught us to work by the sweat of our brow, counting on the community to help in the work. They showed us the way of worker ownership as opposed to what they called wage slavery. They taught us that voluntary poverty (not destitution) is better than conspicuous consumption and that to be with the poor differs greatly from philanthropy or social charity set in bureaucracy. They knew that the heart of transformation of ourselves and the world was found in the Eucharist, the liturgy of the Church. John Paul II's 2003 encyclical, *Ecclesia de*

Eucharistia, provides a ringing affirmation of their and Virgil Michel's understanding of the liturgy:

> Many problems darken the horizon of our time. We need but think of the urgent need to work for peace, to base relationships between peoples on solid premises of justice and solidarity, and to defend human life from conception to its natural end. And what should we say of the thousand inconsistencies of a "globalized" world where the weakest, the most powerless and the poorest appear to have so little hope! It is in this world that Christian hope must shine forth! For this reason too, the Lord wished to remain with us in the Eucharist, making His presence in meal and sacrifice the promise of a humanity renewed by His love. Significantly, in their account of the Last Supper, the Synoptics recount the institution of the Eucharist, while the Gospel of John relates, as a way of bringing profound meaning, the account of the "washing of the feet," in which Jesus appears as the teacher of communion and of service. The Apostle Paul, for his part, says that it is "unworthy" of a Christian community to partake of the Lord's Supper amid division and indifference toward the poor.
>
> Proclaiming the death of the Lord until He comes entails that all who take part in the Eucharist be committed to changing their lives and making them in a certain way completely "Eucharistic." It is this fruit of a transfigured existence and a commitment to transforming the world in accordance with the Gospel which splendidly illustrates the eschatological tension inherent in the celebration of the Eucharist and in the Christian life as a whole: "Come Lord, Jesus!" (no. 20).

Dorothy wrote in the May 1978 *Catholic Worker* that life is not always easy or the way immediately clear, but hope persists: "The grace of hope, this consciousness that there is in every person, that which is of God, comes and goes, in a rhythm like that of the sea. The Spirit blows where it listeth, and we travel through deserts and much darkness and doubt....God speaks, He answers these cries in the darkness as He always did. He is incarnate today in the poor, in the bread we break together. We know Him and each other in the breaking of bread." Dorothy wrote passionately in the April 1968 *Catholic Worker* of the tremendous challenge of receiving and following the word of the gospel, not counting the cost, giving one's very life:

> We have to begin to see what Christianity really is, that *our God is a living fire; though He slay me, yet will I trust Him.* We have to think in terms of the Beatitudes and the Sermon on the Mount and have this readiness to suffer.
>
> We have not yet resisted unto blood. We have not yet loved our neighbor with the kind of love that is a precept to the extent of laying down our life for him. And our life very often means our money, money that we have sweated for; it means our bread, our daily living, our rent, our clothes. We haven't shown ourselves ready to lay down our life.

Peter Maurin and Dorothy Day present a very special model of sanctity. Our study of the Catholic Worker movement and of their lives has led us to the conclusion that both Dorothy and Peter should be canonized. They inspire many, especially those who seek to live their faith in an alternative to materialism and war. As Don Divo Barsotti, confessor to recent popes, said:

> Witnesses are needed to make sure that there is a living reality—the living reality created by the saint. Without the saints the Church becomes a despotic power (I say this with a shiver), as in the frightening image of Dostoevsky's Grand Inquisitor. Only holiness justifies the Church's teaching; otherwise all the documents and statements of the Magisterium become empty words. There are men and women who are evident signs of a reality that is not of this world. That differentness is thrust upon one; it is like finding oneself in front of a miracle. This is not because they are not subject to nature (they are wretches, like all others); but nature cannot explain this.
>
> Salvation is not an assent to a generic moral code, or to the values of peace, of humanism, but to the person of Christ and to one's own person. It is a passionate love for Christ that moves the people who meet the saints.[30]

The vision of the Catholic Worker has inspired many to that love. The movement provides a perspective for living out in a practical way a radical following of Jesus.

Today, as in the 1930s when the movement began, those who would like to start Catholic Worker houses or give their work toward a civilization of love as a gift, can follow Peter's advice to Dorothy, "Just use the methods of the saints—pray, and tell people what you are doing and they will help."

Appendix I
Aims and Purposes of the Catholic Worker Movement

(From *The Catholic Worker*, February 1940)

For the sake of new readers, for the sake of men on our breadlines, for the sake of the employed and unemployed, the organized and unorganized workers, and also for the sake of ourselves, we must reiterate again and again what are our aims and purposes.

Together with the Works of Mercy, feeding, clothing and sheltering our brothers and sisters, we must indoctrinate. We must "give reason for the faith that is in us." Otherwise we are scattered members of the Body of Christ, we are not "all members one of another." Otherwise our religion is an opiate, for ourselves alone, for our comfort or for our individual safety or indifferent custom.

We cannot live alone. We cannot go to Heaven alone. Otherwise, as Péguy said, God will say to us, "Where are the others?" (This is in one sense only as, of course, we believe that we must be what we would have the other fellow be. We must look to ourselves, our own lives first.)

If we do not keep indoctrinating, we lose the vision. And if we lose the vision, we become merely philanthropists, doling out palliatives. The vision is this. We are working for "a new heaven and a new earth, wherein justice dwelleth." We are trying to say with action, "Thy will be done on earth as it is in heaven." We are working for a Christian social order. We believe that all people are brothers and sisters in the Fatherhood of God. This teaching, the doctrine of the Mystical Body of Christ, involves today the issue of unions (where people call each other brothers and sisters); it involves the racial question; it involves cooperatives, credit unions, crafts; it involves Houses of Hospitality and Farming Communes.

It is with all these means that we can live as though we believed indeed that we are all members one of another, knowing that when "the health of one member suffers, the health of the whole body is lowered."

This work of ours toward a new heaven and a new earth shows a correlation between the material and the spiritual, and, of course, recognizes the primacy of the spiritual. Food for the body is not enough. There must be food for the soul. Hence the leaders of the work, and as many as we can induce to join us, must go daily to Mass, to receive food for the soul. And as our perceptions are quickened, and as we pray that our faith be increased, we will see Christ in each other, and we will not lose faith in those around us, no matter how stumbling their progress is. It is easier to have faith that God will support each House of Hospitality and Farming Commune and supply our needs in the way of food and money to pay bills, than it is to keep a strong, hearty, living faith in each individual around us—to see Christ in him. If we lose faith, if we stop the work of indoctrinating, we are in a way denying Christ again.

We must practice the presence of God. He said that when two or three are gathered together, there He is in the midst of them. He is with us in our kitchens, at our tables, on our breadlines, with our visitors, on our farms. When we pray for our material needs, it brings us close to His humanity. He, too, needed food and shelter. He, too, warmed His hands at a fire and lay down in a boat to sleep.

When we have spiritual readings at meals, when we have the rosary at night, when we have study groups, forums, when we go out to distribute literature at meetings, or sell it on street corners, Christ is there with us.

What we do is very little. But it is like the little boy with a few loaves and fishes. Christ took that little and increased it. He will do the rest. What we do is so little we may seem to be constantly failing. But so did He fail. He met with apparent failure on the Cross. But unless the seed fall into the earth and die, there is no harvest.

And why must we see results? Our work is to sow. Another generation will be reaping the harvest.

When we write in these terms, we are writing not only for our fellow workers in thirty other Houses, to other groups of Catholic Workers who are meeting for discussion, but to every reader of the paper. We hold with the motto of the National Maritime Union, that every member is an organizer.

We are upholding the ideal of personal responsibility. You can work as you are bumming around the country on freights, if you are working in a factory or a field or a shipyard or a filling station. You do not depend on any organization which means only paper figures, which means only the labor of the few.

We are not speaking of mass action, pressure groups (fearful potential for evil as well as good). We are addressing each individual reader of *The Catholic Worker.*

The work grows with each month, the circulation increases, letters come in from all over the world, articles are written about the movement in many countries.

Statesmen watch the work, scholars study it, workers feel its attraction, those who are in need flock to us and stay to participate. It is a new way of life. But though we grow in numbers and reach far-off corners of the earth, essentially the work depends on each one of us, on our way of life, the little works we do.

"Where are the others?" God will say. Let us not deny Him in those about us. Even here, right now, we can have that new earth, wherein justice dwelleth.

Appendix II
Peter Maurin's List
of Great Books

(Compiled by Dave Mason from Peter Maurin's Easy Essays, in
Catholic Radicalism: Phrased Essays for the Green Revolution
[New York: The Catholic Worker, 1949])

Art in a Changing Civilization, Eric Gill
The Bourgeois Mind, Nicholas Berdyaev
Brotherhood Economics, Toyohiko Kagawa
Catholicism, Protestantism and Capitalism, Amintore Fanfani
Charles V, Wyndham Lewis
Christianity and Class War, Nicholas Berdyaev
Church and the Land, Father Vincent McNabb, OP
Discourse on Usury, Thomas Wilson
The Emancipation of a Free Thinker, Herbert E. Cory
Enquiries into Religion and Culture, Christopher Dawson
Fields, Factories and Workshops, Peter Kropotkin
Fire on the Earth, Paul Hanly Furfey
The Flight from the City, Ralph Borsodi
The Franciscan Message to the World,
    Father Agostino Gemelli, OFM
Freedom in the Modern World, Jacques Maritain
The Future of Bolshevism, Waldemar Gurian
The Great Commandment of the Gospel,
        His Excellency A. G. Cicognani, Apostolic Delegate to
        the United States
A Guildsman's Interpretation of History, Arthur Penty
Ireland and the Foundation of Europe, Benedict Fitzpatrick
I Take My Stand, by Twelve Southern Agrarians
The Land of the Free, Herbert Agar

Lord of the World, Robert Hugh Benson
The Making of Europe, Christopher Dawson
Man the Unknown, Dr. Alexis Carrel
Nations Can Stay at Home, B. O. Wilcox
Nazareth or Social Chaos, Father Vincent McNabb, OP
Our Enemy the State, Albert Jay Nock
Outline of Sanity, G. K. Chesterton
The Personalist Manifesto, Emmanuel Mounier
A Philosophy of Work, Etienne Borne
Post-Industrialism, Arthur Penty
Progress and Religion, Christopher Dawson
Religion and the Modern State, Christopher Dawson
Religion and the Rise of Modern Capitalism, R. H. Tawney
La Revolution Personnaliste et Communautaire,
      Emmanuel Mounier
Saint Francis of Assisi, G. K. Chesterton
Social Principles of the Gospel, Alphonse Lugan
Soviet Man Now, Helene Iswolsky
Temporal Regime and Liberty, Jacques Maritain
The Theory of the Leisure Class, Thorstein Veblen
Things That Are Not Caesar's, Jacques Maritain
The Thomistic Doctrine of the Common Good, Seraphine Michel
Toward a Christian Sociology, Arthur Penty
True Humanism, Jacques Maritain
The Two Nations, Christopher Hollis
The Unfinished Universe, T. S. Gregory
The Valerian Persecution, Father Patrick Healy
What Man Has Made of Man, Mortimer Adler
Work and Leisure, Eric Gill

Notes

Chapter 1

1. Dorothy Day, *From Union Square to Rome* (Silver Spring, MD: Preservation of the Faith Press, 1938), 46–47.

2. Ibid., 26–27.

3. Ibid., 40–41.

4. John J. Mitchell, "Dorothy Day," in *Critical Voices in American Catholic Economic Thought* (Mahwah, NJ: Paulist Press, 1989), 154.

5. Dorothy Day, *The Long Loneliness* (1952; repr. San Francisco: Harper & Row Publishers, 1997), 63.

6. William D. Miller, *A Harsh and Dreadful Love: Dorothy Day and the Catholic Worker Movement* (New York: Liveright, 1973; repr. Milwaukee: Marquette University Press, 2004) 89–90.

7. Day, *From Union Square to Rome*, 88.

8. William D. Miller, *Dorothy Day: A Biography* (San Francisco: Harper & Row Publishers, 1982), xiii.

9. Keith Morton and John Saltmarsh, "A Cultural Context for Understanding Dorothy Day's Social and Political Thought," in *Dorothy Day and the Catholic Worker Movement: Centenary Essays*, Marquette Studies in Theology no. 32, eds. William J. Thorn, Phillip M. Runkel, and Susan Mountin (Milwaukee: Marquette University Press, 2001), 234–35, 237.

10. Miller, *Biography*, 166.

11. William D. Miller, *All Is Grace: The Spirituality of Dorothy Day* (Garden City, NJ: Doubleday and Company, 1987), 15.

12. Day, *From Union Square to Rome*, 88–89.

13. Day, *Long Loneliness*, 136, 141.

14. Ibid., 149.

15. Day, *From Union Square to Rome*, 133–34.

16. Ibid., 155.

17. Day, *Long Loneliness*, 141.

18. Day, *From Union Square to Rome*, 144–45.

19. Day, *Long Loneliness*, 152.

20. Dorothy Day, *House of Hospitality* (New York: Sheed and Ward, 1939), v.

21. Ibid., xiii.

22. Day, *Long Loneliness*, 165.

23. Ibid., 166.

24. Ibid.

25. Michael Baxter, CSC, "Catholic Radicalism from a Catholic Radicalist Perspective," in *Dorothy Day and the Catholic Worker Movement: Centenary Essays*, 80, 84.

26. Day, *Long Loneliness*, 170.

27. Miller, *Harsh and Dreadful*, 25.

28. Day, *Long Loneliness*, 179.

29. Miller, *Harsh and Dreadful*, 19.

30. Miller, *Biography*, 243, 248.

31. Dorothy Day, *Loaves and Fishes* (San Francisco: Harper and Row, 1963; repr. Maryknoll, NY: Orbis Books, 1997), 16.

32. Mel Piehl, "Peter Maurin's Personalist Democracy" in *A Revolution of the Heart: Essays on the Catholic Worker*, ed. Patrick G. Coy (Philadelphia: Temple University Press, 1988), 50.

33. Arthur Sheehan, *Peter Maurin: Gay Believer* (Garden City, NY: Hanover House, 1959), 205. Note that with this title Sheehan was describing Peter as a "joyful believer" in the spirit of St. Philip Neri, at a time before the word *gay* had a connotation of homosexuality. Dorothy Day said in her September 1975 obituary of Arthur Sheehan: "The title of his book is unfortunate, but Arthur wished to emphasize Peter's joyful spirit."

34. Ibid., 104–5.

35. Ibid., 203–4.

36. Ibid., 19.

37. Ibid., 38–39.

38. Ibid., 95.

39. Ibid., 147.

40. Ibid., 57–58.

41. Ibid., 60.

42. Dorothy Day, *On Pilgrimage: The Sixties* (New York: Curtis Books, 1972), 212.

43. Miller, *Harsh and Dreadful*, 27.

44. Sheehan, *Peter Maurin*, 67.

45. Marc Ellis, *Peter Maurin: Prophet in the Twentieth Century* (New York: Paulist Press, 1981), 36–37.

46. Sheehan, *Peter Maurin*, 84.

47. Ibid., 88.

48. Ibid., 104.

49. Day, *House of Hospitality*, xvii.

50. Day, *Long Loneliness*, 173.

51. Day, *Loaves and Fishes*, 16.

52. Day, *Long Loneliness*, 210.

53. Cyril Echele, "An American Poverello," in *Social Justice Review*, May–June 1949, 117–19.

54. Day, *Long Loneliness*, 182.

55. Miller, *Harsh and Dreadful*, 74.

56. Ibid., 87.

57. See Appendix II.

58. See Paul B. Marx, OSB, *Virgil Michel and the Liturgical Movement* (Collegeville, MN: The Liturgical Press, 1957), 374.

59. Day, *Long Loneliness*, 201.

60. Dorothy Day, quoted in Miller, *Biography*, 321.

Chapter 2

1. Harry Murray, *Do Not Neglect Hospitality: The Catholic Worker and the Homeless* (Philadelphia: Temple University Press, 1990), 74.

2. Dorothy Day, "Room for Christ," in *Selected Writings: By Little and By Little*, ed. Robert Ellsberg (first published New York, Alfred Knopf, 1983 as *By Little and By Little*; repr. Maryknoll, NY: Orbis Books, 1992), 96.

3. Dorothy Day, *Loaves and Fishes* (San Francisco: Harper and Row, 1963; repr. Maryknoll, NY: Orbis Books, 1997), 48.

4. Dorothy Day, *House of Hospitality* (New York: Sheed and Ward, 1939) 275.

5. Ibid., 274.

6. Daniel Di Domizio, "The Prophetic Spirituality of the Catholic Worker," in *A Revolution of the Heart: Essays on the Catholic Worker*, ed. Patrick G. Coy (Philadelphia: Temple University Press, 1988), 224, 222.

7. Keith Morton and John Saltmarsh, "A Cultural Context for Understanding Dorothy Day's Social and Political Thought," in *Dorothy Day and the Catholic Worker Movement: Centenary Essays*, Marquette Studies in Theology no. 32, eds. William J. Thorn, Phillip M. Runkel, and Susan Mountin (Milwaukee: Marquette University Press, 2001), 238, 240.

8. James Douglass, "Dorothy Day and the City of God," in *Social Justice Review*, May 1961, 42.

9. Dorothy Day, "The Scandal of the Works of Mercy," in *Commonweal*, November 4, 1949; repr. *Dorothy Day: Writings from Commonweal*, ed. Patrick Jordan (Collegeville, MN: Liturgical Press, 2002), 109.

10. Day, *House of Hospitality*, 241.

11. Ibid., 139.

12. Ibid.

13. Day, *Loaves and Fishes*, 61.

14. Ibid., 100.

Chapter 3

1. Brigid O'Shea Merriman, OSF, *Searching for Christ: The Spirituality of Dorothy Day* (Notre Dame, IN: University of Notre Dame Press, 1994), 87.

2. Benedict Fitzpatrick, *Ireland and the Foundations of Europe with Map of Hibernicized Medieval Europe* (New York: Funk & Wagnalls Company, 1927), 38–39.

3. Ibid., 48–49.

4. Ibid., 41.

5. Ibid., 68–69.

6. Ibid., 78–79.

7. Harry Murray, *Do Not Neglect Hospitality: The Catholic Worker and the Homeless* (Philadelphia: Temple University Press, 1990), 46.

8. Merriman, *Searching for Christ*, 74.

9. Ibid.,102.

10. The poem can be found in Helen Waddell, *The Desert Fathers* (London: Constable, 1936; repr. New York: Random House, 1998), 208–9. Citations are to the Random House edition.

11. Merriman, *Searching for Christ*, 103.

12. Ibid., 102.

13. Ibid., 86. Quoting *Rule* of St. Benedict, 53.15.

14. Ibid., 107. Merriman is quoting here from Vishnewski's letter to Brother Benet Tvedten, OSB, August 14, 1968 (note 98).

15. Dorothy Day, *Loaves and Fishes* (San Francisco: Harper and Row, 1963; repr. Maryknoll, NY: Orbis Books, 1997), 99.

16. Timothy Fry, OSB, ed., *RB 1980: The Rule of St. Benedict* (Collegeville, MN: The Liturgical Press, 1981), 332.

17. Stanley Vishnewski, *Wings of the Dawn* (New York: The Catholic Worker, [1984]), 195.

18. This 1951 pamphlet has recently been reissued as a book: Dom Rembert Sorg, *Holy Work: Towards a Benedictine Theology of Manual Labor* (Santa Ana, CA: Source Books, 2003).

19. Dorothy Day, *The Long Loneliness* (1952; repr. San Francisco: Harper & Row Publishers, 1997), 107.

20. Merriman, *Searching for Christ*, 101.

21. Ibid., 104–5.

22. Ibid., 119.

23. Dorothy Day, *House of Hospitality* (New York: Sheed and Ward, 1939), 255.

Chapter 4

1. Dorothy Day, "Fellow Worker in Christ," in *Orate Fratres* 13 (1939), 139.

2. Quoted in Paul B. Marx, OSB, *Virgil Michel and the Liturgical Movement* (Collegeville, MN: The Liturgical Press, 1957), 208.

3. Virgil Michel, OSB, "The Cooperative Movement and the Liturgical Movement," in *Orate Fratres* 14 (1940), 155.

4. Virgil Michel, OSB, "Christian Culture," in *Orate Fratres* 13 (1939), 303.

5. See Virgil Michel, OSB, "The Liturgy the Basis of Social Regeneration," in *Orate Fratres* 9 (1935), 536–45.

6. See Virgil Michel, OSB, *The Liturgy of the Church* (New York: The McMillan Company, 1937), 47–50.

7. John J. Mitchell, "Virgil Michel, OSB: Eucharistic Economics," in *Critical Voices in American Catholic Economic Thought* (Mahwah, NJ: Paulist Press, 1989), 82.

8. Virgil Michel, "Timely Tracts: Social Justice," in *Orate Fratres* 12 (1938), 132.

9. Michel, "Christian Culture," 299.

10. Virgil Michel, OSB, *Christian Social Reconstruction: Some Fundamentals of the Quadragesimo Anno* (Milwaukee: The Bruce Publishing Company, 1937), 12.

11. Ibid., 63.

12. Mitchell, "Virgil Michel," 87.

13. Michel, *Christian Social Reconstruction*, 10, 74.

14. Virgil Michel, OSB, "What is Capitalism?" in *Commonweal* 28 (1938), quoted in Mitchell, "Virgil Michel," 87. For further information, see the collection of Dom Virgil's articles on economics published by Saint John's University in 1987, *The Social Question: Essays on Capitalism and Christianity*, ed. Robert L. Spaeth.

15. Mitchell, "Virgil Michel," 85.

16. Michel, *Christian Social Reconstruction*, 10.

17. Virgil Michel, "Timely Tracts: Catholic Workers and Apostles," in *Orate Fratres* 13 (1938), 30.

18. Letter from Dorothy Day to Virgil Michel, OSB, published in the *Houston Catholic Worker*, April 1995.

19. Keith Pecklers, SJ, *The Unread Vision: The Liturgical Movement in the United States of America:* 1926–1955 (Collegeville, MN: The Liturgical Press, 1998), 125–6.

20. Ibid., 127.

21. Stanley Vishnewski, *Wings of the Dawn* (New York: The Catholic Worker, [1984]) 54–57.

22. Ibid., 58–59.

23. Dorothy Day, *The Long Loneliness* (1952; repr. San Francisco: Harper & Row Publishers, 1997), 80.

24. Dorothy Day, "Introduction," in *Catholic Radicalism*, by Peter Maurin (New York: The Catholic Worker, 1949), v.

25. C. S. Lewis, *Reflections on the Psalms* (1958; New York: repr. Harvest Book/Harcourt, Inc., 1986), 25–26.

26. Michael J. Baxter, CSC, "Reintroducing Virgil Michel: Towards a Counter-Tradition of Catholic Social Ethics in the United States," in *Communio* 24 (Fall 1997), 502, 515.

27. Ibid., 518–19.

28. Michael Baxter, CSC, "Catholic Radicalism from a Catholic Radicalist Perspective," in *Dorothy Day and the Catholic Worker Movement: Centenary Essays*, Marquette Studies in Theology no. 32, eds. William J. Thorn, Phillip M. Runkel, and Susan Mountin (Milwaukee: Marquette University Press, 2001), 82.

29. Baxter, "Reintroducing Virgil Michel," 519.

30. Ibid., 521–23.

Chapter 5

1. William D. Miller, *Dorothy Day: A Biography* (San Francisco: Harper & Row Publishers, 1982), 238.

2. William D. Miller, *A Harsh and Dreadful Love: Dorothy Day and the Catholic Worker Movement* (New York: Liveright, 1973; repr. Milwaukee: Marquette University Press, 2004), 7–8.

3. Nicholas Berdyaev, *Samopoznanie* [Self-Knowledge], quoted in Geoffrey B. Gneuhs, "Peter Maurin's Personalist Democracy," in *A Revolution of the Heart: Essays on the Catholic Worker*, ed. Patrick G. Coy (Philadelphia: Temple University Press, 1988), 57.

4. Nicholas Berdyaev, *The Meaning of History*, trans. George Reavey (New York: Charles Scribner's Sons, 1936), 79.

5. Nicholas Berdyaev, *The Bourgeois Mind and Other Essays*, ed. Donald Attwater (1934; Freeport, NY: Books for Libraries Press, Inc., 1966), 70.

6. Ibid.

7. Gneuhs, "Peter Maurin's Personalist Democracy," 54–55 (see note 3).

8. Michael Kelly, *Pioneer of the Catholic Revival: The Ideas and Influence of Emmanuel Mounier* (London: Sheed and Ward, 1979), 36.

9. Brigid O'Shea Merriman, OSF, *Searching for Christ: The Spirituality of Dorothy Day* (Notre Dame, IN: University of Notre Dame Press, 1994), 212.

10. Helene Iswolsky, *No Time to Grieve: An Autobiographical Journey* (Philadelphia: The Winchell Company, 1985), 184.

11. Ibid., 183–84.

12. Berdyaev, *Bourgeois Mind*, 97–98.

13. Marc Ellis, *Peter Maurin: Prophet in the Twentieth Century* (New York: Paulist Press, 1981), 87.

14. Berdyaev, *Bourgeois Mind*, 12, 14.

15. Nicholas Berdyaev, *Christianity and Class War*, trans. Donald Attwater (London: Sheed and Ward, 1933), 51.

16. Ibid., 81.

17. Ibid., 82–83.

18. Howard A. Slaaté, *Personality, Spirit and Ethics: The Ethics of Nicholas Berdyaev* (New York: Peter Lang, 1997), 108.

19. Berdyaev, *Christianity and Class War*, 51–52.

20. Dorothy Day, *From Union Square to Rome* (Silver Spring, MD: Preservation of the Faith Press, 1938), 14.

21. Dorothy Day, "Holy Obedience," in *Selected Writings: By Little and By Little*, ed. Robert Ellsberg (first published New York, Alfred Knopf, 1983 as *By Little and By Little*; repr. Maryknoll, NY: Orbis Books, 1992), 172.

22. Ibid., 171.

23. Nicolas Berdyaev, *Freedom and the Spirit*, trans. Oliver Fielding Clarke (New York: Charles Scribner's Sons, 1935; repr. London: Geoffrey Bles, 1946), 338.

24. Nicholas Berdyaev, *The Destiny of Man*, trans. Natalie Duddington (1954; repr. Westport, CT: Hyperion Press, 1979), 114–16.

25. See also chapter 14 in this book on Father Hugo and the retreat.

26. Berdyaev, *Freedom and the Spirit*, 186.

27. Miller, *Harsh and Dreadful*, 6.

28. Berdyaev, *The Meaning of History*, 190.

29. Ibid., 188–89.

30. Christopher Dawson, *Progress and Religion: An Historical Enquiry* (Westport, CT: Greenwood Press, 1929), 3.

31. Ibid., 8.

32. Berdyaev, *The Meaning of History*, 74–75.

33. Miller, *Biography*, 238.

34. Ibid., 240.

35. Berdyaev, *Bourgeois Mind*, 13.

36. Miller, *Biography*, 247.

37. Ibid., 239.

38. Ibid., 247.

39. Miller, *Harsh and Dreadful*, 11.

40. Miller, *Biography*, 502–503.

41. Miller, *Harsh and Dreadful*, 10–11.

42. Berdyaev, *Freedom and the Spirit*, 161.

43. Miller, *Biography*, 242.

44. William D. Miller, *All Is Grace: The Spirituality of Dorothy Day* (Garden City, NJ: Doubleday and Company, 1987), 34.

45. Berdyaev, *Freedom and the Spirit*, 153.

46. Berdyaev, *The Destiny of Man*, 119.

47. Miller, *All Is Grace*, 86.

48. Berdyaev, *Bourgeois Mind*, 126.

Chapter 6

1. Dorothy Day, *The Long Loneliness* (1952; repr. San Francisco: Harper & Row, 1997), 171.

2. Ellen Cantin, CSJ, *Mounier: A Personalist View of History* (New York: Paulist Press, 1973), 64.

3. Emmanuel Mounier, *Be Not Afraid: A Denunciation of Despair*, trans. Cynthia Rowland (New York: Sheed and Ward, 1962), 135.

4. Emmanuel Mounier, *A Personalist Manifesto*, trans. Monks of Saint John's Abbey (New York: Longmans, Green, and Co., 1938), 69.

5. Emmanuel Mounier, *Personalism*, trans. Philip Mairet (Notre Dame, IN: University of Notre Dame Press, 1952), 22–23.

6. Mounier, *Personalism*, 23–24.

7. Cantin, *Mounier*, 29.

8. James Hanink, unpublished manuscript, "A Personalist Vision: Beyond the Established Disorder." See also Mounier, *Personalism*, 23.

9. Mounier, *Personalism*, 22.

10. Leslie Paul, Foreword, Emmanuel Mounier, *Be Not Afraid*, vii.

11. See Cantin, *Mounier*, 18–22.

12. Michael Kelly, *Pioneer of the Catholic Revival: The Ideas and Influence of Emmanuel Mounier* (London: Sheed and Ward, 1979), 13.

13. William D. Miller, *Dorothy Day: A Biography* (San Francisco: Harper & Row Publishers, 1982), 419.

14. Kelly, *Pioneer*, 42.

15. Mounier, *Manifesto*, 10.

16. Ibid., 7–8.

17. Kelly, *Pioneer*, 12.

18. Paul Ricoeur, *History and Truth*, trans. Charles A. Kelbley, Northwestern University Studies in Phenomenology and Existential Philosophy (Evanston: Northwestern University Press, 1965), 137.

19. Mounier, *Manifesto*, 2.

20. Mounier, *Be Not Afraid*, 193.

21. Ibid., 150.

22. Cantin, *Mounier*, 26.

23. Mounier, *Be Not Afraid*, 170.

24. Kelly, *Pioneer*, 43.

25. William Griffin, "A Study of Emmanuel Mounier's Philosophy of Personalism, Its Philosophical Roots and Its Contemporary Relevance," Master's thesis, Fordham University, 1992, 50.

26. Cantin, *Mounier*, 23.

27. Mounier, *Manifesto*, 177.

28. Ibid., 165.

29. Griffin, "Study," 30. Griffin is translating from Emmanuel Mounier's "Revolution personnaliste et communautaire," in *Oeuvres de Mounier*, vol. 1: 1931–1939, ed. P. Mounier (Paris: Editions du Seuil, 1961).

30. Mounier, *Manifesto*, 17–18.

31. Mounier, *Be Not Afraid*, 115.

32. Griffin, "Study," 11–12.

33. Mounier, *Be Not Afraid*, 132.

34. Emmanuel Mounier, *The Character of Man*, trans. Cynthia Rowland (New York: Harper and Brothers Publishers, 1956), 156.

35. Mounier, *Manifesto*, 5.

36. William D. Miller, *A Harsh and Dreadful Love: Dorothy Day and the Catholic Worker Movement* (New York: Liveright, 1973; repr. Milwaukee: Marquette University Press, 2004), 5.

37. Mounier, *Manifesto*, 95.

38. Cantin, *Mounier*, 94.

39. Harry Murray, *Do Not Neglect Hospitality: The Catholic Worker and the Homeless* (Philadelphia: Temple University Press, 1990), 71.

40. Ibid., 213.

41. *Dorothy Day, Meditations*, selected and arranged by Stanley Vishnewski (New York: Newman Press, 1970; repr. Springfield, IL: Templegate, 1997), 94.

42. Mounier, *Personalism*, 87.

43. Mounier, *Be Not Afraid*, 12.

Chapter 7

1. Kenneth Woodward, *Newsweek*, quoted on front cover of *Dorothy Day, Meditations*, selected and arranged by Stanley Vishnewski (New York: Newman Press, 1970; repr. Springfield, IL: Templegate, 1997).

2. Theodore Maynard, *Richest of the Poor: The Life of St. Francis of Assisi* (Garden City, NY: Doubleday, 1948), 12.

3. G. K. Chesterton, *St. Francis of Assisi* (New York: George H. Doran Company, 1924; repr. Garden City, NY: Doubleday, Image Books, 1928, 1957), 109–10.

4. Maynard, *Richest of the Poor*, 46.

5. Father Cuthbert, OSFC, *Life of St. Francis of Assisi* (1912; London, New York, Toronto: Longmans, Green and Co., 1956), 202.

6. Brigid O'Shea Merriman, OSF, *Searching for Christ: The Spirituality of Dorothy Day* (Notre Dame, IN: University of Notre Dame Press, 1994), 177.

7. Dorothy Day, "Reflections During Advent, Part Two: The Meaning of Poverty" in *Ave Maria*, December 3, 1966, 29. Reprinted in "Dorothy Day Library on the Web," http://www.catholicworker.org/dorothyday/.

8. Chesterton, *St. Francis of Assisi*, 61–62. See also "The Little Flowers of St. Francis" in *St. Francis of Assisi: Writings and Early Biographies. English Omnibus of the Sources for the Life of St. Francis, vol. 2.*, ed. Marion A. Habig, trans. Raphael Brown et al. (Quincy, IL: Franciscan Press, 1991), 1304.

9. Merriman, *Searching for Christ*, 26.

10. Eileen Egan, *Peace Be with You: Justified Warfare or the Way of Nonviolence* (Maryknoll, NY: Orbis Books, 1999), 77.

11. Arthur Sheehan, *Peter Maurin* (Garden City, NY: Hanover House, 1959), 11.

12. Johannes Jorgensen, *St. Francis of Assisi*, trans. T. O'Connor Sloane (New York: Longmans, Green, 1913).

13. Dorothy Day, *On Pilgrimage*, with an introduction by Mark and Louise Zwick, Ressourcement Series: Retrieval and Renewal in Catholic Thought (New York: The Catholic Worker, 1948; repr. Grand Rapids, MI: William B. Eerdmans, 1999), 158.

14. Myles Schmitt, OFM Cap, *Francis of the Crucified* (Milwaukee: Bruce Publishing Company, 1956), 26, 33.

15. Dorothy Day, *Loaves and Fishes* (San Francisco: Harper and Row, 1963; repr. Maryknoll, NY: Orbis Books, 1997), 91.

16. Dorothy Day, *On Pilgrimage: The Sixties* (New York: Curtis Books, 1972), 207.

17. Dorothy Day, *The Long Loneliness* (1952; repr. San Francisco: Harper & Row, 1997), 204–5.

18. Day, *Loaves and Fishes*, 83–84.

19. Hans Urs von Balthasar, *Bernanos: an Ecclesial Existence* (San Francisco: Ignatius Press, 1996), 614.

Chapter 8

1. Dorothy Day, *Loaves and Fishes* (San Francisco: Harper and Row, 1963; repr. Maryknoll, NY: Orbis Books, 1997), 104.

2. For an analysis of the impact of Max Weber's thought, see Alasdair MacIntyre, *After Virtue* (1981; Notre Dame, IN: University of Notre Dame Press, 1984) 25–27, 114–15.

3. Arthur J. Penty, *A Guildsman's Interpretation of History* (New York: Sunrise Turn, Inc., 1919), 13–14.

4. Ibid., 256.

5. Ibid., 32.

6. Ibid., 155–56.

7. Ibid., 165–66.

8. Ibid., 165–67.

9. Ibid., 167.

10. G. K. Chesterton, "What's Wrong with the World," in *Collected Works: G.K. Chesterton*, vol. IV (San Francisco: Ignatius Press, 1987), 91.

11. See Christopher Dawson, *Religion and the Rise of Western Culture* (New York: Sheed and Ward, 1933; New York: Doubleday, 1957, 1991, Image Books) 170–73.

12. See, for example, Dorothy Day, *House of Hospitality* (New York: Sheed and Ward, 1939), 145.

13. R. H. Tawney, *Religion and the Rise of Modern Capitalism* (New York: Harcourt, Brace and Company, 1926; new ed. New Brunswick, NJ: Transaction Publishers, 1998), 254.

14. Ibid., 239, 238.

15. See Tawney, *Religion*, 243–45.

16. Ibid., 114–15.

17. Ibid., 264–67.

18. Arthur Sheehan, *Peter Maurin* (Garden City, NY: Hanover House, 1959), 165.

19. St. John Chrysostom, "Sermon on Almsgiving and Hospitality," trans. from the Greek by Tasos Sarris Michopoulos for the *Houston Catholic Worker*, May–June 2000.

20. "Gregory of Nyssa Against the Usurers," trans. from the Greek by Tasos Sarris Michopoulos for the *Houston Catholic Worker*, November 1999.

21. Tawney, *Religion*, 84.

22. Penty, *Guildsman's Interpretation of History*, 33.

23. Day, *Loaves and Fishes*, 85.

24. Ibid., 72.

25. Thorstein Veblen, "The Theory of the Leisure Class," reprinted in *The Portable Veblen*, ed. and with an introduction by Max Lerner (1948; repr. New York: The Viking Press, 1965), 196–97.

26. Dorothy Day, *On Pilgrimage*, Ressourcement Series: Retrieval and Renewal in Catholic Thought (New York: The Catholic Worker, 1948; repr. Grand Rapids, MI: William B. Eerdmans, 1999), 248.

27. Day, *Loaves and Fishes*, 104.

28. Dorothy Day, *The Long Loneliness* (1952; repr. San Francisco: Harper & Row Publishers, 1997), 226.

29. Veblen, "Theory of the Leisure Class," 84–86.

30. Day, *Long Loneliness*, 206.

31. Stanley Vishnewski, *Wings of the Dawn* (New York: The Catholic Worker, [1984]), 157–58.

32. Ibid., 158.

33. Dorothy Day, *House of Hospitality* (New York: Sheed and Ward, 1939), 142–43.

34. Ibid., 146.

35. Ibid., 255–56.

Chapter 9

1. Arthur Sheehan, *Peter Maurin* (Garden City, NY: Hanover House, 1959), 52–53. For more information on Harmel and *Rerum novarum*, see Joan L. Coffey, *Léon Harmel: Entrepreneur as Catholic Social Reformer* (Notre Dame, IN: University of Notre Dame Press, 2003).

2. Dorothy Day, *The Long Loneliness* (1952; repr. San Francisco: Harper & Row Publishers, 1997), 55.

3. Ibid.

4. Ibid., 54.

5. Peter Kropotkin, *Fields, Factories and Workshops* (London: Thomas Nelson and Sons, 1912; repr. New York: Harper & Row, 1974), 1–2.

6. Ibid., 24.

7. William D. Miller, *A Harsh and Dreadful Love: Dorothy Day and the Catholic Worker Movement* (New York: Liveright, 1973; repr. Milwaukee: Marquette University Press, 2004), 28.

8. Dorothy Day, *On Pilgrimage*, Ressourcement Series: Retrieval and Renewal in Catholic Thought (New York: The Catholic Worker, 1948; repr. Grand Rapids, MI: William B. Eerdmans, 1999), 175.

9. Day, *Long Loneliness*, 56.

10. Father Vincent McNabb, OP, *The Church and the Land* (First published as a Benziger Bros. Pamphlet, 1926; repr. Norfolk, VA: IHS Press, 2003), 19.

11. G. K. Chesterton, "Why I Am Not a Socialist," in *The New Age: A Weekly Review of Politics, Literature, and Art*, January 4, 1908, no. 695, New Series 2 (9), 189.

12. G. K. Chesterton, *The Outline of Sanity* (London: The Royal Literary Fund, 1926; repr. Norfolk, VA: IHS Press, 2001), 25.

13. Ibid., 26.

14. Ibid., 145.

15. Ibid., 45.

16. Hilaire Belloc, *The Servile State* (London: T.N. Foulis, 1912; New York: Henry Holt and Company, 1946), 72.

17. Day, *Long Loneliness*, 220–21.

18. Ibid., 223–24.

19. Ibid., 176.

20. Ibid., 227–28.

21. McNabb, *Church and the Land*, 19.

22. Sheehan, *Peter Maurin*, 12.

23. Ibid.

24. Day, *Long Loneliness*, 225.

25. Dorothy Day, *House of Hospitality* (New York: Sheed and Ward, 1939), 149.

26. Sheehan, *Peter Maurin*, 12.

27. Day, *House of Hospitality*, 146.

28. Day, *Long Loneliness*, 72.

29. Dorothy Day, *From Union Square to Rome* (Silver Spring, MD: Preservation of the Faith Press, 1938), 86–87.

30. Anne Klejment, "The Radical Origins of Catholic Pacifism: Dorothy Day and the Lyrical Left During World War I," in *American Catholic Pacifism: The Influence of Dorothy Day and the Catholic Worker Movement*, eds. Anne Klejment and Nancy L. Roberts (Westport, CT: Praeger, 1996), 21.

31. William D. Miller, *Dorothy Day: A Biography* (San Francisco: Harper & Row Publishers, 1982), 384.

32. Quote from Marquette University Archives.

33. Joseph Pearce, *Literary Converts: Spiritual Inspiration in an Age of Unbelief* (San Francisco: Ignatius Press, 1999), 363–64.

34. Chesterton, *Outline of Sanity*, 89.

35. Ibid., 79.

36. Day, *On Pilgrimage*, 175–76.

37. Day, *Long Loneliness*, 171.

Chapter 10

1. Raïssa Maritain, *We Have Been Friends Together* (1942; New York: Longmans Green and Co., 1945), 39.

2. Ibid., 175.

3. Ibid., 150, 152.

4. Jacques Maritain, *The Person and the Common Good* (New York: Charles Scribner's Sons, 1947; repr. Notre Dame, IN: University of Notre Dame Press, 1966) 23–26.

5. Ibid., 91.

6. Ibid., 12–13.

7. Ibid., 29, note 22.

8. William D. Miller, *Dorothy Day: A Biography* (San Francisco: Harper & Row Publishers, 1982), 266.

9. Stanley Vishnewski, *Wings of the Dawn* (New York: The Catholic Worker, [1984]), 130–31.

10. *The Social and Political Philosophy of Jacques Maritain: Selected Readings*, selected by Joseph W. Evans and Leo R. Ward (New York: Charles Scribner's Sons, 1955), 336.

11. Dorothy Day, *House of Hospitality* (New York: Sheed and Ward, 1939), 239.

12. Raïssa Maritain, *Raïssa's Journal: Presented by Jacques Maritain* (Albany, NY: Magi Books, 1974), 235.

13. See chapter 14.

14. Brigid O'Shea Merriman, OSF, *Searching for Christ: The Spirituality of Dorothy Day* (Notre Dame, IN: University of Notre Dame Press, 1994), 64.

15. Ibid., 63.

16. *Social and Political Philosophy of Jacques Maritain*, 336.

17. Jacques Maritain, *Integral Humanism*, trans. Joseph W. Evans (New York: Charles Scribner's Sons, 1968; Notre Dame, IN: University of Notre Dame Press, 1973), 110.

18. Dorothy Day, "Reflections for Advent, Part Four, Obedience," in *Ave Maria* (December 17, 1966). Reprinted in "Dorothy Day Library on the Web," http://www.roundtable.org/dorothyday/.

19. Merriman, *Searching for Christ*, 63.

20. Jacques Maritain, *Freedom in the Modern World* (New York: Charles Scribner's Sons, 1936), 153.

21. Ibid., 152.

22. Merriman, *Searching for Christ*, 60.

23. Jacques Maritain, *Art and Scholasticism with Other Essays*, trans. J. F. Scanlon (1930; London: Sheed and Ward, 1946), 55.

24. William D. Miller, *A Harsh and Dreadful Love: Dorothy Day and the Catholic Worker Movement* (New York: Liveright, 1973; repr. Milwaukee: Marquette University Press, 2004), 77.

25. Father James K. Daprile has done an extensive study of the impact of Eichenberg's engravings together with Dorothy's text in *The Catholic Worker* in his doctoral dissertation at Duquesne University entitled "The Power of the Visual Image and its Correlation to Text: The Graphic Illustrations of Fritz Eichenberg and the Texts of Dorothy Day as found in *The Catholic Worker* 1949–1980."

26. Miller, *Harsh and Dreadful Love*, 220–21.

27. Jacques Maritain, *The Peasant of the Garonne: An Old Layman Questions Himself About the Present Time*, trans. Michael Cuddihy and Elizabeth Hughes (1966; New York: Macmillan, 1969), 62–63; see also p. 63, note 68.

Chapter 11

1. Dorothy Day, *The Long Loneliness* (1952; repr. San Francisco: Harper & Row Publishers, 1997), 140.

2. Brigid O'Shea Merriman, OSF, *Searching for Christ: The Spirituality of Dorothy Day* (Notre Dame, IN: University of Notre Dame Press, 1994), 183–84.

3. Dorothy Day, *From Union Square to Rome* (Silver Spring, MD: Preservation of the Faith Press, 1938), 153–54.

4. Teresa of Avila, "The Book of her Life," in *The Collected Works of St. Teresa of Avila*, vol. 1, trans. Kiernan Kavanaugh, OCD, and Otilio Rodriguez, OCD (Washington, DC: ICS Publications, 1976), 47.

5. Dorothy Day, *On Pilgrimage*, Ressourcement Series: Retrieval and Renewal in Catholic Thought (New York: The Catholic Worker, 1948; repr. Grand Rapids, MI: William B. Eerdmans, 1999), 112.

6. See Jodi Bilinkoff, *The Avila of St. Teresa: Religious Reform in a Sixteenth-Century City* (Ithaca, NY: Cornell University Press, 1989).

7. Dorothy Day, *House of Hospitality* (New York: Sheed and Ward, 1939), 117.

8. Merriman, *Searching for Christ*, 186.

9. Stanley Vishnewski, *Wings of the Dawn* (New York: The Catholic Worker, [1984]), 118.

10. Day, *Long Loneliness*, 140.

11. Ibid.

12. Ibid, 140–41.

13. Day, *House of Hospitality*, 74.

14. Ibid., 135–36.

15. Teresa of Avila, "The Interior Castle," in *Collected Works of St. Teresa of Avila*, vol. 2 (Washington, DC: ICS Publications, 1980), 351.

16. Day, *Long Loneliness*, 188.

17. Merriman, *Searching for Christ*, 291, note 34.

18. Raymundo Panikkar, "Preface," *The Interior Castle*, by Teresa of Avila, trans. Kieran Kavanaugh, OCD, and Otilio Rodrigues, OCD, (New York: Paulist Press, 1979), xiii.

Chapter 12

1. Dorothy Day, *Loaves and Fishes* (San Francisco: Harper and Row, 1963; repr. Maryknoll, NY: Orbis Books, 1997), 12.

2. Dorothy Day, *The Long Loneliness* (1952; repr. San Francisco: Harper & Row Publishers, 1997), 172.

3. Brigid O'Shea Merriman, OSF, *Searching for Christ: The Spirituality of Dorothy Day* (Notre Dame, IN: University of Notre Dame Press, 1994), 181.

4. Ibid.

5. Ibid., 182.

6. Dorothy Day, *On Pilgrimage*, Ressourcement Series: Retrieval and Renewal in Catholic Thought (New York: The Catholic Worker, 1948; repr. Grand Rapids, MI: William B. Eerdmans, 1999), 177.

7. William D. Miller, *A Harsh and Dreadful Love: Dorothy Day and the Catholic Worker Movement* (New York: Liveright, 1973; repr. Milwaukee: Marquette University Press, 2004), 347.

8. William D. Miller, *Dorothy Day: A Biography* (San Francisco: Harper & Row Publishers, 1982), 236.

9. Catherine of Siena, *The Dialogue*, trans. Susan Noffke, OP (Mahwah, NJ: Paulist Press, 1980) 35–36.

10. Susan Noffke, OP, "Introduction," Catherine, *Dialogue*, 10.

11. Ibid.

12. Merriman, *Searching for Christ*, 182.

13. Nicholas Berdyaev, *Freedom and the Spirit* (New York: Charles Scribner's Sons, 1935; repr. London: Geoffrey Bles, 1946), 83.

14. Thomas C. Cornell, Robert Ellsberg, and Jim Forest, eds., *A Penny a Copy: Readings from The Catholic Worker* (Maryknoll, NY: Orbis Books, 1995), 310–11.

15. Merriman, *Searching for Christ*, 181.

16. See chapter 14.

17. Day, *On Pilgrimage*, 127.

18. Ibid., 227.

19. Catherine, *Dialogue*, 62.

20. Day, *On Pilgrimage*, 225, 224.

21. Catherine, *Dialogue*, 30.

22. Giuliana Cavallini, "Preface," Catherine, *Dialogue*, xv–xvi.

23. Susan Noffke, OP, "Introduction," Catherine, *Dialogue*, 8–9.

Chapter 13

1. Dorothy Day, *The Long Loneliness* (1952; repr. San Francisco: Harper & Row Publishers, 1997), 42–43.

2. William D. Miller, *Dorothy Day: A Biography* (San Francisco: Harper & Row Publishers, 1982), 36.

3. Dorothy Day, *From Union Square to Rome* (Silver Spring, MD: Preservation of the Faith Press, 1938), 18.

4. Miller, *Biography*, 326.

5. Day, *From Union Square to Rome*, 154.

6. Day, *Long Loneliness*, 108.

7. Dorothy Day, *Loaves and Fishes* (San Francisco: Harper and Row, 1963; repr. Maryknoll, NY: Orbis Books, 1997), 75.

8. Miller, *Biography*, 334.

9. Henri de Lubac, SJ, *The Drama of Atheist Humanism* (New York: Sheed and Ward, 1949; repr. San Francisco: Ignatius Press, 1995), 285.

10. Ibid., 292.

11. William D. Miller, *A Harsh and Dreadful Love: Dorothy Day and the Catholic Worker Movement* (New York: Liveright, 1973; repr. Milwaukee: Marquette University Press, 2004), 24–25.

12. Day, *From Union Square to Rome*, 8–9.

13. Ibid., 9.

14. Miller, *Biography*, 373.

15. William D. Miller, *All Is Grace: The Spirituality of Dorothy Day* (Garden City, NY: Doubleday, 1987), 49.

16. Dorothy Day, "Reflections During Advent, Part Two: The Meaning of Poverty" in *Ave Maria* (December 3, 1966), 21. Reprinted in

"Dorothy Day Library on the Web," http://www.catholicworker.org/dorothyday/.

17. Day, *From Union Square to Rome*, 104.

18. Dorothy Day, *The Catholic Worker*, April 1941, quoted in Brigid Merriman, *Searching for Christ: The Spirituality of Dorothy Day* (Notre Dame, IN: University of Notre Dame Press, 1994), 49.

19. Dorothy Day, *House of Hospitality* (New York: Sheed and Ward, 1939), 170.

20. Nicholas Berdyaev, *Dostoievsky: An Interpretation*, trans. Donald Attwater (London: Sheed and Ward, 1934), 67.

21. Ibid., 189–90.

22. Ibid., 190.

23. Ibid., 72.

24. Miller, *Biography*, 246–47.

25. Dorothy Day, *On Pilgrimage*, Ressourcement Series: Retrieval and Renewal in Catholic Thought (New York: The Catholic Worker, 1948; repr, Grand Rapids, MI: William B. Eerdmans, 1999), 130.

26. Ibid., 199.

27. Ibid., 238–39.

28. Vladimir Soloviev, *The Meaning of Love*, trans Thomas R. Beyer, Jr. (London: Geoffrey Bles, 1945; new edition, Hudson, N.Y.: Lindisfarne Press, 1985), 63. Citations are to the Lindisfarne Press edition.

29. Hans Urs von Balthasar, *Studies in Theological Style: Lay Styles*, trans. Andrew Louth, et al., ed. John Riches, *The Glory of the Lord: A Theological Aesthetics*, volume III: (1962; San Francisco: Ignatius Press, 1986), 294–95.

30. Ibid., 342.

31. Marina Kostalevsky, *Dostoevsky and Soloviev: The Art of Integral Vision* (New Haven, CT: Yale University Press, 1997), 63.

32. Ibid., 87.

33. Berdyaev, *Dostoievsky*, 95–96.

34. Ibid., 224–25.

35. Ibid., 14.

Chapter 14

1. Dorothy Day, *The Long Loneliness* (1952; repr. San Francisco: Harper & Row, 1997), 259, 263.

2. Jim Forest, *Love Is the Measure: A Biography of Dorothy Day* (Mahwah, NJ: Paulist Press,1986; revised edition, Maryknoll, NY: Orbis Books, 1994), 83.

3. Dorothy Day, *On Pilgrimage*, Ressourcement Series: Retrieval and Renewal in Catholic Thought (New York: The Catholic Worker, 1948; repr. Grand Rapids, MI: William B. Eerdmans, 1999), 112.

4. Dorothy Day, *House of Hospitality* (New York: Sheed and Ward, 1939), 109.

5. Day, *Long Loneliness*, 246–47.

6. Ibid., 246.

7. Forest, *Love Is the Measure*, 82.

8. Day, *Long Loneliness*, 252.

9. John Hugo, *Your Ways Are Not My Ways*, vol. 1 (Pittsburgh, PA: Encounter with Silence, 1986), 9.

10. Ibid., 84–85.

11. The mentioned article is reprinted in John Hugo, *Weapons of the Spirit: Living a Holy Life in Unholy Times. Selected Writings of Father John Hugo*, eds. David Scott and Mike Aquilina (Huntington, IN: Our Sunday Visitor, 1997), 138–40.

12. Ibid., 137.

13. Day, *On Pilgrimage*, 102.

14. Hugo, *Your Ways*, 244.

15. Day, *On Pilgrimage*, 249.

16. Ibid., 76.

17. Day, *Long Loneliness* 258–59.

18. William D. Miller, *All Is Grace: The Spirituality of Dorothy Day* (Garden City, NJ: Doubleday, 1987), 45.

19. Hugo, *Your Ways*, 25.

20. Ibid., 245.

21. Letter from Father Hugo to Dorothy Day, n.d., published in Miller, *All Is Grace*, 59.

22. Brigid O'Shea Merriman, OSF, *Searching for Christ: The Spirituality of Dorothy Day* (Notre Dame, IN: University of Notre Dame Press, 1994), 150.

23. Hugo, *Your Ways*, 239, 242.

24. Ibid., 241.

25. Ibid., 262, 228–29.

Chapter 15

1. Arthur Sheehan, *Peter Maurin* (Garden City, NY: Hanover House, 1959), 50–51.

2. See Ibid., 50–70.

3. See Anne Klejment, "The Radical Origins of Catholic Pacifism: Dorothy Day and the Lyrical Left During World War I," in *American*

Catholic Pacifism: The Influence of Dorothy Day and the Catholic Worker Movement, eds. Anne Klejment and Nancy L. Roberts (Westport, CT: Praeger, 1996), 20.

4. Anne Klejment and Nancy L. Roberts, "The Catholic Worker and the Vietnam War," in *American Catholic Pacifism*, 154.

5. Klejment, "Radical Origins," 24.

6. Patricia McNeal, "Catholic Peace Organizations and World War II," in *American Catholic Pacifism*, 40.

7. Stephen T. Krupa, SJ, "American Myth and the Gospel: Manifest Destiny and Dorothy Day's Nonviolence," in *Dorothy Day and the Catholic Worker Movement: Centenary Essays*, Marquette Studies in Theology no. 32, eds. William J. Thorn, Phillip M. Runkel, and Susan Mountin (Milwaukee: Marquette University Press, 2001), 184–85.

8. Francis J. Sicius, "Prophecy Faces Tradition: The Pacifist Debate During World War II," in *American Catholic Pacifism*, 65.

9. Tom Cornell, "Solidarity, Compassion and a Stubborn Hold on Truth: The Roots of Dorothy Day's Pacifism," in the *Houston Catholic Worker*, September–October 1997.

10. Jim Forest, *Love Is the Measure: A Biography of Dorothy Day* (Mahwah, NJ: Paulist Press,1986; revised edition, Maryknoll, NY: Orbis Books, 1994), 74.

11. See David Wyman, *Abandonment of the Jews: America and the Holocaust, 1941–1945* (New York: Pantheon Books, 1986).

12. William D. Miller, *A Harsh and Dreadful Love: Dorothy Day and the Catholic Worker Movement* (New York: Liveright, 1973; repr. Milwaukee: Marquette University Press, 2004), 182.

13. Dorothy Day, *The Long Loneliness* (1952; repr. San Francisco: Harper & Row, 1997), 181.

14. Ibid., 264.

15. John Hugo, *Your Ways Are Not My Ways*, vol. 1 (Pittsburgh, PA: Encounter with Silence, 1986), 66–67.

16. John J. Hugo, *The Gospel of Peace* (privately printed, 1944), 76.

17. Sandra Yocum Mize, "'We Are Still Pacifists': Dorothy Day's Pacifism During World War II," in *Dorothy Day and the Catholic Worker Movement: Centenary Essays*, 468–69.

18. See, for example, Charles Chatfield, "The Catholic Worker in the United States Peace Tradition" (8), and Mel Piehl, "The Catholic Worker and Peace in the Early Cold War Era" (87), both in *American Catholic Pacifism*.

19. William Cavanaugh, "Dorothy Day and the Mystical Body of Christ in the Second World War," in *Dorothy Day and the Catholic Worker Movement: Centenary Essays*, 456.

20. Ibid., 464.

21. Klejment, "Radical Origins," in *American Catholic Pacifism*, 26.

22. John O'Sullivan, "An Uneasy Community: Catholics in Civilian Public Service During World War II," in *Dorothy Day and the Catholic Worker Movement: Centenary Essays*, 476.

23. Piehl, "The Catholic Worker and Peace in the Early Cold War Era," in *American Catholic Pacifism*, 78.

24. William D. Miller, *Dorothy Day: A Biography* (San Francisco: Harper & Row Publishers, 1982), 317.

25. See Klejment and Roberts, "The Catholic Worker and the Vietnam War," in *American Catholic Pacifism*, 153–57.

26. Ibid., 154.

27. See Julie Leininger Pycior, "Dorothy Day and Thomas Merton: Overview of a Work in Progress," in *Dorothy Day and the Catholic Worker Movement: Centenary Essays*, 368.

28. Tom Cornell, "How I Became a Pacifist," in the *Houston Catholic Worker*, November 1999.

29. Day, *Long Loneliness*, 270.

30. Miller, *Biography*, 141.

31. Daniel Berrigan, SJ, "Introduction," *The Long Loneliness*, by Dorothy Day (San Francisco: Harper & Row Publishers, 1952), xix–xx.

32. Ibid., xxiii.

33. Hugo, *Your Ways*, 281.

Chapter 16

1. Dorothy Day, *Therese: A Life of Therese of Lisieux* (Notre Dame, IN: Fides Publishers, 1960; repr. Springfield, IL: Templegate Publishers, 1979, 1991), xii.

2. Ibid., 174.

3. Ibid., 174–75.

4. Dorothy Day, *The Long Loneliness* (1952; repr. San Francisco: Harper & Row Publishers, 1997), 140–41.

5. Day, *Therese*, viii.

6. Dorothy Day, *Loaves and Fishes* (San Francisco: Harper and Row, 1963; repr. Maryknoll, NY: Orbis Books, 1997), 127.

7. Day, *Therese*, 163.

8. Peter Casarella, "Sisters in Doing the Truth: Dorothy Day and St. Thérèse of Lisieux," in *Communio* 24 (1997), 470.

9. Day, *Therese*, 167.

10. Ibid., 93.

11. Ibid., 117.

12. Ibid., 93, 144.

13. Ibid., 132.

14. Day, *Long Loneliness*, 149.

15. See Casarella, "Sisters in Doing the Truth," 486–87.

16. Day, *Therese*, 134–35.

17. Ibid., 85.

18. Ibid., 130, 131.

19. Ibid., 166–67.

20. Thérèse of Lisieux, *Story of a Soul: The Autobiography of St. Thérèse of Lisieux*, third edition, trans. John Clarke, OCD (1975; repr. Washington, DC: ICS Publications, 1996), 99–100.

21. Day, *Therese*, 119.

22. Ibid., 90.

23. Ibid., 127.

24. Quoted in Brigid O'Shea Merriman, OSF, *Searching for Christ: The Spirituality of Dorothy Day* (Notre Dame, IN: University of Notre Dame Press, 1994), 193–94.

25. Quoted in Merriman, *Searching for Christ*, 197. The original source is William James to Mrs. Henry Whitman in the *Letters of William James*, vol. 2, ed. Henry James (Boston: Atlantic Monthly Press, 1920), 90.

26. Day, *Therese*, 100.

27. Thérèse of Lisieux, *Story of a Soul*, 122.

28. Ibid., 222.

29. Casarella, "Sisters in Doing the Truth," 488, 498.

30. Day, *Therese*, 135, 139.

31. Dorothy Day, *On Pilgrimage*, Ressourcement Series: Retrieval and Renewal in Catholic Thought (New York: The Catholic Worker, 1948; repr. Grand Rapids, MI: Eerdmans, 1999), 225, 228.

32. William D. Miller, *All Is Grace: The Spirituality of Dorothy Day* (Garden City, NJ: Doubleday, 1987), 93.

Chapter 17

1. David L. Schindler, *Heart of the World, Center of the Church* (Grand Rapids, MI: William B. Eerdmans, 1966), 133–34. Schindler notes that John Paul II here also references Paul VI in *Evangelii nuntiandi*.

2. Mel Piehl , "The Politics of Free Obedience," in *A Revolution of the Heart: Essays on the Catholic Worker*, ed. Patrick G. Coy (Philadelphia: Temple University Press, 1988), 182.

3. Ibid.

4. William D. Miller, *Dorothy Day: A Biography* (San Francisco: Harper & Row Publishers, 1982), 431.

5. Dorothy Day, *On Pilgrimage*, Ressourcement Series: Retrieval and Renewal in Catholic Thought (New York: The Catholic Worker, 1948; repr. Grand Rapids, MI: William B. Eerdmans, 1999), 155.

6. Dorothy Day, *House of Hospitality* (New York: Sheed and Ward, 1939), 135.

7. Raniero Cantalamessa, OFM, *Poverty*, trans. Charles Sérignat, OFM Cap (New York: Alba House, 1997), 6–7.

8. Karol Wojtyla, *The Acting Person*, trans. Andrzej Potocki (Dordrecht, Holland: Reidel Publishing Company, 1979), 149. See also, Karol Wojtyla, *Person and Community: Selected Essays*, trans. Theresa Sandol, OSM (New York: Peter Lang, 1993), 265–69.

9. James Hanink, unpublished manuscript, "A Personalist Vision: Beyond the Established Disorder." See also Emmanuel Mounier, *Personalism*, trans. Philip Mairet (Notre Dame, IN: University of Notre Dame Press, 1952), 133–40.

10. William Portier, "Are We Really Serious When We Ask God to Deliver Us from War? The Catechism and the Challenge of Pope John Paul II," in *Communio* 23 (Spring 1996), 60, 52.

11. John Paul II, 1998 statement during his visit to Cuba. Quoted in Race Mathews, *Jobs of our Own: Building a Stake-Holder Society, Alternatives to the Market and the State* (Sydney, Australia: Pluto Press, 1999), 236.

12. Richard John Neuhaus, *Appointment in Rome: The Church in America Awakening* (New York: Crossroad, 1999), 16.

13. See Thomas Rourke, *A Conscience as Large as the World: Yves Simon vs. the Neoconservatives* (Lanham, MD: Rowman and Littlefield, 1997), 78–79.

14. Michael Novak, *The Spirit of Democratic Capitalism* (New York: American Enterprise Institute, 1982), 69.

15. Michael Novak, *Este hemisferio de libertad: Filosofía de las Américas* (Mexico City: Diana, 1994), 101.

16. Michael Novak, *Business as a Calling: Work and the Examined Life* (New York: The Free Press, 1996), 58.

17. Emmanuel Mounier, *Be Not Afraid: A Denunciation of Despair,* trans. Cynthia Rowland (New York: Sheed and Ward, 1962), 176.

18. See Michel Chossudovsky, *The Globalisation of Poverty: Impacts of IMF and World Bank Reforms* (Penang, Malaysia: Third World Network, 1997).

19. See Day, *On Pilgrimage*, 199.

20. Interview with Dorothy Day by Jim Wallis and Wes Michaelson at the Catholic Worker farm in Tivoli, New York, published in *Sojourners*, December 1976.

21. Morris Berman, *The Twilight of American Culture* (New York: W. W. Norton, 2000).

22. Wendell Berry, "The Idea of a Local Economy," in *In the Presence of Fear; Three Essays for a Changed World* (Great Barrington, MA: The Orion Society, 2001), 15–16.

23. Alasdair MacIntyre, "Politics, Philosophy and the Common Good," in *The MacIntyre Reader*, ed. Kelvin Knight (Notre Dame, IN: University of Notre Dame Press, 1998), 236.

24. See Greg MacLeod, *From Mondragon to America: Experiments in Community Economic Development* (Sydney, Nova Scotia: University College of Cape Breton Press, 1997), 14–20.

25. See Luigino Bruni, "The Experience of the Economy of Communion and its Relation to the Civil Economy," in *Communio* 27 (2000), 464–73.

26. Joseph Pearce, *Small Is Still Beautiful* (London: Harper Collins, 2001). The original book is still available: *Small Is Beautiful: Economics As If People Mattered* (London: Blond & Briggs, 1973; reissued New York: Harper and Row, 1973 and Harper Perenniel paperback, 1989.)

27. Robert Coles, *Dorothy Day: A Radical Devotion* (Reading, MA: Addison Wesley, 1987), 101–102.

28. Dorothy said she was quoting here from William Storey's book, *Days of the Lord*, 3 vols. (New York: Herder and Herder, 1965–1966).

29. Mark S. Massa, *Catholics and American Culture: Fulton Sheen, Dorothy Day, and the Notre Dame Football Team* (New York: Crossroad Publishing Company, 1999), 126.

30. Antonio Socci, "Divo Barsotti," in *30 Days*, April 1990, 53.

Index